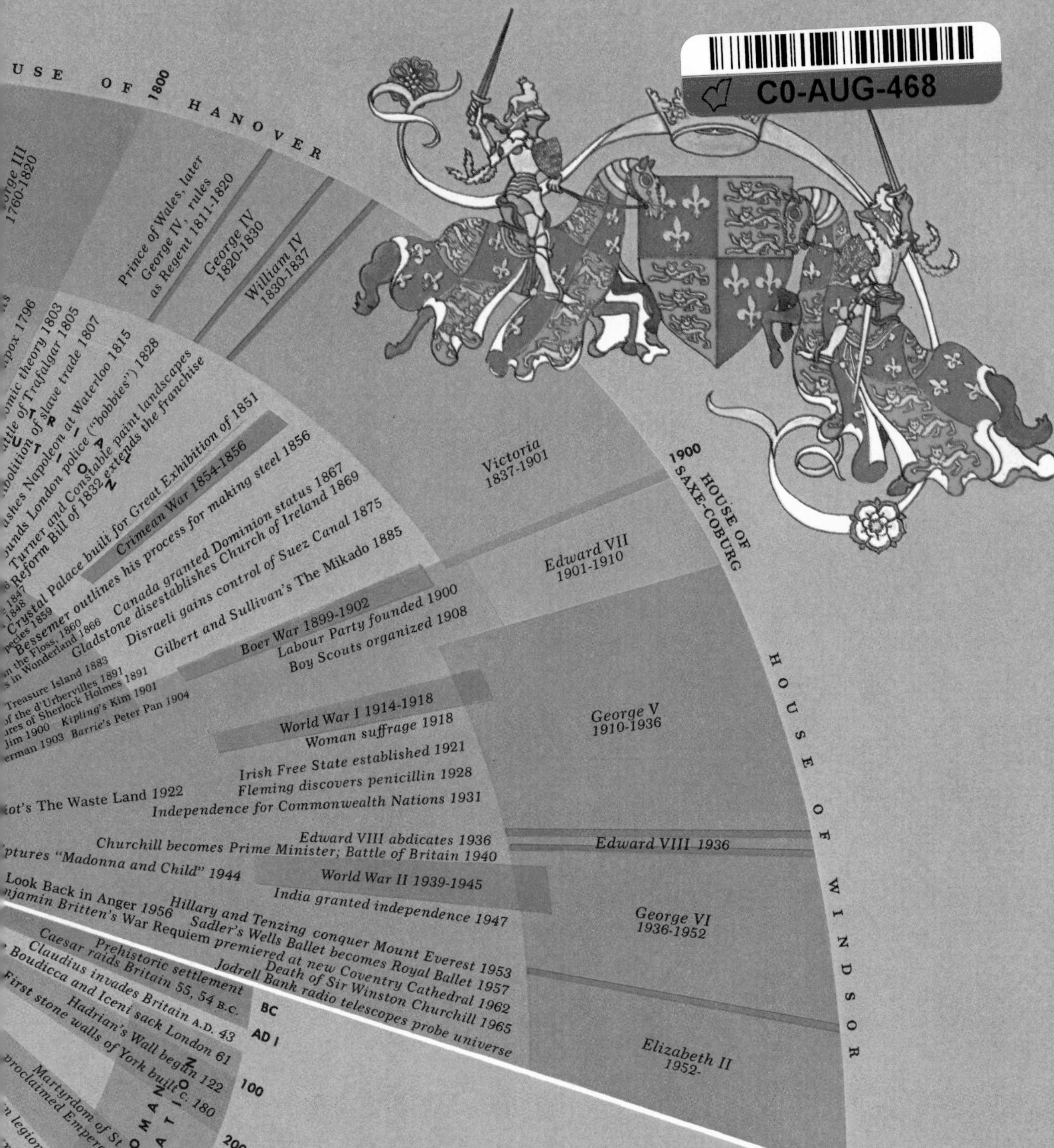

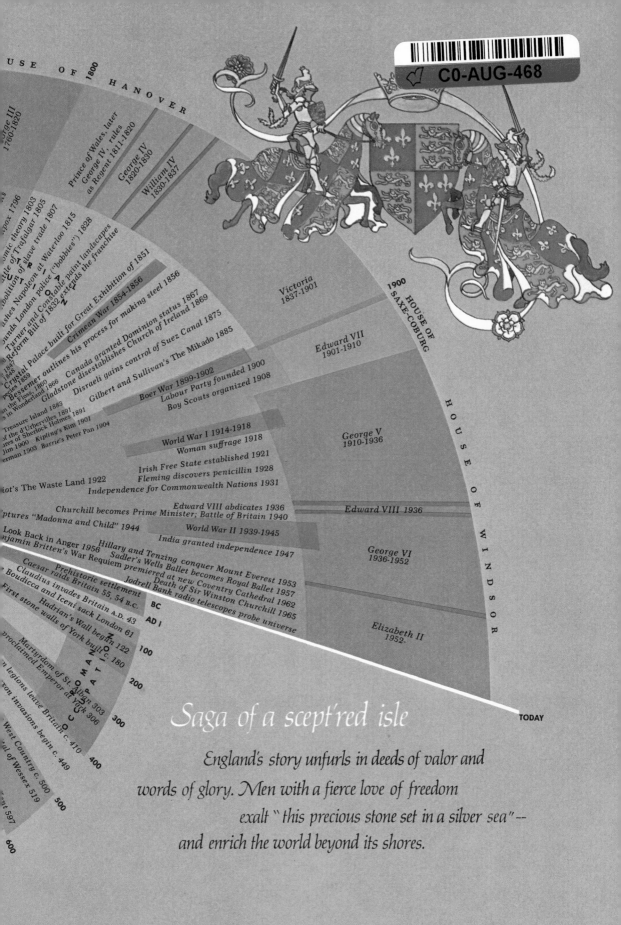

Saga of a scept'red isle

England's story unfurls in deeds of valor and words of glory. Men with a fierce love of freedom exalt "this precious stone set in a silver sea"-- and enrich the world beyond its shores.

This royal throne of kings,

this scept'red isle,

This earth of majesty, this seat of Mars,

This other Eden, demiparadise,...

This blessed plot,

this earth, this realm,

this England...

RICHARD II (ACT II, SCENE I)
by William Shakespeare

THIS

NATIONAL
GEOGRAPHIC SOCIETY
WASHINGTON, D.C.

ENGLAND

658 illustrations, 620 in full color

A volume in the World in Color Library
prepared by NATIONAL GEOGRAPHIC BOOK SERVICE
Merle Severy, Chief

Foreword by

MELVILLE BELL GROSVENOR
President and Editor, National Geographic Society

Chapters by

ALLAN C. FISHER, JR., MELVILLE BELL GROSVENOR,
STUART E. JONES, and MERLE SEVERY of the Society staff, *and*

ERNLE BRADFORD
author of biographies of Drake and Nelson; *Ulysses Found*

LEONARD COTTRELL
author of *Seeing Roman Britain; The Great Invasion; Anvil of Civilisation*

H. V. MORTON
author of *In Search of England; In Search of London; In Search of Scotland*

GEORGE RODGER
author of *Far on the Ringing Plain: 75,000 Miles with a Photo Reporter*

ALAN VILLIERS
author of *Men, Ships, and the Sea; Falmouth for Orders; The New Mayflower*

LOUIS B. WRIGHT
Director, Folger Shakespeare Library;
author of *Middle-Class Culture in Elizabethan England*

Photographs by

JAMES P. BLAIR, DEAN CONGER, ROBERT GOODMAN, BATES LITTLEHALES, DAN McCOY, GEORGE F. MOBLEY, WINFIELD PARKS, GEORGE RODGER, MERLE SEVERY, ADAM WOOLFITT, *and others*

This book was prepared under the editorial guidance of
MELVILLE BELL GROSVENOR and FRANC SHOR
by the following staff:

MERLE SEVERY, *Editor and Art Director*
SEYMOUR L. FISHBEIN, EDWARDS PARK, *Associate Editors*
PATRICIA COYLE NICHOLSON, *Designer*
ANNE DIRKES KOBOR, *Picture Editor*

THOMAS B. ALLEN, ROSS BENNETT, BERRY L. REECE, JR.,
DAVID F. ROBINSON, *Editor-Writers*

JAMES P. KELLY, *Production*
WILLIAM W. SMITH, *Engravings;* JOE M. BARLETT, *Printing*

MARGERY G. DUNN, HAZEL EAGLE, JOCELYN C. WHITE, *Editorial Research;* ANN MARTIN, MARY E. RILEY, *Picture Research;* JOSEPH BAUMER, *Additional Layouts;* WERNER JANNEY, *Style;* DOROTHY M. CORSON, *Index;* BARBARA BOHNENGEL, ROBERT W. LANNI, PAULA C. SIMMONS, KAY TRAVIS, WERNER L. WEBER, *Production Assistants*

W. E. ROSCHER, *Director, European Office, London*

Composed by National Geographic's Phototypographic Division,
HERMAN J. A. C. ARENS, *Director;* ROBERT C. ELLIS, JR., *Manager*
Printed and bound by R. R. Donnelley and Sons Co., Chicago
First printing 150,000 copies

LIBRARY OF CONGRESS CATALOG CARD NO. 66-26776

SYMBOLS OF ENGLAND: *Big Ben and the Houses of Parliament beside the Thames (overleaf); Royal Horse Guardsman (opposite); Crown of State (page one).*

ROBERT F. SISSON, NATIONAL GEOGRAPHIC PHOTOGRAPHER; SUSAN McCARTNEY, PHOTO RESEARCHERS; CROWN COPYRIGHT RESERVED

FOREWORD

WIND SANG in the rigging as the sturdy ketch hissed across Spithead toward Portsmouth. With Alan Villiers I had cruised waters the Spanish Armada had sailed. We had put in at Devon ports that Drake and his sea dogs knew, and called at Cornish coves once haunted by smugglers.

Now at the helm in dripping oilskins, I peered at the darkening harbor ahead. Ferries churned by. A big Cunarder stood out from Southampton. Following the lead marks up-channel, we shot safely inside.

Suddenly dark spars towered above us. Nelson's *Victory*! We slipped almost under the transom of the old flagship of Trafalgar. What a thrill to see her, light streaming from the great cabin as though the Admiral were aboard.

Buoy ahead! "Down mains'l!" I spun the wheel, and the ketch came grudgingly into the wind, sails slatting. Soon we were snugly moored.

With our crew was my son Eddie, then eight. His eager response to England reminded me of my own first visit at the age of eleven.

London . . . bustling, big, full of pageantry. Horse Guards in gleaming breastplates clopping down the Mall. Sentries in scarlet at Buckingham Palace marching and stamping like mechanical toys. How could they see from under those bearskin caps?

Westminster Abbey, crammed with monuments to more heroes than I thought existed in all the world. Regent's Park zoo. That camel ride was fun. Hampton Court, a palace with a thousand rooms! And the Thames—swans beating the water to a froth with their great wings, barges with big red sails, Tower Bridge, the grim old Tower itself. I'll never forget the Yeoman Warder's tales of treachery, the tally of the headsman's ax, the murder of the Little Princes. Inside you can see Henry VIII's armor: one suit that he wore at 19, a much bigger one tailored to his bulk at middle age.

Stratford . . . here the shadowy schoolbook figure of Shakespeare came alive for me. At Warwick my eye went to swords and halberds bristling in the castle halls. Kenilworth's ruins I peopled with all the knights and fair ladies at a tournament in *Ivanhoe*. Then the boat train, clacking across the Midlands to Liverpool past factories, storybook villages, and the greenest countryside in all my memory.

I have returned many times. Each time England's impact is as fresh as ever, for I find here, in Marlowe's phrase, "infinite riches in a little room."

You may bask in the cheer of a Lake District inn, shiver in the ocean winds at Land's End, explore cathedrals, castles, pulsing cities, lonely moors – all packed into an area smaller than Wisconsin. You may stroll cobbled lanes where half-timbered houses lean on one another in the slumber of centuries, sip tea in humble homes "crushed with their burden of thatch," and sleep, as I have, in cottages whose honey-hued stones seem to grow from the soil. A light shines through an arrow slit in a crenellated wall – and you realize this is no museum. Many a castle is an Englishman's home!

Stately homes standing amid deer parks at the end of beech-canopied drives invite us in. How grateful we should be to Britain's National Trust, which helps preserve them. Homes that entertained Good Queen Bess may still shelter the same families. Glance from ancestral portraits on the walls to your host, and you see the same faces.

Celt, Roman, Saxon, Norman – all left their mark on the land. These ancient battlements withstood a siege. On that field "manie a nobil erle and valrous knyghte ... fell ... in bloudie fyghte." In this chamber a king was foully done to death; there an archbishop martyred. At this table, with this pen, a poet wrote his masterpiece.

A mere eight miles separates the Stonehenge of prehistory from Salisbury Cathedral, glory of the Middle Ages, its spire rising above the meadows just as Constable painted it. Magna Carta is not just a phrase – it's a parchment you can read there in the cathedral, and a living symbol of the freedoms and traditions we share.

HOW TO ENCOMPASS these "infinite riches" within a book? For long months our authors and photographers sought England's essence in all its diversity. They returned with a treasure of lore and an incomparable photographic record. Nine hundred years after the Battle of Hastings we "tell sad stories of the death of kings" – and also relate the vigorous lives of men. In England the wine tasted like vinegar, complained Erasmus, the famed Renaissance scholar. But he extolled the charming women who welcomed guests with "delicate and fragrant" kisses. "If you were once to taste them," he wrote, "you would certainly desire ... till death to be a sojourner in England." Kisses, alas, are not standard greeting now, but the welcome is as warm.

In Smarden, amid the orchards of Kent, George and Jinx Rodger shared with me the mellow charm of the Tudor home they had restored with their own hands. They told me of their search for old beams and explained the origin of the village name. Fascinated, I invited George to retell the story in this book.

A name like Fordingbridge, where you cross the River Avon, explains itself. But what about Musbury? Here, its Saxon-derived name tells you, once stood a fort inhabited by mice. The book also gives keys to the meaning of coats of arms, the strange language of blazonry, the rollicking symbolism of inn signs. You will discover delightful customs, learn that Britain's money talks in many tongues, and how marquesses and viscounts rank in the peerage. Cricket, anyone? Come watch an innings and learn what a "googly" bowler can do to a batsman on a sticky wicket!

I admit to a deep personal involvement in *This England.* Like many Americans I am proud to trace my roots in English soil and was delighted to find in an early classic of heraldry that "with *William the Conqueror* ... came one *Gilbert le Grosvenour.*" My father, Gilbert Grosvenor, and my mother were married in London, and during his long years as Editor of *National Geographic* he always strove to strengthen understanding among peoples linked by "the bond of our glorious tongue."

To most Americans, a journey to England becomes, in a sense, a homecoming. This royal land is part of our heritage. Ten of her monarchs were our rulers too, and we share a priceless cultural legacy. We echo in our hearts the words of Nathaniel Hawthorne: "Visiting these famous localities ... I was often conscious of a fervent hereditary attachment to the native soil of our forefathers, and felt it to be our own Old Home."

Melville Bell Grosvenor

"**THIS FORTRESS BUILT BY NATURE**" *guards a heritage as enduring as the heathered Cornwall cliffs where Melville Grosvenor and his son Edwin stand. Nowhere in England are you more than 75 miles from the everlasting voice of the sea.*

ALAN VILLIERS

GOLDEN LIONS OF RICHARD THE LIONHEART, *walking with heads turned (passant guardant), gleam on England's shield. London's coat of arms (below) combines St. George's red cross and the sword of St. Paul, the city's patron. Ox crossing a ford spells Oxford. Stratford took three lion heads from the royal arms; Cirencester, Roman city reborn, displays a phoenix. Three crows (opposite), Thomas à Becket's arms, announce Canterbury; castles protect Winchester. Three wells signify Wells; castled device declares Exeter "ever faithful." Birmingham industriously wields a hammer; Cambridge recalls its medieval waterborne trade. York parades royal lions on St. George's cross. Kendal wove wool hooks and teasels into its shield.*

Contents

SEMPER FIDELIS

PAGEANT OF A

In the beginning, a people wandering westward came to a land where the sun vanished into the sea. When ice glazed that land, they huddled in caves. Then forest clothed the warming earth. The sea swept into a long valley behind them, and the island of Britain was born.

A new race, wise to the rhythm of earth, crossed to the island and, like the trees, took root. As trees grow strong in groves, so these people throve in camps. Here they herded goats and sheep, cows and swine, and here they dropped grain into the earth to be born again. When a man died, they placed him in the earth and mounded high his grave. They, and those who came after them, marked the course of sun and stars, faithful heralds of the seasons. Birth, death, earth, and sky engrossed them. They began a temple of stone, perhaps to venerate the sky, perhaps to study it.

STORIED REALM

Amid the barrows of the dead they dug a great circle, chipping the chalk with antlers, scooping the soil with shoulder blades of oxen. For decades, generations, centuries, men toiled. From rock-studded uplands and from distant mountains they hauled huge stones. Worshiping gods whose names have vanished from man's ken, they arrayed the stones within the circle. Stark against the dawn, Stonehenge stands today as a mighty mark of man blazoned upon a long, unchronicled age.

Forging bronze, then iron, men made knives and spears, hunting not food but men of other tribes. Rude forts arose. Leather-sailed boats landed on the sentineled shore. Belgic battle cries rang on the downs. These chariot-driving warriors built a town and named it Camulodunum for their god of war. Our chronicle now opens, its first pages writ in blood.

ROME'S DISCIPLINED SWORDS AND SPEARS cut to the heart of this misty land great Caesar had called Britannia. Twice Caesar had invaded and fought its blue-dyed barbarians. Twice baffled, he had sailed back to Gaul. Now, a century later, Rome's legions prevail. Camulodunum becomes their first colony. Roads built for eternity soon march between garrison towns that impose a grid of power on tribal lands. And, like a mighty wave of stone, Hadrian's Wall courses from sea to sea, marking the northern frontier of an empire that extends to the Nile and the Euphrates.

Centurions from Mediterranean climes shiver as they check sentries guarding against Pict raids. Townsmen in togas gossip at the baths, and in villas craftsmen copy classical mosaics with exuberant infidelity. Then imperiled Rome recalls her legions; Anglo-Saxon hordes pour in. Though a Briton renowned as King Arthur battles the tide, Angleland is born.

DAN McCOY, BLACK STAR. INSET: ROMAN CAVALRYMAN'S TOMBSTONE, FIRST CENTURY A.D., IN GLOUCESTER CITY MUSEUM
PAGES 10-11: THOMAS J. ABERCROMBIE, NATIONAL GEOGRAPHIC STAFF

RVFVS·SITA·EQVES·CHO VI
TRACVM·ANN·XL·STIP·XXII
HEREDES·EXS·TEST·F·CVRAVER
H S E

AT HASTINGS, Norman knights cut down Saxon foot soldiers. Scion of sea-roving Northmen who carved Normandy from the bleeding flank of France, William the Conqueror mounts fierce campaigns to crush the England of *Beowulf*, the Venerable Bede, and Alfred the Great. A hundred castles subdue the fiefs he distributes to his vassals. Colchester's

BATTLE OF HASTINGS, OCTOBER 14, 1066; PAINTING FOR NATIONAL GEOGRAPHIC BY BIRNEY LETTICK

keep, largest of all, rises atop a Roman temple of Camulodunum. Scorning Saxon timber shrines, proud prelates build a thousand square-towered churches arched in enduring stone. Saxon serfs tend the cows, swine, and sheep that put *boef, porc*, and *mouton* on the Norman lord's table. "Tax" and "prison" cross the Channel – also "charity," "jury," and "joy."

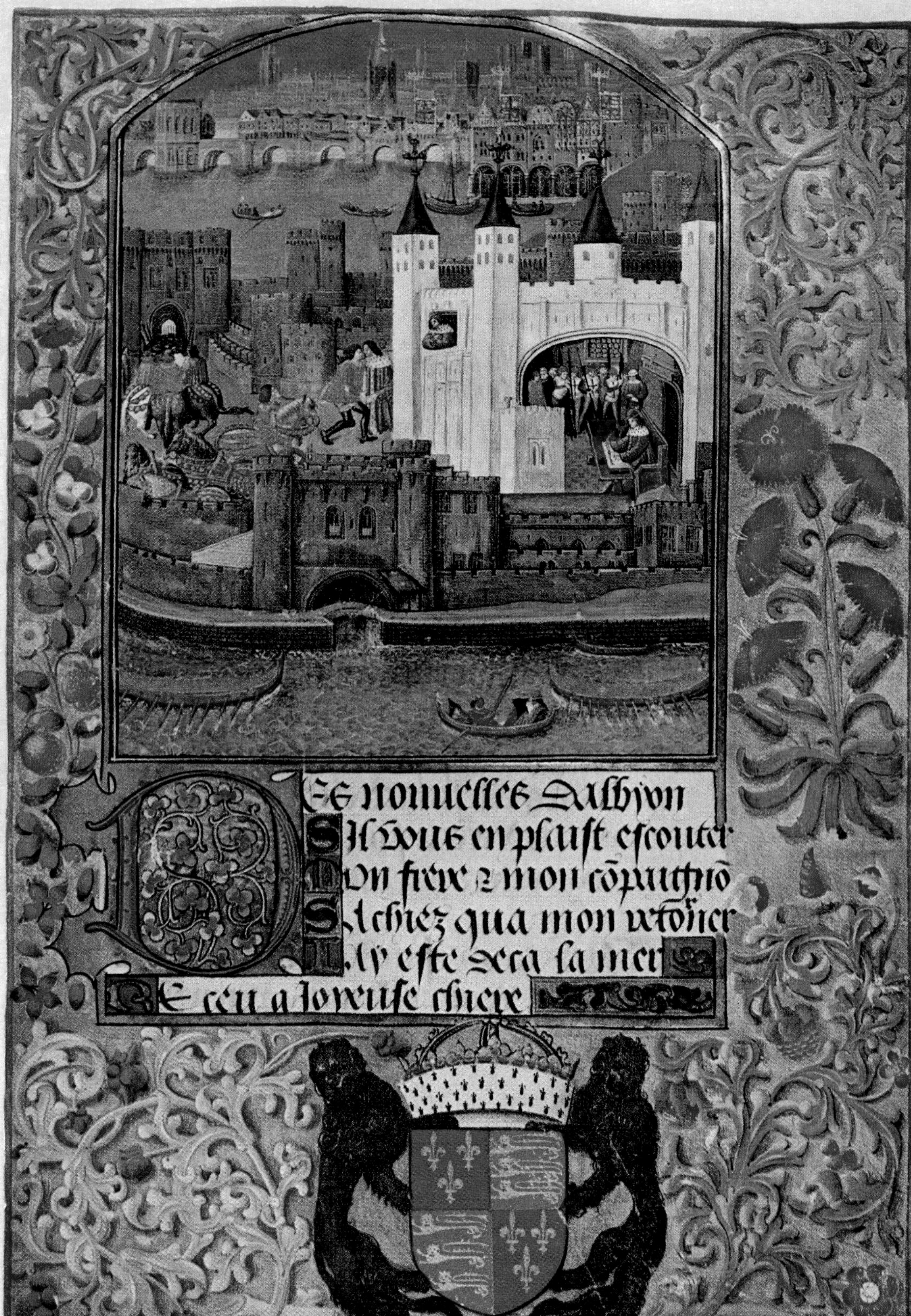
Des nouuelles dalbyon
Sil vous en plaist escouter
Mon frere & mon cōpaignō
Sachez qua mon retourner
Ay este deca la mer
Receu a ioyeuse chiere

FOR THREE CENTURIES England's kings speak French; they range an empire that reaches the Pyrenees. Men of the roving royal household win lasting titles: *chamberlain*, guardian of the bedchamber, where the king keeps his treasure; *chancellor*, who emerges from the chancel to become scribe, keeper of the seal, and kingly confidant; lords of the *exchequer*, who reckon rents due the king by moving counters about a checkered cloth.

Henry II spends but a third of his long reign in England; Richard the Lionheart only six months in ten years. Barons grown strong in their absence force Magna Carta on John "Lackland," short of crops and cash. Longbows at Crécy put sting in Edward III's claim to the French throne. A century of war sunders Albion from the Continent, and "in alle the gramere scoles of Engelond, children leveth Frensche and ... lerneth in Englische." Grasping for power, Plantagenets pluck a white and a red rose – destined to bloom on reddened fields.

BRITISH MUSEUM (ALSO OPPOSITE)

NATIONAL PORTRAIT GALLERY, LONDON (ALSO ABOVE)

"MIRROUR OF PROWESSE," *Henry V (left) triumphed at Agincourt, seizing the Duke of Orleans, who penned poems while languishing unransomed in the Tower of London (opposite). Henry entangled "giddy minds in foreign quarrels" to bolster his Lancastrian claim to the throne his father had wrenched from Richard II (above), who perished in Pontefract Castle. The hollow crown rested on uneasy heads, then fell with Richard III at Bosworth. Henry VII (upper left), who snatched it, ending the Wars of the Roses, "drew more gold than blood" and sired the Tudor age.*

BORNE IN SPLENDOR by peacock courtiers, Elizabeth sweeps across the stage of a dazzling age and a surging realm. Adorned in silks, velvets, and chains of gold, her swaggering nobles raise mansions on fruitful lands Henry VIII wrested from the Church. They "indulge in pleasures as if they were to die tomorrow, and build as if they were to live forever," a bishop mutters. Not slits for archers but mullioned windows frame glittering halls and a "riot of banquetting." Madrigals muffle Puritan sermons.

Flirting, dancing a merry galliard, reveling, "Gloriana" mirrors the

quicksilver passions of her people. Yet as Spain's Armada nears, she is the steely soul of England. "I have the body of a weak and feeble woman," she tells her cheering men, "but I have the heart and stomach of a king!" Raleigh of the chivalrous cloak names a new land Virginia for his Virgin Queen. Drake, her knighted pirate, "brings home the spoil, Riching Eliza and Eliza's soil." And, riching all the days to come, a treasure flows from a matchless pen. Only amid such a happy breed of men, only in this other Eden could William Shakespeare find his realm, his England.

BY AN UNKNOWN ARTIST C. 1600, COURTESY SIMON WINGFIELD DIGBY

JAMES P. BLAIR, NATIONAL GEOGRAPHIC PHOTOGRAPHER. RIGHT: FOX PHOTOS

ROYAL ENGLAND still stages her stately spectacles: The Lord Mayor of London rides in gilded grandeur, attended by helmeted pikemen, and Elizabeth, second of the name, convokes her Parliament from a golden throne in the House of Lords. Splendor arrays the vaulting chamber, filled with scarlet-robed peers, peeresses in glittering coronets, bishops, ambassadors from distant lands. Bewigged judges sit on the Woolsack, relic of days when sheep meant wealth—and a throne meant power.

Behind the Lords, and unseen in this portrait of pageantry, stand the "faithful Commons," who showed their historic independence of the Crown by refusing to attend until commanded by the Queen's personal messenger, the Gentleman Usher of the Black Rod.

When Black Rod neared the House of Commons, the door slammed in his face. Neither monarch nor emissary may enter unbidden. He knocked three times, was admitted, and returned to the House of Lords with the Commons, summoned but not subjugated.

The pantomime evokes a heroic drama. In 1642 Charles I with several hundred swordsmen invaded Commons to

arrest five members who had defied him. The Speaker, asked their whereabouts, replied, "I have neither eye to see, nor tongue to speak here, but as the House is pleased to direct me."

Charles stalked out, divinely certain of his right. Had not his learned father, James I, reminded Commons that when the Spartans proposed legislation to their ruler they appeared before him with nooses round their necks?

Parliament—rooted in the Saxon *witan,* council of wise men; named from the Norman *parler,* to discuss; proud of privileges and power over the purse so painfully won—would not yield. With audacity born of Runnymede, these "arrant rebelles" fought the king, tried him, finally slew him.

A groan welled from the throng that saw the royal head roll. Cromwell, "damned to everlasting fame," not only proclaimed a land ever free of kings but scorned Parliament's mace as "a bauble." The Lord Protector, as Winston Churchill wrote, was "in lasting discord with the genius of the English race." Great leaders of Parliament—Walpole, Pitt, Disraeli, Gladstone, Churchill himself—saw the strength in a symbol of sovereignty as enduring, as radiant as the scepter.

Now, with Imperial State Crown flashing and ermine train cascading, the Queen who "reigns but does not rule" addresses her Lords Spiritual, Lords Temporal, and Commons. The words come from those who legislate, empowered by the ballot box. But she speaks them, for she is the voice of England.

"Our Government is like our Climate," said the Marquess of Halifax. Its misty imprecision softens the sharp edge of doctrine. With a constitution left unwritten so that nothing will be too well defined, England has saved her old freedoms while other nations became up-to-date by losing theirs.

Scorched by war, the flag that awed an empire flies over an island buffeted by new winds. Behind the proud, unchanging face of pomp and circumstance Britons tinker at everyday problems with stoic good humor, ever seeking Aristotle's middle road. They greet the sun, but carry umbrellas. And when their way of life is threatened, they willingly pay for its survival in "blood, toil, tears and sweat."

CROWN COPYRIGHT RESERVED. OPPOSITE: ROBERT B. GOODMAN

LONDON, HEART OF THE

My wife Mary is not a jealous woman, but we did go through a period when she spoke darkly of "that rival of mine." At such times I would be packing a bag, intent on putting home and children behind me. With candor, if not tact, I would analyze for Mary her rival's appeal: good looks, charm, character, individuality.

Oh, but I was enamored! I still am. But my tolerant and understanding wife knows how it is with a traveling man. Sometimes he loses his heart to a certain place, one that lures him back again and again. And for some years now I have been totally and unabashedly in love with London.

Let me concede at once that other cities surpass London in certain qualities. Paris is more beautiful, Rome friendlier, Rio de

FATHER THAMES *meets the Mother of Parliaments in foggy London Town. Big Ben bongs the hours*

KINGDOM

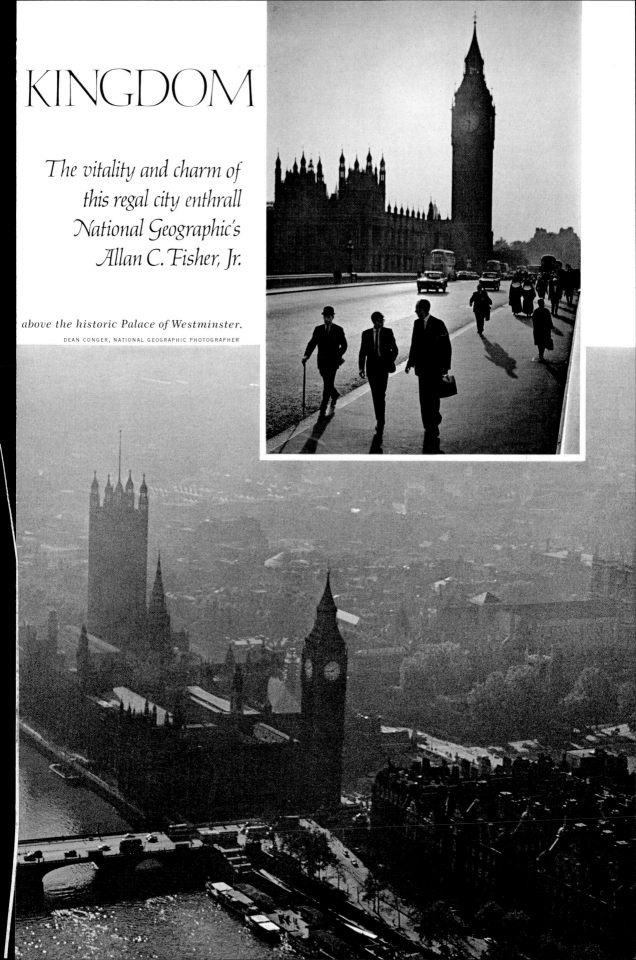

The vitality and charm of this regal city enthrall National Geographic's Allan C. Fisher, Jr.

above the historic Palace of Westminster.

DEAN CONGER, NATIONAL GEOGRAPHIC PHOTOGRAPHER

Janeiro more colorful, New York more exciting. No matter. In the aggregate, London tops them all. Great Britain's capital somehow manages to be greater than the sum of its parts.

Not that London's sum, in terms of sheer physical size and complexity, ever fails to impress. Greater London covers about 720 square miles. Here live more than eight million people, a population exceeded by only two other cities, Tokyo and New York.

I had long wanted Mary to know her rival. So at last we bade our maturing children goodbye, and free as mudlarks flew to my favorite city for a prolonged stay. We rented a flat in Mayfair and began a memorable tasting of London's landmarks, institutions, neighborhoods, pubs, museums, and galleries. After a time Mary said, "This city is too big. Too crowded. And the climate—an absolute horror most of the time! But I'm almost as smitten with the place as you are."

LIKE MOST VISITORS I enjoy pilgrimages to Westminster Abbey and St. Paul's Cathedral, pre-eminent monuments to a great faith and a great people. I often go to the Mother of Parliaments, surely a shrine for every free man. I dote on the pageantry associated with the monarchy and other old institutions—the changing of the guard at Buckingham Palace, the pomp of the Lord Mayor of London. In these feelings I am typical. But much of my appetite for this city is individual and personal.

I am an inveterate plaque spotter. The municipal government identifies many historical and literary landmarks with blue plaques, and I am seldom happier in London than when strolling the streets with one wary eye on the traffic and the other alert for telltale flashes of blue on the walls of buildings. Often I have experienced moving moments by chancing upon a site associated with one of my literary heroes: the home of William Blake on South Molton Street, the house in Kensington where Thackeray wrote *Vanity Fair*, the building on Doughty Street where Dickens penned *Oliver Twist*. Dickens House is now a museum, as are former homes of Carlyle, Keats, and Johnson.

If one cares to embark upon a literary binge in London, it is quite easy to do so in a literal as well as a figurative sense. The city offers fine pubs dedicated to the memories of such celebrated patrons as Pepys, Dickens, Tennyson, Boswell, and, of course, the convivial Dr. Johnson.

Ye Olde Cheshire Cheese, revered as Johnson's favorite, is one of London's most picturesque pubs. Boswell doesn't record any visits to it by Johnson, but he allegedly dined there often. I sat in his "favorite seat" at lunch one day. Above me, a grim-looking

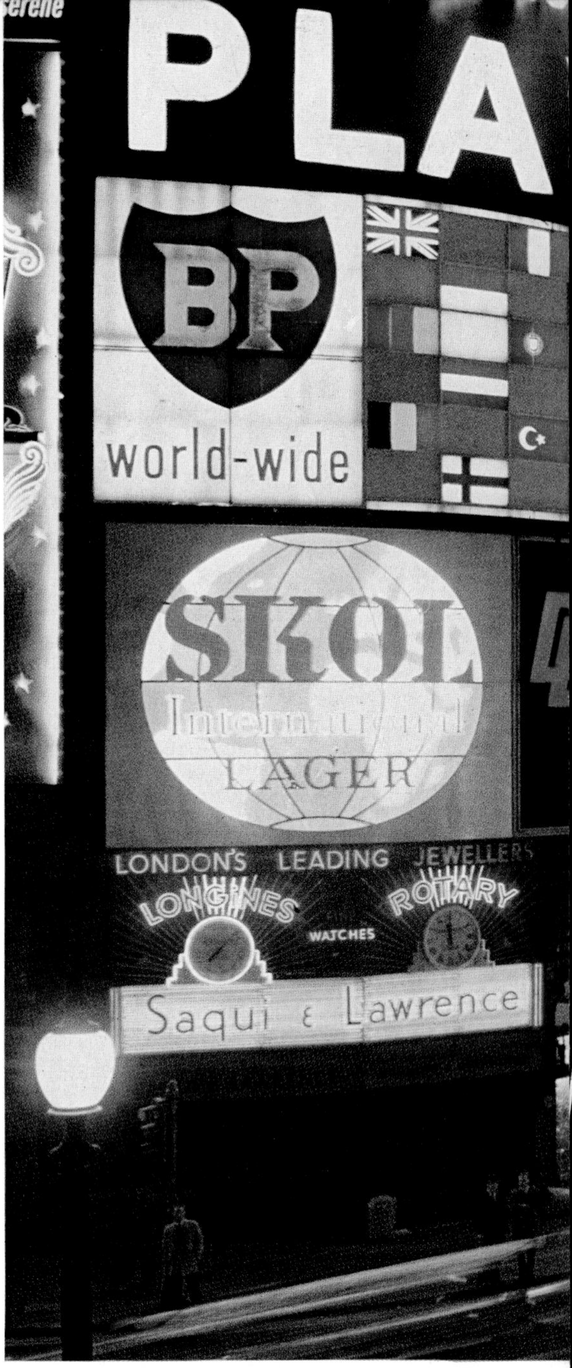

JAMES P. BLAIR, NATIONAL GEOGRAPHIC PHOTOGRAPHER

LONDON SWIRLS *round Piccadilly Circus, light-spangled center of the theater district and rendezvous of baffled sightseer and patient bobby. Here lived a 17th-century tailor whose "pickadills," stiff ruffed collars, inspired the name of the circular intersection. From a fountain island reigns a Victorian Angel of Christian Charity honoring the philanthropic seventh Earl of Shaftesbury. The winged archer bends to bury a shaft, but the pun on Shaftesbury's name got lost; Londoners call him Eros (Cupid), Greek god of love. Eros was the mythical son of Chaos—fitting comment on Piccadilly traffic jams.*

Johnson gazed down from a framed canvas. He seemed to eye me, in particular, with sour disapproval.

Though pubs have their delights, I am also a confirmed fancier of London parks, those magnificent open spaces aptly called "the lungs of London." Sometimes on good days (in London any day when it doesn't rain is a good day) I pick a park at random, then wander through it as aimlessly as the addlepated pelicans that stroll beside the lake in St. James's Park. If the sun is out, thousands of Londoners lounge on the greensward, their pale faces turned, like Thomas Moore's sunflower, toward their god in the sky. Sometimes I join them, and I try not to watch the entwined young lovers, probably the boldest on display in Europe.

Londoners owe some of their best parkland to their monarchs' love of the hunt. Royal decrees set aside numerous hunting preserves that ultimately became public parks—among them Hyde, St. James's, Green, and Regent's—in the heart of modern London. Green islands in an ocean of stone and brick, they give the central part

VEILED IN SNOW, *Life Guards of the Queen's Household Cavalry ride past St. James's Park, their mien*

of the city sweep and spaciousness and a bit of a countrified look.

The Crown still retains title to the 5,684 acres in London's Royal Parks, but the public enjoys this land as freely as it does the 7,300 acres in the splendid park system administered by the Greater London Council or the innumerable squares and commons, usually of two acres or less, maintained and manicured by the 32 boroughs.

My particular delight is the Old English Garden at Golders Hill, where color riots in a setting as formal and stylized as a minuet. The last time I was there superintendent Herbert Pocock discussed with me what to plant after taking up his tulips. "The superintendent plants what he likes," said Mr. Pocock, "but if he is a good man he gets ideas from the public."

The Englishman loves his garden, and if he can't be near one he'll settle for a window box. London abounds in colorful window boxes. You may find them on the grimy brick façade of a docker's home or the imposing front of a bank in the financial district. Tulips, daffodils, and narcissi, favorites in

as imperturbable in winter as in summer, when camera-armed brigades of tourists harry their flanks.

JAMES P. BLAIR, NATIONAL GEOGRAPHIC PHOTOGRAPHER

spring, yield to geraniums, petunias, and hydrangeas.

It often seems that some kind of flower show gladdens each day in London during the summer. These shows range from an improbable but charming one put on by the porters and fishmongers of Billingsgate, the historic fish market, to the elaborate and impressive Chelsea Show, attended on opening day by everyone who is someone—or who would like to become someone.

London's most unusual gardens, 100 feet above congested Kensington High Street, cover 1¼ acres atop Derry & Toms Department Store. Americans seeking the gardens invariably tell cab drivers, "Take me to Tom and Jerry's." But they end in the right place, delightedly exploring the Spanish, Tudor, or Woodland Garden. In the latter, which has a stream, I parted some bushes one day and found myself confronting a harlequin duck that had spiraled down for rest and refreshment. He paddled off, squawking.

For a man who prefers

PRESSES THROB *on Fleet Street, heart of a newspaper industry whose per capita circulation leads the world. British tastes range from tabloids dripping with gore and scandal to the staid* Times, *some of whose leaders, or editorials, exude an "aroma of carpet slippers and elderly geniality." St. Paul's Cathedral rises on Ludgate Hill beyond the "Street of Ink."*

Dr. Johnson, literary arbiter of 18th-century London, scowls above his traditional seat in Ye Olde Cheshire Cheese (opposite) off Fleet Street. The brick house where he wrote his great dictionary stands in nearby Gough Square.

W. D. VAUGHN

the more sedentary pleasures, I display a remarkable avidity for walking when in London. Sometimes I wander through the narrow byways of Chelsea, the city's arty area, feeling, as I pass between tiny row houses painted in vivid hues, as though I'm nearing the end of the rainbow. At other times I explore old neighborhoods that retain their fenced and tidily kept private squares, such as Brompton Square.

It's ultrafashionable in today's London to live in a mews, or area of horse stables. Of course the horses have long since moved out, and the coach rooms and lofts have been thoroughly—and expensively—renovated. London abounds in these mews,

tucked away behind the Victorian edifices they once served. Some have been refurbished to the point of poshness.

I have a British friend who, after years of country living in Surrey, paid a stiff price for a home in Kensington's Ennismore Mews. He had dreaded the lack of neighborly spirit, the aloofness of city life. "My first Sunday in the mews," he told me later, "blast me if all of my neighbors didn't drag chairs and tables out on the cobblestones and sit around sipping apéritifs. Just like Paris, y'know. Later we played darts against a team from another mews. 'Straordinary!"

The Royal Mews is one of the few in London that still have four-footed residents. You can visit these stables behind Buckingham Palace and see the Coronation Coach, a masterpiece of the carriage-maker's art. Royal coachmen will explain things to you—and I wish you luck. The coachmen are Irish;

HYDE PARK, *haven for haranguers and arena for sheep-dog trials, gives freedom to city dwellers. Crowds gather to applaud crusaders and heckle prophets of doom near Marble Arch, where mobs once cheered the hangings at "Tyburn Tree," a gallows big enough for 24 victims.*

Fashionable riders prance along Rotten Row. Bird watchers and lovers stroll where Henry VIII hunted deer. Charles I let the public into the royal preserve; William III installed oil lamps to foil footpads. Victoria staged the first great international exhibition here in 1851, and Victorian propriety lingered; not until 1930 were women permitted to swim in The Serpentine, the park lake. Kensington Gardens and Hyde Park together form a square mile of green.

Londoners' fondness for their parks is reflected in Prime Minister Walpole's reply to Queen Caroline when she asked the cost to put St. James's back as a royal pleasure ground: "Only a crown, Madam."

Snowballs fly in Soho Square (opposite lower), one of more than 400 oases that refresh the city.

JAMES P. BLAIR, NATIONAL GEOGRAPHIC PHOTOGRAPHER

FLOODLIT TRAFALGAR SQUARE, *hub of London, swarms with Britons on election night. In the darkness high above, the cocked-hatted, empty-sleeved figure of Admiral Lord Nelson watches the unfolding destiny of his nation. Nelson lost an arm and an eye in naval engagements; he died in action at the Battle of Trafalgar, off the coast of Spain, where he defeated the French and Spanish fleets in 1805. His victory, a masterpiece of seamanship, ended forever Napoleon's hopes of invading England. And his words then, "England expects that every man will do his duty," still inspire his countrymen.*

KODACHROMES BY JAMES P. BLAIR © N.G.S.

I couldn't understand half of what they said.

Nearly all London's horses are gone but I am charmed that a number of their drinking troughs remain, some along thoroughfares. Many of these hardy survivors, shaped like fountains, are still impressively handsome—nostalgic bits of Victoriana, more flavor for an already flavorful city.

NO ONE EVER TASTED London with more appreciation than Samuel Johnson, who declared, "When a man is tired of London, he is tired of life." The good doctor, reveling in the vitality of the city, did not confine his forays to the fashionable parts of London—and neither should you.

In but not *of* the fashionable West End lies the colorful enclave of Soho. It teems with striptease clubs, nightclubs, coffeehouses, pubs, movie theaters, betting shops, and some of London's finest restaurants. Printers, shoe menders, tailors, and palmists follow their trades in small shops.

Soho, London's Bohemian quarter, bears a reputation for general naughtiness that has survived the city's war on prostitution. The languages one hears suggest a new Babel: African dialects, French, Italian, American hipster slang. But the most bizarre Soho habitués are some of London's own: the Mods, those young men with the tight, foppish clothes and long, girlish hair.

"Soho used to be a wild place when the girls were on the street," says the doorman at a strip club on Old Compton Street. "A lot gayer. It's just a place to work now."

And while one talks the traffic rumbles through the streets: Rolls-Royces, bikes,

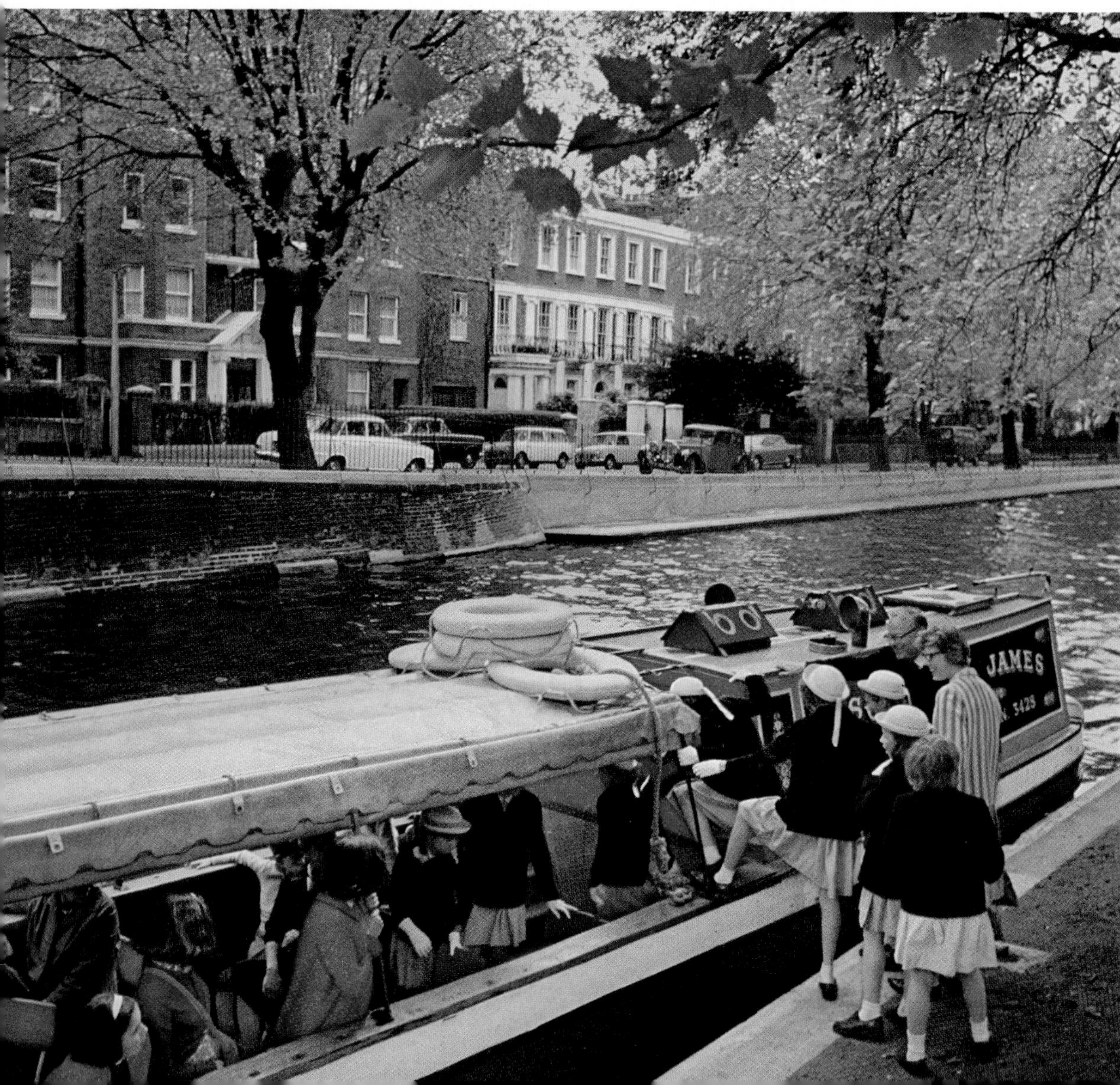

scooters, junk heaps driven by bearded beatniks, the black motorcycles and unmarked Zodiacs of the police, the taxis and chauffeur-driven Rovers of the tourists.

Across town, in the East End, you can still find the irrepressible Cockney, his heritage rich on his tongue. But the distinctive manner of speech is no longer commonplace. Take the Underground to Bethnal Green Station, then stroll down Bethnal Green Road, where the produce stalls seem little

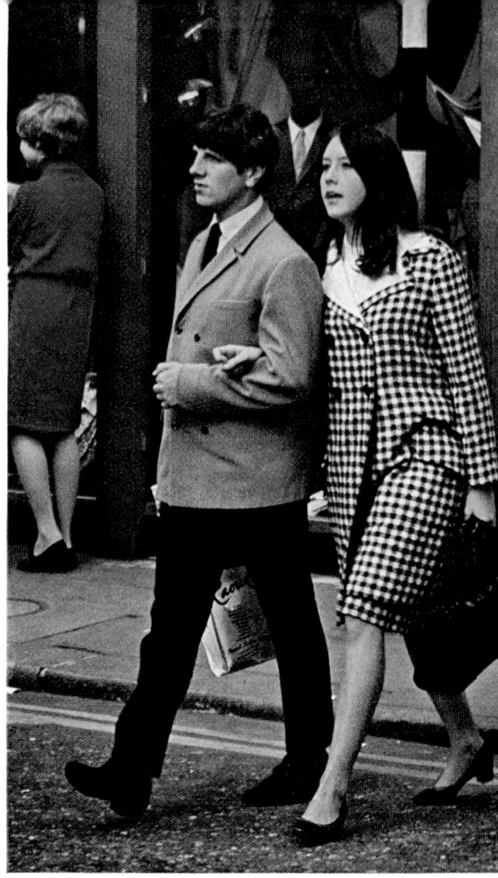

THE REGENCY—*the elegant early 1800's when the Prince of Wales reigned as Regent and John Nash as architect—inspired Regent Street, designed to sweep grandly from the Prince's mansion in Pall Mall to a proposed palace in Regent's Park. Instead of a regent, the park got a zoo (page 52). The Quadrant of Regent Street, here decorated for Christmas, houses fashionable shops.*

Schoolgirls board a narrowboat (opposite) for a cruise on another relic of the era, Regent's Canal, which traverses London's "Little Venice."

Carnaby Street shops (right) cater to Mods (short for moderns), whose penchant for fancy dress recalls a Regency dandy, Beau Brummell.

WINFIELD PARKS (UPPER) AND JAMES P. BLAIR (OPPOSITE), NATIONAL GEOGRAPHIC PHOTOGRAPHERS. BELOW: ADAM WOOLFITT

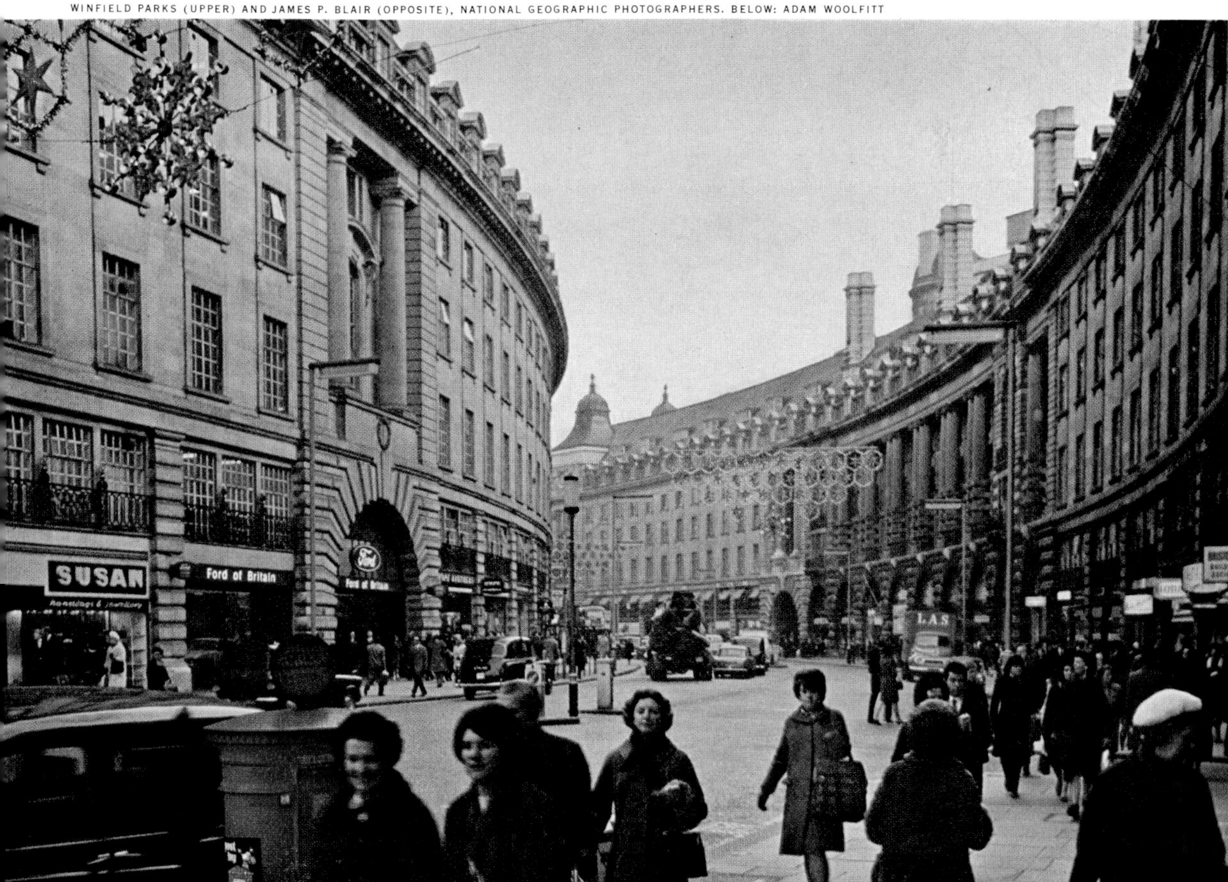

changed from the street marts of the Cockney costers at the turn of the century. Bins overflow with vegetables brought before dawn from Spitalfields Market, about a mile away. Gossiping women block the sidewalk, while children tug at their skirts.

Stepping on rhubarb stalks, breathing air that seems gray and clotted, you mingle with descendants of the original Cockney hawkers. You smell the fish and meats laid out for the flies and the sun and the housewives. "S. R. Kelly Live Eel and Meat Pies" – the sign catches your eye as you continue down this tawdry yet vital street. Listening to the talk and laughter, you begin to understand the inimitable Cockney spirit celebrated in such memorable shows as *Oliver!* and *My Fair Lady.*

"Cockney is still alive, but dying," a young woman shopper tells you while the coster wraps her fish. "Take me; I don't speak at work – or to you – the way I do at home. But we Cockneys are great talkers. We say what we mean and mean what we say, always in negatives, like 'You don't 'arf look a treat,' which means you look great. Or at the market, when my mother is looking over some nice meat pies, she'd say 'not 'arf nice.'

"Cockneys all come from big families, and they have big families of their own. Sons and daughters will live with mum forever, so generations of large families grow

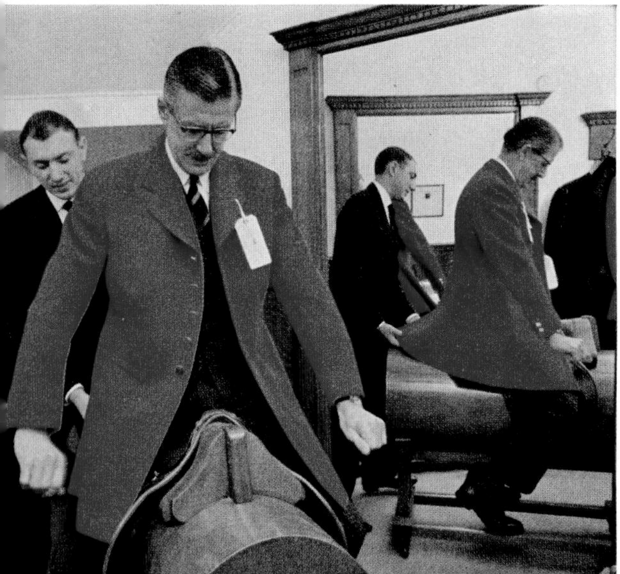

HUNTERS OF BARGAINS—*or foxes—stalk London shops. In Petticoat Lane (opposite upper), baubles are the lure. Antiques (lower) draw others to stalls in Portobello Road. On Savile Row (far left), a gentleman of the chase mounts a wooden horse to be fitted for a hunt coat.*

FESTOONED WITH PHEASANTS, *a Brompton Road shop displays seafood on a marble slab. Prepackaging has not invaded this and many another stronghold of the fishmonger and the greengrocer. London housewives can also pick fruit from curbside barrows and fresh vegetables from open-air stalls.*

JAMES P. BLAIR, NATIONAL GEOGRAPHIC PHOTOGRAPHER. OPPOSITE: W. D. VAUGHN (UPPER) AND ADAM WOOLFITT

WINFIELD PARKS, NATIONAL GEOGRAPHIC PHOTOGRAPHER (ALSO RIGHT)

IN SERRIED ROWS, *or stacked in towers, London flats reflect changing styles. Classical façade of Kensington Place (left) contrasts coolly with gingerbread exuberance of Hornton Street's cast-iron railings, mansard roofs, bay windows rusticated with stucco and keystoned with male and female masks (above). Homes for thousands rise in modern simplicity on Alton Estate (upper), a low-income development six miles from the heart of the city. Bungalows for the aged share the 130-acre parkland.*

WHERE HORSES *were housed, the fashionable now flock. The neighborhood of Ennismore Mews (right) today knows no neighs. Hawks cooped while mewing, or molting, originally occupied mews; at the Royal Mews, stables replaced cages but the name stuck. Stability came to sagging sheds when the sports-car set shifted to cobbled courtyards and discovered the joys and prestige of living in spruced-up stalls.*

But mews dwellers are not amused by much of London's new look. No longer bound by a 100-foot limit, skyscrapers sprouted from war's rubble. The new Post Office Tower, Britain's tallest, rises 582 feet, topped by a revolving restaurant. The 30-story London Hilton (below) is a Yankee newcomer to the staid West End. Before the Y-shaped hotel stretches Hyde Park; beyond, the smart district of Mayfair.

JOHN E. FLETCHER AND (ABOVE AND OPPOSITE UPPER) JAMES P. BLAIR, NATIONAL GEOGRAPHIC PHOTOGRAPHERS

up together. If someone dies, you put on a good funeral with lots of flowers, because the neighbors judge everything. Weddings have to be big too, and on Saturday, the established day. Oh, I'm proud I'm a Cockney."

NEARLY EVERYONE criticizes London's size and congestion—and has done so for 400 years. In 1580 Queen Elizabeth I, aghast that the old warren harbored 140,000 people, forbade new construction within the city walls or within three miles of its gates. No one took the order very seriously, but King James I later enforced it; he also ordered all noblemen without business in London to remain at their country homes unless Parliament was in session. The King, and generations of wishful-thinking town planners, might as well have tried to restrain the tide on the Thames. London continued to engulf its suburbs.

This growth has brought the city to the boundaries of the Green Belt, an 840-square-mile preserve, mostly of natural field and heath, held as soul-satisfying elbow room for confined urbanites. It encircles

TARTANS SWINGING, *gaiters gleaming, Scottish pipes of the Cameronians wheel past the memorial to Victoria before Buckingham Palace, London residence of the Queen. Crowds gather at 11:30 daily for the changing of the guard—thumping regimental band, six-foot guardsmen in scarlet tunics, bearskin hats, and pipe-clayed crossbelts, shouted orders, stamping feet, toy-soldier precision. Wide-eyed children find it hard to believe that "A soldier's life is terrible hard. . ."*

ADAM WOOLFITT

the city like a constrictive girdle. Now, as never before, London is practicing girth control. Although the city's new skyline boasts impressive new skyscrapers, laws severely restrict construction. Other laws encourage – indeed, prod – companies and individuals to seek their fortunes outside Greater London. To accommodate this "overspill," the national government has built eight new towns at least 30 miles from London. Twenty-five existing towns, 30 to 100 miles out, have agreed to absorb more people and businesses.

Because of these programs, London's population has fallen slightly. But the traffic seems no less congested. Each day nearly 16 million journeys are made within, into, or out of London. At Hyde Park Corner, the busiest intersection, more than 145,000 vehicles stream by in a twelve-hour period. Aside from the occasional stockbroker who absentmindedly wields his rolled umbrella like a rapier, the British commuter seems notable for his patience and good manners. In return, he enjoys a notably efficient transportation system.

"TROOPING THE COLOUR," *the Queen's Household Brigade stages a martial spectacle at Whitehall in honor of the monarch's "official" birthday each June. Her actual birth date is April 21. In the uniform of the Welsh Guards, the Queen and the Duke of Edinburgh here inspect her Life Guards, red-plumed Horse Guards, and her foot troops—Irish, Scots, Welsh, Grenadier, and Coldstream Guards. Sun gilds helmet and white plume of Life Guardsman at right.*

Beyond pageantry, the Royal Family plays a personal role in the life of each citizen. He comments freely on the Queen's health, Prince Charles at school, Princess Margaret's coiffure. "We live in what virtually amounts to a museum," Prince Philip has said. Other royal dukes, such as Gloucester and Kent, are also in the public eye, visiting factories and opening exhibitions. Royal dukedoms date from 1337 when Edward, the Black Prince, became the Duke of Cornwall. Today the monarch's eldest son assumes that title at birth; later he is named the Prince of Wales.

JAMES P. BLAIR, NATIONAL GEOGRAPHIC PHOTOGRAPHER

London's Underground, the world's first, operates 215 miles of track. Each year this subway records 675 million fares. Topside, 8,000 buses and 7,000 taxicabs ply the city's 7,000 miles of streets.

Gladstone is credited with advising some visitors: "The way to see London is from the top of a bus—the top of a bus, gentlemen." I agree. It's like sitting in a traveling red grandstand. As for the London cab, I maintain it's the most sensible vehicle ever designed. Someone who never heard of Detroit gave the cab a flat floor, large doors, and a spacious interior. Even with a topper on, you can enter without feeling that you are climbing into a well. And the car will turn on a sixpence.

Although the interior glass panel makes conversation with the driver difficult, I persist in talking to cabbies. They know such wonderful stories about Americans.

"Had a nice old lady in my cab who kept talking 'bout morale posters," one cabbie told me. "She says, 'The war's been over for years. Why do you still have those signs to help your morale?'

"I asks her, 'What signs? Show me one.' So she did, guv'nor. Like that one." He gestured toward a rooftop sign: "Take Courage." It advertised a British beer.

Although London was not planned for the convenience of tourists, some of its most famous places—the Tower, St. Paul's, Parliament, Westminster Abbey, Buckingham Palace—lie within easy cab distance, or even walking distance, of one another in the City of Westminster or the venerable City of London.

An Englishman refers to the City of London simply as the City, with a capital "C," and everyone knows he means the oldest part of London, a political entity extending back to Roman times.

Within the City, or Square Mile, as it is also called, one can still see remains of the stone wall that encircled Roman Londinium and medieval London.

The Lord Mayor presides over this little fief with medieval pomp and ceremony. When he takes office, London stages its most famous spectacle, the Lord Mayor's Show, a rousing parade through the city to the Royal Courts of Justice in the Strand.

I witnessed one in a drenching rain. Bands blared, military units strode by in sodden but impeccable ranks, and throngs cheered from beneath massed umbrellas.

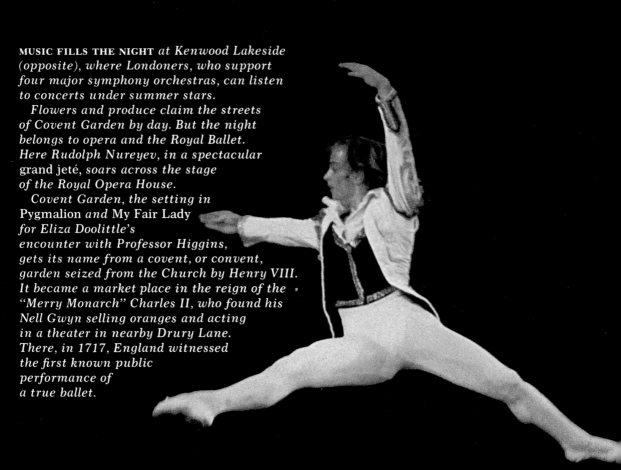

MUSIC FILLS THE NIGHT *at Kenwood Lakeside (opposite), where Londoners, who support four major symphony orchestras, can listen to concerts under summer stars.*

Flowers and produce claim the streets of Covent Garden by day. But the night belongs to opera and the Royal Ballet. Here Rudolph Nureyev, in a spectacular grand jeté, *soars across the stage of the Royal Opera House.*

Covent Garden, the setting in Pygmalion *and* My Fair Lady *for Eliza Doolittle's encounter with Professor Higgins, gets its name from a covent, or convent, garden seized from the Church by Henry VIII. It became a market place in the reign of the "Merry Monarch" Charles II, who found his Nell Gwyn selling oranges and acting in a theater in nearby Drury Lane. There, in 1717, England witnessed the first known public performance of a true ballet.*

In park, theater, and gallery, London royally champions the arts

JAMES P. BLAIR, NATIONAL GEOGRAPHIC PHOTOGRAPHER

FASHIONABLE PREVIEW *of the summer exhibition at the Royal Academy of Arts draws art patrons, multimillionaire J. Paul Getty among them. The show included works by Sir Winston Churchill. Founded in 1768 with Sir Joshua Reynolds its first president, the Academy sponsors free schools for young artists. Blake, Turner, and Constable were pupils.*

Art lovers find a feast in London's rich collections. They delight in European masterpieces at the National Gallery, survey British art at the Tate Gallery, study historic faces in the National Portrait Gallery, marvel at furnishings in the Victoria and Albert Museum.

Huge floats rumbled by. Last of all came the Lord Mayor in a massive coach drawn by six horses. With its fresh gilt and red paint, the coach blazed like a tropical sunset.

Beyond the City's boundaries the Lord Mayor has no jurisdiction; within them he ranks second only to the sovereign. If the Queen visits the City, she must pause at its outskirts to receive the Lord Mayor's welcome. In fealty he offers her the Pearl Sword – traditionally with point downward lest someone suspect his intentions.

When old "Tempull Barre" was a stout gate across the road at the City's western edge, Elizabeth I accepted the sword there as she journeyed to St. Paul's to give thanks for the destruction of the Spanish Armada. Even the dour Cromwell halted there when he went to the City to dine in state in 1649. A sooty and spectacularly ugly statue of a winged dragon has replaced the gate at Temple Bar.

Once a year a robed and bewigged delegation strides purposefully into the Royal Courts of Justice and seeks out that specialist in matters ceremonial, Queen Elizabeth II's Remembrancer. With a grave bow of acknowledgment, the Remembrancer accepts in Her Majesty's behalf these items: six horseshoes ("suitable for the forefeet of a great Flemish warhorse"), 61 horseshoe nails, a hatchet, and a billhook.

Warrants attesting receipt of the token hardware are recorded. Once again the Lord Mayor's resolutely independent City has paid its annual land rents to the Crown.

The Remembrancer always remembers to appear for the October ceremony; it has been held without break for more than 500 years. In some mysterious fashion the horseshoes and nails find their way back to City officials and are bestowed upon the Queen again the next year. However, custom requires that she annually receive a new hatchet and billhook.

In medieval times, guilds selected the City's principal officials – and they still do. Today, representatives of 82 of these trade associations, or "misteries," gather as electors each year to name sheriffs and other dignitaries, and to choose the Lord Mayor. Long ago the guilds adopted distinctive

SAVOYARDS *shine in an opera company bearing the name of Richard D'Oyly Carte, who teamed W. S. Gilbert and Arthur Sullivan in 1875.*

In Ruddigore, *a spoof on Victorian melodramas, Richard Dauntless (above) shushes Sir Ruthven Murgatroyd. It opened in 1887 at the Savoy, London's first electrically lighted theater, built especially for Gilbert and Sullivan operettas after the success of* Trial by Jury, H.M.S. Pinafore, The Pirates of Penzance, *and* Patience. *Sullivan's melodies and Gilbert's librettos blended onstage, but offstage feuding grew. After* The Gondoliers *in 1889, collaboration ended.*

Where hay wagons rolled, traffic now grinds to Haymarket Theatre (right), site of a stage since 1720. Stung by satire here, Prime Minister Walpole thrashed the actor who spoke the lines, and sponsored an act giving the Lord Chamberlain power to censor, which he still has. Playgoer's paradise, London boasts some 50 theaters, with prices far below Broadway's.

ADAM WOOLFITT (ALSO BELOW). RIGHT: JAMES P. BLAIR, NATIONAL GEOGRAPHIC PHOTOGRAPHER

"**ANGRY YOUNG MEN**," *led by John Osborne, make the London stage a forum to flay Britain's stratified society. His* Look Back in Anger *set a postwar trend. Older but still angry, he created in* Inadmissible Evidence *(above) a hero adrift in a world of confusing values. Like plays as old as Shakespeare, it became an export to America.*

THE FINE ART *of auctioneering is demonstrated by Peter Wilson, chairman of Sotheby's, world's oldest art auction house, founded in 1744. Rembrandt's "Portrait of a Man" goes up for sale, and the practiced Wilson eye scans the packed room for the slightest nod or gesture. Bids and tension rise; within two minutes the masterpiece commands $392,000. The day's 124 old masters tally $2,591,400.*

SPLENDORS OF THE AGES *awe visitors to the British Museum, massive treasure-house of art and learning. The colossal head of Thutmosis III, carved in red granite about 1450* B.C., *gazes upon schoolchildren exploring the Egyptian Sculpture Gallery (below). Spoils of war wrested from the French at Alexandria in 1801 include the Rosetta Stone. Inscriptions on it gave the key to deciphering Egyptian hieroglyphics.*

Ashurbanipal in his chariot hunts lions in magnificent Assyrian reliefs. Sculptures from the Parthenon grace another gallery—the Elgin Marbles, named for Lord Elgin, who acquired them in Athens in 1801-03, and was denounced by Lord Byron for taking them from Greece.

In the museum's circular Reading Room, Karl Marx wrote Das Kapital, *now one of 6,000,000 books in a library that fills a mile of shelves with new books each year. Enshrined nearby are the ninth-century* Anglo-Saxon Chronicle, *said to be authored in part by King Alfred himself; the unique manuscript of the oldest English epic,* Beowulf; *a First Folio of Shakespeare; and the log of Nelson's* Victory.

The animal oddities with which the museum began in 1753 find a home in the Natural History Museum in South Kensington. Next to it stands the Science Museum, whose thousands of exhibits include the world's oldest locomotive.

JAMES P. BLAIR, NATIONAL GEOGRAPHIC PHOTOGRAPHER

robes and insignia, so they became known as livery companies. The City recognizes 12 "Great Companies" and assigns them this precedence: Mercers, Grocers, Drapers, Fishmongers, Goldsmiths, Skinners, Merchant Taylors, Haberdashers, Salters, Ironmongers, Vintners, and Clothworkers.

As you might suspect, most guilds no longer regulate their old trades. They exist as fraternal and charitable organizations of businessmen.

Many livery companies maintain baronial meeting halls, showplaces of the City. *The* Guildhall, however, always refers to the City's historic center of government, a magnificent place of assembly whose crypt and scarred walls survive from the 15th century. The Great Fire and the Nazi blitz badly damaged the Guildhall. But skilled hands each time faithfully restored it.

One night Mary and I visited the Guildhall to attend a formal reception and dinner given by the Right Honourable the Lord Mayor of London. The magnificent old hall was ablaze with pikemen in scarlet uniforms and helmets and breastplates of burnished metal. They stood about at strategic spots, looking determinedly picturesque.

The Lord Mayor and some of his entourage added to the antique decor by wearing knee breeches and buckled shoes. The Toastmaster, his portentous voice fairly dripping with upperclass inflections, announced each of the important guests, who then strode across a stage to receive a greeting from the Lord Mayor and his lady.

ZOO AND KEW PARADE NATURE'S MARVELS *before eager London eyes. A fine holiday may bring 50,000 visitors to Regent's Park where the Zoological Gardens opened to an incredulous public in 1828. Today, children frolic with zoo babies, ride camels and donkeys, learn how to raise chinchillas and hamsters, and watch chicks hatch and chimps take tea and play skittles. Here a zebra shyly shows its stripes, and a trunk extends in welcome at the moat before the starkly modern Elephant and Rhinoceros Pavilion.*

The Chelsea Show (opposite, upper) at the Royal Hospital for army pensioners displays spring blooms to strollers.

Bananas ripen and exotics flower in the Palm House of the Royal Botanic Gardens (lower). Begun as a royal hobby by George III's mother in 1759, the Thameside gardens blossomed into a 300-acre wonderland that brings queues to Kew. Sparked by Sir Joseph Banks, who had circumnavigated the globe with Captain Cook, Kew's green-fingered scientists explored earth's leafy mantle. They sailed with Captain Bligh, founded the quinine and rubber industries of the Far East. Millions of plant specimens at Kew serve botanists as a matchless "fingerprint" file of world flora.

JAMES P. BLAIR, NATIONAL GEOGRAPHIC PHOTOGRAPHER. LEFT: ADAM WOOLFITT

My wife was entranced. "I wonder what these people do in real life," she said.

To an American, the City's dress-up shows inevitably seem unreal, but the costumed participants never forget they are heirs of England's oldest traditions and custodians of ground hallowed by history. Almost every time workmen lay a foundation in the City, they unearth objects dating back nearly 2,000 years. London Museum maintains a large collection of these artifacts of Londinium—pottery, tile, coins, tools, knives.

THE LORD MAYOR'S "kingdom" has evolved from a plague-ridden, medieval warren into a vastly powerful financial center. In this citadel of the sterling area, often called the wealthiest square mile on earth, stand Britain's greatest fiscal and commercial institutions: Lloyd's of London; worldwide shipping firms; the London Stock Exchange; merchant houses older than the United States, such as the Hudson's Bay Company; and banks, including that awesome symbol of stability, the Bank of England.

A cartoon of 1797 depicted the bank as a rich dowager sitting atop a money box. Since then, the bank has been known far and wide as the Old Lady of Threadneedle Street.

A detachment from the Brigade of Guards rumbles through the City nightly to take up posts inside the bank, a custom that began during the anti-Catholic Gordon Riots of 1780. Bank messengers wear pink tail coats, scarlet vests, and top hats, believed to be the livery the bank's first governor prescribed for his servants.

Perhaps the City tradition most scrupulously observed is one that the financial houses share—best summed up by the Stock Exchange's Latin motto: *Dictum Meum Pactum*, "My Word is my Bond." Exchange members meet daily on their

GREAT HALL OF MIDDLE TEMPLE, *a cradle of English common law, fetes barristers and their guests. Queen Elizabeth I may have witnessed a performance of Shakespeare's* Twelfth Night *under these magnificent oaken beams. Plaques on the wall honor readers, or instructors. Armorial bearings of Sir Walter Raleigh and other prominent Middle Templars decorate windows.*

Middle Temple and Inner Temple began teaching law more than 600 years ago when jurists acquired property of the Knights Templars as an inn. Only the Inns of Court—the Temples, Gray's, and Lincoln's—can call a person "to the bar," enabling him to practice in the higher courts. A bar once separated public from court. Student "barristers" were called to it to hear cases.

JOHN E. FLETCHER, NATIONAL GEOGRAPHIC PHOTOGRAPHER, AND W. D. VAUGHN

London's river saw the pageantry of a lusty age perish in plague and fire

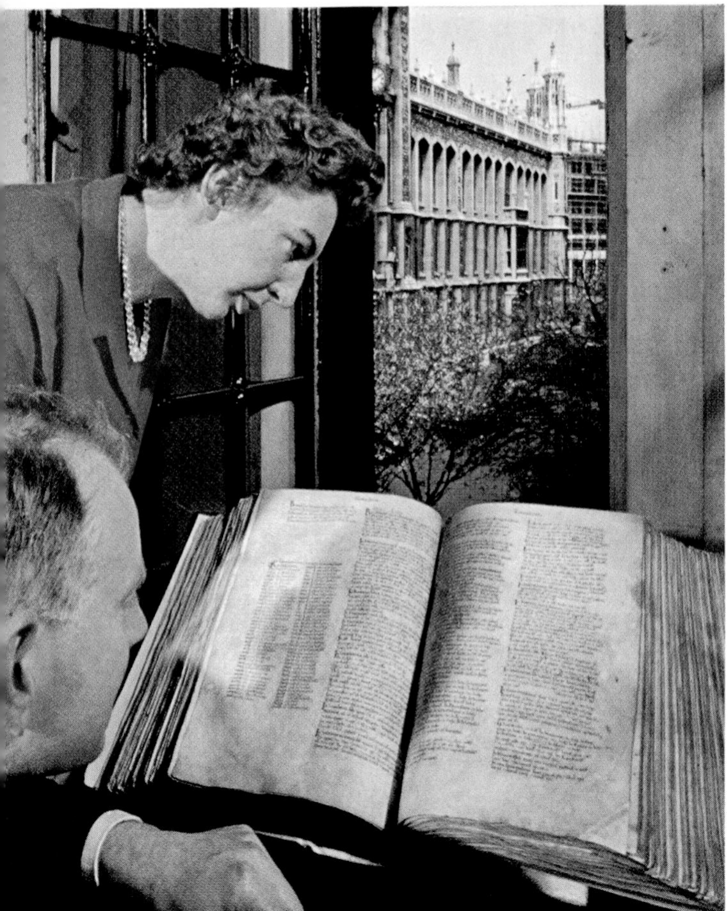

W. E. ROSCHER AND E. D. HESS. BELOW: VIEW OF LONDON ENGRAVED BY C. J. VISSCHER IN 1616; COURTESY GUILDHALL LIBRARY. OPPOSITE: JAMES P. BLAIR, NATIONAL GEOGRAPHIC PHOTOGRAPHER

IN THE "RATTLING, rowling, rumbling age" of Tudors and Stuarts, the mainstream of London life surges with the River Thames. Fishermen, lightermen, and swans ply the "silver christall streame." Wherrymen split the air with cries as they vie for water-taxi fares from north bank to Southwark.

Pageantry blazons the river highway as royal barges float in stately processions with "minstrels making . . . sweet harmony."

Sport roils the waters as Henry VIII and a boisterous company bait a swimming bear. A wherry rowing a cleric from Westminster to the City passes. Before he can utter a paternoster, "The bear brake loose and came into the boat," forcing him over the side.

Tragedy rides the river. Malefactors hanged at Wapping lie in cages to be washed by three tides. Prison barges ply between courts and Tower, grim headsman with his victim on board. Traitors' Gate at waterside clangs behind wretched souls doomed by Bloody Mary. But her half sister Elizabeth, Londoners say, refuses to enter as a traitor. Tower warders kneel as she passes by.

Enthroned, "Good Queen Bess" makes "progresses" 'twixt palaces at Whitehall, Greenwich, Richmond, Hampton Court, and Windsor. She goes to Deptford to knight Francis Drake aboard his globe-girdling *Golden Hind.* When the Armada threatens, she hastens to Tilbury to cheer her troops.

Familiar landmarks (below) greet her eyes: The Bear Garden *(1)*, where crowds roar to see "a greate mastyfe dogge and a foule ouglye bear . . . fyght wyth terrible teaarynge" the Globe *(2)*, where Shakespeare conjures up "the vasty fields of France" in his *Henry V;* Southwark Cathedral *(3)*, also called "St. Mary's of the Ferry." Her barge tosses in the waters swirling under London Bridge *(4)*, "falling down" in the nursery rhyme, but here crammed with shops, homes and brawlers ("Many a man was slayne and caste in Temys"). Heads of traitors molder on spikes at the Surrey side.

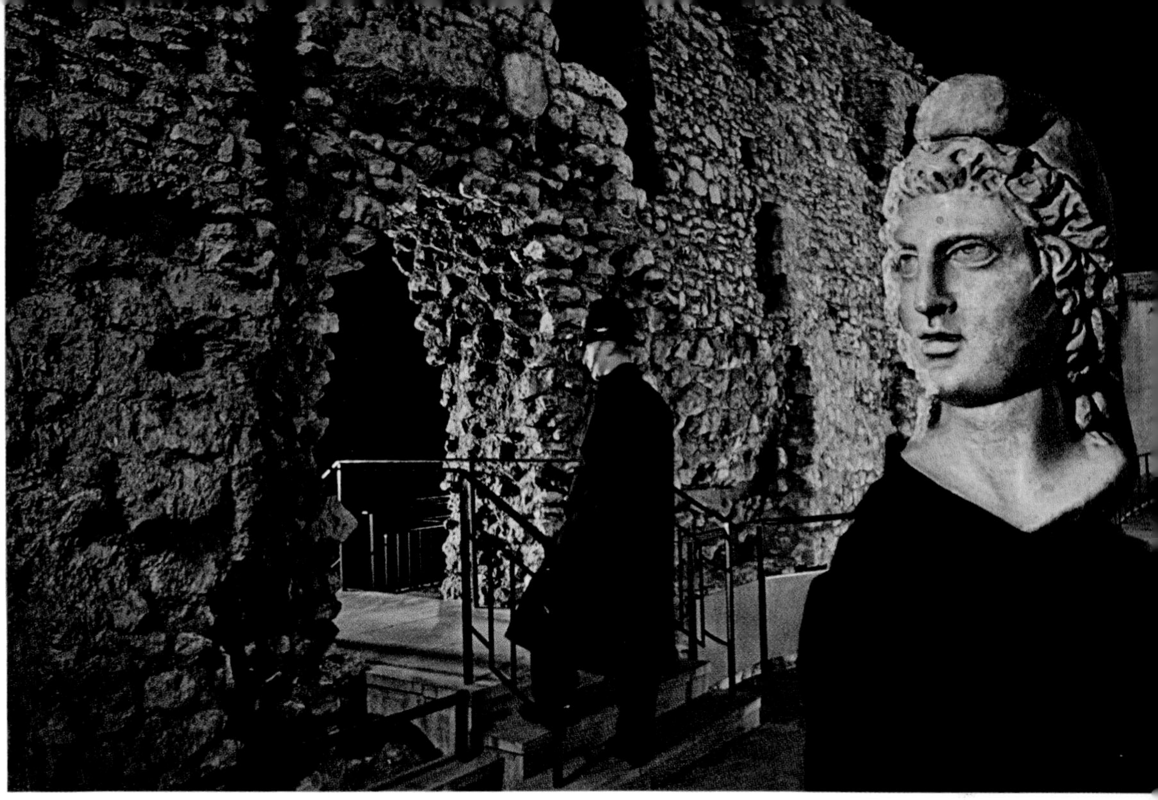

She grimly recalls her days in the Tower *(5)*. In the Guildhall *(6)* a Jewish doctor was tried for trying to poison her (the inspiration, some say, for Shylock in *The Merchant of Venice*). Beyond rises St. Paul's *(7)*, its spire shorn by lightning.

Londinium knew other gods. A Mithras head was unearthed in 1954 amid a temple to this sun god. Romans founded the city soon after A.D. 43. They spanned the river with a wooden drawbridge and barged stone from Kent to ring their capital with a three-mile wall. Part still stands (above).

Up the Thames came stone from Normandy for the Conqueror's White Tower. William ordered a tax survey in 1086, and "there was not one hide nor yard of land . . . that was not set down. . . ." Today at the Public Record Office (opposite) scholars consult this Domesday, or Doomsday, Book – so called because it seemed as complete a record as would be kept for the Last Judgment.

Doomsday seems near when bubonic plague strikes in 1665. House after house is chalked with a red cross and the words "Lord have mercy upon us." Bells toll endlessly; at night they signal the passage of "deadcarts" stacked with corpses. Wracked with pain from the buboes, fatal swelling of lymph glands, victims run naked through the streets to fling themselves in the Thames. Some 7,000 die in a week, almost 70,000 in the year.

Winter slows the march of the rat-borne infection; soon Charles II and others who had fled return.

In September, 1666, fire breaks out in a bakery. Wind whips it into "malicious, bloody flame." Buildings crumple, screaming people flee. Stone explodes, bits flying "like grenados." In five days 13,000 houses, 89 churches, and St. Paul's lie in ruins.

Phoenixlike, the city rises from its ashes, shaped by the genius of Sir Christopher Wren and dominated by his masterpiece, a new St. Paul's.

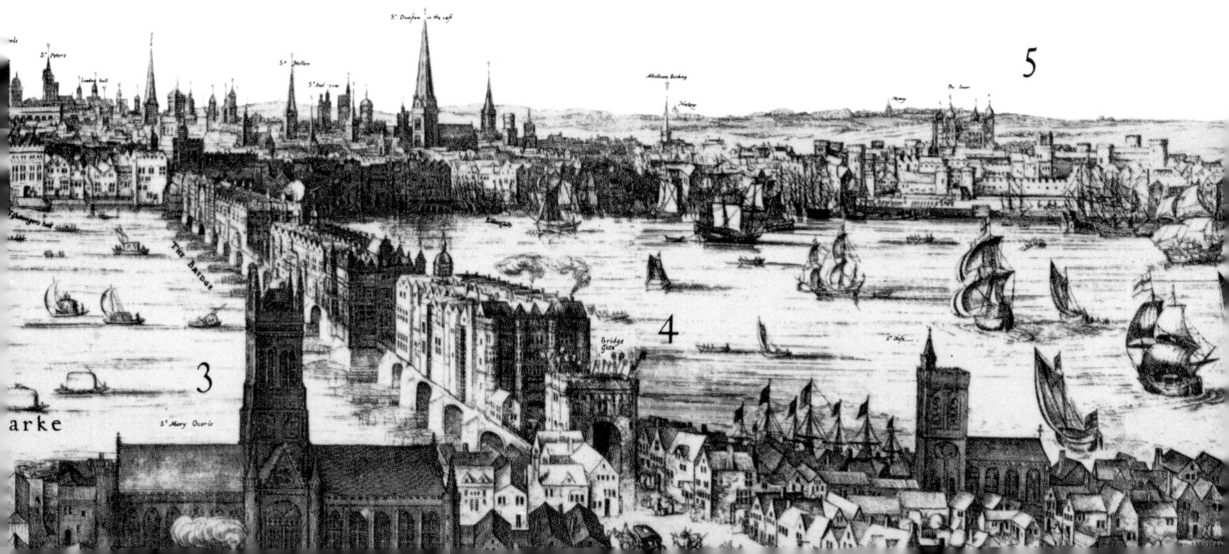

JAMES P. BLAIR, NATIONAL GEOGRAPHIC PHOTOGRAPHER. OPPOSITE: ADAM WOOLFITT

THEY BANK ON EACH OTHER: *Britain's financial lions deal in a currency of trust and tradition.*

At Lloyd's of London (above), whose motto Fidentia *means confidence, an attendant rings the famous* Lutine Bell. *Salvaged from H.M.S.* Lutine, *which sank in 1799 off the Netherlands with £1,000,000 in Lloyd's-insured gold, the bell tolls once for bad news, twice for good.*

It stands in the "Room," a huge marble hall where brokers scurry to and fro, bargaining with various underwriters for the best possible odds on a given risk. "I'll have a go at it," one says and scrawls the amount of his liability and his initials on the slip. Others write their initials under his. Often hundreds "underwrite" part of the risk.

Brokers, some in top hats, and jobbers jam the Stock Exchange (left), jotting "deals" in "bargain books." Jobbers in the "House" buy and sell stock to brokers, who represent the public.

Bank of England's columns stand like stone sentinels along a windowless wall on Threadneedle Street (opposite). Royal Exchange, whose pediment represents commerce, faces the square guarded by the Duke of Wellington, cast from captured French cannon. The sculptor forgot stirrups.

trading floor. Here some 2,500 men mill about in chattering groups, buying and selling immensely valuable holdings. A signature or receipt? Not needed. A man's word is good enough. Let the paper work come when clerks record sales the next day.

"We can't always predict the reaction of members to a visitor," one of the officials explained, when I asked if I could go on the floor. "They usually spot him, and someone may cry, 'Fourteen hundred!' You see, years ago the Exchange had precisely 1,399 members. An outsider on the floor became number 1,400, and up went the cry.

"Recently we let a photographer on the floor, and 500 men began following him about. I think he wore a sports shirt. But they were delighted with another visitor, a famous Australian cricket player. Members set up a cricket pitch, with wadded paper for a ball and a newspaper for a bat.

"But you might even pass as a member," the official added graciously.

Thus cheered, I ventured on the floor with the general superintendent.

Members of the Exchange adhere strictly to the customary garb of City men: dark suits, sober ties, and black shoes, sometimes called "the uniform." I soon realized I was the only man on the floor wearing brown shoes. Despite my breach of the uniform, I attracted few stares and no outcries.

Like members of the Stock Exchange, Lloyd's of London underwriters gathered in the coffeehouses of 17th-century London to conduct their business. Eventually the underwriters settled in the coffeehouse of Edward Lloyd, whose name became indelibly associated with insurance ventures.

Today Lloyd's counts some 5,000 underwriting members. They comprise a society of associates, not a company. More than 200 brokerage firms bring them proposals from just about every corner of the globe, and they have a reputation for accepting risks considered too chancy by others.

The Stock Exchange and Lloyd's are by far the best known of the City's many marts. But the old firms of Mincing Lane do a brisk wholesale business in exotic goods.

Hale & Son, established in 1780, is one of the deans of Mincing Lane, where the smell of lands over the far horizon hangs heavy on the air. There I felt and sniffed birds' nests that enrich Chinese soup; dark ambergris and russet beaver glands that contri-

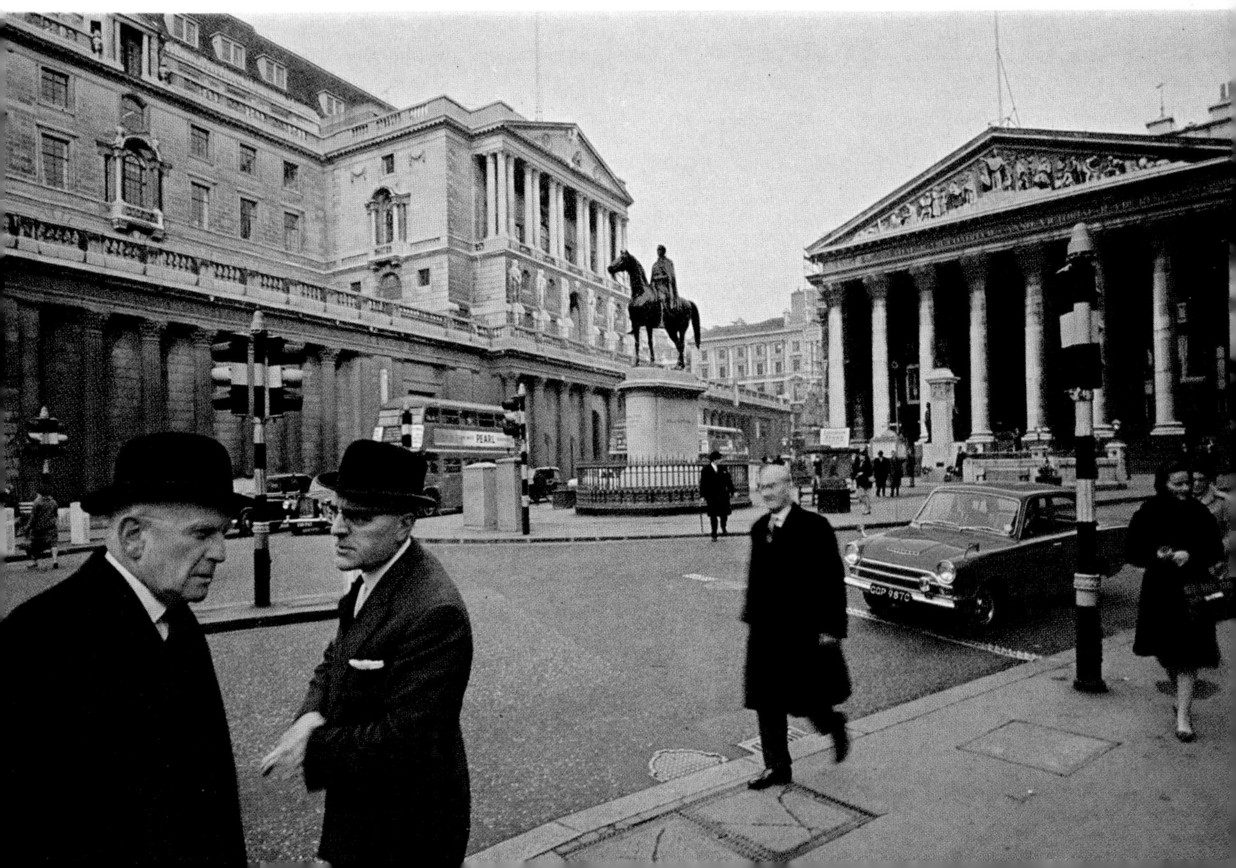

bute to perfume; rhino horn, valued by the Chinese as an aphrodisiac.

If you like walking, I can recommend the City on Sunday; then the buildings stand deserted, and empty streets return the sound of footfalls. Begin at the Tower, that grim pile of long and bloody fame. Every bleak chamber in the buildings comprising the Tower of London has its tales of intrigue, often ending on the headsman's block.

From Norman times the Tower has been a state prison, its captives ranging from Ralph Flambard, Bishop of Durham, in 1100 to Rudolf Hess, the Nazi leader, in World War II. The torture instruments and a headsman's block and ax remain as grisly curios in the White Tower.

The Little Princes, Edward V and his brother, the Duke of York, were murdered in the Bloody Tower in 1483. Their uncle, who became King Richard III, is believed by some historians to have ordered their deaths. Assassins killed Henry VI, according to old belief, in Wakefield Tower, and this deed is often attributed to Richard.

If you still have the strength after tramping through the throngs of visitors at the Tower, leave the crowds behind by walking down Lower Thames Street past old Billingsgate Market, a site where fish have been sold for a thousand years.

"Billingsgate" has long been a word synonymous with vituperative language. But the market superintendent once told me, with a resigned air, "The codwives years ago used the bad language, not the market men. The talk you hear around the market is no worse than any other place where you have 3,000 men under one roof."

NEAR BILLINGSGATE stands the Monument, a fluted Doric column 202 feet high, designed by Sir Christopher Wren to commemorate the Great Fire of 1666, which reputedly started exactly 202 feet away, in Pudding Lane. The Monument's spiral staircase will make you feel like a fly crawling up a corkscrew, but if you can manage the 311 steps, one of London's finest views will reward you at the top.

A visit to the marvelous chaos of the open-air market in Petticoat Lane is another fine way to begin a Sunday in London. Barkers man flimsy counters on either side of the narrow thoroughfare and hawk their wares: toys, watches, clothes, rings, silver, china. "I'll sell these articles so cheap you'll think they're stolen–but they're only partly stolen!" shouts a pitchman to the gawkers.

According to legend, the lane (actually, Middlesex Street) got its name because the pitchmen were such clever sleight-of-hand artists that they could steal a housewife's petticoat and sell it back to her–as new.

THE SHAPELY DOME and gilded cross of St. Paul's Cathedral is seldom out of sight as you stroll the City's historic streets. St. Paul's (officially, London Cathedral) stands on a site where prayer and worship have been offered to God for more than 1,300 years. Construction of Wren's masterpiece began in 1675. His son put the last stone in place in 1708. Wren designed 52 other churches in London after the Great Fire. By 1939 only 33 still existed. Of these, 17 were destroyed or gutted in the bombing that devastated London in World War II.

From the exterior gallery of St. Paul's dome, 283 feet above Ludgate Hill, you can pick out other landmarks: to the west, Fleet Street, canyoned by newspaper and publishing houses; to the south, the College of Arms, "keeper of the blood," or coats of arms; to the north, Old Bailey court and Smithfield, the wholesale meat market.

At the handsome 17th-century building that houses the College I had talked with an official bearing the romantic title of Bluemantle Pursuivant. He told me the college gets a constant flow of American visitors, most seeking to trace family trees.

The Old Bailey takes its name from the adjacent street. In turn, this street probably was named for the *ballium*, an areaway or wall in the City's defenses. Dread Newgate Prison, mentioned in Dickens' works, occupied the site until 1902. Executions used to be held outside its walls.

Smithfield, too, was once a place for public executions. Queen Mary I, best known as Bloody Mary, ordered 200 persons burned at the stake there over a four-year period.

From the dome of St. Paul's you can also

Pounds, shillings, and pence tell a sterling story

BRITAIN'S MONEY TALKS in many tongues. The pound ($2.80) was once a weight of silver. The sign £ stands for *libra*, its Latin name.

Shilling derives from a Saxon word, but the symbol *s.* refers to *solidus*, a Roman coin. Twenty shillings make a pound.

Penny, probably of Germanic origin, gets its symbol *d.* from *denarius*, a Roman coin which, like the early penny, was silver. Twelve pence make a shilling.

On the 10-shilling note (never "bill") rests a half crown, worth 2*s.* 6*d.* (or 2/6). A pair of florins, 2*s.* each, show head and tail atop the pound note. Florin may trace to *fiorino*, flower, a gold coin struck in Florence in 1252. Below them lies a sixpence; under it a penny adorned by Britannia. Then comes a threepenny bit ("thruppence") whose 12 sides helped bus conductors distinguish it in wartime blackouts. Portcullis on its face appears in the Palace of Westminster badge and symbolizes Parliament. Halfpenny ("hayp'ny") below it is the cheapest coin, for in 1960 the farthing died. Medieval farthing, a quarter-penny, could buy a plump chicken. Bottom coin is a shilling, first given firm value by Henry VII. At right, Churchill glowers from a crown (5*s.*), minted as a commemorative and like the gold sovereign (£1) valued as a collector's item. He is the first commoner to appear on a British coin with the monarch.

The gold guinea, named for Guinea gold, is long defunct. But "guinea" (21*s.*) graces price tags for luxury goods and bills for professional services.

In slang a pound is a quid, a shilling's a bob, a penny's a copper (though it's bronze), and, oddly, a crown is a dollar. All the money is called sterling, perhaps from "starling," which recalls the small star on early Norman pennies.

Gold worth millions is stacked in the Bank of England (below). Bars weigh 25 to 30 pounds. Scale, affectionately called the Lord High Chancellor, is accurate to 1/40th ounce.

W. D. VAUGHN

perceive the life-giving role of the Thames, a pulsing artery that loops through the very heart of the metropolis. Old Father Thames to many is a surpassingly ugly river. But to me it has the beauty of utility and vitality. Unlike the serene Seine of Paris, the Thames is a working river.

Oceangoing freighters head as far upstream as London Bridge. Downstream, the docks of the Port of London Authority form watery mazes along the river. For miles, giant cranes tower above the wharves like monstrous praying mantises. Some 5,500 barges serve the Port of London, and at times it seems that all, shepherded by chuffing tugs, are on the move at once.

The men of Scotland Yard's Thames Division perhaps know the Thames best. This division, formed in 1798, is the oldest branch of the Metropolitan Police. It evolved from a force of tough rivermen organized by the West India Company of Merchantmen to protect cargoes against looting and pilfering. One lowering morning I went on a prowl cruise with a sergeant from the Waterloo Pier.

We were cruising one of the most storied areas of the Thames. On the South bank I glimpsed the site of the bearbaiting pit where bloody spectacles competed with the plays of William Shakespeare, performed nearby. I tried to draw the sergeant out on the river history of that romantic past. But he was intent on the present.

"See that?" he asked, pointing to a canvas-covered, nondescript barge tied up at a wharf. "Brandy," he said. "Forty thousand pounds' worth. But nobody's going to pinch a drop of it."

On another visit to the Thames I made a foray deep into the Royal Albert Dock, where I met J. H. Norman, master of a battered and delightfully obsolete 68-year-old tub, the *Ethel,* one of the last of the

W. D. VAUGHN. ABOVE AND RIGHT: JAMES P. BLAIR, NATIONAL GEOGRAPHIC PHOTOGRAPHER

BILLINGSGATE PORTER *"nuts" (carries) a crate of fish on his hat, a hard-leather heirloom. Sherry flows into a measuring jug in Crescent Vault (upper), a vast cellar for wine merchants. Freighters crowd quays (left), 42 miles from the sea. The port's man-made lakes, linked to the Thames by locks, can take more than 100 ships at a time.*

sailing barges to ply the Thames. These squat vessels, operating between the English Channel ports and London, still run under sail when they can, though all have engines.

Norman, a typical London waterman, wore a threadbare dark jacket and trousers, a scarf, and a battered old cap. He rolled a cigarette and talked while we waited for a lock to clear so that *Ethel*, laden with soybeans, could enter the river.

"I c'yam to London on a sighling barge 1913 or 1914, and I been sighling 'em back here ever since. No, I don't mind using 'er engine. Unless you have a fair wind of it, she won't do much alone, but with sighl and 'er motor together, she does eight knots. A right proper good old girl."

The lock cleared and Norman eased *Ethel* out into the stream under power. At that moment I made a resolution to find J. H. Norman again and sail with him down the river route of the sea dogs and beat up the Channel under *Ethel*'s patched old canvas.

Some of the most fascinating Thames-side activity goes on deep underground. There in six dimly lit man-made caverns, the Port of London Authority stores some 83,000 casks of wine and spirits.

My favorite of these huge caves, the Crescent Wine Vault, was built more than 150 years ago by prisoners taken during the Napoleonic Wars. The prisoners, being French, thought the construction of a home for wine an excellent idea and fell to with right good will. Casks in seemingly endless files stretch away beneath brick arches festooned with fungus and eerily illuminated by gas lamps flickering to an occasional spectral breath. Newly formed fungus looks like Spanish moss; later it solidifies and takes on the dank, dark look of congealed blood.

"The fungus feeds on the wine," explained a guide. "The wine breathes—evaporates through the wood of the cask. The vapor gets on the ceiling, and the fungus grows there."

I have an uneasy feeling that the Crescent Wine Vault's days are numbered, for the modern way to store wine is in bulk, like fuel oil or gasoline. Ships fitted as wine tankers berth alongside a warehouse and disgorge their contents into huge glass-lined tanks. When a merchant wants some wine, a tanker truck delivers it.

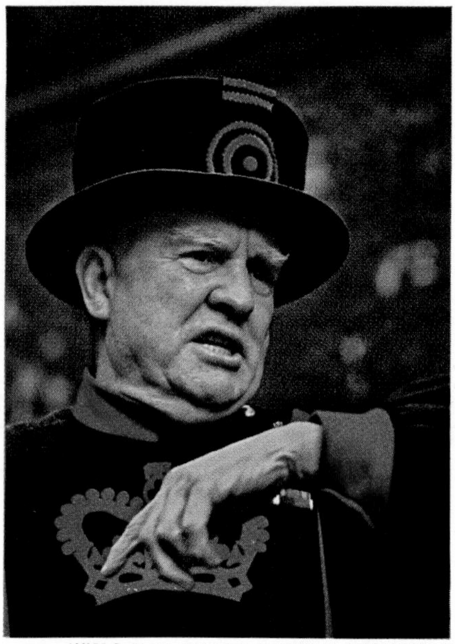

JAMES P. BLAIR, NATIONAL GEOGRAPHIC PHOTOGRAPHER

THE TOWER OF LONDON *would look like this to the Tower ravens—if they could fly. But their wings are clipped; legend says Britain will fall if the ravens leave.*

Yeomen Warders in Tudor garb spellbind visitors with tales of the grim fortress, dominated by the square White Tower William the Conqueror built nearly 900 years ago. Retired warrant officers, the warders often are mistakenly called Beefeaters, a term for Yeomen of the Guard, who attend the Queen. Large beef rations inspired that name.

Twin piers of Tower Bridge rise behind. Center drawspan can let through seagoing ships.

The man showing me around this warehouse pointed to the maze of pipelines. "Some day," he said thoughtfully, "we are going to pump some claret or burgundy into some sauterne. That's never happened yet, but it's the kind of nightmare I live with."

I confess the thought cheered me. I hate to see the death of the old colorful ways of handling wine. That evening, unnerved by this glimpse of the future, I indulged myself in a very fine burgundy that had never tried to breathe in a glass-lined tank.

Port of London facilities are not open to casual visitors, but you can get an excellent look at a vibrant part of dockland by taking an excursion boat from Westminster Pier or Charing Cross Pier downstream to Greenwich, home of the Royal Naval College and site of the Greenwich Zero Meridian, the line from which geographers measure the longitude of every point on earth. Doughty little sightseeing craft also push upstream to the Royal Botanic Gardens at Kew and to Hampton Court Palace, given by the luckless Cardinal Wolsey to his mercurial sovereign Henry VIII.

"Earth has not anything to show more fair," Wordsworth wrote in describing London's most celebrated river view from a vantage point on the old Westminster Bridge. From the graceful new bridge, built in 1862, the view now may well be more fair. When

Wordsworth wrote his poem, the turreted, richly Gothic Palace of Westminster (Houses of Parliament), stretching 940 feet along the riverside, had not been built. Begun in 1840 and completed in 1860, the palace replaced the centuries-old Parliamentary home, St. Stephen's Chapel, destroyed by fire in 1834. Fate dealt more kindly with nearby Westminster Hall, begun by William Rufus in 1097, and Westminster Abbey, the British shrine-of-shrines started by Edward the Confessor before the Norman Conquest. The saintly Confessor, with scores of the nation's most famous sons, lies buried in the abbey, Great Britain's house of history.

MANY AMERICAN TOURISTS seek tickets to the visitors' galleries of the House of Commons, and the United States Embassy in London gets a prescribed ration of tickets to distribute to them. I will never forget asking an embassy official for tickets not only to Parliament but also to Trooping the Colour, an annual military spectacle in honor of the Queen's Birthday. Apparently I had parlayed two of the most impossible requests that one can make of a harried State Department employee. I won't do it again; I hate to see a grown man cry.

If you want to watch the Mother of Parliaments in session, write to the embassy months in advance. Better yet, get a British friend to obtain tickets from an M. P. When

TALES OF THE TOWER, *embellished by a sword, fascinate children in the White Tower, gallery of arms and armor. Anne Boleyn and Catherine Howard, wives of Henry VIII, were beheaded on Tower Green—Anne with a requested sword, Catherine with the usual ax. Elizabeth I, who had paced the Tower herself as prisoner, sent Sir Walter Raleigh there in 1592 after he overly charmed a lady-in-waiting. Soon released, he returned to royal favor as an explorer and admiral. Raleigh's famed cloak did him no good when enemies at court began to sling mud; James I flung him into the Bloody Tower. Here (lower) during his 12-year imprisonment he wrote his* History of the World, *displayed in the showcase. Set free in 1616 to seek gold in the New World, he returned empty-handed to the Tower in 1618 and was beheaded on an old charge of treason (page 183).*

TREASURES OF THE TOWER, *the Crown Jewels dazzle tourists. St. Edward's Crown (below) honors Edward the Confessor, whose ancient regalia were destroyed by Cromwell. Made for Charles II and weighing seven pounds, it intimidated Victoria. Her lighter Imperial State Crown (page one) bears 3,000 jewels, including the Black Prince ruby Henry V wore at Agincourt. For her coronation in 1953 Elizabeth II chose St. Edward's Crown. Golden, gem-studded arches, symbolizing sovereignty, vault above the velvet Cap of Maintenance. Orb and cross show Christ's dominion.*

ASSOCIATED NEWSPAPERS. LEFT: THOMSON NEWSPAPERS LTD. OPPOSITE: GERRY CRANHAM

St. Paul's and Winston Churchill – when Britain looked to them, they stood firm

you attend you may find, as I always seem to, that the day's business in the House is prosaic and the debate lethargic. But that wonderful little unvarying show, the Speaker's procession, makes it worthwhile. It takes place in the Central Lobby.

A voice calls out, "Mr. Speaker!" Then quick-marching in perfect cadence, six men in black go by: the Senior Doorkeeper; the Serjeant-at-arms, carrying the mace; the Speaker, wearing wig and silk knee breeches with buckled shoes; his Train-bearer, holding up his robe; his Chaplain; and his Secretary. Within moments these unsmiling men, looking neither to the right nor left, have walked into the House Chamber, leaving one with the feeling that he has seen ghosts from centuries past.

If WE DIDN'T HAVE a monarch, we would have to hire one for you Yanks," a British friend once told me. He was right. I can't imagine London without all its omnipresent reminders of royalty: cavalrymen in scarlet clattering through the streets ... the iron immobility of sentries in the guard

THEIR FINEST HOUR—*St. Paul's, Churchill's, London's—shone forth in Britain's darkest night. The glow of cities aflame reddened the skies of Coventry, Bristol, Birmingham, Liverpool. Yet as Churchill wrote, "There was a white glow, overpowering, sublime, which ran through our island from end to end."*

December 29, 1940: *London's burning. The pall of smoke from 1,500 fires enshrouds her homes, her churches, her dead. But, its golden cross burnished by the flames, St. Paul's dome rides above the searing storm. Like London, St. Paul's was scarred, hit by a bomb two months earlier. Like London, the cathedral would endure.*

May 10, 1941: *Moonlight bathes the majesty of Westminster Hall, Westminster Abbey, the Houses of Parliament. Then comes the dreaded drone in the skies, the thunder, the crumbling of walls that can stand no more. Bombs gouge the Hall and the Abbey, destroy the Chamber of the House of Commons. Soon a somber leader stands amid the rubble, his silhouette in the shambles as familiar and inspiring as St. Paul's. A gallant city heeds his words: "We shall not flag or fail. We shall go on to the end. . . ."*

January 30, 1965: *Glory transcends grief in St. Paul's. Near the tombs of Nelson and Wellington, near a memorial chapel to Americans who fell in World War II, a choir sings: "Who would true valour see, Let him come hither." Winston Churchill lies in state beneath a triumphant dome.*

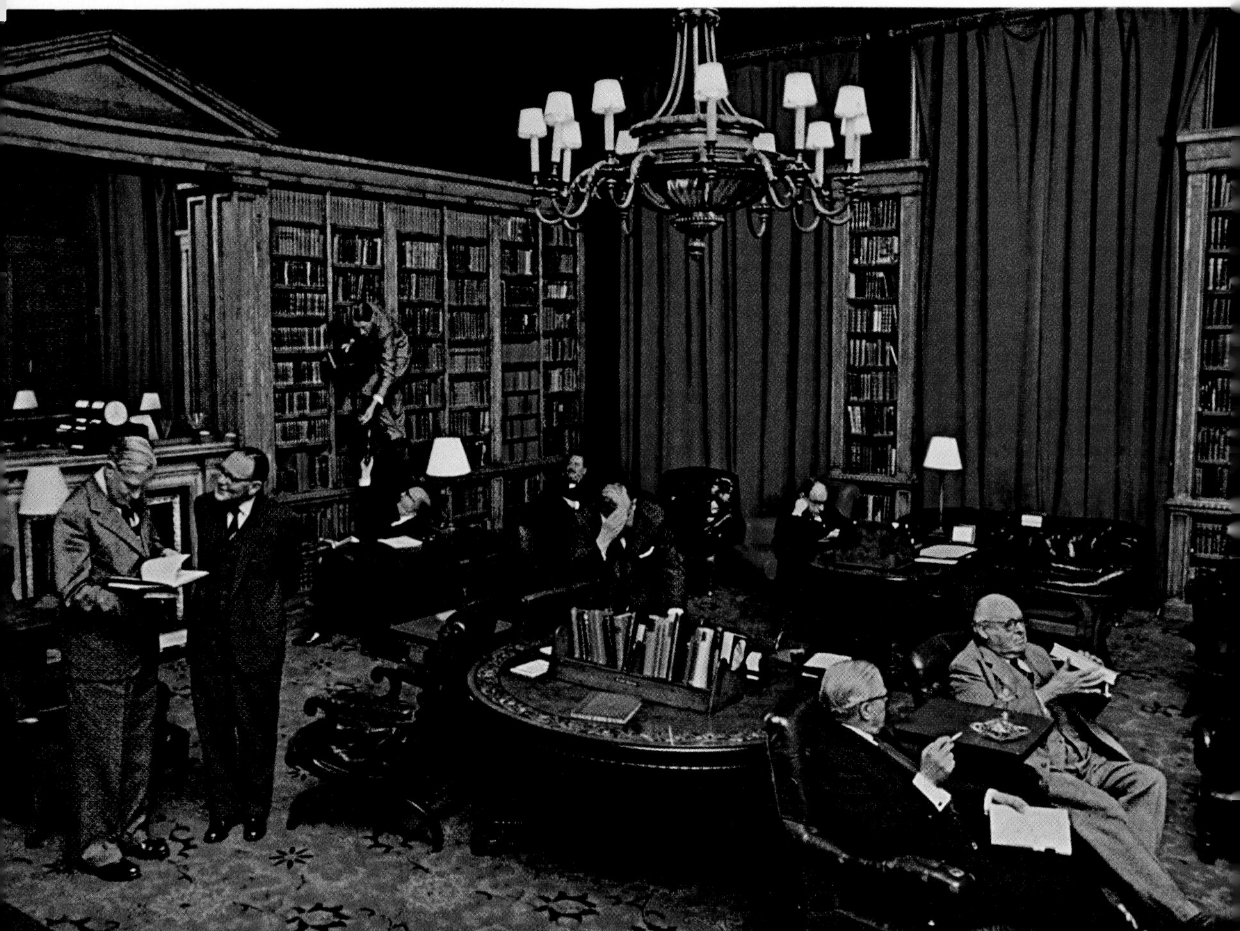

JAMES P. BLAIR AND JOHN E. FLETCHER, NATIONAL GEOGRAPHIC PHOTOGRAPHERS (ALSO OPPOSITE). BELOW: ADAM WOOLFITT

boxes at Buckingham Palace . . . a stirring "God Save the Queen" at football match, concert, formal banquet . . . the familiar royal face on the pounds you spend.

Most Americans think of the British monarchy as a colorful, pleasant, but almost entirely ceremonial appendage of the government. But it is much more. I was reminded of that fact when a friend pointed out to me a messenger from Buckingham Palace getting out of a royal carriage in Whitehall. "Returning government dispatches," he said. "The Queen sees them all, y'know. Secret. Most Secret. The lot."

There are only oblique references in statute law to the powers of the monarch. Those powers that remain are almost entirely the result of evolution. Yet even today any number of things and any number of appointments cannot legally take place without the Queen's signature. The British consider this a safeguard to freedom. Confronted by

LONDON IS A MAN'S TOWN, *and the British gentleman finds haven from the press of affairs in that leather-chaired sanctum, the club. Clustered round Pall Mall and St. James's Street, clubs dispense fine port and* The Times *to doze beneath.*

Only the rustle of pages and a cultured murmur in "Oxbridge" inflections break silence at the Oxford and Cambridge Club (opposite).

Cards or backgammon are proper pursuits. An 18th-century duke at Boodle's enjoyed sitting in the bow window watching "the damn'd people get wet."

Advised that militant females threaten the male redoubts, one old clubman sputtered, "By George, if one came into the backgammon room, she'd be stoned!"

A GENTLEMAN'S SHOP *fits him out to look his best, whether for a picnic or a war. And he gets only the best—from bowler to handmade shoes, from tightly furled umbrella to a gun as well tailored as his suit. Purdey and Sons (right) shapes a shotgun to a sportsman's stance and style.*

MEN OF ADVENTURE *gather round Everest in miniature at the Royal Geographical Society (opposite lower). Sir John Hunt (diary in hand) led the victorious 1953 assault on the world's tallest peak. With him are Sir Dudley Stamp, Society president, and L. P. Kirwan, director and secretary.*

Bravery marks the gentleman. In 1912 L. E. G. Oates, unable to struggle on, sought death in a blizzard rather than remain a burden to his comrades on Scott's South Pole expedition. His cairn bears this epitaph: "A very gallant gentleman."

THE SPORT OF KINGS *brings Queen Elizabeth to Ascot on Gold Cup Day in June. Four grays draw her landau (right). Queen Anne inspired the royal race in 1711 when she urged members of her court at nearby Windsor to gallop across Ascot Heath for a 100-guinea prize. Nell Gwyn's son won. Nell's admirer, Charles II, had often taken her to Epsom, whose salts had made it a spa. King and courtiers watched wild races here over the Surrey downs. In 1780 Lord Derby sponsored the race that bears his name.*

A horse flashes past the royal party (below) before the 186th running of the 1½-mile Derby (pronounced "darby"). Beside the Queen Mother stands the Duke of Norfolk. The famed race draws a fashion-plate crowd, emotions tempered by proper British reserve (center).

Since 1877 champions have graced the lawns of Wimbledon (far right), tennis capital of the world. Chaucer tells of the "to and fro" of the ancient game, which Henry VIII played at Hampton Court.

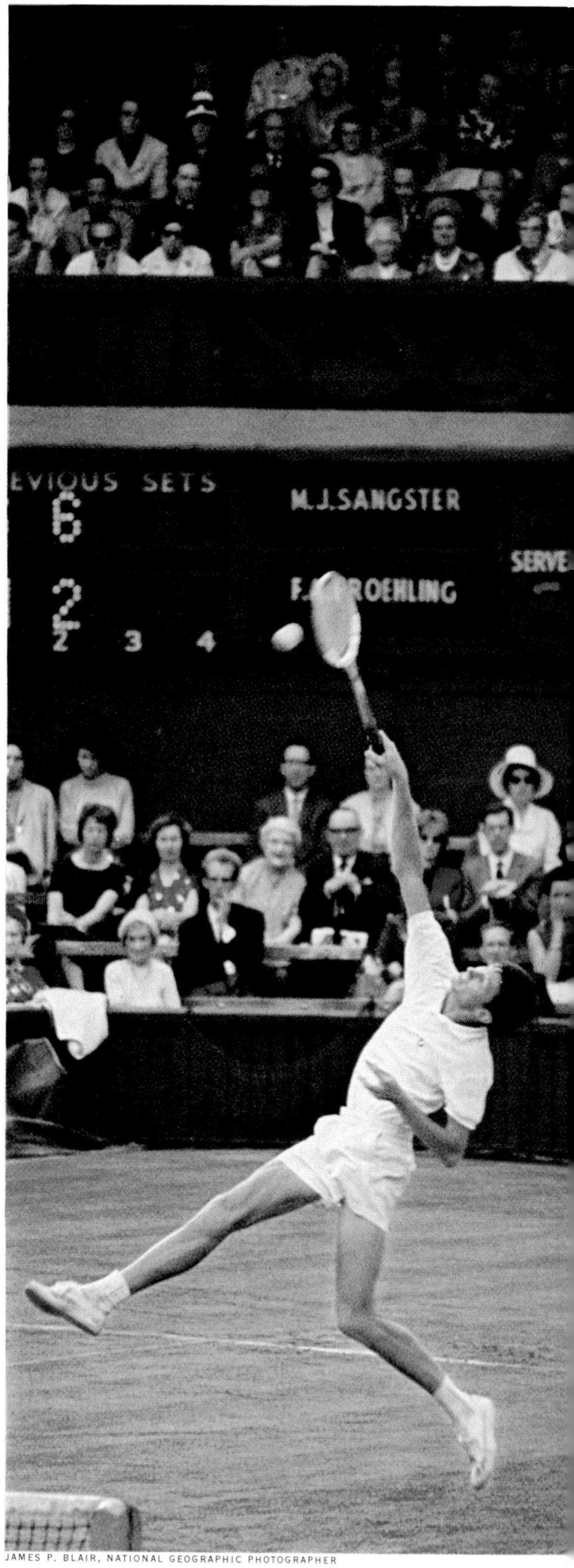

JAMES P. BLAIR, NATIONAL GEOGRAPHIC PHOTOGRAPHER

HISTORY LIVES *at No. 10 Downing Street and Westminster Abbey. Trees in Dean's Yard (below) frame the 13th-century nave and 18th-century towers of "the nation's Valhalla." In 1965 the refurbished Abbey, scene of 38 coronations since William the Conqueror's, celebrated the 900th anniversary of its founding by the sainted Edward the Confessor. Kings, statesmen, and heroes share the peace of its tombs. The Poet's Corner enshrines men of letters.*

No. 10 was built in the 1660's by Sir George Downing, second graduate of Harvard College, master spy for Cromwell, a "perfidious rogue" to diarist Samuel Pepys. It became the Prime Minister's official residence in 1733, but Walpole found it dilapidated, Disraeli "draughty," and Churchill "shaky." The unpretentious house, its Cabinet Room the scene of many unshakable decisions, was rebuilt in 1960-63. An unarmed bobby, symbol of law and order, stands outside. His nickname honors Robert Peel, founder of the Metropolitan Police and twice resident at No. 10.

ADAM WOOLFITT. ABOVE: JAMES P. BLAIR, NATIONAL GEOGRAPHIC PHOTOGRAPHER

madness or treason in a Prime Minister, the sovereign can force a general election.

"A monarch who has been on the throne for a number of years is the best-informed person in the realm on affairs of state," a British friend told me. "You see, under our system, an incoming Prime Minister does not have access to the confidential papers of his predecessor, but the sovereign sees everything. A wise and capable sovereign will use this knowledge effectively."

WHEN WE LEFT LONDON for home, it was raining, as usual. As a cabbie drove us to the airport, I kept my head close to the rain-flecked window, bidding a last goodbye to the bobbies with their tall helmets, the scurrying figures at intersections, the flower dealer huddling by his stand, the glistening plane trees. In my heart I embraced old London—and never mind its climate or what Henry James called its "horrible numerosity of society."

At that moment I recalled something a Greater London Council official had told me. "I know there are many people who can't stand London," he said. "But you often hear the phrase 'not half way' to describe the reluctance to live anywhere else but in the heart of London."

I reminded my wife of his remark. "I'm tempted to say, 'not half way,' and go back."

Mary sighed. "That rival of mine! What can a poor girl do?"

THAMES VALLEY, SHAKESPEARE COUNTRY, AND THE COTSWOLDS

SHRINES OF A PROUD PEOPLE

LIKE A SCROLL OF HISTORY, the Thames winds through the heart of England. Born of springs amid the serene Cotswold Hills, Britain's longest river flows 215 miles to the wild North Sea, traversing a gentle valley haunted by the living past.

Windsor Castle, seat of sovereigns for centuries, rises above it, rank on rank of towers and battlements. Hampton Court, finest palace in the land, spreads along its bank. Father Thames flows past Runnymede, cradle of English liberties, past the playing fields of Eton and the "dreaming spires" of Oxford, fount of learning in the 20th century as it was in the 13th.

Julius Caesar and the Emperor Claudius stood beside the "dark river." Two great Roman cities rose in its valley – Londinium near one end and Corinium, now Cirencester, at the other.

Pathway for conquering Romans, Saxons, Danes, and Normans, the Thames became a national highway in the days when England's roads were fit for little but horseback travel. Produce rode to market on its glistening back, for "this fruiteful and pleasante country yeldeth . . . such comfortable haboundaunce of all kinde of grayne, that it maketh the inhabitants to clappe theyr handes for joye. . . ." And when canals linked the Thames with the Severn and with Midland cities, imported goods once reserved for the rich spread through the countryside. By 1800 one found even in humble cottages "the cups that cheer but not inebriate" – tea had become a national drink.

The chuffing of locomotives sounded the canal era's knell. And while estuary shipping turned London into the great port of empire, the upper Thames lapsed into medieval tranquility.

Today, visitors delight in the beautiful valley's storied manors and abbeys. They tour the Avon countryside that Shakespeare knew, and massive Warwick Castle, stronghold of Richard Neville, "the Kingmaker." And where the Cotswolds ripple the western horizon, they visit stone villages forgotten by time.

Part of Gloucestershire

Part of
Warwickshire
London
Buckinghamshire
Oxfordshire
Berkshire

THE THAMES MIRRORS

BRITAIN'S GLORY

Wending upstream from London, Louis B. Wright, Director of the Folger Shakespeare Library, traces bright threads of history

On a July morning filled with the promise of sunshine I set off to explore my favorite river. Innumerable trips to Britain have never diminished my fascination with this historic highway through the heart of England, and I welcomed the chance to probe its upper reaches. I would visit towns and villages, many of whose origins are lost in antiquity. I would trace the river to its source in the Cotswold Hills, where it trickles from a meadow.

Vikings bent on plunder once swept up the lower Thames. Ships still do; you can sit by the river in London and see them arrive from all over the world. Cargoes of coal and lumber move upstream as far as Kingston. There, near the Guildhall, I saw the stone on which seven Saxon kings were crowned—the "King's Stone." And there I was joined by an old friend, Frederick Hard.

Boarding our rented powerboat above Teddington Lock, Fred and I moved out among swarms of canoes, punts, skiffs, houseboats, speedboats, swans, and ducks. The Thames teems with life, and in summer every creature seems to enjoy a river holiday, including the dogs that sit on the prows of boats. We chugged past cottages that line the banks and dot the islands. Their gardens, gay and fragrant with flowers, extend right to the water's edge.

Our first goal was Hampton Court with its royal palace of Henry VIII. From the river we had a postcard view of Hampton

THE "STRIPLING THAMES" *flows past Lechlade, drowsing amid Gloucestershire meadows. For another 125 miles it winds through England's heartland to London, thence to the sea.*

ROBERT F. SISSON, NATIONAL GEOGRAPHIC PHOTOGRAPHER

ADAM WOOLFITT. UPPER RIGHT: NATIONAL PORTRAIT GALLERY, LONDON.
RIGHT: ROBERT F. SISSON, NATIONAL GEOGRAPHIC PHOTOGRAPHER

HAMPTON COURT *spreads its gardens in a bright tapestry to the bank of the Thames. Cardinal Wolsey, Lord Chancellor of England, built the original palace on a scale to match his wealth and power. Then he fell from favor, and to save his skin gave Hampton to Henry VIII.*

That lusty monarch (above right) enlarged it and brought to it five of his six queens. In huge kitchens his cooks roasted oxen and venison which the royal party in the Great Hall washed down with wine from the vast cellars.

Here Jane Seymour gave birth to Edward VI, Mary honeymooned with Philip of Spain, Elizabeth entertained, and James I presided over the conference that resulted in the King James Bible. For William and Mary, Sir Christopher Wren added wings and redesigned the grounds—including Henry's Pond Garden (right).

Best way to get to England's largest palace is the old way: up the river. Sight-seeing boats run from London (above). As at many other national monuments, "Sound and Light" programs in summer evoke history's great moments.

Court Park, the little spire of Hampton Parish Church, and then the palace itself, sprawling in red brick vastness.

We strolled to the Great Gatehouse, crossing the moat on a bridge lined with "kynge's beestes" – an honor guard of carved lions, griffons, and other heraldic animals. Above the entrance hangs Henry's coat of arms.

Legend peoples Hampton Court with ghosts. Two of Henry's six queens – Jane Seymour and Catherine Howard – are said to walk its galleries. We could almost see Henry himself, clad in huntsman's green, striding off to mount for the chase in the nearby forests of those distant days.

We passed through Anne Boleyn's Gateway into Clock Court, named for the eight-foot astronomical clock made for Henry, who nurtured a personal interest in science. It tells the hour, date, phase of the moon, even the moment of high tide at London Bridge. In the Communication Gallery we gazed at portraits of the ladies of Charles II's court – Restoration beauties, sleek, coquettish, and all very much alike. Exploring the great rooms, we admired the arms collection, Flemish tapestries, paintings by Titian, Tintoretto, and Veronese.

Runnymede we found generously carpeted with picnickers. Somewhere on that meadow, between June 15 and 19, 1215, the barons of England met with King John and forced him to seal the Magna Carta.

Some guides still claim that Magna Carta

Island, just below Runnymede, was the scene of the confrontation. "That's the place, guv'nor," one assured me. "The King, 'e was 'untin' on that island when them dukes come up to 'im, sittin' there on 'is white 'orse, and the King 'e gave 'em the charter, right there where you're lookin'."

Where it was sealed and what it signified seems of little concern to the crowds who flock to the picnic grounds, buy "Iced Lollies," and swarm around the tea wagons. Yet it has influenced the lives of all.

We passed Datchet near Windsor, where in Shakespeare's *The Merry Wives of Windsor* Falstaff was dumped "hissing hot" from a laundry basket into the Thames during an amorous misadventure. "The rogues slighted me into the river with as little remorse as they would have drowned a blind bitch's puppies, fifteen i' the litter," the luckless lover fumed. "I had been drowned but that the shore was shelvy and shallow—a death that I abhor, for the water swells a man, and what a thing should I have been when I had been swelled! I should have been a mountain of mummy."

Falstaff would run greater risk of drowning today, for the wash of powerboats has ruined the shelf and undercut the banks.

WILLIAM THE CONQUEROR built a fortress where the Round Tower of Windsor Castle now stands. Henry III added more towers in 1272. Edward III, born in the Castle, founded the Order of the Garter at Windsor in the 14th century.

Here we visited St. George's Chapel, one of England's finest examples of late Gothic architecture, noted for its fan vaulting. Edward IV began the chapel; Henry VIII completed it, and here he lies buried.

Across the Thames from Windsor loom the towers of Eton College, most celebrated of England's public schools. In the American sense Eton is neither a public school nor a college, but an exclusive private preparatory school. Henry VI founded it in 1440 as a charitable school where penniless scholars were instructed to pray for their king.

Along with Winchester, Rugby, Harrow, and other great public schools, Eton became

WILLIAM EPPRIDGE. OPPOSITE: BATES LITTLEHALES, NATIONAL GEOGRAPHIC PHOTOGRAPHER

HARROW, *an island of learning surrounded by London's sea of houses, stands on a hill where pagans worshiped and archbishops of Canterbury hunted stag, roebuck, and wild boar. Chartered by Queen Elizabeth in 1571, the famed boys' school once taught five future prime ministers in the same generation. A later entrant into this citadel of the classics, 13-year-old Winston Churchill, was deficient in Latin and Greek. This kept him overlong in the lowest form, where "we were considered such dunces that we could learn only English." He mastered the language.*

The scholar in straw boater running to class (opposite) wears informal dress known as "half change." Formal "school dress"—top hat and tails—was still worn at cricket in 1881. Harrow football calls for a tasseled fez.

At Runnymede a Queen bequeaths to America a hallowed bit of England and a vow: Forever shall a fallen leader's memory live at the shrine of Magna Carta

JAMES P. BLAIR, NATIONAL GEOGRAPHIC PHOTOGRAPHE
KING JOHN'S SEAL REPRODUCED BY PERMISSION
OF THE PROVOST AND FELLOWS OF ETON COLLEGE

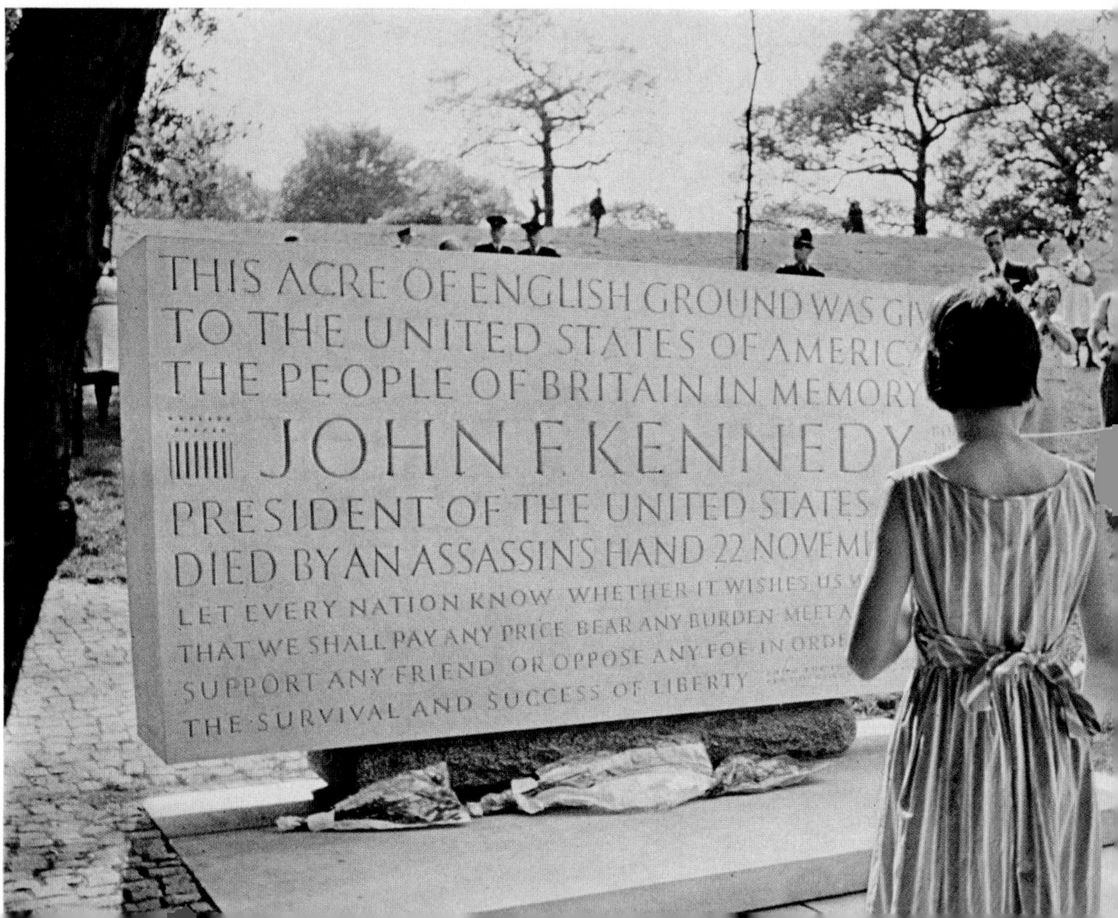

THIS ACRE OF ENGLISH GROUND WAS GIV
TO THE UNITED STATES OF AMERICA
THE PEOPLE OF BRITAIN IN MEMORY
JOHN F. KENNEDY
PRESIDENT OF THE UNITED STATES
DIED BY AN ASSASSIN'S HAND 22 NOVEMI
LET EVERY NATION KNOW WHETHER IT WISHES US W
THAT WE SHALL PAY ANY PRICE BEAR ANY BURDEN MEET A
SUPPORT ANY FRIEND OR OPPOSE ANY FOE IN ORDE
THE SURVIVAL AND SUCCESS OF LIBERTY

ON A MOMENTOUS DAY in May, 1965, before a quiet throng gathered from all the world, Queen Elizabeth II gave a historic plot of green English hillside above the Thames to the American people. The gift was a lasting memorial to President John F. Kennedy "whom in death my people still mourn, and whom in life they loved."

The site gave the bequest special meaning. For below spreads Runnymede, where 750 years earlier King John faced rebellious barons and, perforce, bowed to their demands, setting his seal upon the document called Magna Carta.

The Great Charter by no means opened the floodgates of freedom. The barons were no defenders of the "little man." John was no swaggering tyrant. The able, if luckless, King sought new revenue to finance his campaigns in France; much of the charter reflects the barons' efforts to hold the line at ancient feudal dues.

The Charter of 1215 marked but a truce. The barons reopened hostilities; the Pope promptly annulled the agreement. Magnates of the realm had to have subsequent versions – notably Henry III's Charter of 1225 – confirmed by John's successors no fewer than 55 times. In the long struggle between Crown and subjects this feudal document advanced the cause of freedom not so much by what it actually said as by what men thought it said.

The original charter did, however, state that no freeman may be imprisoned "except by the lawful judgment of his peers or by the law of the land," foreshadowing the rights of trial by jury, due process, and habeas corpus. It said no tax may be levied "without general consent," providing precedent for the famous cry, "No taxation without representation." And it drew from a medieval ideal the paramount principle: The law is above both the governor and the governed. Thus Magna Carta may rightly be considered the cornerstone of liberties which England and America share.

Mrs. Jacqueline Kennedy, thanking the British people for this gift of "sacred soil," said that one day her children "will realize what it means to have their father honored at Runnymede."

KNIGHTS OF THE GARTER *in velvet robes parade at 900-year-old Windsor Castle. The royal standard, signaling the Queen is in residence, flies atop Henry II's Round Tower, successor to William the Conqueror's wooden keep. Mightiest in a ring of fortresses round London, the Thames-side castle grew with the centuries.*

Edward III, returning from his triumphs at Crécy and Calais, created England's premier chivalric order here in 1348. A chronicler wrote that the King, retrieving a lady's fallen garter, had warned jesting courtiers they'd soon "attribute muche honour unto such a garter." His rebuke, Honi soit qui mal y pense *("Shame on him who thinks ill of it!") became the order's motto. Its blue garter symbolizes the bond of honor between the monarch and 25 companions in arms, a brotherhood like King Arthur's Round Table.*

Heraldic "king's beasts" atop St. George's Chapel (left) gaze upon the Queen and her companions, led by two newly invested knights. The chapel, dedicated to England's dragon-slaying patron saint, is the spiritual home of the order.

JAMES P. BLAIR, NATIONAL GEOGRAPHIC PHOTOGRAPHER

DAN McCOY, BLACK STAR (ALSO BELOW). RIGHT: ADAM WOOLFITT. LOWER RIGHT: "QUATRE BRAS," BY LADY BUTLER; NATIONAL GALLERY OF VICTORIA, MELBOURNE

a preserve of the rich and the powerful—"The Establishment"—and a nursery of statesmen. The traditional school dress—striped trousers and tailcoats for the older boys, high starched collar and short black jackets for the smaller ones—reflects early 19th-century formality.

Before then, unruly boys rioted against unpopular masters. "Have you had a rebellion lately, eh, eh?" George III would ask any Eton boy he met. At Harrow the boys once laid gunpowder, intending to blow up the headmaster!

ETON COLLEGE *bears scars honorably earned in 500 years of educating young gentlemen. Two future statesmen of the 18th century—Walpole and Pitt—carved their names on this desk. Eighteen Old Etonians have been prime ministers.*

In the "Field Game" (above) young Etonians display dash and leadership on the playing fields where, Wellington said, "the Battle of Waterloo was won."

Eton still supplies cadets to nearby Sandhurst (upper right), Britain's West Point. Some may have commanded those "British squares" (lower) that shattered Napoleon's onslaughts.

Expelled from Harrow for his part in a three-day riot in 1771, the 11-year-old Marquis of Wellesley was sent to nearby Eton. As a result his younger brother Arthur, later Duke of Wellington, went to Eton instead of Harrow. And it was the "Iron Duke" himself, idol of the nation in the heady years following England's defeat of Napoleon, who set the gentlemanly fashion of the stiff upper lip.

Charles II once amused himself by fishing for gudgeon in the Thames near Windsor. Here, said Izaak Walton, many trout lurked, and to prove it he fished the quiet pools with Sir Henry Wotton, Eton's provost. Walton observed in *The Compleat Angler*

Wood

Chambers

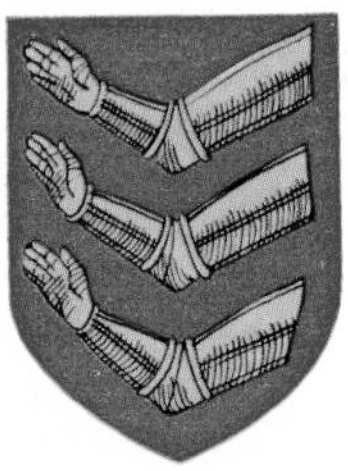

Armstrong

Moore

Ellis

Clifford

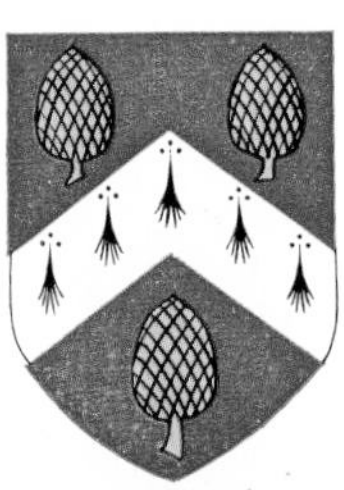

Pine

Smith

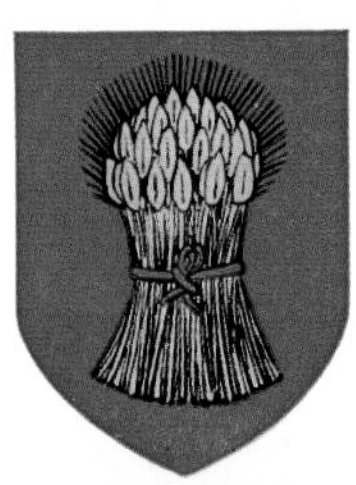

Grosvenor

Marsh

ADAM WOOLFITT

CLIVEDEN'S *formal gardens (above) overlook the Thames near Maidenhead. Viscount Astor, the last owner, deeded the mansion to the National Trust, an endowed organization that maintains and exhibits many stately homes.*

Another Trust property in Buckinghamshire is Hughenden Manor (opposite), home of Benjamin Disraeli, brilliant statesman of Victoria's reign.

that the fattest salmon in England came from the Thames, and no other salmon had "so excellent a taste." Today's fishermen still patiently dangle their lines all along the stream and with vast yet subdued excitement haul in catches six inches long.

Swans we found in abundance. Toss them a crust and they come at you like frigates in line of battle. They are imperious birds, sometimes dangerous, beating an intruder with their great wings. Swans once graced the holiday tables of the nobility. A "swanmark" was a prized possession, for the ownership of swans was a privilege granted by the Crown.

Upriver from Windsor on the Berkshire bank lies the town of Bray, with 17th-century almshouses now called Jesus Hospital.

A coat of arms wraps a family in a heraldic status symbol

DISRAELI'S COAT OF ARMS, embroidered on a banner screen in Hughenden's drawing room (opposite), was granted to him in 1876 after Queen Victoria made him Earl of Beaconsfield.

Such armorial bearings originated in the Middle Ages as a device to tell friend from foe in battle. Over his armor a knight wore a coat of arms – a tunic marked with his emblem. He also displayed this insignia on his shield.

At tournaments, heralds acted as masters of ceremony. Recognizing an escutcheon – from the Latin *scutum*, or shield – they blazoned (called out) the knight's name and honors. They became experts in genealogy and, as "kings of arms," had the right to grant arms to those worthy of entry into the ranks of the gentry.

Richard III incorporated the heralds into a College of Arms in 1483. They were empowered to inspect and remove "all false armory and arms devised without authority." Ever since, the College of Arms has remained Britain's official custodian of heraldry and pedigrees (from *pied de gru*, crane's foot, the shape made by lines in a genealogical chart).

When iron suits went out of fashion, the coat of arms remained a family's hereditary emblem of honor, emblazoned on seals and possessions and over manor doors. The examples opposite, from John Guillim's *A Display of Heraldrie* (1611), show that many ensigns involved a play on words.

The tree, cannon chambers, strong arms, and pinecones are puns on the family name. The mermaid was a favorite with seafarers. Rampant lions, panthers, swan, and horse represent courage and strength. "Garb" of wheat may symbolize plenty. Rooflike chevrons suggest that the family built a church or castle.

The archaic language of blazonry describes the Clifford shield as *chequy or and azure; on a bend gules three lioncels rampant of the first* – "checked gold and blue; on a diagonal red band, three rampant lions in gold." The *bend* runs from *dexter chief* to *sinister base*. Dexter is at the right of the man behind the shield. The word sinister, for his left, recalls an ancient belief that danger came from that ill-omened direction.

Family alliances may be shown by impalement (two sets of arms on a vertically split shield) or quartering (dividing into four or more parts).

Shield and external ornaments form an "achievement." Disraeli's has an eagle and a lion as supporters. The coronet denotes high rank. The triple tower is the crest (originally an emblem displayed on the knight's helmet). The motto reads, "To the brave nothing is difficult."

Families of the same name may have different arms, or none at all. Americans may claim theirs from the College of Arms, London, proving descent from the original grantee. If no arms exist, the College can devise new ones.

Here lived the parson whose principles were so flexible, according to a satirical song, that whatever turn politics took he'd "still be the Vicar of Bray." And here we left the river for an excursion to the north.

First to Beaconsfield, a few miles from Windsor. Edmund Burke, the great defender of the American colonies at the time of the Revolution, lived here and loved it so well that he asked to be buried in the parish church and not in Westminster Abbey.

In the nearby churchyard of Hughenden lies another statesman, Benjamin Disraeli. He had married a rich Beaconsfield widow and thus could afford a gentleman's life at Hughenden Manor. Disraeli liked to boast that he made Queen Victoria Empress of India. She made him Earl of Beaconsfield.

At Chalfont St. Giles we visited the half-timbered cottage where John Milton spent the plague year of 1665. We turned south again to take a pleasant walk from Beaconsfield to Burnham Beeches where some of England's oldest trees grow on a 600-acre tract. Poet Thomas Gray strolled here as a youth. Later, staying with his mother in neighboring Stoke Poges, he completed *Elegy Written in a Country Churchyard.* And in that churchyard he now lies.

We returned to the river and slipped past Maidenhead, a fashionable watering place in Edwardian times. Not far beyond we

ROBERT F. SISSON, NATIONAL GEOGRAPHIC PHOTOGRAPHER (ALSO RIGHT). UPPER: WILLARD PRICE

THE THAMES *rolls past fine homes near Henley. Boathouses nudge the water like garages on a suburban street.*

Gardens splash color along the banks at Sonning, where an excursion boat squeezes through a lock (left), one of about 50 on the river, nearly all hand operated.

Thames swans belong to the Queen and to two London guilds, the Vintners and the Dyers. Each July a new generation of birds is taken from the river and divided in a centuries-old ceremony called "swan-upping" (opposite). Here scarlet-shirted Queen's men corral fledglings between skiffs. The guilds' cygnets are nicked on the beak; the Queen's go free, unmarked. About 1,000 swans glide in the stretch between London and Henley.

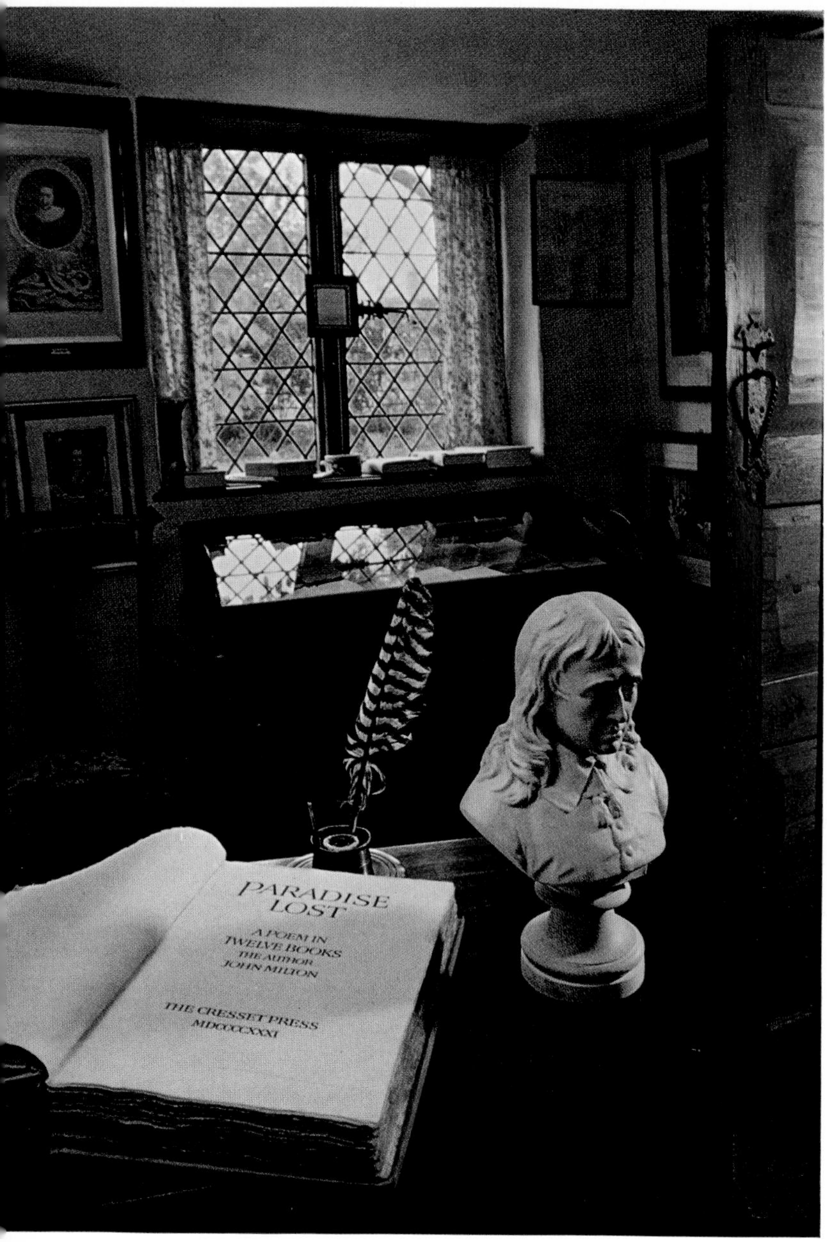

JOHN MILTON'S *bust broods beside a copy of his great epic in Milton Cottage, today a museum at Chalfont St. Giles.*

Britain's Civil War between Charles I and his Parliament had interrupted Milton's poetic work, for he devoted his talents to the service of Cromwell's Roundheads against the Cavaliers. When the Restoration ended the Puritan cause, the poet lived in fear of imprisonment by the Royalists, who fined him heavily and ordered two of his books burned by the hangman.

Now blind and fleeing the plague in London, Milton moved to this Buckinghamshire village in 1665 with his third wife and his daughter Deborah. Here he finished the masterpiece he had begun long before and conceived Paradise Regained.

At nearby Jordans the Quaker meetinghouse (lower) stands in quiet dignity. Here William Penn, founder of Pennsylvania, and his family are buried. The Penns also lived in the manor at Stoke Poges. The adjoining churchyard (right) draws many visitors, for here Thomas Gray, ruminating that "paths of glory lead but to the grave," wrote his Elegy.

spotted Cliveden. The mansion stands on a red brick terrace overlooking the Thames, amid magnificent gardens and trees. Before World War II the "Cliveden set" met here, with Lord Astor its host and the Prince of Wales its focal point.

Few stretches of the river convey such a feeling of contentment as that from Cliveden to Henley. The Chilterns present a green escarpment of woods, broken by fields and pastures. At Marlow a riverside hotel, the Compleat Angler, serves tea on a terrace overlooking a weir. A 15th-century pub, the Hare and Hounds, dispenses both atmosphere and refreshment.

We hurried past Reading, a thriving industrial center above Henley, and gave our time to appealing villages like Pangbourne. Here Betty Price, a Berkshire witch, shrieked curses when arrested in 1663. Within a year her captors died. And here lived Kenneth Grahame, whose *The Wind in the Willows* evokes scenes along the river.

Cows grazed amid summer's plenty as we

ADAM WOOLFITT

neared Wallingford with its narrow streets and Shillingford with its graceful bridge.

Dorchester, near the confluence of the Thame and the Thames, was an armed camp in Roman days. Later, in 634, Pope Honorius I sent St. Birinus to convert the English heathen, and near here he baptized Cynegils, King of the West Saxons. Thus for a time Dorchester became a cathedral city. Today the saint's shrine attracts visitors to the magnificent abbey church.

Little remains of the Benedictine abbey

Staff man Edwards Park takes a sentimental journey up the Thames

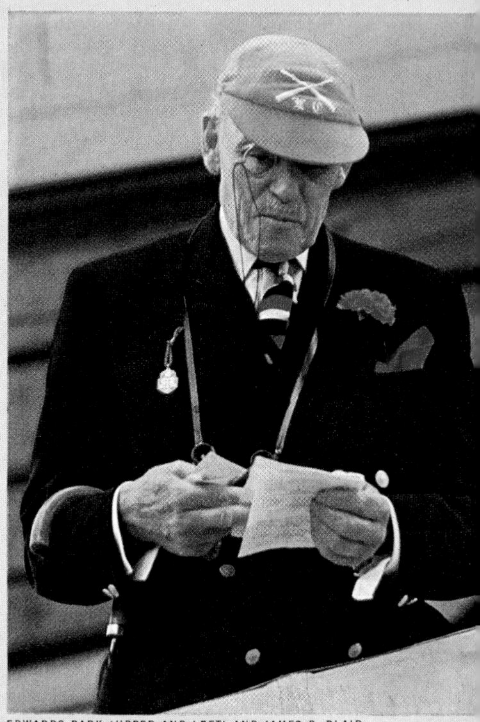

EDWARDS PARK (UPPER AND LEFT) AND JAMES P. BLAIR, BOTH NATIONAL GEOGRAPHIC STAFF

to Henley, where the regatta is ever young, and only the oarsmen grow old

YOU COULD HEAR HENLEY before you ever saw it. During those four days of the annual Royal Regatta the old riverside town throbbed with exciting sounds. The steam calliope whistled, the ferris wheel groaned, the vendors shouted, and endless traffic squealed and grumbled across the old bridge beside Henley's medieval church. Behind all these sounds hovered the chorus of the crowd—the lilting murmur of cultivated voices, the shouts of Cockney children, the guffaws of young gentry, the giggling of shopgirls. All England seems to gather in this little town the first week in July to watch young athletes strain at the oars, racing up one of the few straight stretches of the Thames. Years ago I was among them, one of a crew of Yale lightweight oarsmen, all wide-eyed and determined.

We arrived on the banks of the Thames at Henley and found our sleek eight-oared shell stowed in a huge blue-and-white striped marquee with scores of others. We rowed our practice sessions instinctively. For our minds were enraptured by the delights ashore—the gorgeous girls in broad-brimmed hats who gave us bored glances, then dashed off in snarling, low-slung sports cars driven by Oxford blades with seven-foot scarves round their necks. Tottering old gentlemen in brightly colored rowing caps watched us from the Stewards' Enclosure or the exclusive Phyllis Court Club. We could hear them barking that rowing was not what it used to be—"Hey? Hey?"

When the heats began, we paddled to the start near Temple Island with timorous strokes, our muscles quivering like jelly. Hundreds of launches, punts, skiffs, canoes, kayaks, balsa rafts, even steamboats lined the $1\frac{5}{16}$-mile course. At a sharp command our muscles hardened, and nothing else mattered but to row.

I remember little about the races except the unbearable fatigue, the spots dancing before my eyes, and the roar of the crowd. At last we would sweep by the point of greatest noise, our coxswain would yell, "Way enough!" and we would droop gasping over our oars.

After a shower, ice-cold in British fashion, we would wander along the banks to meet those gorgeous girls.

This past summer I took my son to Henley, and I heard the sounds of Henley again as I watched the races from Phyllis Court Club. I saw the winners lift high their silver trophies. I saw the girls in their broad-brimmed hats, and the young men in their blazers. The old gentlemen still wore bright caps, and they still barked at each other about how things had changed. "They go jolly fast, you know," one said. "But you can hardly call it rowing, can you? Not like '38—Hey? Hey?"

Thirty-eight? Good Lord, that was my year!

at Abingdon, yet the town has a venerable air. At the picnic grounds old men and nursemaids watch the swans converge in flotillas. We noticed the birds' red, yellow, or blue leg bands. A barmaid said it had to do with their age. "Some gentlemen from Oxford put them on. Same swans been coming for years. No telling how old they are."

OXFORD, crowded and traffic-clogged, harbors the serene quadrangles of its famed university. Near Folly Bridge we passed the college barges lining the riverbank, looking like relics of Edwardian days. During Eights Week in the spring they blossom into ornate grandstands from which young elegants of the university applaud their stalwart oarsmen.

We moored our "barge" nearby and headed for Carfax in the heart of the city. The word is a corruption of *quadrifurcus,* or four-forked. It applies to the crossroads from which High Street—"The High"—curves past the gates and turrets of seven of the 35 colleges: Brasenose (named for a lion-faced bronze knocker), the college where George Washington's great-great-grandfather studied; Oriel, where Sir Walter Raleigh and Cecil Rhodes went; All Souls, which has no students, only research fellows and a warden who parade once a century round the quadrangles bearing a dead mallard on a pole; University, endowed in 1249; Queen's, whose members troop to dinner at the sound of a trumpet; St. Edmund Hall, last of the medieval halls used as residences; and Magdalen ("Maudlen"), loveliest of all with its bell tower soaring above the River Cherwell, a tributary of the Thames. Every May Day Magdalen's choir sings a dawn hymn from the tower while undergraduates in punts drift below.

UNDERGRADUATES *in "sub fusc," Oxford's full academic dress, hold a post-mortem on exams as traffic roars along "The High." Behind rises the classic dome of Queen's College and the spire of St. Mary's, university church for six centuries.*

ADAM WOOLFITT

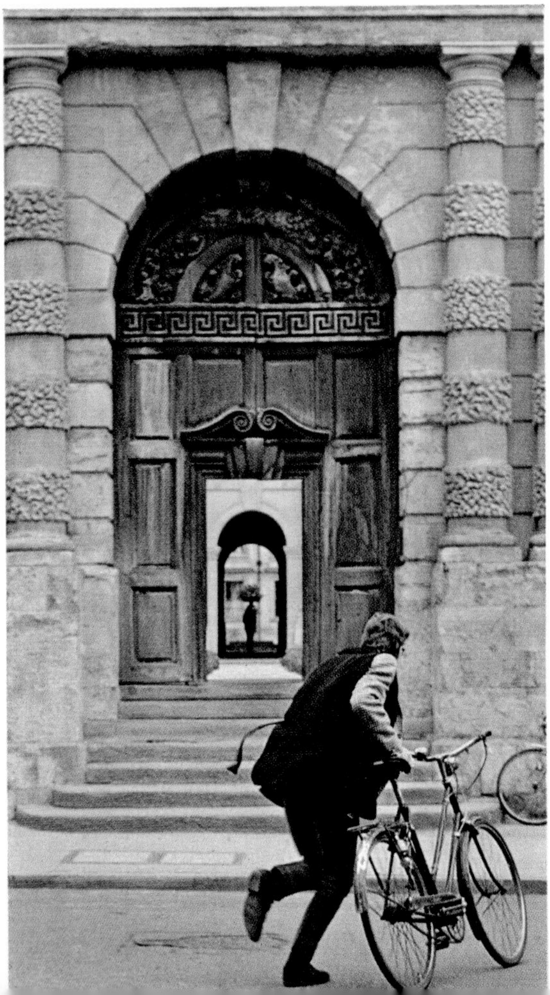

Harwell: atomic energy for peace

MEN OF THE FUTURE unload radioactive fuel at the Harwell Atomic Energy Research Establishment in Berkshire. Behind gleams the bank of a reactor core. Round channels set in its face contain metal rods that hold uranium. The splitting of uranium atoms in the reactor produces energy in the form of heat.

England's John Dalton gave the world its first working lesson in atomic science in 1803. He described elements in terms of their atoms and assigned them atomic weights. A century later Lord Rutherford, "Father of the Atom," predicted that "an enormous amount of energy" would be released by the "disintegration of radioactive elements."

After World War II ended in an atomic blast, Britain turned an air base at Harwell into a pioneering research station and soon led the world in producing atomic energy for peaceful uses. Atomic plants sprouted like white-domed mushrooms. Some fed electricity to factories. Others joined Harwell in research, working toward the day when atoms supersede the coal bin, when isotopes serve ever more widely in industry, agriculture, and medicine.

At Harwell, as at Jodrell Bank with its radio telescopes (page 343), the pulse of science beats firmly amid serene landscapes and timeless towns—proof that Britain, venerable and mellow, still strides forward with vigor.

Bewildered Americans ask, "But where is the *university*?" It is all around them—the association of these highly individual colleges. It began when Henry II called home English scholars studying in Paris in the 12th century. Many gathered at Oxford, where monastic schools existed.

The hostels where the medieval scholars lodged gradually became colleges. Merton was so designated in 1264. Most have remained small. Christ Church is the largest, with some 500 undergraduates.

A Christ Church lecturer in mathematics, Charles Dodgson, wrote, under the pen name of Lewis Carroll, *Alice's Adventures in Wonderland* and *Through the Looking Glass* to please Alice Liddell, the little daughter of the dean of the college.

Unworldly though Oxford may seem, with dons wandering the street in gowns and tasseled caps, it is changing. Women today have five colleges of their own. Students work harder. The ivory-tower atmosphere is disappearing. Gone are the Town and Gown riots; not for decades have townsmen surged past the gates of Balliol howling for scholarly blood. And the vast Morris Motors plant has forged an industrial city out of "a kind of elfin workshop, full of respectful craftsmen tapping away in back alleys."

But as we strolled along Broad Street, as we passed the Sheldonian Theatre and visited the Bodleian Library and Radcliffe Camera, the sense of Oxford's timelessness overwhelmed us—as it always has.

Returning to our boat, we continued up the Thames by gushing locks, step by step,

COMMUNAL REPAST *at Wadham College reflects Oxford's philosophy: Place young scholars in close contact with fellows and tutors and they will "catch" learning as they might a cold. Essayist Stephen Leacock maintained that dons educate students by smoking pipes at them during the weekly tutorials, when a student's essay is discussed. "Men who have been systematically smoked at for four years turn into ripe scholars," he wrote.*

Lower: Gown flies as a scholar hastens to Queen's College from the Ashmolean Museum.

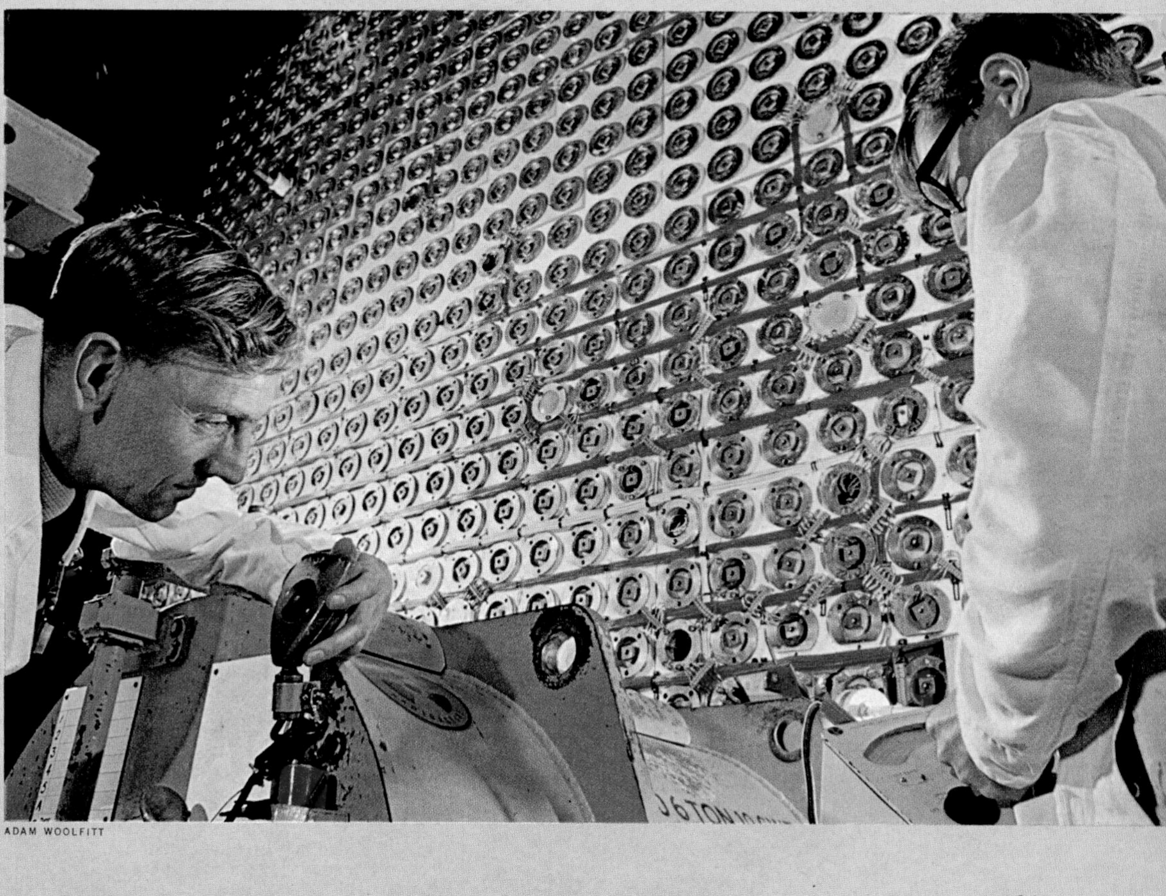

ADAM WOOLFITT

"**MARLBOROUGH'S VICTORIOUS SWORD,"** *never tarnished by defeat, led England in crushing the ambitions of Louis XIV to rule Europe. For his triumph at Blenheim, Bavaria, in 1704, a grateful Queen Anne presented to John Churchill (right), first Duke of Marlborough, a vast estate at Woodstock, Oxfordshire. Here a monument would rise to his glory.*

Blenheim Palace, designed by dramatist-architect John Vanbrugh to rival Versailles itself, took 17 years to build and cost the nation a quarter of a million pounds. Its stupendous scale awes the visitor. Massive buildings and courts cover seven of the park's 2,700 acres, landscaped with lake and cascades by Capability Brown. The Great Hall rises 67 feet, the Long Library extends 180 feet. State rooms blaze with tapestries, paintings, and carvings. The Duke died before it was completed.

FROM A SECTION OF SCREEN AT ROYAL MILITARY ACADEMY, SANDHURST

KARSH OF OTTAWA

"**AT BLENHEIM** *I took two very important decisions: to be born and to marry," said Sir Winston Churchill. Descendant and biographer of the mighty Marlborough, he frequently visited the ancestral home, though he never lived there. His mother was the American heiress Jennie Jerome.*

BATES LITTLEHALES, NATIONAL GEOGRAPHIC PHOTOGRAPHER

into the Cotswold Hills. Barges once carried freight above Lechlade; now the quiet old town marks the end of navigation, though the source of the Thames lies about 14 miles to the west, near Cricklade.

Our journey could not end without a special pilgrimage. Sir Winston Churchill was born at Blenheim Palace, his ancestral home beside the old town of Woodstock, just north of Oxford. Only a mile away the parish church of Bladon perches on a hill above the green and quiet countryside. In the churchyard Sir Winston lies in peace.

We joined a stream of people, young and old, rich and poor, English and foreign, mounting the hill to stand before the white marble slab. Every visitor remained for a moment, paying silent tribute to greatness. Many remembered the voice that rallied England in its time of greatest peril, a voice that roused men's spirits and gave them courage to suffer, to endure, and to struggle on to victory. Few statesmen have ever used the English language with such magical effect.

Then I remembered another Englishman who was a magician with words, one who influenced Churchill's own style. At Stratford upon Avon, an easy drive northward, had lived a poet who more than any other had fashioned English into an instrument of brilliance and beauty. Shakespeare and Churchill had both loved and drawn strength from this heartland of England.

STRATFORD AND THE

DEAN CONGER, AND (RIGHT) BATES LITTLEHALES, NATIONAL GEOGRAPHIC PHOTOGRAPHERS

POET OF AVON, *in bronze, gazes upon his town. Every April 23—observed as both Shakespeare's birthday and deathday—a procession (below) winds through Stratford. Beadle, mace-bearers, and other dignitaries lead it to the birthplace and tomb.*

FOR UNTOLD NUMBERS of Americans, Great Britain is a land of romance and history—all because of William Shakespeare. They think of England in the words spoken by John of Gaunt in *Richard II:*

This royal throne of kings, this
scept'red isle,
This earth of majesty, this seat
of Mars,
This other Eden, demiparadise...
This blessed plot, this earth,
this realm, this England...

After 30 years of studying Shakespeare's age I finally found a chance to make a systematic survey of Shakespearean geography. My curiosity led me in search of subtle things—traces of the Elizabethan age that linger perhaps in some hidden village in the poet's native Warwickshire, among plain country Britons such as filled his comedies.

SHAKESPEARE COUNTRY

Shakespearean scholar Louis B. Wright continues his pilgrimage to the banks of the Avon where the soul of an age was nurtured

My wife and I, with Miss Virginia LaMar, my co-editor of "The Folger Library General Reader's Shakespeare," set out for England in early autumn, when by the law of averages the sun should favor us. Our arrival over London did not produce sunshine, but such a black September fog that our jet could not land. Finally, we flew to Amsterdam for an excellent Dutch breakfast. By midafternoon a hole had opened over London Airport, and we landed.

From the weather we concluded that William Shakespeare was obviously an optimist; otherwise he could not have put so much sunshine into his poetry. His characteristic imagery emphasizes good weather, and we could not believe that Elizabethan England was vastly different meteorologically from our time. Only when Shakespeare wanted to induce an atmosphere of gloom or impending disaster did he call up images of lowering weather. As his King Richard III says:

The sun will not be seen today;
The sky doth frown and lower upon
our army.
I would these dewy tears
were from the ground.

Despite the fog we arrived in the greatest heat wave of the season. The mercury soared to 70°–front-page news. "Shocking day, sir!" the porter commented. And the chambermaid echoed: "Very 'ot, sir; close, I calls it; very un'ealthy, I says."

Shakespeare's native county, Warwickshire, "is the core and centre of the English world; midmost England, unmitigated England," according to that Anglophile Henry James. It is a land of green pastures and wooded hills; of gentle streams that, as Shakespeare wrote in *Two Gentlemen of Verona*, make "sweet music with th' enameled stones"; of orchards, grainfields, and quiet villages with straw-thatched cottages; in short, a prosperous countryside where every prospect pleases.

We found Warwickshire as vivid as a Pre-Raphaelite painting. Shakespeare would still recognize the face of the land. Sheep still graze on the hillsides; cattle roam the pastures; and wheat and barley ripen in the sun as they did in the 1560's. But no longer is the grain cut and placed in "stooks," as the shocks were called. Modern combines leave the straw in long windrows.

As in Shakespeare's time, Stratford is a market town, noted for its ale. Shakespeare himself was interested in brewing, and he invested in malt grains after his retirement from London to Stratford. A local legend, recorded by the Reverend John Ward in his diary, says that "Shakespear, Drayton, and Ben Jhonson had a merry meeting, and itt seems drank too hard, for Shakespear died of a feavour there contracted." Whether he died of too much ale remains unproved, but Autolycus in *The Winter's Tale* sings that "a quart of ale is a dish for a king," and Stratford's good brew has tempted many besides the dramatist.

STRATFORD UPON AVON once marked the head of navigation on this tributary of the Severn. Cloth from the Cotswolds, malt, grains, ale, beef, mutton, raw wool, fruit, and gloves such as were made by Shakespeare's father flowed from here to the great world. Yet Stratford remained a small town, its citizens countrymen close to the land. Each house had a garden. Some had barns. Shakespeare's father was once fined for keeping a compost pile in the streets, the mark of a thrifty gardener somewhat short of hygienic concern. The sights, sounds, and smells of the country were all familiar to young Shakespeare.

The town and its surroundings are particularly gorgeous in late September. The land brightens with color, as flowers make a last, almost desperate effort to show their beauty before frost cuts them down.

Asters, Michaelmas daisies, geraniums, goldenrod, dahlias, roses, and countless

"WHEN DAFFODILS *begin to peer . . . Why then comes in the sweet of the year," Shakespeare wrote. And when spring comes to Stratford the streets bloom for the poet on his birthday. Children join the procession in their school uniforms; this youngster's hatband proclaims her a pupil at the Croft School. They carry April bouquets or just flowers that Shakespeare knew–daffodils, roses, and "rosemary, that's for remembrance."*

BATES LITTLEHALES, NATIONAL GEOGRAPHIC PHOTOGRAPHER

BENEATH THIS STONE *in Holy Trinity Church lies Shakespeare, who died in 1616, aged 52. The inscription won respect: He rests in peace, his wife Anne nearby. She died in 1623, the year his First Folio (right) was published. Earliest-known Shakespeare portrait, engraved by Martin Droeshout, is probably accurate.*

Stratford (opposite) has six times as many people today as when the poet was born. Detergents now whiten the Avon with foam, but the church yet stands amid verdant beauty.

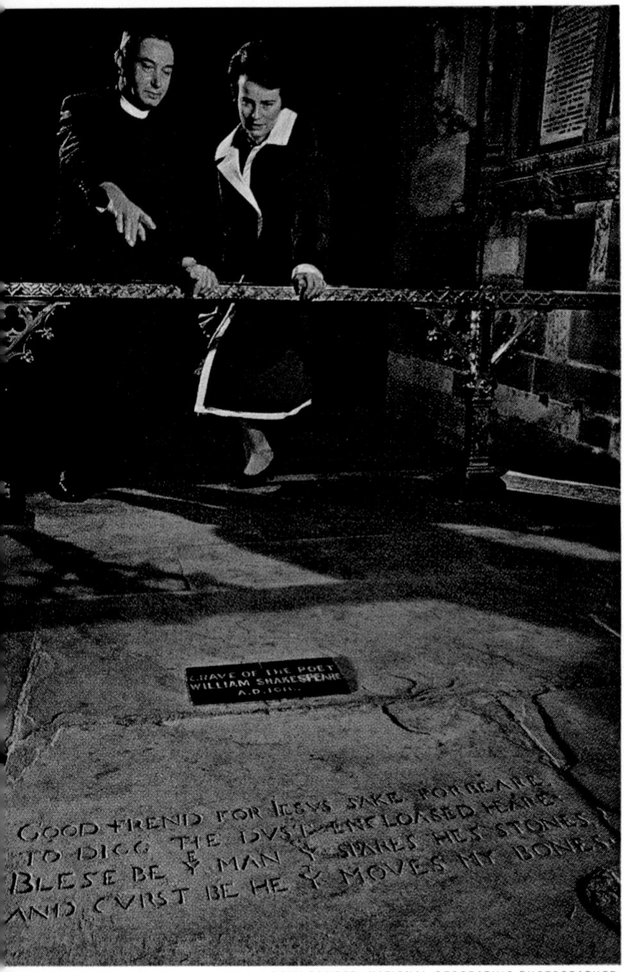

GOOD FREND FOR IESVS SAKE FORBEARE
TO DIGG THE DVST ENCLOASED HEARE
BLESE BE Y MAN Y SPARES THES STONES
AND CVRST BE HE Y MOVES MY BONES

DEAN CONGER, NATIONAL GEOGRAPHIC PHOTOGRAPHER; ABOVE BY PERMISSION OF THE VICAR AND CHURCHWARDENS

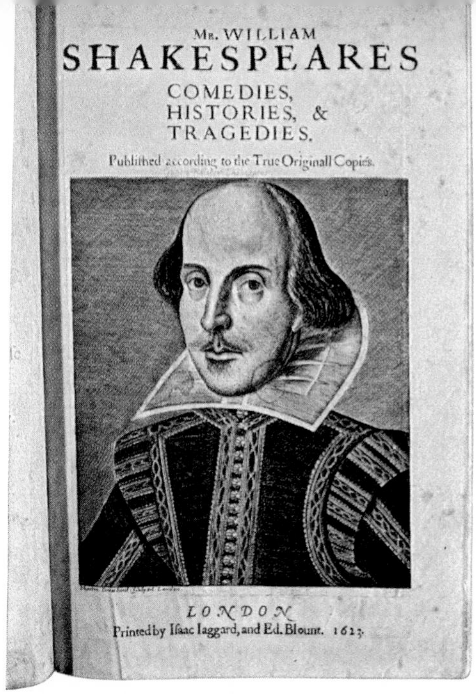

Mr. WILLIAM
SHAKESPEARES
COMEDIES,
HISTORIES, &
TRAGEDIES.
Published according to the True Originall Copies.

LONDON
Printed by Isaac Iaggard, and Ed. Blount. 1623.

other species still bloom in every garden, and wild flowers wave along the roads. Beech, elm, and oak here and there show a bronze and yellow tinge amidst the green.

Each year something like a million visitors pour into Stratford. The authorities try to keep their community as nearly like Shakespeare's town as possible, while still accommodating the visitors.

The citizens of Stratford, we found, don't always share their guests' devotion to the poet. "No, I can't say I care much for Shakespeare," observed a taxi driver who drove us from the station to our hotel. "We 'ear too much about him around 'ere." And a town constable remarked, "If you ask me, I think it's all a lot of humbug. All of these people comin' 'ere because a man wrote some plays. I'd rather get a nice program on the telly."

A townsman at Holy Trinity Church was even more vehement. He had seen the crowds packing his church all summer, asking questions, wanting to take pictures of the poet's grave. "What has Shakespeare done for this church? Just brought crowds 'ere," he asserted. "They bang, bang on the doors when they are shut. We can't 'ave a decent service 'ere on Sunday for them a-bangin' on the doors.

"I wish they would move 'im out of 'ere. Just take 'im out; that is, if they can find 'im. All he is, is mud, anyway. Mud, I say, because the river gets up and floods where he is buried down there. Just move 'im out, I say, and let us 'ave some peace."

The worshipers of Shakespeare all come to Holy Trinity to see the documentary evidence of Shakespeare's reality: the baptismal and burial record in the parish register, still visible but fading from long exposure to light; the graves of Shakespeare and his

family within the chancel; and the bust erected by his friends.

The "anti-Stratfordians," theorists intent on proving that Shakespeare's plays were written by Sir Francis Bacon, by the Earl of Oxford, or a score of other candidates, sometimes come to the church with a request to open the tomb. What they expect to find, no one can tell. If the Stratford man is right, all they would find would be mud.

The tomb is protected by a doggerel curse, which legend says the poet composed:

Good frend for Iesus sake forbeare
To digg the dust encloased heare!
Bleste be ye man yt spares thes stones,
And curst be he yt moves my bones.

Shakespeare had watched the sexton digging graves and unceremoniously throwing out old bones, as did the gravediggers in *Hamlet*, and was leaving a warning to prevent that happening to his own remains. The curse has been respected to this day.

STRATFORD, for all the cynics among its citizens, has long benefited from the public fascination with its most famous citizen. Statues and pictures of Shakespeare appear all over town. Hardly a public park or place of business escapes some Shakespearean symbol. Curio shops are littered with busts, pictures, and other souvenirs of every sort. None of the pictures or images, except the frontispiece of the First Folio, published in 1623, and the bust in Trinity Church, has any validity; most represent idealized concepts of the poet.

The propensity of Stratfordians to invent legends is illustrated by a sign that suddenly appeared on one hotel's back lawn while we were there. It declared that *A Midsummer Night's Dream* was first performed under the neighboring cedar tree! The most famous legend, also unfounded, is the story that Shakespeare poached deer from Sir Thomas Lucy at Charlecote, four miles from Stratford. The fact is that Sir Thomas did not then have a deer park, though deer abound there now.

Nonetheless, even if Shakespeare did not poach deer from Sir Thomas Lucy, he gives evidence of a knowledge of hunting. In his

DEAN CONGER, NATIONAL GEOGRAPHIC PHOTOGRAPHER

SCHOOLBAGS FLYING, *Stratford pupils pedal past Hall's Croft, the half-timbered house of Dr. John Hall. He married Susanna Shakespeare, daughter of the poet. The word croft signifies that the house originally had an adjacent field for pasture or crops.*

Preserved by the Birthplace Trust, the house is furnished so that Susanna would still feel at home. The 16th-century mortars and pestles fascinate children (opposite). The doctor's casebook lists remedies made from such ingredients as frog's spawn, earthworms, and hen's dung with which he treated his patients' "humours."

The Halls had one child, Elizabeth, who ended Shakespeare's line. Of his four grandchildren only she married, and she died childless.

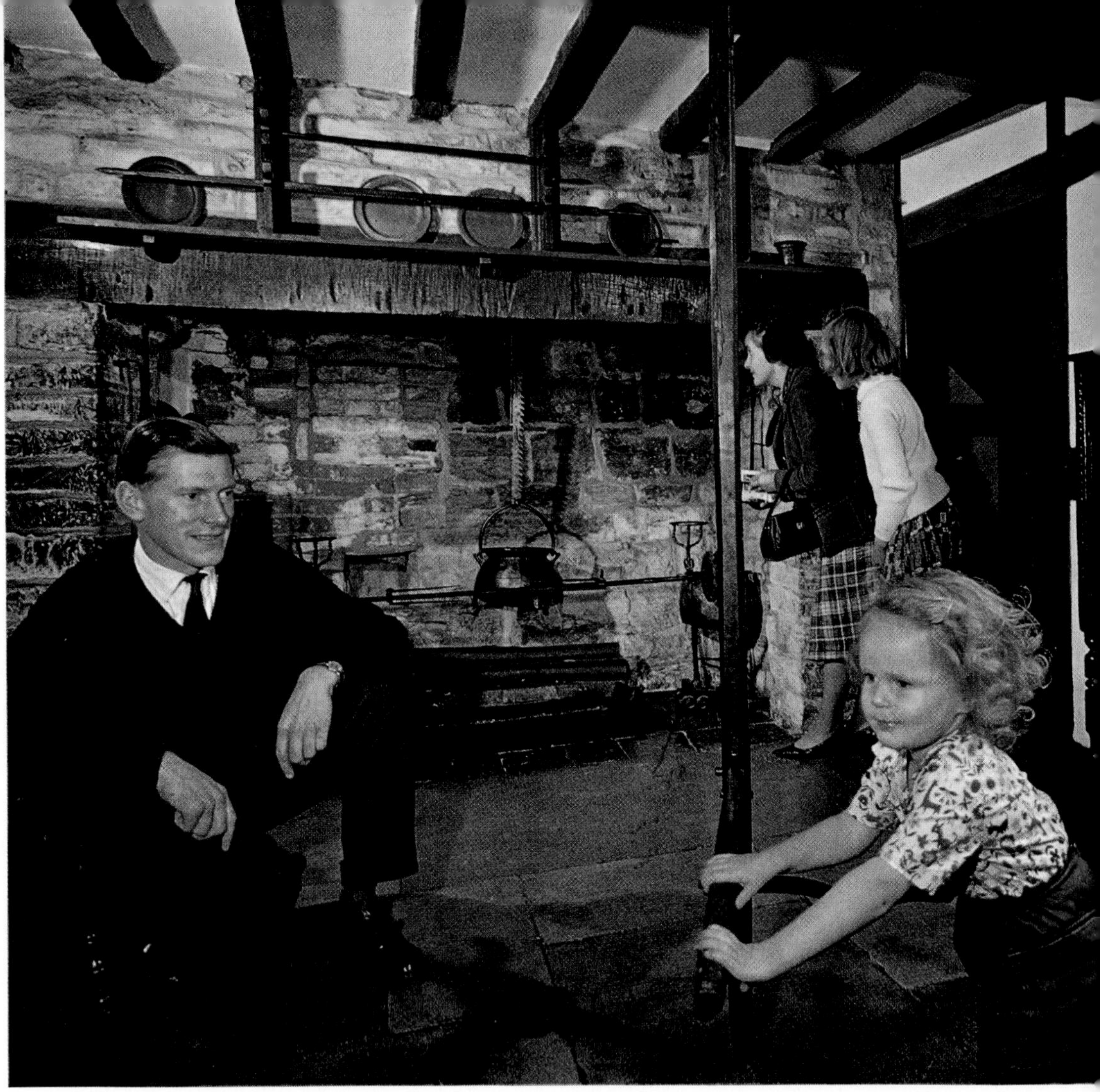

plays he often draws metaphors and similes from the chase. For instance, in *Julius Caesar*, Antony refers to Caesar's murder in terms of a deer hunt:

> *Here was thou bayed, brave hart;*
> *Here didst thou fall; and here thy hunters stand,*
> *Signed in thy spoil and crimsoned in thy lethe* [blood].

In *As You Like It* there occurs a famous description of "a poor sequestered stag, That from the hunter's aim had ta'en a hurt," and in *Venus and Adonis* Shakespeare compares the love-worn Adonis to "a wild bird being tamed with too much handling, or as the fleet-foot roe that's tired with chasing."

The legend that has produced the most relics is the story that New Place, the handsome estate that Shakespeare bought in Stratford for his retirement, contained a mulberry tree which the poet had planted with his own hand. Tourists as early as the 18th century became such a nuisance that the owner, the Reverend Francis Gastrell, finally cut down the sacred mulberry. A local craftsman, Thomas Sharp, bought the wood and made it up into souvenirs that were sold widely. In time the Folger Library alone acquired enough mulberry mementos to account for at least a cord of wood. The carpenter was accused of faking relics of New Place, but he swore by the Twelve Apostles that all were genuine.

Actual relics of Shakespeare's life in Stratford are numerous and interesting. The Birthplace Trust carefully makes no claims that cannot be substantiated. The birthplace itself in Henley Street, a double

DEAN CONGER, NATIONAL GEOGRAPHIC PHOTOGRAPHER

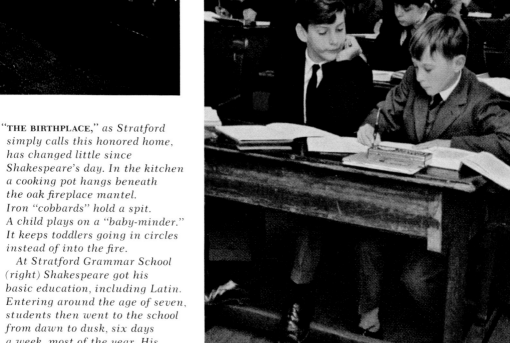

*"**THE BIRTHPLACE**," as Stratford simply calls this honored home, has changed little since Shakespeare's day. In the kitchen a cooking pot hangs beneath the oak fireplace mantel. Iron "cobbards" hold a spit. A child plays on a "baby-minder." It keeps toddlers going in circles instead of into the fire.*

At Stratford Grammar School (right) Shakespeare got his basic education, including Latin. Entering around the age of seven, students then went to the school from dawn to dusk, six days a week, most of the year. His "whining schoolboy . . . creeping like snail Unwillingly to school" may have described himself.

A tearoom sign reminds visitors that Anne Hathaway's Cottage stands at Shottery, a mile away. Shakespeare married her in 1582.

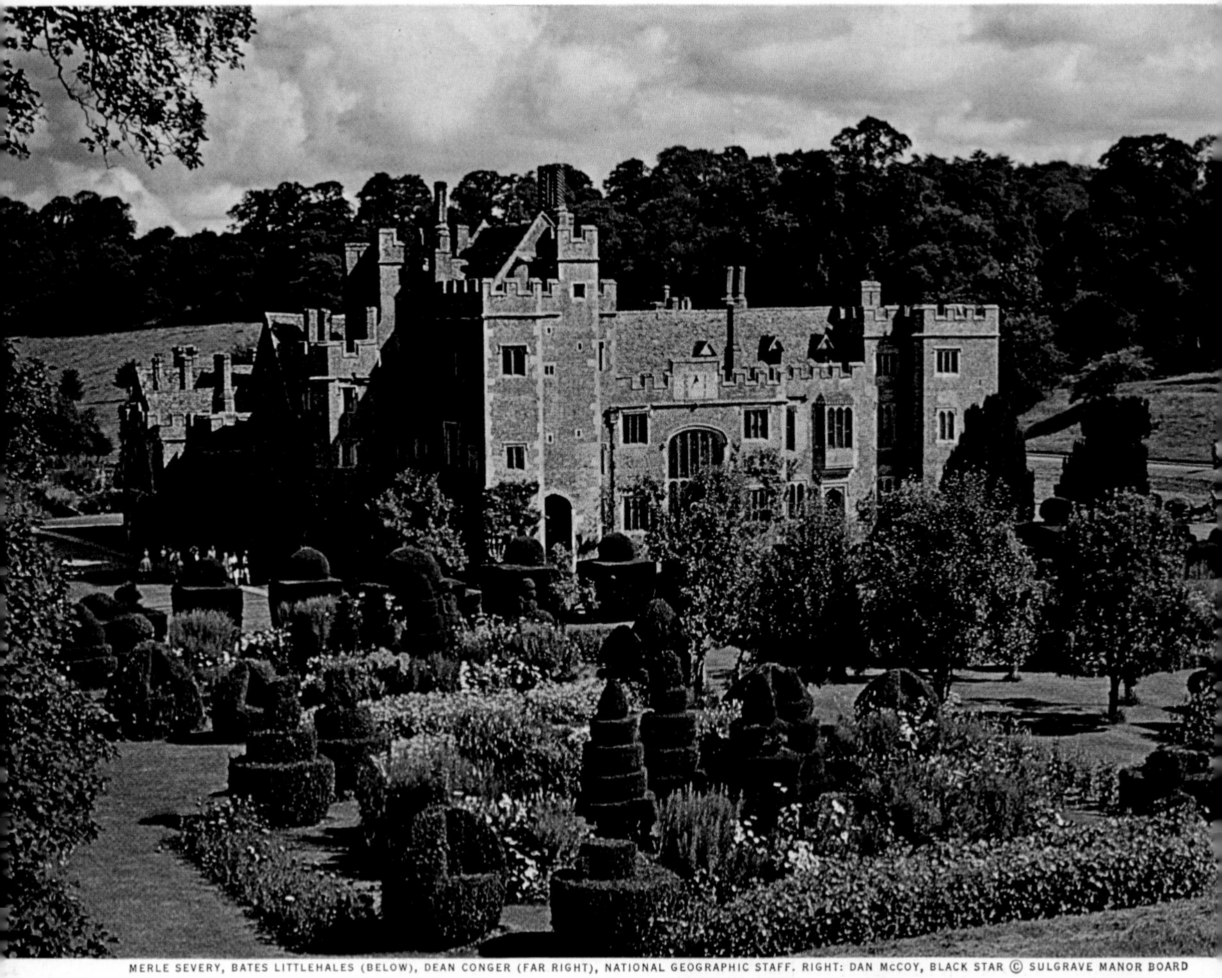

MERLE SEVERY, BATES LITTLEHALES (BELOW), DEAN CONGER (FAR RIGHT), NATIONAL GEOGRAPHIC STAFF. RIGHT: DAN McCOY, BLACK STAR © SULGRAVE MANOR BOARD

house owned by Shakespeare's father, served as both residence and the family glove shop. The birthroom has Elizabethan furniture, though not that of the Shakespeare family.

The same care has gone into furnishing Anne Hathaway's Cottage, where Shakespeare went courting; Mary Arden's House, home of Shakespeare's mother; and Hall's Croft, the house and office of Shakespeare's physician son-in-law, Dr. John Hall. All these are museums of genuine historical value. Hall's Croft is one of Stratford's most interesting houses. Its herb garden is the sort a physician would have maintained, and its doctor's office has authentic equipment. Unfortunately, Hall's clinical notebook makes no mention of Shakespeare's last illness.

The Grammar School, where the poet undoubtedly was educated, stands in

GEORGE WASHINGTON'S *ancestors slept here – 23 miles east of Stratford at Sulgrave Manor (left), home of the Washingtons from 1539 until 1659. George's great-grandfather John left for Virginia three years before the manor was sold. Over its door appear the royal arms and the family shield, its stars and stripes an intriguing coincidence.*

At nearby Compton Wynyates (opposite) visitors delight in Tudor brickwork, carved oak paneling, and secret stairs. The estate has been in the same family for nearly eight centuries.

DOVECOTE *at the Wilmcote farm of Mary Arden, Shakespeare's mother, has 657 nest holes where pigeons lived until needed to bolster winter fare.*

Deer roam Charlecote Park (opposite). Legend says Shakespeare was caught poaching them by Sir Thomas Lucy, who had him whipped; and that the playwright later vengefully made this local magistrate the model for boobish Justice Shallow of Henry IV Part II *and* The Merry Wives of Windsor.

Church Street. The much-carved desks are still there, but the initials "W. S." appear on none of them. Beneath the schoolroom, now known as the Big School, is the old Guildhall where itinerant players gave performances. There Shakespeare saw his first plays, and there he received the inspiration, perhaps, that took him to London to join a dramatic company.

On 15th-century Clopton Bridge, Shakespeare stood and watched the swirling waters of the Avon and the swans swimming below. The Avon now has a new ingredient, detergents that boil up in a vast mass of foam at the weirs below Trinity Church. The concentration is so great that at times the swans lose the natural oil in their feathers and become waterlogged.

We made a foray through Cotswold villages south of Stratford and back through the woodlands that still remain in this region. Shakespeare probably poached deer in these woods. The Forest of Arden north of Stratford gave him a name and the atmosphere for *As You Like It*. He knew the trees by name and understood woodcraft.

Cedars, common in the parks of Warwickshire, he usually pictures as the "lofty

STORIED CASTLES *of Shakespeare country, Kenilworth and Warwick met differing fates. Cromwell's men razed Kenilworth (above), now a magnificent ruin. A Cromwell ally held great Warwick (right), still the residence of the Earl of Warwick.*

Kenilworth, founded as a Norman keep in 1122, became a mighty citadel. A man-made lake held off attackers. Edward II abdicated while imprisoned here, and here Elizabeth I visited the Earl of Leicester. One 19-day fete—when merrymakers quaffed 320 casks of beer—inspired a scene in Sir Walter Scott's Kenilworth.

Coronation portrait of the Queen by her goldsmith hangs in Warwick's Great Hall amid arms, suits of armor, and elk antlers. The bear appears on the Warwick family emblem.

cedar," the "majestic cedar," or the "stately cedar" *(Cymbeline)*. He can refer to "Jove's stout oak" *(The Tempest)* or "the splitting wind" that "Makes flexible the knees of knotted oaks" *(Troilus and Cressida)*. And he reveals an observation from nature in *A Midsummer Night's Dream:*

So doth the woodbine the sweet
honeysuckle
Gently entwist; the female ivy so
Enrings the barky fingers of the elm.

A nearby town that Shakespeare must have known is Kenilworth, the site of the castle where Robert Dudley, Earl of Leicester, entertained Queen Elizabeth on more than one occasion. As a boy of eleven in 1575, Shakespeare may have seen—and perhaps been inspired by—some of the pageantry at Kenilworth when Leicester staged the most elaborate of all his festivities for the Queen.

Dusk had fallen as we turned back toward Stratford. A faint mist enveloped low-lying spots and the sliver of a crescent moon hung in the sky: "The moon, like to a silver bow New-bent in heaven . . ." as Hippolyta calls it in *A Midsummer Night's Dream.*

Across a stubble field someone had lighted a fire that glowed against the dark background of beech and oak trees. Such a scene Shakespeare might have remembered as he wrote of the campfire before the Battle of Agincourt in *Henry V* where

The poor condemned English,
Like sacrifices, by their watchful fires
Sit patiently and inly ruminate
The morning's danger...

Indeed, the sights and scenes of Shakespeare's country are enough to inspire poetry in any soul. He has left us descriptions of his England that establish in the land points of eternal interest.

BATES LITTLEHALES, NATIONAL GEOGRAPHIC PHOTOGRAPHER

A day at the Globe – when a penny bought the riches of a play by William Shakespeare

TRUMPETS BLARE in the unroofed arena of the newly built Globe. Eyes turn toward the stage, a raised platform that thrusts into the yard or "pit." It is September, 1599, and one of the first performances of *Julius Caesar* is about to begin.

Players step out from their "tiring room" backstage where they don their costumes. "Hence!" shouts an actor. "Home you idle creatures. . . ." Groundlings – so called because they stand in the trampled dirt of the pit – laugh uproariously at this opening line. Many, truant apprentices, have deserted their masters for the afternoon.

William Shakespeare knew his audience: What Flavius shouted onstage at the idlers of Rome had long been the cry of Puritan preachers and priggish London officials. The Lord Mayor and aldermen could not close the Globe and other theaters on the south bank of the Thames outside their jurisdiction. So they petitioned the Queen's Privy Council to shut them, for theaters "maintain idleness . . . and draw apprentices and other servants from their ordinary works. . . ."

But Elizabeth and her successor James I loved plays and ignored such petitions. Happily, Shakespeare's genius would flower before the Puritans could suppress theatricals. He died in 1616; the Elizabethan theaters died in 1642.

James Burbage, an actor and carpenter, built London's first theater in 1576, when Shakespeare was 12. Burbage probably based his design on the inn courtyard where, up to then, public dramatic performances had been staged. He also drew from the design of the bearbaiting amphitheater. Shakespeare, in the prologue to *Henry V*, aptly called the theater of his day the "wooden O."

The only contemporary drawing of an Elizabethan theater's interior (left) shows the Swan as it looked in 1596. The flag, visible to Londoners across the Thames, proclaims a performance in progress. Playgoers able to pay more than the groundling's penny admission filled the roofed galleries around the stage. Some gallants sat on three-legged stools placed on the stage itself. Nobles and lowborn mingled. Hawkers sold food, drink, and penny pipes. Cutpurses skulked about. The gentry promenaded.

People spoke of going to "hear," not "see," a play because, on the stark stage, pageantry was conjured by the playwright's words and the actors' skill. Boys played women's parts.

A bad performance instantaneously got bad reviews: Onstage spectators stomped off; others hurled insults and ripe fruit. Then as now, good theater was rewarded with applause.

CURTAIN CALL *at the Royal Shakespeare Theatre brings forth players carrying on a tradition that began in 1769, when David Garrick organized the first Shakespearean festival in Stratford. Festival performances, April to October, annually attract some 400,000 playgoers from all over the world. A touch of makeup, a costume grim or regal—and immortal words take new life.*

DEAN CONGER AND JOHN E. FLETCHER, NATIONAL GEOGRAPHIC PHOTOGRAPHERS. OPPOSITE: UTRECHT UNIVERSITY LIBRARY

BY COTSWOLD LANES

HOW PLEASED I am that you are coming to England – and the Cotswolds! Come stay with us in our cottage in this unspoiled village of Leafield, Oxfordshire."

These hospitable words from my old friend Alan Villiers greeted me on my arrival in England. "You will live in a real Cotswold cottage (a bit tough, but not too bad) and will sample English country life. We have a nice vegetable garden, a warm attic room, and a good welcome for you."

Ask any British naval officer what he would like most when he retires. Likely he will say, "Give me a cottage in the Cotswolds, with a garden, a dog, and a pipe."

The region straddling the Cotswold Hills west of Oxford is a country all its own. To an Englishman it typifies old England. Little cottages with flaked-stone roofs merge into the wolds, or open uplands, as if they had grown there. Each has its rose garden with ramblers climbing the walls and perhaps blue delphiniums, petunias, phlox, and lilies nodding in the breeze.

Even the quaint names of Cotswold rivers and towns caught my fancy. Think of living beside the Evenlode or the Windrush – purling streams lazing beneath great oaks and winding through lush meadows – or calling your home town Chipping Campden, Snowshill, Birdlip, or Lower Swell!

In London I acquired a pocket-size car ideally suited to the narrow lanes of the Cotswolds. All the way to Oxford I drove through beautiful English country gently rolling with pastures and sylvan glades. Set back from the road on hills, fine manor houses peeped through the trees.

Bicycles swarmed everywhere, for it was a warm, sunny day and "trippers" were taking advantage of the weather. But, as always in England, a shower was just around the corner. When it came, like a flash, the cyclists stuck heads through slits in ponchos, stretched the tentlike coverings across handlebars, and kept on pedaling!

Leaving Witney, noted for its blankets, I

COTSWOLD CHARM *glows from the time-mellowed stone buildings of Chipping Campden. Arches of the Market Hall frame High Street, where houses of 14th-century wool traders still stand.*

ADAM WOOLFITT

TO WOLD'S END

Amid gentle hills and purling streams
Melville Bell Grosvenor finds timeless towns
built of honey-hued stone in the days when wool was king

LEAFIELD BELFRY *trembles with vibrant song as ringers go through their changes. The man at left has just let go his "sally"; the colored grip flies to the ceiling. Cocked upward in the tower overhead, his bell swings down thunderingly. Other ringers intently wait their turns; timing is vital. If a lad fails to release his sally at the right instant, the pull of the bell may yank him to the ceiling! Little wonder a novice may observe for months before he touches a rope. Change ringers ply their art in many parts of England, filling the air with the pealing of bells.*

WHIPPETS *steal the show in Waynes Close (opposite), a 16th-century Burford home that once housed a wheelwright. Diamond panes latticed in lead make a muted mosaic of the house across the way. Cozy ingle seats flank the wide stone fireplace in many a Cotswold cottage; often a spiral staircase rises near the hearth.*

took to a narrow stone-walled lane. From a hill I spotted the tall thin steeple which Alan Villiers had written was the guidepost to Leafield. But he had not mentioned the bell music that came floating across the meadows. As I approached, the din grew. In Leafield green, directly below the church, it was earsplitting. "Ding, dang, dong, bom, welcome to the Cotswolds," the bells sang over and over.

Entranced, I stopped the car and listened along with the townsfolk who had gathered beneath the arched gate of the churchyard. All were enraptured by the tintinnabulation. When I asked a lad where Mr. Villiers lived, he replied, "The sailor fellow? He lives down there, third cottage on the right."

Slowly I drove down the lane, its stone walls topped with red ramblers. There, in his garden, I saw my salty friend Alan. "Welcome aboard," he beamed. "And watch the overheads when you enter—Cotswold doors were designed for dwarfs!"

Inside, Nance, Alan's charming wife, was waiting for me. For the next ten days she would serve as my hostess and, when Alan spelled her at the chores, would act as guide while I explored the Cotswolds.

OVER COFFEE that first evening we could still faintly hear the pealing and clanging of the bells. "Don't they ever grow tired?" I asked Nance.

"No; this is practice night. Teams of bell ringers are rehearsing for next Sunday. They will ring 720 changes. It will take a half hour. Alan, show him up to the belfry, so he can have a look at the men in action."

It was dark in the lane and we had to feel our way, but the bells kept us company. As we fumbled around the tower, looking for the door, the bells beat upon our ears. "Tin, tan, din, bom," they sounded over and over. The reverberations stirred me deeply. Perhaps that's why bells are rung; they draw people like a magnet.

Up endless stairs we climbed to a room dimly lit by lamplight. Six men and boys in a circle were pulling and letting go red, white, and blue ropes. Not a head turned as we entered; each man kept his eyes glued to his neighbor's rope. Above, we heard the bells sounding.

From the group of onlookers a grizzled man came forward, and Alan introduced him as the tower foreman.

"Welcome to our belfry! Are you a ringer?"

"No, I can't ring a bell," I replied.

"Sorry; good ringers are scarce. We're always looking for a new man to lay hand to a rope."

For a while we stood and watched the silent, solemn-faced ringers pulling and letting go their ropes and sallies (grips). Finally the course, or tune, completed, everyone began talking, congratulating the experts, joshing those who made mistakes.

"Change ringing originally was peculiar to the English," the foreman explained. "Belgians play tunes on their carillons by

WINFIELD PARKS, NATIONAL GEOGRAPHIC PHOTOGRAPHER. UPPER: ADAM WOOLFITT

striking a hammer against the bell's rim. But in change ringing the whole bell is swung in an almost complete circle, the clapper striking near the end of the stroke. This swinging of the bell as she – a bell is always a lady – is struck mellows the tone, but makes it stronger, more piercing. Come up to the bell chamber and I'll show you."

Up a steel ladder we climbed and through a trap door into the cavernous steeple. Six monster bells in a cluster hung from big wheels; ropes led to the ringers' chamber below.

As I watched, the big tenor bell slowly swung upright, her bronze mouth yawning. I could clearly see the inscription on her side: "Presented to Leafield Church by H. M. Queen Victoria, 1874."

"She is set at the backstroke," the foreman said in my ear. "Hang on now and I'll signal for a handstroke." Suddenly the ponderous bell rolled over and bellowed a vibrant "Bom." The whole tower jarred. My hands and arms vibrated. Again the bell swung, in reverse this time, the backstroke. Again came a deep "Bom," like a 16-inch gun firing.

"The sound of the bells terrifies some," Alan said. "If you were locked up here during a prolonged peal, the concussion might drive you mad. In Dorothy Sayers' novel, *The Nine Tailors*, one of the big bells was the murderer. The victim was tied in the belfry. Old Batty Thomas drove him mad and finally killed him with her bonging."

Change ringing is more mathematical than musical. In simple courses the order of ringing is changed each time until all possible combinations are exhausted. Leafield's six bells can ring 720 changes without repetition, the notes tumbling out in succession without regard for melody.

Back in the ringers' chamber another group, including a girl, were set to play "Plain Bob Doubles," a simple course usually practiced by beginners.

"Bells up and ready for ringing. Stand to your ropes," called the foreman. A youngster not 14 years old gave a pull on his sally and then let go. High overhead his bell rang true and clear.

"Look now, treble is gone," the conductor called. The other five ringers started pulling their ropes in sequence to "sound the rounds." The bell music continued long after we returned to the cottage. Three hours they played that night. "As long as anyone will pull a rope," Alan commented.

"OUR HOUSE was once a duplex – two families lived under the same roof," Nance told me. "One owner cut doors through, making a single roomy cottage. Seventeen lived here a generation ago. Many Leafield people moved to the cities to work."

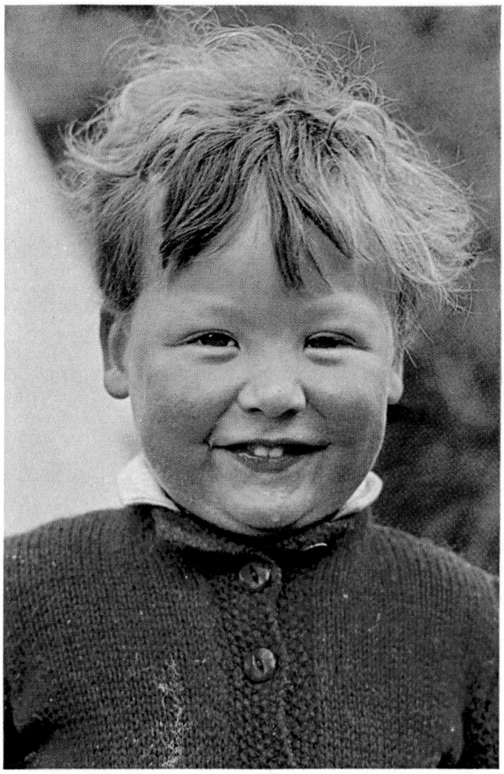

WINFIELD PARKS, NATIONAL GEOGRAPHIC STAFF. OPPOSITE: ADAM WOOLFITT

LEAFIELD SPIRE *spikes the clouds above the green quilt of a Cotswold valley. The River Windrush meanders beneath the leafy colonnade at center, a remnant of great forests that once mantled the downs. Kings galloped across the stream in pursuit of deer; story-book hamlets straddle its banks. The square tower of Swinbrook's church rises at right. Local stone harmonizes the rambling farmstead in foreground with its setting.*

Vagrant breeze tousles a Bibury lad (left). Sweater bespeaks cool summers; rare hot spells last only a day or so.

The 300-year-old house had no central heating. Tiny stoves in kitchen and living room – and two-foot stone walls for insulation – kept the home warm and cozy.

Unlike the true Cotswold cottage, which has no plumbing, the Villiers home boasted a bathroom on the second floor. But I looked in vain for a refrigerator – until Nance opened the door of her "Cotswold icebox," a cupboard set in the stone wall. The butter inside was firm, the meat cool. Temperatures in the Cotswolds seldom get high enough to spoil perishables.

One morning after a night of rain the sun streamed in my dormer. Roses in the gardens and the green shutters of the cottages across the way sparkled in the sun.

Nance turned Alan and me out in her raspberry and black currant patch. Lazily we picked the luscious berries.

"What a fine day for color photography," I commented. "Not a cloud in the sky."

A growl from the sea captain. "It always rains in the Cotswolds after a sunny morning. It will be cloudy by 10 o'clock, and rainy in the afternoon." And how right he was!

After the weather cleared we set out for Swinbrook. Down stone-walled lanes we drove, with the sun gilding the cows and Shires, shaggy-fetlocked draft horses whose forebears bore knights to battle. Red poppies carpeted the hillsides as in Flanders fields; rosebay willow purpled the roadside.

"Life in a Cotswold village revolves around its church. You must explore one thoroughly," my host said.

Overlooking Swinbrook, sprawled along the Windrush, perched St. Mary's Church – off the beaten path, full of surprises.

Inside we were startled by knights in armor, white and stiff, lying on shelves beside the chancel. These were the Fettiplaces, the famous family who owned and ruled the Swinbrook area for 315 years. So powerful were they and their neighbors that villagers still quote this old rhyme:

The Traceys, the Lacys, and the Fettiplaces
Own all the manors, the parks, and the chases.

On a wall we saw "A Table of Benefactions" listing many Fettiplace charities: "In 1743 Sir George Fettiplace gave £2:10s

ADAM WOOLFITT. OPPOSITE: WINFIELD PARKS, NATIONAL GEOGRAPHIC PHOTOGRAPHER

ARMORED EFFIGIES *of once-powerful Fettiplaces have kept stiff vigil in Swinbrook Church for four centuries; stone pillows offer small comfort. World War II bombing shattered the church's stained glass but left these worthies undisturbed. The village appears in Domesday Book as Svinbroc, or "swine brook." Pigs watered nearby in the Windrush.*

Fallow deer enliven Wychwood Forest (above), once part of a royal preserve. Their kind probably arrived with the Romans; fences have kept them in private herds ever since.

A year to repair the Family Monuments in Swinbrook Church, and £3 A year to A Clergyman for preaching four Sermons in every year in commemoration of himself and his Sister."

In addition, Sir George "gave £13 A year to be distributed in ten sixpenny Loaves every Sunday among the poor, who must be present at divine Service to receive it."

Parishioners collected their free loaves of bread each Sunday for more than 200 years—until after World War II.

From Swinbrook we drove through meadows along the winding Windrush to see the castle at Minster Lovell. Nothing is left of it but walls and turrets with stairs leading nowhere. Stories told about the old ruin clothe it with mystery that attracts thousands of visitors.

Novels have been written about Minster Lovell, the most famous being *The Blanket of The Dark* by John Buchan. It tells of Peter Pentecost, who fought against King Henry VII at the Battle of Stoke in 1487 and, escaping, hid out in a dovecote at Minster Lovell. But the story that draws most visitors to the castle shell is the mysterious disappearance of Francis, 13th Lord Lovell, who also fought and lost at Stoke. Escaping, he dove his horse into the Trent and never was seen again. Many legends grew

up about his disappearance, but one held through the years. Lovell, this story went, was rescued from drowning and hidden in a secret room in his castle by a trusted servant. But this retainer died with the secret, and Lord Lovell was entombed alive.

When repairs were made in 1708, workmen broke into a hidden chamber. Seated at a writing table was a man's skeleton with the remains of a dog at his feet. Though it was never identified, many people felt that the relic was the great Lord Lovell, who had "starved like a rat."

One morning I took Alan to the station in lovely Ascot under Wychwood. From the brow of a hill overlooking the Evenlode we saw the London train puffing down the valley. I became alarmed that he might miss it. "Don't worry!" he said. "They'll hold the train if they see anyone coming."

Just before the train pulled out, a girl rushed up on her bike. "Better run, Anne! I'll park your bicycle for you," the stationmaster called calmly. She did and he did—an example of Cotswold courtesy.

Driving on, I called upon Mrs. Muriel Groves in Shipton under Wychwood. "I have lived in Wychwood Forest for 300 years at least!" Mrs. Groves greeted me. "Many of my family, the Hambidges, are buried outside Swinbrook Church."

In the old days the Wychwood was a large royal hunting preserve. Its trees covered the hills between the Evenlode and the

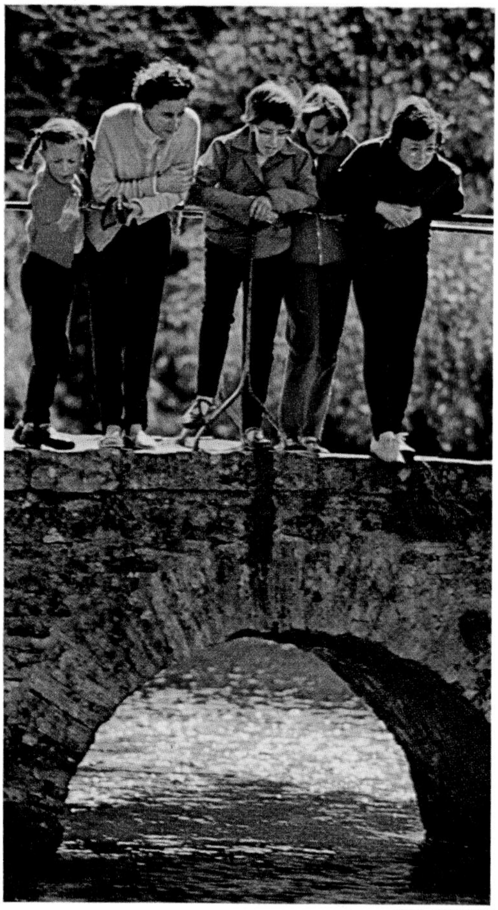

ADAM WOOLFITT

DORMERED COTTAGES *of Bibury's Arlington Row wear centuries like a blessing. "Surely the loveliest village in England," said William Morris. Visitors here scan the crystal Coln. Trout, wise to man's ways, gobble crusts but spurn lures.*

Windrush. Shipton and Ascot nestled beneath those forested heights. Thus they won their name "under Wychwood."

William the Conqueror loved Wychwood; "Sciptone" is mentioned in his Domesday Book. King John, local historians claim, built the hunting lodge at Langley, near Shipton. Henry VII stayed there with his Queen, Elizabeth of York; their initials, H E, can still be seen carved in a bay window of the palace, now a farmhouse. Henry VIII, while hunting here, was presented with a greyhound by Anne Boleyn in 1532.

"Shipton old-timers love to tell stories of poaching days in the ancient forest," Mrs. Groves said. "Everyone above 12 was required to respect His Majesty's wild beasts – the hart, the hind, the hare, the boar, and the wolf. Yet all hunted on the royal preserve; fresh meat was scarce. Many a Shipton villager had more venison in a week than a Londoner in a year."

The poachers strung nets between trees and then drove the deer down the "ride" into the nets. Others used trained greyhound-like dogs called lurchers to drive the deer to the nets. Cunning places were picked for hiding venison – a hayrick hollowed out, false bottoms in carts, even an empty tomb in the Burford churchyard.

Forest keepers often searched the villages for cooked venison, even looking into "Cotswold iceboxes." On one raid a housewife picked a venison pie off the table and shoved it under baby in the high chair. Keeper left, none the wiser.

Returning home to Leafield, I circled through Charlbury to view the shrunken Wychwood. In Victorian times the forest was cut and the land plowed until only a small copse was left. Under the remaining great trees I imagined shadowy poachers stalking deer through the ferns and purple rosebay that carpeted the glades.

In Leafield everyone has a little garden in which he tries to keep something green the year around. Old Harry Wiggins was setting out Brussels sprouts when I called on him in mid-July. "Oi loikes Brussels sprouts. They be proper hardy ones, they be," he told me. The plants grow all winter; he picks buds even in the snow. Savoy cabbage, leeks, and broccoli sown in the summer also survive frost and ice and they are "fit to pick in spring if I lev 'em bide."

WITH MRS. GROVES as guide, Nance and I wound through the narrow Cotswold lanes to Chastleton. The huge manor of yellowish stone with a flaked-stone roof was built 11 years before the Pilgrim Fathers landed at Plymouth.

We wandered through spacious rooms, with huge fireplaces, paneled walls, and furniture from the time of William and Mary and earlier. On a wall we saw the 1609 marriage settlement between Henry Jones and Anne Fettiplace. Sir Edmund Fettiplace, the same whose tomb and epitaph we admired in Swinbrook's church, agreed to pay a dowry of £1,000 to Father Jones *after* the marriage. The matchmakers evidently knew child psychology – the agreement was made without the knowledge of the youngsters. So the wedding took place and they lived happily at Chastleton, having 13 children.

Pointing to a portrait of a young lady, our guide said: "That's Anne Fettiplace in her bridal gown. We took the picture down recently for cleaning. The bride had red nails – there's nothing new under the sun!"

Secret rooms always fascinate me, so I was thrilled when we walked through a sliding panel into a tiny hidden chamber. The guide was not long unfolding its story. After the Battle of Worcester in 1651, a member of the Jones family fled here and took refuge in this room. Hard on his heels Cromwell's men clattered up to Chastleton and, seeing a steaming horse in the barn, demanded that Mrs. Jones produce the fugitive. They thought they had cornered King Charles II himself.

To prove no one there, Mrs. Jones showed them through the house. Not satisfied, they stayed the night and chose of all places the room with the secret panel. Fearing her

FAIRY-TALE VILLAGE *shimmers on a bow window in Burford. Half-timbered and stone buildings of High Street blend styles; antiques vie with their reflections for the shopper's eye. Charles II and Nell Gwyn, refugees from plague-ridden London, enjoyed horse races here.*

ADAM WOOLFITT

ADAM WOOLFITT

husband might betray himself by making a noise, Mrs. Jones tried to inveigle the men down to the banquet hall, but they demanded service in that room. Mrs. Jones sent food up, all right, but she put laudanum in the wine. Soon the men were fast asleep, sprawled on the floor.

"Can't you see little Mrs. Jones stepping gingerly over those snoring soldiers and releasing her husband?" Mrs. Groves asked. He escaped and was never caught.

STOW ON THE WOLD, where the winds blow cold!" said our lady guide, as we approached a castlelike town crowning a hill. "Roads radiate from it like spokes from a wheel hub."

Old Stow encloses a hollow square, the market place where cattle were corralled for safety in olden days. A narrow street led my little car into the court like a gateway. We admired the yellowish houses, the church, and the stocks where prisoners were once exposed to public scorn.

Our road to Upper and Lower Swell was overhung with big trees. It was easy to believe the local saying, "The squirrel can hop from Swell to Stow, without resting his foot or wetting his toe."

SHELTER FOR THE CENTURIES *takes shape under the tiler's hammer (above) as Brook House in Cricklade gets a new roof. A tile's name varies with its length; "Farewell," the smallest, goes on last. Winter's frosts help fashion these flakes by splitting limestone blocks left out in the open. At Farmington, one of the few Cotswold-stone quarries still operating, men lever up two-ton chunks (below); whining saw cuts them into building blocks (opposite).*

My chief recollection of Lower Swell, besides its church and trim yellow cottages with doorstep gardens, was the sweet scent in the air. Creamy blossoms carpeted the meads beside the Dikler. With good reason the herb is called meadowsweet.

Lower Slaughter is a quiet little village hardly as bloody as its name implies. A tiny brook wends down its one street. Every book I read spoke of the white ducks that sport in its millstream. Sure enough, Pekin ducks were tipping, rippling the reflections of rose gardens and cottages.

Coming to Bourton on the Water, I was surprised by a miniature Venice. Through the village green the Windrush flows beneath arched bridges, clean and clear, rippling in its shallow bed.

Picturesque as Bourton is, it hardly seems a Cotswold town, because its houses are red brick and its roofs blue slate. The railroad has brought modernity here.

In the vegetable garden of the New Inn, the proprietor has built a miniature Bourton on the Water. So realistic is his toy village that photographs of it are mistaken for aerial views of the town itself. Every house is built to scale. Small saplings reproduce real trees, and a Windrush winds through the village. Street lights glimmer, and an organ plays hymns in the church.

Through a periscope visitors get a "villager's view." All is well till a live giant in seven-league boots stalks across the scene!

APRIL BRINGS SPRING *to the Cotswolds, and early trippers greet it at Bourton on the Water (above) where footbridges span the sparkling Windrush.*

Modern Gullivers explore the Model Village (right), Bourton's tiny twin and most famous attraction. Church and cottages are built at one-tenth scale. Shrubs equal trees. The green alms box proffers a slot for "Baptist Church Expenses."

In August sodden players drench each other in Bourton's annual football frolic (far right), played in the river shallows. Local teams compete. Biggest winners are the shops and inns, welcoming visitors who flock to watch the fun.

BATES LITTLEHALES, NATIONAL GEOGRAPHIC PHOTOGRAPHER RIGHT: ADAM WOOLFITT

Alan joined us on our trip to the west. Our first visit was to old Burford, a prosperous town back in the days of coaches. Travelers moving north and south, east and west, stopped here overnight. Kings and queens of England who have slept in Burford sound like a Who's Who of Royalty. The railroad sent Burford into a decline, but the motorist brought prosperity again. In summer one has to make reservations far ahead at the Bull, the Lamb (in Sheep Street), the Bay Tree, and other inns whose history reflects Elizabethan days.

Burford's church is one of the finest in Oxfordshire. Its tower goes back to Norman times, and its history is as exciting as that of Burford itself. Cromwell's men put down a mutiny here and incarcerated the prisoners in the church. On the font we saw a crudely carved name, "Anthony Sedley Prisner 1649."

We joined the famous Roman road, Fosse Way, now a modern highway, at Northleach. Straight and true, over hill and dale

Autumn auction recalls the great fairs of yesteryear

NOVEMBER CRISPS THE WIND at a farm auction in Stow on the Wold. Knowing eyes make cool appraisals as horses, mules, saddles, and tools go on the block; buyers elbow for standing room at the rail. Men at left risk a tumble for a ringside seat; Cotswold stone fences often lack mortar and will topple. "Stow on the Wold, where the Devil caught cold," townsfolk describe their windy hilltop. Many a tradesman must have caught the sniffles there too in the open-air markets and fairs of bygone centuries. Into Stow's market square came generations of drovers with their herds; some 20,000 sheep once were sold there in a day.

Towns all over England held such fairs. The great ones offered a bewildering variety of wares – apes, bears, and exotic birds for pet fanciers; Italian silk, Flemish linen, French wine, spices from the Orient. Isaac Newton bought his first book on the stars at a fair. Tumblers and bawds entertained the shoppers; cutpurses and mountebanks preyed on them. Special "piepowder" courts, so named for the dusty feet – *piepoudrous* – of litigants, dispensed quick justice. Market places often centered around a cross (like Banbury's in the nursery rhyme); men closed deals by a handshake on its base. Though fairs are now few, today's countryman still likes to trade out of doors.

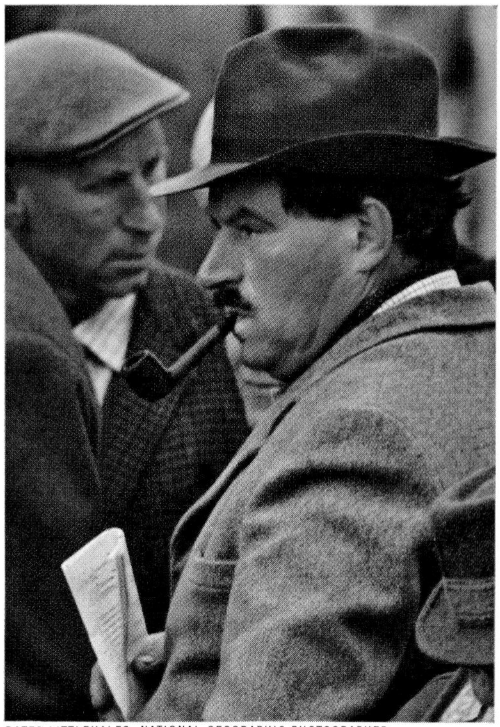

BATES LITTLEHALES, NATIONAL GEOGRAPHIC PHOTOGRAPHER

ROMAN GHOSTS *and medieval customs live on in Cirencester. On Fridays old Market Square earns its name anew as merchants set up stalls to hawk foods and textiles. Strolling shoppers come in from the countryside for Market Day, as did their forebears in the Middle Ages.*

Even the distant past lies just below the surface. Here stood Corinium, second largest town in Roman Britain; only Londinium, today's London, outshone it. Later centuries buried the Roman ruins, including a large mosaic that floored one of the buildings. Then in 1849 repairmen dug into Dyer Street and struck gods—Ceres, Silenus, a seaweedy Neptune (right). The second-century mosaic now spreads its splendor in the Corinium Museum, one of England's best on Roman Britain.

A stairway through Cirencester's history still keeps diggers busy behind her church. Roman building, Saxon church, and abbeys of the 12th and 14th centuries rose and fell on the site. Girl (below) cleans a roof boss from the last. Student volunteers on holiday help in summer's five-week dig. Town's name baffles many. Varied pronunciations amuse locals; to them it's "Syrensester" or "Sisiter."

ADAM WOOLFITT

it runs. Romans built it that way so guards could keep an eye on long pack trains and gallop to the rescue in case of ambush by hostile Britons.

Not far from Northleach we digressed to see Chedworth's Roman villa, built in the second century but "modernized" in the fourth. Its foundations outline a sumptuous villa enclosing three sides of a square. The caretaker brought the ruins to life with vivid descriptions of Roman days.

"Do you realize the Romans occupied Britain some 400 years? That's almost as long as the New World has been known," Mrs. Groves remarked. "We are coming now to Cirencester. It was the important Roman town of Corinium." When a street is torn up or a cellar dug in Cirencester, Roman relics are often unearthed.

Bibury lived up to its reputation as "one of the loveliest villages in England." We admired gray cottages reflected in the still waters of the River Coln and the early 17th-century Arlington Row houses, which draw sightseers from around the world. From Bibury bridge we saw fat trout, so old and wise they never rise for fly or worm.

Crusts thrown to them by visitors are their favorite diet. I marked one big fellow on the bottom lazily sculling against the stream; he kept station perfectly. A passing bicyclist tossed in a cigarette butt. In a flash the "sleeping" trout snatched it, then angrily cast it forth.

What's in a name? Fascinating clues to a town's origin

UPPER SWELL, Lower Slaughter, Birdlip, Owlpen—droll images spangle a Cotswold map. But forget bloodshed; Slaughter comes from *slohtre*, or slough, a muddy spot. Owlpen is where a man named Olla built an enclosure. Birdlip may mean "cliff of birds"—or "bride's leap." Upper Swell stands beside a swell, or hill.

Cotswold itself originally meant "Cod's *wald*" or forest (for such it was), and many town names reflect the region's woolly past. From "sheep" came Shipton. *Ceping*, an old word for market, explains Chipping Campden.

How its name ends may tell how a town began. The suffix *ton* suggests a farm or village, *burg* or *borough* a fort. Roman stations end in *caster*, *cester*, or *chester*, Viking homesteads in *by* and *ing*, Norman towns in *ville*. From dairy farms came *wich* and *wick*, from enclosures *worth*.

Some *tons* indicate what they produced—Hayton, Flaxton, Butterton, Barton in the Beans. Bickerston was a beekeeper's farm. Keswick and Chiswick made cheese. Oxford, Hartford, and Horsford tell what animals crossed there. And we can read eels in Ely, beavers in Beverley.

Ecclesiastical origins show in Eccles, Godstow, Abbotsbury, Monkton, Nuneaton, Minster Lovell, Holywell, and Kirkby Overblow, "church town of the smelters." Saxon paganism pervades others: Thundridge, from Thunor, god of thunder; Wednesbury, evoking Woden, god of the dead.

The oldest names, often rivers and hills, are Celtic. Cornwall has most: Penzance, from *sant* and *pen*, "holy cape"; Lizard, from *ard* and *lis*, "high court." The Saxon names Higham and Hinton, "high homestead," crop up in the south. Dwellers in Nasty take comfort that *atten ast hey* meant "at the east enclosure." Prophetically, Hastings sprouted from *haest*, "violence."

Viking names abound in the east and north. Tooting, Yelling, and Barking stem from clans. Brocklesby recalls a "man without breeches"; Scamblesby was "shameless," Sloothby "good-for-nothing." Essex folk can thank Gallic taste for Beaumont, "beautiful hill." It had been Fulepet, "filthy hollow." To Old English names Norman overlords often added their own. Acaster Malbis recalls "Aca's Roman fort" and a Norman called "evil beast." Bentley Pauncefote links "grassy clearing" and "round belly."

Centuries of tongues wear rough edges off a place name. Gislheresuuyrth appears in a charter of 695; now it's Isleworth. Uuiggangeat is now Wyegate. And where a hospital stood on old Watling Street, today's town is called Spital in the Street. The Normans pared the Saxon Scrobbesbyrigscir down to Salopescira, then to Salop. The name evolved to Shropshire, but Salop still abbreviates it. Some names are still eroding. Locals write Arkholme but call it Arum; Chalvington is pronounced Chont'n.

Following the lovely Coln we came to Fairford. Though noted for its fishing, Fairford is celebrated chiefly for its curious church windows. Like medieval comics in stained glass are the windows of Fairford's church. Walt Disney could draw no funnier figures, nor more horrible, than these portrayed in glass at about the time America was discovered. John Tame, the wealthy wool stapler who sponsored this sermon in pictures, had a keen sense of humor.

Most celebrated is the great west window, picturing Judgment Day. From open tombs at the bottom the exalted wind slowly up to a heaven depicted in gorgeous ruby and blue. But the damned are whisked off to hell (a glassmaker's oven!) by the most devilish devils imaginable. Little blue and red demons, dog-faced and monkey-faced, beat the victims (mostly naked women), pitchfork them, and carry them off by wheelbarrow and on the shoulders.

REGRETFULLY I said goodbye to the Villiers next day. I was off to explore the north Cotswolds. Bells sounded across the still air as I drove through Leafield green. From the fast pealing I knew old-timers were showing off to beginners. My friends the bell ringers were bidding me farewell.

Purposely I kept off the main highways, zigzagging across rolling downs to find hidden villages. A favorite was Bourton on the Hill, a hamlet with window-box "gardens." Its yellow cottages and church clung to a steep hillside like barnacles. Squeezed between house fronts and the lane, terraced gardens burst with flowers of every kind.

Driving leisurely on, I caught a glimpse

A GAME OF DARTS, *a pint of bitter: day's end for "regulars" at the Fleece in Bretforton. Village pubs (public houses) all over England echo the scene as friendly folk gather for a bit of gossip and a try for a bull's-eye or maybe a "triple twenty."*

The syllables of Bretforton's name, recorded as early as 709, mean board, ford, and homestead, telling us that here stood a settlement by a stream crossed by planks. Today the unspoiled village, in the Vale of Evesham, boasts six dovecotes, one now a cottage. The half-timbered Fleece, built as a farmhouse, has changed little since Tudor times.

WINFIELD PARKS, NATIONAL GEOGRAPHIC PHOTOGRAPHER

Sermons in glass chastened an unlettered age; memorial brasses record its costumes

DOOMED DAMSELS wail in vain as demons, wielding flail and pitchfork, whisk them off to limbo. Fairford Church's 15th-century windows, among the best of medieval stained glass, opened the Bible to common folk in an age when few but the clergy could read. Eve in Eden, Moses and Solomon, sundry saints shine from adjacent windows. But doomsday in the famed "Last Judgment" window draws the eye; Satan's scaly hordes in lurid reds and blues eclipse even the elect on golden stairs nearby.

John Tame's wool fortune built the church and bought its windows. He and his wife, incised full-length in brass, survey the great work from atop their tomb.

Like a costume catalog of the ages, several thousand of these monumental brasses survive. Hobbyists make excursions to churches all over England to trace the brazen tides of fashion from the 13th to the 17th centuries. The Vardon family (opposite) journeyed from Dover to make rubbings – images formed by covering a plaque with paper and rubbing with crayon – of 15th-century brasses in Chipping Campden's church.

Many churches ask a fee to permit rubbings; some bar photographing.

The oldest brass in England, at Stoke d'Abernon in Surrey, portrays Sir John d'Abernon life-size, clad in chain mail with sword, spear, and shield. He died in 1277. Through the following years parade knights and courtiers, ladies in sweeping dresses and butterfly headgear, clerics in religious robes. Woolmen and other self-made men soon swell the ranks, joined by university provosts, justices, and Tudor merchants in ruffs and fur-trimmed gowns.

Some Cotswold brasses show merchants standing on sheep or wool sacks, others on shears. One at Chipping Campden proclaims William Grevel "the Flower of the wool merchants of all England."

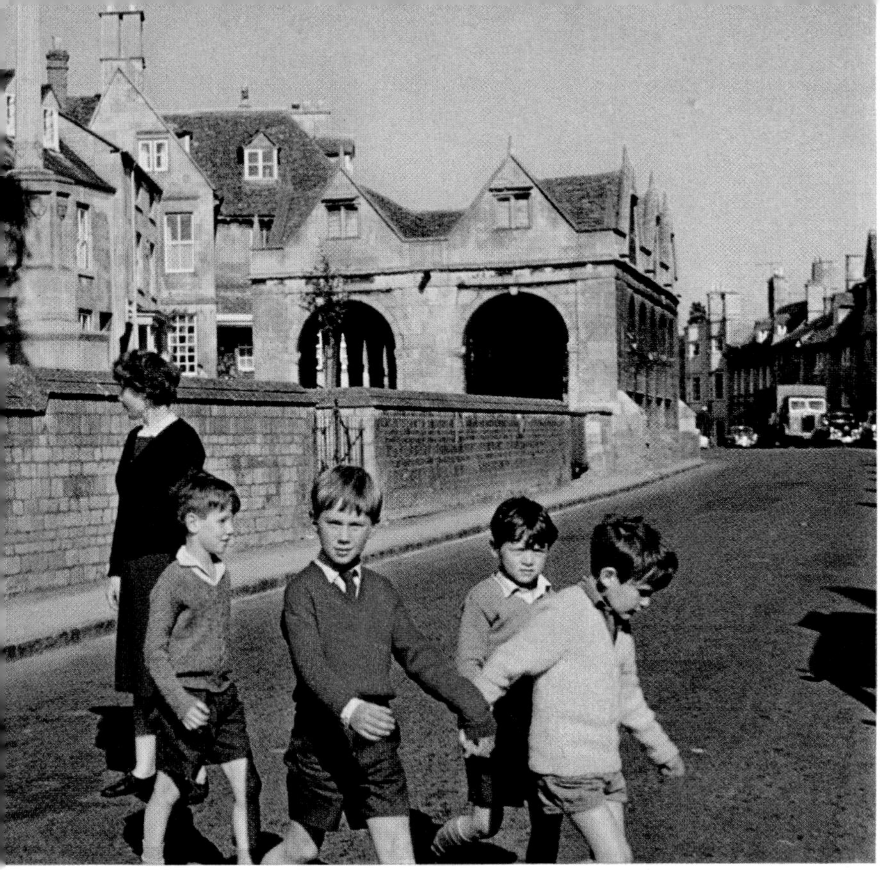

HIGH STREET *in Chipping Campden, where packhorses clip-clopped, sounds to the carefree steps of schoolchildren. Behind them, its arches yawning, dozes the old Market Hall (page 120), where traffic in wool brought prosperity to the town.*

In medieval times the region pastured thousands of Cotswold sheep, a distinct breed now all but vanished. An average fleece weighed 14 pounds. Merchants flocked from all over Britain and Flanders to dicker for the wool in Cotswold towns. Now men farm where drovers toiled, and the marts are monuments.

ADAM WOOLFITT (ALSO OPPOSITE). ABOVE: WINFIELD PARKS, NATIONAL GEOGRAPHIC PHOTOGRAPHER

LOW SUN *in Stow on the Wold etches the whiskered face of an early riser (left) and brings a squint to a shopper's eye (lower). Fruits and flowers blazon the cheery windows; boxes of produce line the sidewalk. Sign on one touts "English tomatoes."*

Most Cotswold towns lie on slopes and in sheltered valleys. But Stow sits high on a windblown hill; commerce along several ancient thoroughfares converging there sired the town. Shops enclose a vast market square. The Puritan victory at Stow in 1646 marked the final collapse of King Charles I's armies.

Fine old silver tempts sterling from the purses of window watchers outside a shop in Chipping Campden (right). Lack of waterpower kept industry from this market town when the great wool trade waned. Today it prospers anew as visitors stroll its ancient streets and browse its quaint marts.

of a flat-topped tower rising above buff cottages set in a green valley. It was Chipping Campden, "the flower of Cotswold towns." From my hotel window I looked past chimney pots smoking thin wisps to the grassy hills and patchwork fields above Campden. Below stood the arched wool market and the city hall, the town's center of life. Music floated from the latter when dances were held there in the evenings.

Back in the days when sheep made the wolds rich and famous, Chipping Campden was the center of the local wool industry. Success brought prosperity to the towns-

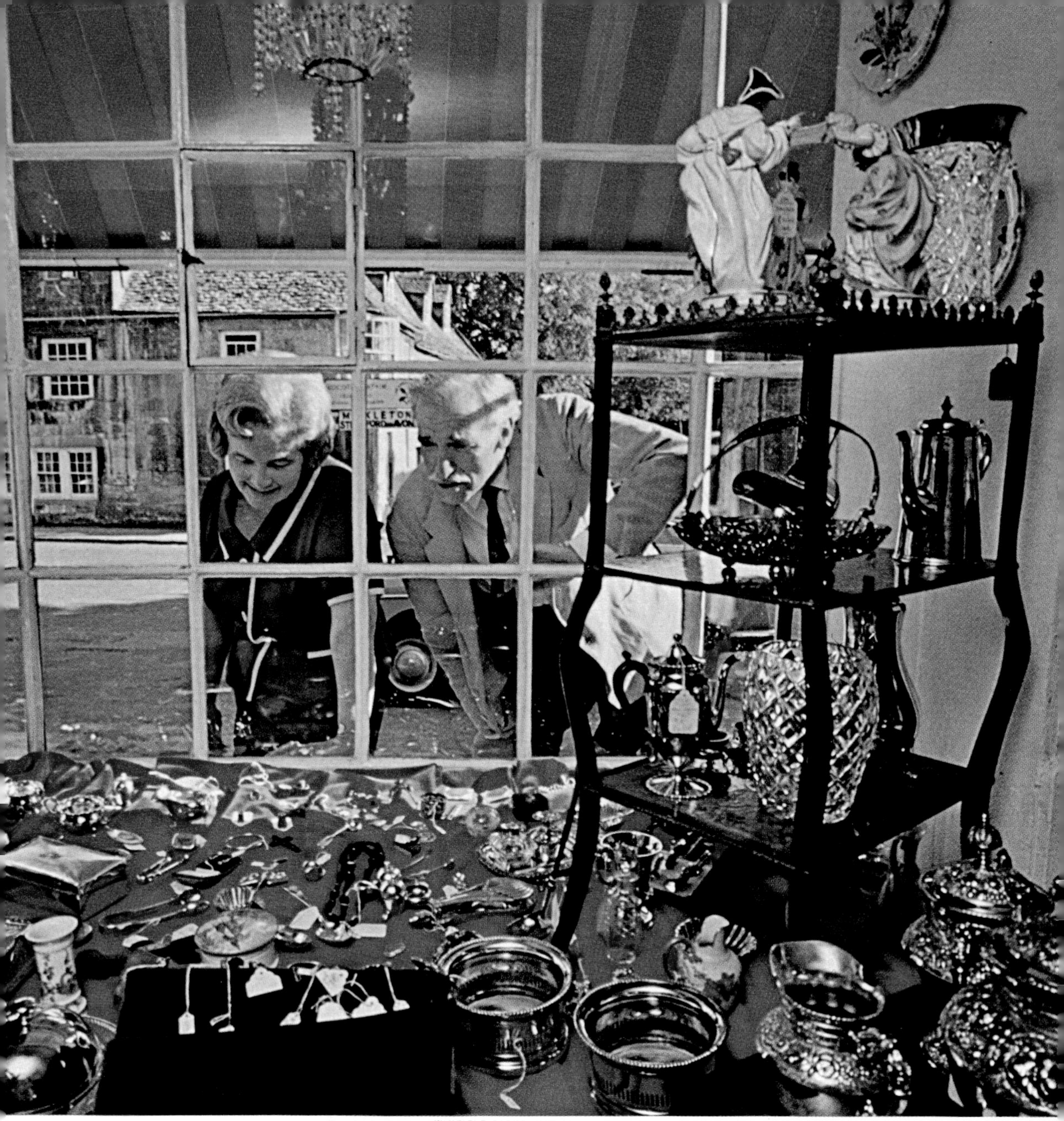

WINFIELD PARKS, NATIONAL GEOGRAPHIC PHOTOGRAPHER. OPPOSITE LOWER: ADAM WOOLFITT

people; they built fine homes and manors.

Campden folk cling to tradition and fight attempts to commercialize their town. In fact, Chipping Campden is an English Williamsburg, but with this difference: The houses are originals, not restorations. I strolled down High Street, window-shopping in the old bay fronts. As houses abutted the sidewalks, I could look right through leaded glass into front parlors or little shops. Perhaps grandmother was knitting in a wing chair or a storekeeper arranging bread, sweets, meat, or tobacco in her round window. Shops and homes looked very much alike, for signs are few and inconspicuous.

One old house full of antiques especially appealed to me. As I entered, a bell tinkled, but no one greeted me. I was supposed to browse among the antiques undistracted. I was fascinated by the big bow window which filled the front of the room like a movie screen. Passersby unaware of me in the depths stopped to peek at the copper coal scuttles, ladder-back chairs, pewter mugs, and brass warming pans.

Just like actors on a screen, an elderly couple in tweeds, young hikers in shorts with knapsacks, schoolchildren with their

book bags, and trippers, all did their little act framed in the bay.

The proprietor led me to the Wool Staplers' Hall in a lofty vaulted room upstairs. Here the staplers spread out their wool samples and settled prices before going out to the Market Hall in High Street for a supposed auction. "Prices obviously were rigged or settled in advance," he told me. "This hall, by the way, built in the 14th century, is one of the oldest buildings in Chipping Campden."

One day my little car squeezed along narrow, winding lanes to visit Dover's Hill, where in Shakespearean times and later the Cotswold Games were held. On the

I came over a hill and found myself on a vast green scarp: "Wold's End," the sharp western border of the Cotswolds.

The wind whistled as I walked across to turreted Broadway Tower standing like a sentinel on the brink. Cattle grazed on the slopes around it; behind stretched the green pastures of the highland Cotswolds, once a vast sheepwalk, or pasture. Far below reached the lovely Vale of Evesham, its face splotched with cloud shadows, green fields, and many villages and hamlets.

The Countess of Coventry, according to local tradition, built this tower so she could watch her earl hunt. From its windy summit, she kept track of his waving plumes,

CHILDREN *find Cotswold villages delightful places to romp. Great Tew (left), landscaped by the 19th-century horticulturist John Claudius Loudon, affords fragrant blooms, and lawns to cushion the bumps of handstands gone awry. Plantings set off 17th-century thatched cottages, uncommon in the region today. In Minster Lovell (below) a young comic plays to an enthusiastic gallery.*

ADAM WOOLFITT

Thursday after Whitsun, athletes from all over England came here to vie in cudgel and backsword play, wrestling, and of course greyhound and horse racing. But the toughest sport of all was shin kicking. Opponents kicked each other with heavy boots until one gave in. Campden's star kicker conditioned himself by batting his legs with a hammer; others whacked their shins with planks. No guards were used, either.

As I waved goodbye to my friends in Chipping Campden, one called out, "When you come to a steep scarp with the Vale of Evesham far below, that's Wold's End."

My car purred down the old streets and out into the rolling uplands. Suddenly

as he galloped across the downs, to see that he tarried not in tavern or cottage. Actually, the tower was built in 1800 by the Earl of Coventry to please his wife, who liked to climb to its top and survey his domain.

In bygone years many famous poets and artists spent vacations in this "medieval castle." While they waxed enthusiastic over the magnificent view, all grumbled at the long uphill pull from Broadway, the nearest town for supplies.

ALL THAT DAY I explored "the edge," as some Cotswold folk call that western bastion of their realm. I wandered into Snowshill, a picture village of golden cottages tucked in a narrow combe. Henry Ford, who often visited the Cotswolds, loved Snowshill (pronounced "Snozill"). He bought a farm group here and shipped the cottages stone by stone to Greenfield Village, Michigan. When the houses were assembled, though every stone and roof flake was numbered, even his most skilled mechanics could not put them together again! Mr. Ford had to send to Snowshill for a stone tiler to hang the roofs.

Dropping down from the wolds by a narrow lane, I passed through Stanway, a small town of yellow houses and red roses. In a pasture a cricket game was in progress, the players dressed in snowy white. Making a sharp turn, I literally burst into Broadway. As its name implies, it is one long street, an expanse of lawns and flowers edged with old houses.

The charm of old Broadway has attracted many American artists. Francis Davis Millet had a house and studio in the village, where John Singer Sargent, Edwin Austin Abbey, and other painters visited.

The principal highway from London to Worcester passes through Broadway; so the town prospered as a coaching stop. Its 400-year-old inn, the Lygon Arms, is one of the most sumptuous in England.

If you are one of those who like to sleep in famous persons' rooms, you can have your wish at the Lygon Arms. Reserve in time and you may have the Cromwell Room, where tradition says the Puritan leader slept before the Battle of Worcester in 1651.

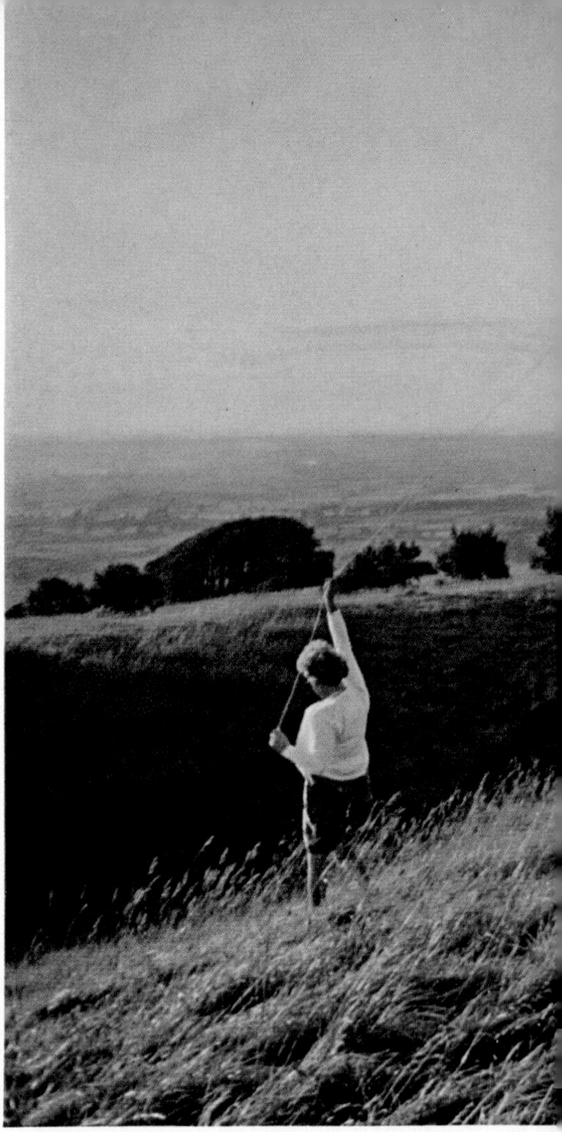

BROADWAY TOWER, *a landmark for miles, stands atop 1,024-foot Broadway Beacon. The splendid view from its battlements takes in 13 counties, from the Vale of Evesham spread out below to the Black Mountains of Wales some 50 miles away. Just downslope lies Broadway, where the Lygon Arms (right) has fed and sheltered travelers since the 1530's. The old coaching inn bids modern trippers tarry for a night's rest at Wold's End. Many do, for the charming village with its broad main street draws crowds of holidayers.*

Many members of the British Royal Family have stayed at this excellent inn.

The reddening sun hovered low over the western horizon. My visit to the Cotswolds had come to an end, all too soon. As I gazed back toward Wold's End, my shadow stretched out before me; like its owner, it seemed eager to return.

ADAM WOOLFITT

THE SOUTH

CHALK CLIFFS, DOWNS, AND QUIET VILLAGES

TITANIC FORCES THRUST the ocean floor skyward. A great chalk dome formed. Glaciers and the rains of ages gnawed it away, leaving the North and South Downs. These long whalebacks of green-turfed chalk, cradling the broad and fertile Weald, end abruptly at the Channel in white cliffs.

They beckoned Romans, then Saxons, who landed in Kent. William the Conqueror went ashore in Sussex, near towering Beachy Head. Napoleon eyed the chalk cliffs of "perfidious Albion" in frustration as his invasion plans crumbled before the "wooden walls" of England – Nelson's ships built of oak from the Weald and Hampshire's New Forest. Hitler's troops sang that they would sail against England. "We are waiting for the long-promised invasion," said Winston Churchill. "So are the fishes."

Today Dover's white cliffs welcome tourists, who drive off the ferries past signs reminding them, in French, to keep to the left. And at Southampton, sally port for the Normandy invasion, liners dock with throngs of vacationing Americans. Here amid the rolling downs they find Winchester, England's first capital; Canterbury, her mother church; and meet bowler-hatted London commuters in unchanging garden villages.

KENT, GARDEN OF

THE BATTLE OF BRITAIN brought me to Kent for the first time, as a war correspondent. Even now, when I stand on the chalk cliffs of our Channel coast, the calendar whirs back to those momentous days when, with little else than a handful of Spitfires and Churchill's thunderous rhetoric, we awaited Hitler's invasion.

High on Shakespeare Cliff, just west of Dover, the noise of one battle left me battered and dazed. Dive bombers screamed. Bombs whistled and roared. Machine guns crackled. Ack-ack guns barked. And through it all, gulls mewed plaintively.

I remember the drive back to London through the stillness of country lanes after that raid. I looked on the Kentish scene and saw grain rippled by the wind, white sheep grazing on green velvet pasture, red-tiled farmhouses snuggling into folds of ground, and white-nippled oasthouses silhouetted against the sky. Yeoman houses and moated manors sat in exactly the right places with an air of always having been there and intending always to remain. I vowed that someday I would live here.

Many a year of war and wayfaring slipped by before my path led again to Kent. Then

ENGLAND

Writer-photographer George Rodger describes a year in the heart of the Weald, where he found a den of his own

my wife Jinx and I returned to England after six months of exploring the Sahara and received an invitation to stay in the Kentish Weald, the lowland that lies between the heights of the North and South Downs. Friends had recently acquired a Tudor farmhouse with ample room for a couple of nomads. We were delighted! We shook the sand out of our hair and settled in.

One day our friends drove us along twisting lanes to Biddenden, Bethersden, Benen-

KENT IN APRIL *explodes with blossoms as trees and shrubs like these in Sutton Valence parade their springtime colors. Beyond spreads the Weald, where thick forests have given way to orchards, gardens, and lush pastures.*

GEORGE RODGER, MAGNUM

den, Frittenden, and several other "dens."

"It's a Saxon word," they explained. "Den means a clearing in a valley. In the early days the valley of the Weald was all forest. Farmers living on higher ground sent their herds of pigs down each winter to feed off acorns. The swineherds built huts in the dens, and each clearing took the name of the family living there."

We walked for awhile between hedgerows sweet with brier and honeysuckle. Larks soared and sang in a cloudless sky, and I thought again of Shakespeare Cliff and my vow on the Dover road. "We simply *must* have a home of our own," I said.

"Den of your own," our friend corrected.

WE MIGHT have had a long search if we hadn't met Barnes Brown in Smarden, waist deep in red dahlias. I asked him if he was a Man of Kent or a Kentish Man.

"Oi'm a Man of Kent, zur, born and raised in Smarden," Barnes Brown replied.

My approach wasn't as fatuous as it might seem. About A.D. 450 two Saxon leaders, Hengist and Horsa, arrived at the invitation of King Vortigern of Kent to help protect his kingdom from attack by Picts and Scots. During the ensuing Saxon immigration early Britons retreated west of the Medway. The river became the boundary between the two races, and the division still survives. Inhabitants west of the river call themselves Kentish Men, those to the east, Men of Kent.

Smarden was so tucked away that it seemed to have been forgotten for a very long time. There were lovely Tudor houses around the church. There was a village post office with an entrance 5 feet 8 inches high, a pub, a butcher's, a bakery, two general stores, and little else.

"Do you think there might be a house for sale in Smarden?" we asked Barnes Brown.

"Not that I knows of, there ain't," he said. Then, after a moment, he added, "unless Mrs. Bucknall would sell."

Mrs. Bucknall's house lay across the lane behind a garden gate under arched willows. Shooing away three ducks sitting on the gate, we followed a brick path beside a lily-covered pond to the back.

GEORGE RODGER, MAGNUM

AUTHOR'S HOUSE, *Waterside, becomes "Iceside" in the grip of an unusually cold winter. Its lights glance off the frozen duck pond as it snuggles against the crenellated tower of Smarden's church. Villagers in summer sun (opposite) tend flowers while a thatcher renews a roof. Rethatching every 20 years or so prevents leaks and discourages vermin.*

Mrs. Bucknall, a ponderous woman, had a heart of gold. Her house was always open to the sick, the hungry, the unwanted—including 27 Muscovy ducks, 12 cats, a pair of hedgehogs, and a huge white goose that had been auctioned one Christmastime at the church bazaar. She said she couldn't bear to see its life bandied like that under the hammer—"going, going, gone!" So she redeemed it afterward for double the price.

I bumped my head on the solid oak lintel as we went in the back door and again as we entered the parlor. Cats were everywhere. Mrs. Bucknall stood in the middle of the room saying, "Shoosh! Shoosh!" and flicking them off chairs with a duster.

A cheerful log fire burned in the open grate; we sat in front of it drinking strong tea that Mrs. Bucknall brewed in a big brown pot. We told her how impressed we

GEORGE RODGER, MAGNUM

"POP" MARSHALL, *one of Smarden's oldest inhabitants, mends the bicycles of a community geared to run on two wheels. Postman (left) and newsagent (right) pedal their rounds. Older villagers shun wider travel. Invited to London, Pop was shocked. "I wouldn't go to that place if you paid me a pound for every mile!" Yet villages like Smarden attract more and more commuters.*

were with Smarden and how we would like to live there. She said she wouldn't mind a change if she could find somewhere else to live. Suddenly she added, "Would you like to see the rest of my place?"

Four little half-timbered cottages built in late Tudor times sat in a row under one roof of old Kentish handmade peg tile. She owned them all but lived in only one. The others she let at a pittance. The cottages were all crying out to be renovated. We tried to suppress our excitement as we went back inside. Then as she poured us more tea, thick and brown and sweet, she asked, "How would you like to buy the lot?"

A quick succession of pictures raced through my mind. The four cottages thrown into one house . . . an old-world garden in the back . . . a rockery by the pond . . . wisteria on the walls. . . . Yes! When we left we were virtual owners of 16 tiny rooms, four staircases and 36 doorways, not one of which was more than 5 feet 8 inches high.

During the 350 or so years that our cottages had stood on Water Lane they must have changed hands many times. But never, I think, can a moving day have taken place in such an aura of operatic splendor.

It rained all day. Being a Saturday, it was practice time for the bell ringers at the church. To the accompaniment of crashing thunder and the peals and quarter peals clanging through a drenching downpour we moved into our new home.

Then, as though on cue, the River Beult burst its bank and came surging up the road and across our garden. The waters filled our pond and united it with the great flood stretching over the Weald. In true Wagnerian style the sun broke through from the west. It gleamed on our ducks, swimming in single file across the garden, through the churchyard, and out into the wide wet world that now lay before them.

CASKS OF KENTISH CIDER *form serried ranks at The Winery; Col. Richard White's product sells as far afield as New York. Morris dance (below) halts Smarden traffic. One story says dancers once wore blackface and resembled Moors; hence the name Moorish (or morris) dance.*

GEORGE RODGER, MAGNUM

RIPENING APPLES *herald the end of a Kentish summer. In a good year Smarden's cider mill may fill some 2,000 barrels from 1,000 tons of these apples. But the "Garden of England" is better known for its hops.*

Used to flavor beer, hops sprout on tall vines, forming conelike clusters. At harvest, near the end of summer, cutters (right) hack down the laden vines so that the crop can be stripped off.

The ripe hops go into one of the oasthouses, whose conical, white-tipped roofs punctuate the Kentish countryside. Here the hops dry out above a fire made from special Welsh anthracite that does not impair their flavor. Fumes escape through a vent in the oast's tip.

The oasts at Smarden (opposite) date back to around 1800—not nearly as old as the Cloth Hall in the foreground, whose hook, dangling under the eaves, once hoisted bales of Kentish wool for storage. Now a residence, Cloth Hall has half-timbered construction similar to that of nearby Waterside House. This technique, where brick or plaster fills in the walls between heavy beams and joists, often characterizes Tudor buildings. It also occurred throughout Europe wherever oak forests were plentiful.

OUR FIRST WINTER in Smarden was a period of entrenchment. Occupying two of our four cottages, we draft-proofed and heated them as protection against the fog and cold. Each evening when the sun set, long white streamers of mist groped across the fields and orchards and spilled into the lanes until fog blanketed the whole of the Weald. When we explored the countryside we made a point of getting back before dark. We spent the evenings before an open log fire drawing up plans for the conversion of our house and reading local history.

Our own cottages, though I can find no authentic date, must have been built sometime in the 16th century. The church, visible through our dining room windows, has watched over the village for six centuries, maybe even seven. Dedicated to St. Michael, it's known locally as "the Barn of Kent" because of the construction of its oak-timbered roof. With no buttresses, tie beams, or supporting columns, it spans 36 feet.

To restore a period house it's necessary to use materials of the same type and date.

GEORGE RODGER, MAGNUM

GYPSIES *by the hundreds once camped beside Kentish hedgerows at harvest time. As the hops ripened, these nomads converged on the Weald, joining local farmers and other itinerants, many from the streets of London.*

The army of harvest hands worked through the fields like locusts. Cutters attacked the vines; strippers, standing beside their bins—canvas bags stretched over frames—pulled off the clustered hops.

Now machines have mostly taken over. Vines trundle to the bins behind tractors. Mechanical fingers pluck them clean. Few harvesters show up, but among them even now are a handful of gypsies. Their caravans, spotlessly clean and often freshly painted, still roll behind a plodding horse—but on automobile tires.

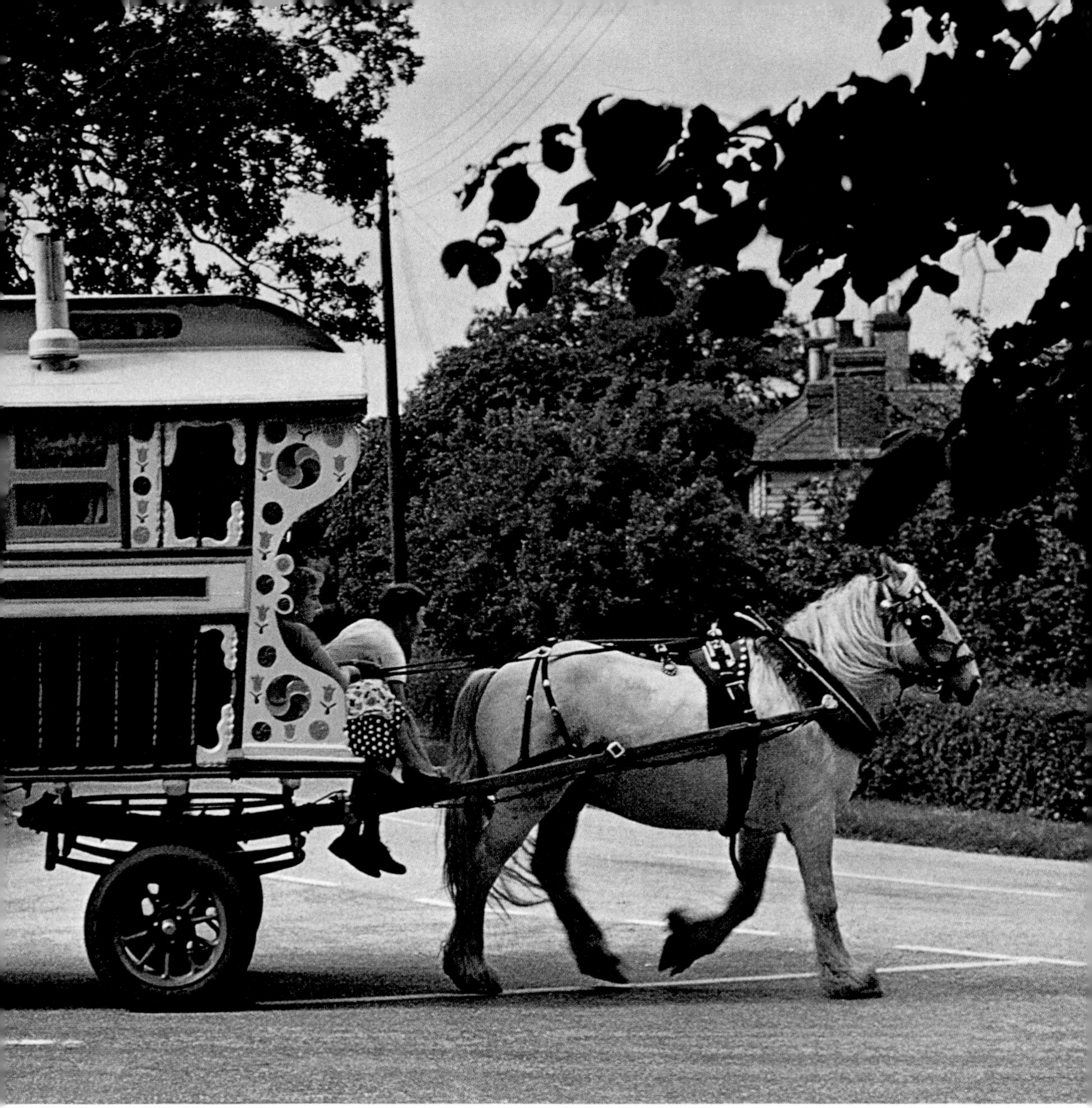

My search for old handmade bricks and tiles and centuries-old oak timbers took me all over Kent and gave me many a lesson in county history.

I had noticed when I stripped the ceilings and walls of our cottages that every piece of oak timber bore Roman numerals cut with a broad chisel. These I learned were the assembly numbers. The builders had prefabricated the house in the forest where they cut the timbers. They shaped pieces by adz, fitted them together, then numbered them for reassembly in the village.

The forests of the Weald once provided charcoal for the local iron industry. But the trees probably were vanishing by the mid-17th century, and the foundries declined for lack of fuel to feed the "bloomeries," or smelters. Eventually the industry moved to the coalfields of the Midlands.

Some charcoal burning still goes on, I discovered while looking for a man named Charlie Light who might know where I could buy old timbers.

"You'll find Charlie in t' woods down by t' pit," a cheery woman said at the door of his isolated cottage.

I found him, black as a raven from head to foot, "cooking" a mound of charcoal. As we talked the acrid blue smoke swirled

SOARING VAULTS *echo a canticle (opposite) in Canterbury Cathedral, hub of the Church of England and seat of its archbishop. Sixteen centuries of worship hallow this site. Britons and Saxons raised churches here, then Vikings put them to the torch. Norman conquerors rebuilt the cathedral; visitors still admire the vaulted Norman crypt, largest of its kind.*

Stormy site of clashes between Church and Crown, the cathedral echoed the clang of broadswords one night in 1170 as four knights of Henry II slew Archbishop Thomas à Becket. Christendom stood aghast; papal wrath stirred. Finally a penitent Henry in sackcloth walked barefoot to Becket's bier for a flogging by the monks.

The martyrdom, portrayed in a psalter (left) of about 1200, drew three centuries of pilgrims to Canterbury. Geoffrey Chaucer described them in his Canterbury Tales, *illustrated below, 16th-century style. Travelers often jogged at a "Canterbury gallop," now called a canter.*

Young Henry VIII venerated Becket's shrine. Later, with Reformation zeal, he wrecked it and scattered the prior and monks. A stone in the floor marks the spot where Becket fell.

BRITISH MUSEUM (ALSO RIGHT). OPPOSITE: GEORGE RODGER, MAGNUM, AND JOHN E. FLETCHER, NATIONAL GEOGRAPHIC PHOTOGRAPHER

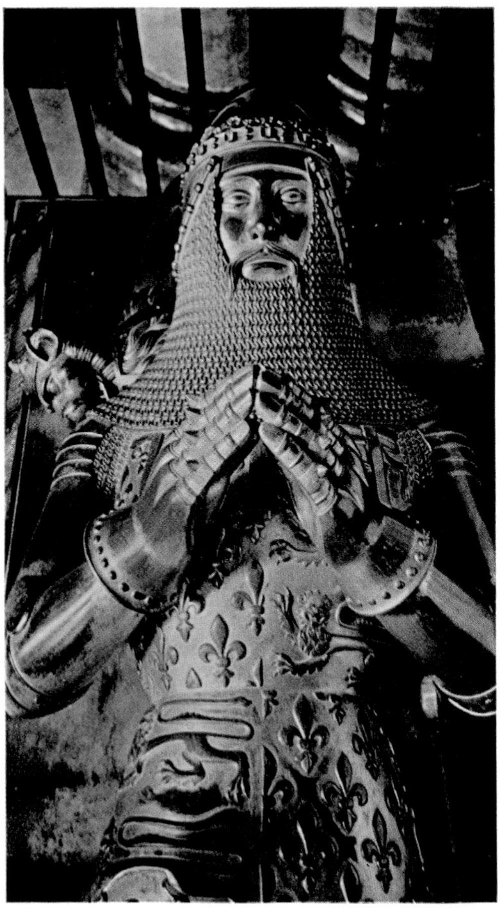

PATRICK THURSTON

BRONZE EFFIGY *of Edward of Woodstock, emblazoned with English lions and French fleurs-de-lis, lies atop his tomb in Canterbury Cathedral. Dubbed "the Black Prince" partly for his armor's hue, the ruthless Prince Edward became England's darling in 1346 when, at 16, he skillfully deployed his longbow archers to rout mounted French knights at Crécy. Later, his brilliant use of bowmen at Poitiers again crushed the French. Son of Edward III who founded the Order of the Garter, the Prince shared leadership of its knights until he died of illness at 46. Parts of his armor rest in a showcase nearby.*

around us. He kept patting the mound with a broad shovel. "Got to keep t' fire from running away," he declared.

I asked if there were any special system to piling up the oak logs for burning.

"You put t' dopey woot in t' mittle, see?" he stated. ("Dopey wood," I learned, is the sapwood which is softer than the core.) The stacked logs are covered with chaff and a thick layer of half-burned debris from the pit floor. Then the mound smolders for four or five days.

Burning the mound evenly seems an art: If it burns through the side, the fire "runs away" and the charcoal is hard and useless. Charlie Light kept hopping around his smoldering mound either patting it together or poking holes in it to let in the draft.

I asked if this wasn't the same system the Romans used 1,500 years ago. He said

SOMBER-COATED LADS *of King's School (left) live where Canterbury monks dwelt. The school dates from St. Augustine, who converted Kentish King Ethelbert in 597. The cathedral once housed looms of Huguenots and Walloons; the Tudor homes of these weavers overlook the Stour (opposite). Kent remains England's door to Europe. Air ferries at Lydd (below) swallow cars of tourists bound for the Continent.*

DAN McCOY, BLACK STAR. UPPER: PATRICK WARD. OPPOSITE: GEORGE F. MOBLEY, NATIONAL GEOGRAPHIC PHOTOGRAPHER

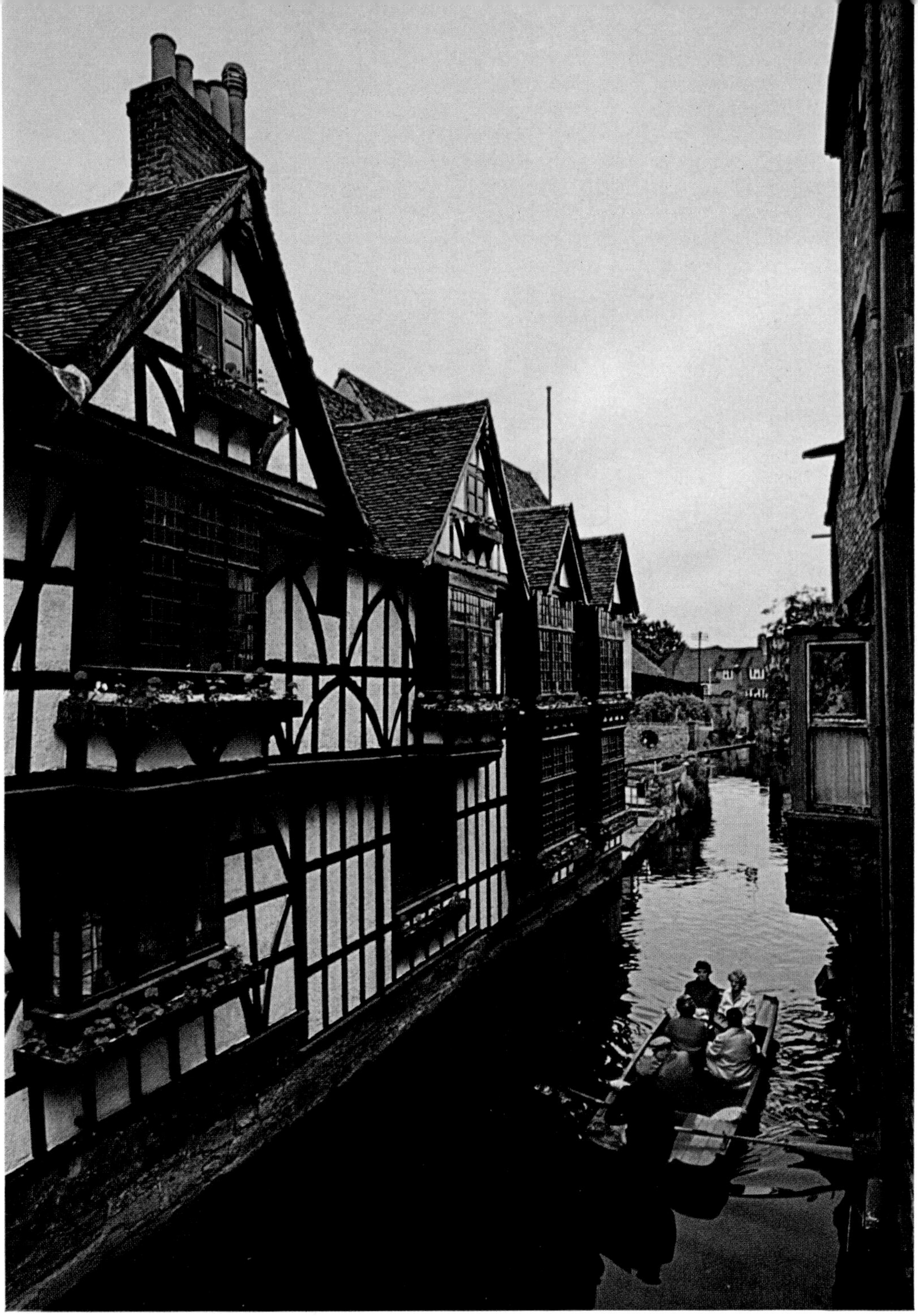

he didn't see how they could possibly do it any other way and told me there was a Roman road at the end of the wood. During a lull in the patting we went to see it. Removing only a foot of topsoil with his spade, he revealed the hard surface of a road made from the dross of a smelter. Charlie Light was not only operating in the same way as the Romans but also in the same place.

My hunt for restoration material often took me down to Romney Marsh. Local people always speak of going "down" to the Marsh as though Romney were a foreign land. It seems incredible that you could go "down" anywhere from Smarden, which has an altitude of only 75 feet. Nevertheless there is a definite drop at Appledore, where in Roman times the sea battered the

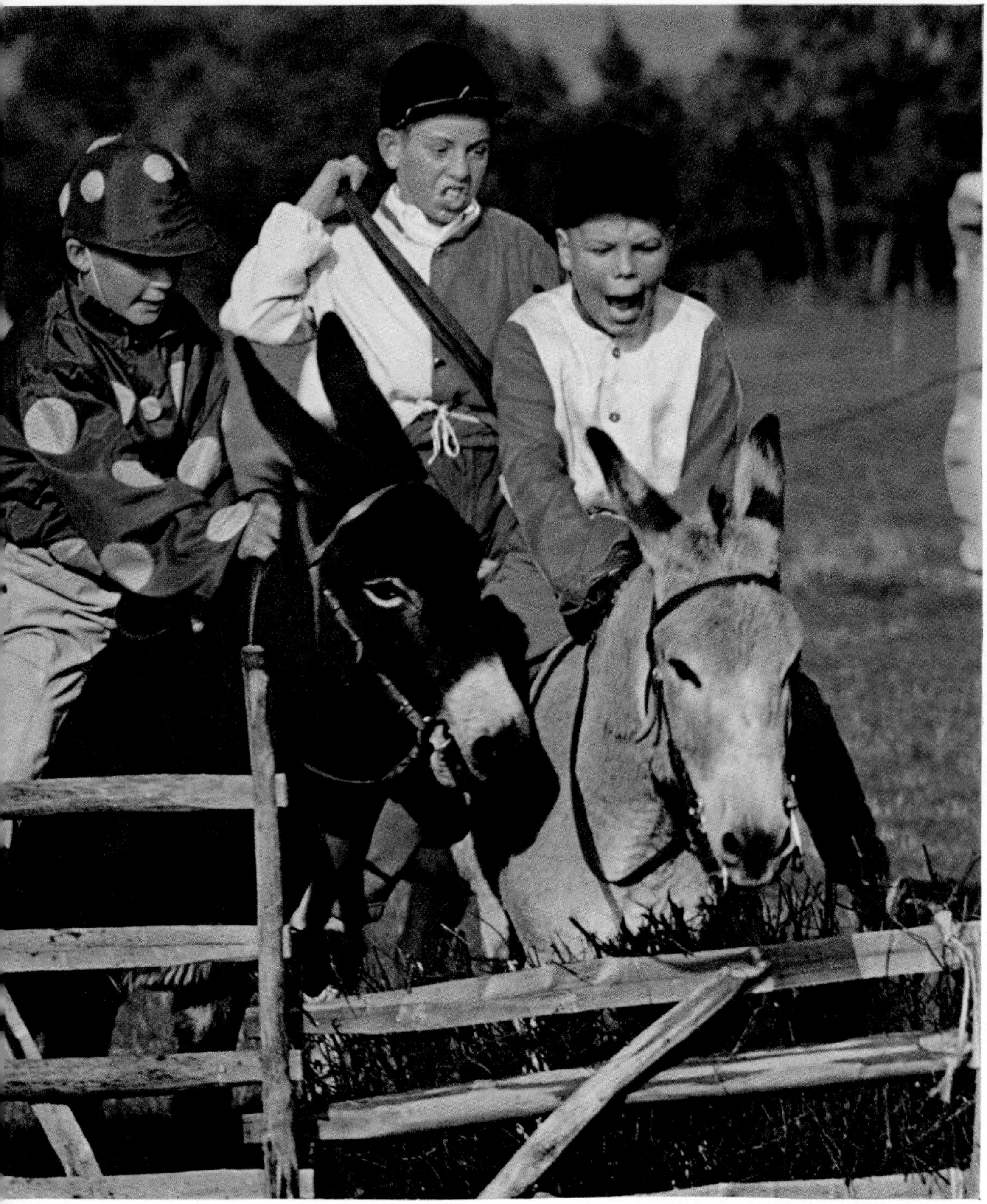

coast. The road leads over the wall built by the legions to keep the sea out. Then it crosses the canal built by George III's engineers to keep Napoleon out.

Crossing the Marsh in spring is always delightful. The landscape looks like Holland —as flat as the sea itself. Hedges gleam white with small blackthorn blossoms. Wild ducks rise from reed-fringed canals. Nearly always there is a silver-gray heron patrolling low over the ditches on lazy wings, looking for frogs and big sweetwater mussels.

I was never sorry when Mr. Waters, who lived in the Marsh, phoned to say he had found an antique for us. He often found interesting things holed up in the walls of condemned houses which he pulled down for the bricks and tiles. He would never tell me on the phone what it was this time. I would have to drive 20 miles to find out. Then he would run to meet me, his eyes crinkled up with excitement. "Come and tell me what you think of this!"

Once it was a Georgian fireback, now in our dining room. Another time it was an iron-studded oak door with handwrought iron hinges, now our front entrance.

WE DISCOVERED the loveliness of the Kentish spring that first year in Smarden. Thrushes sang from the elm trees; lambs frisked under a pink froth of apple blossoms. Then as summer wore on, activity increased through a succession of harvests—hay, strawberries, cherries, wheat, plums, and early apples. The peak arrived with the ripening of the hops in September.

People no longer chatted on the village street. The local pub fell empty. Everyone left for the fields. The oasthouses, which

RACE MEETINGS *enliven the villages of Kent. Onlookers at Charing gather to chat and cheer (below) during one of the point-to-point races sponsored by local hunts.*

Donkey derbies occur annually in many towns, to the delight of those who watch, those who bet, and those—aged usually 9 to 12—who ride. Wearing homemade silks and straddling their "mokes" bareback, young jockeys at Headcorn exhort their steeds to jump (opposite). The donkeys, often older and more determined than their riders, generally oppose such nonsense.

GEORGE RODGER, MAGNUM

CHALK CLIFFS *tower over holiday lodgings at Dover. City seal (left) reflects its more famous role as a port. Roman legions debarked here; today from this gateway boats ferry thousands of tourists 20 miles to the Continent. Of the original Cinque Ports in Kent and Sussex—Hastings, Romney, Hythe, Dover, and Sandwich—only Dover harbor remains in use. From pre-Norman days they furnished ships for defense. In return, Edward I granted them some self-government and tax privileges. A Lord Warden traditionally administers the ports and may reside at Walmer Castle, erected by Henry VIII near Dover. The Duke of Wellington and Sir Winston Churchill held the title, which includes the office of Constable of Dover Castle. That fortress, built around a Roman lighthouse, sprawls atop these cliffs.*

GEORGE F. MOBLEY, NATIONAL GEOGRAPHIC PHOTOGRAPHER. LEFT: NATIONAL MARITIME MUSEUM, GREENWICH

had waited patiently with their white cowls turning to the whims of the wind for 48 weeks, now came to life.

The picking of hops used to draw hordes of laborers. Fifty thousand hop pickers once came from the East End of London each September, and every gypsy in the south of England converged on Kent for the harvest. Now, machines do much of the work.

On the mechanized farm of Peter Hukins, near Tenterden, we found 12 men doing a job that formerly would have occupied several hundred. They worked with the rhythm and precision of a corps de ballet. Cutters severed the 12-foot vines, top and bottom, from the supporting wires and laid them in scented rows ready for loading onto special tractor-drawn trailers. These transported the vines to the picking machine, which separated the heavy, clustered hops from the leaves and the stalks.

At the end of the hop harvest the Weald settled down to its normal routine. Having nearly completed our rebuilding program, we relaxed and began to explore farther afield. We went to point-to-point races and donkey derbies, a feature of Kentish life.

Our local butcher had entered a fleet-footed "moke" in the donkey race at Headcorn, our neighboring village, and we promised to back it with a shilling or two if the odds were good. On the day of the race a true "Derby" atmosphere pervaded the village. The track had been laid out across open fields with miniature hurdles. Jockeys proudly wore satin blouses in the colors of their racing stables. Rolls-Royces and Bentleys sparkled in the car park, and bookmakers lined up behind the grandstand.

The jockeys – girls as well as boys, and mostly between 9 and 12 years old – brought their long-eared steeds to the tape. A gun fired. Some started sideways, some stern first. Some riders got off and pulled to get their mounts moving. No donkey was disqualified unless it lay down. We had staked our shilling on the butcher's entry, but after the start we never saw the beast again!

HUNGRY FOR THE SUN *after a long, gray winter, thousands of holidaymakers, mostly from London, carpet Kent's beaches on summer weekends. Such resorts as Margate (above), frequented by bathers since 1750, and Ramsgate and Hythe sprawl along an almost continuous fringe of beach. Broadstairs, which holds a Dickens festival each June, was described by that author as "one of the freest and freshest little places in the world."*

As temples for sun worship the resorts prosper—and surely benefit the patient Britons who struggle with miles of traffic and then must often don coats against the Channel chill.

GEORGE RODGER, MAGNUM. OPPOSITE: GEORGE F. MOBLEY, NATIONAL GEOGRAPHIC PHOTOGRAPHER

The Kentish coast is so popular during summer that highways from London carry a continuous stream of traffic. The resorts of Margate, Broadstairs, Ramsgate, Folkstone, and Hythe overflow into nearby villages. Sandy beaches disappear under a coating of deck chairs and picnic parties.

In autumn, after the crush had thinned out, we ventured to the seashore and followed the course of the River Stour down to its mouth in Pegwell Bay. We were seeking to retrace the web of England's first recorded history. Looking over the valley with the little river undulating through low-lying farmland, we found it hard to realize that momentous events had taken place here in the past.

In ancient times the Stour Valley held a navigable waterway called the Wantsum Channel; much shipping followed this on the way to the Thames estuary in preference to rounding the Isle of Thanet in the open sea. In A.D. 43 a large Roman invasion force landed on an island in the Wantsum

THE PANTILES *of Tunbridge Wells (above) recall elegant decades. A young 17th-century lord sipped at a Kentish spring and avowed that the iron-rich water cured the ravages of his high living. Dyspeptic nobles flocked to the Wells, and a town arose. One walk was terraced with flat tiles—pantiles—and here strolled men of fashion and the arts.*

At nearby Penshurst Place (right) was born Sir Philip Sidney (upper right), courtier, statesman, sonneteer, beau ideal of the Elizabethan age. Mortally hurt fighting the Spanish in Flanders in 1586, he refused water so another wounded man could drink.

Knole at Sevenoaks (far right) has 365 rooms; some may date from King John's time. Five archbishops of Canterbury lived here, then Henry VIII acquired it. A superb example of a baronial mansion, it presents austere outer walls that belie the decorated courtyards and graceful furnishings within.

Channel which became Richborough. For 400 years this remained one of the main ports of Roman Britain.

We saw the crumbling walls of the Roman harbor and the stonework that had once formed an impressive gateway to Britain. The Wantsum has long been silted up.

Only a few fields away at Ebbsfleet, Hengist and Horsa landed to join King Vortigern. A crew of Danes recently rowed a replica of a Viking ship across the North Sea to commemorate the event. It rests atop the cliff in honor of the two chieftains.

Augustine landed at the same place in 597, bringing a band of monks and Christianity. A replica of an ancient cross stands there above Pegwell Bay, where the lonely wind whistles through the sedge. But the road home leads through Canterbury, perhaps our finest Christian shrine.

We had many visitors that first year in Smarden, and always they wanted most to see Canterbury. We would take them by way of the old Roman Watling Street to give them the same first impression that Chaucer and his pilgrims had. We would go through Harbledown, the town pilgrims

MERLE SEVERY, NATIONAL GEOGRAPHIC STAFF. ABOVE: SIR PHILIP SIDNEY BY AN UNKNOWN ARTIST C. 1570, COURTESY VISCOUNT DE L'ISLE, PENSHURST PLACE

Cricket, stately old lady of sport, still dances on the village green

THE SUN seems to shine a bit brighter, somehow, when it beams on a village cricket match. The broad green glistens like emerald against the shade of encircling trees. Cricketers move through their ritual clad in dazzling white. And when you stop to watch – here at Smarden, or on village greens throughout England – you feel the welcome warmth and relax in the languid calm of summer.

Villagers lining the fence make room for you with quiet courtesy. All eyes are riveted on the center of the green where a tall young man abruptly leaps forward in giant strides and, swinging a stiff arm, hurls a small red ball at blistering speed toward a target formed by three upright sticks.

Guarding this "wicket," a batsman with padded shins meets the missile with his flat-bladed bat. A *thwack* sends the ball toward one of the crouching fielders. He snaps it up, bare-handed, and the batsman decides it is not safe to run.

This is cricket; he doesn't have to.

The tall bowler tries again – the same leaping run, the sizzling red streak, and *whack!* This time the ball skitters between two fielders.

The batsman takes off full tilt for the opposite wicket, and a second batsman who has been lolling there springs into action and swaps ends with his teammate. They pass each other halfway, each carrying his bat. Then they touch with their bats the "crease" marked off in front of each wicket and dash back, passing again. By this time the retrieved ball is hurtling toward one of the wickets. It strikes. Sticks fly. But both men have made it back to their creases. Two runs – and your fellow onlookers murmur approval.

The match continues like this for seemingly endless hours – if you stay and watch. But the enthusiasts around you come and go freely, without any compunction to prove their loyalty to the home team by seeing it through. So do the same. Wander around the green to the pub that is likely to adjoin it – as does the Cricketers Inn (insets) at Meopham, Kent. Inside you may well meet your fence companions and learn more about what you have been watching.

"Cricket is not a game, it's a way of life," one will surely begin. "Aye, and often a dull life at that," another will chime in, for the English get as impatient with slow play as anyone else.

Gradually the picture will emerge: two wickets set 22 yards apart, each defended by a batsman; two bowlers attacking the wickets – one bowls an "over" of six balls, then fields while his mate bowls from the other end of the "pitch." This bowler, perhaps with a slow, spinning delivery, tries to bounce the ball past the batsman and demolish the wicket – or force him to misdirect his shot. A skilled bowler might come in with

a "googly," a ball that looks as though it will bounce away from the batsman but breaks toward him. He tries to block or swipe the ball away. If it strikes him instead of his bat, and the umpire rules "Leg before wicket," he's out. He can hit in any direction. If he knocks a ball to the boundary, he gets an automatic four runs. If he lofts one over the fence, it's an automatic six. Fielding is generally quick and sure; if a fly ball is caught, the batsman's out. When ten of a team's eleven men are out, the "innings" ends, and the other side comes to bat.

Time limit for village teams is generally one day—so the crops won't wither in the fields. County teams, usually professional, play for three days. Test (international) matches can last five days. If the last innings is not over within the time limit, the match is a draw, and all previous heroics go for naught.

The time rule opens the door to strategy. A side with a high score may declare its innings closed, before all its men are out. Then its bowlers try to "dismiss" opposing batsmen, allowing as few runs as possible, before the wicket stumps are pulled at the match's end. Uncertain weather adds to the fun. Captains eye the sky, ready to "declare" and thus force opponents to bat on wet ground—catching them on a "sticky wicket."

Cricket has scarcely altered its basic rules since the 1700's, and the game was old then. Royal household accounts show that Prince Edward—later King Edward II—played it at Westminster in 1300. In 1744 Kent beat an All England eleven and inspired a burst of poetry:

"Fierce Kent, ambitious of the world's applause,
Against the World combin'd, asserts her cause . . ."

Cricket reporters seldom resort to verse now. The top hats of the early 19th century have gone. And amateurs and professionals are no longer categorized as "gentlemen" and "players." They're even allowed to share the same dressing room! But the old game still stirs English hearts. Headlines proclaim the loss of a test match with words that frighten foreign investors: "ENGLAND TOPPLES!" one screamed. That's cricket.

GEORGE RODGER, MAGNUM. INSETS: PATRICK WARD

DICKENS DOWNS A DRAM *at Gad's Hill Place (below), his "stupendous property" in the Kentish countryside near Rochester, a cathedral city reflected in his stories. Family and friends surround him as he leans against a column of the house he vowed as a boy to own. He loved to entertain guests here; one was Hans Christian Andersen.*

A stroll away lies the town of Cobham and the Leather Bottle, a "clean and commodious village ale-house" where pudgy Pickwick lodged a night and quaffed his pint.

TRUSTEES OF THE DICKENS HOUSE

used to call "Bob-up-and-down" because of the way the cathedral appeared and disappeared as the road rose and fell. We would enter the city by the West Gate and slip into the precincts through Christ Church Gateway. We would then lead our guests through the cathedral's southwest porch and confront them suddenly with the towering sweep of the nave. And then we would leave them alone with their thoughts.

AUTUMN BROUGHT incredible coloring to the Weald. Splashes of gold and red and yellow made every hedgerow, wood, and thicket seem aflame. The orchards held a heavy crop of Barnack Beauty apples

RADIO TIMES HULTON PICTURE LIBRARY. OPPOSITE: JOHN D. LE VIEN, PRODUCER, "THE FINEST HOURS," A FILM BASED ON CHURCHILL'S MEMOIRS

PERSONAL BANNER *of Sir Winston Churchill adorns his study at Chartwell (opposite), his home for four decades. Here he once saw some old boards on the lawn, jumped on them—and dropped into a well! At his stand-up desk (above) he dictated* The Second World War *in torrents of words to secretaries laboring in relays.*

which aren't picked until late October—the last of the Kentish harvests. We took walks through the lanes, gathering wild blackberries for making jam. Our house was gay with sprays from the hedges—wild cornel, spindleberries, the red hips of the dog rose, and nightshade. Woodsmoke curled from crooked chimneys, and the smell of baking bread escaped when housewives opened their doors to the bicycling postman.

In Smarden men still cycle to and from work. Farmers' wives pedal to the village to shop. Some people even cycle for fun.

Summer and winter the newsagent pedals off to the railroad station, four miles away, at five in the morning. He meets the early train from London, picks up the papers, fits them into a special carrier on his handlebars, then grinds back to Smarden. Since we are one of the first houses on his rounds, we get our paper at six. Often when I get up with the sun to work in the garden I am startled by the newsagent's call: "Don't you ever sleep?"

Bicycles help keep "Pop" Marshall busy. Almost every bike in the village has been in his workshop. Pop, we soon discovered, could always be relied on to answer questions dealing with events in Smarden over the past 65 years. He had lived there about the longest of all the village's 350 inhabitants. Once I asked him about a right-of-

GAILY GARBED *folk dancers swing their partners on the sculptured grounds of Chilham Castle. The group, made up largely of students from Canterbury six miles to the northeast, aided charity with their dazzling show. Famed architect Inigo Jones designed the castle in 1616 as a residence for Sir Dudley Digges. It centers around a Norman keep on Roman foundations. Beyond the castle's terraced garden roll the North Downs, green and glorious in summer vestments.*

way across our property which had been used, as I understood it, "during the war."

"That's perfectly correct," Pop told me. "The Boer War."

To Pop Marshall and other Smarden natives this village is "home," and even a next-door hamlet is "foreign parts." I asked Ben Batt if he knew a certain man I had heard might be willing to work for me.

"Can't say as I do," Ben replied, removing his cap and scratching his head in thought. "Never 'eard a' that name an' I knows 'em all wot lives 'ereabouts."

"I'm told he's from Pluckley," I said. That's five minutes drive away.

"Oh. *Pluckley!*" he scoffed, as though I had said Hong Kong. "I thought 'e couldn't be no local man."

But situated in the southeast of England, Kent has always been in close con-

GEORGE RODGER, MAGNUM

tact with the Continent. Most trade goods once passed through Kent. Early monarchs taxed certain imports from the Continent and the Indies. When the export of English wool was prohibited, people rebelled. For years "owlers" worked at night, meeting barks that beached in sheltered bays. Mules carried smuggled goods along forest paths. Only in the Victorian era did soldiers at last subdue the owlers.

As our evenings drew in, and the smell of wet leaves hung in the chill air, we realized we had already lived a year in Smarden. The oak beams I had found were waxed and polished. The living room walls were paneled.

Now, on foggy nights we sit before our fireplace, watching five-foot logs burn and mulling elderberry wine. At last we have a den of our own.

WINCHESTER AND THE

Ernle Bradford walks with history amid towns and downs that recall Alfred's greatness, William's conquest, and Nelson's victories

NOWHERE IN BRITAIN does the stream of history run stronger and deeper than in Winchester, ancient capital of England and seat of its Saxon kings. During the Roman occupation this was one of the most important garrison towns in the island. In the troubled centuries following the Romans' departure this was the great city of the Saxon kingdom of Wessex, which included Hampshire, Sussex, and Surrey.

From Winchester ruled Alfred the Great from 871 to 899. Defender of his realm against Danish invaders, he was not only a superb general but also a scholar, author, and able administrator.

With sword held high, hilt up like a crucifix, he towers in bronze at the end of the High Street. Had his successors matched his caliber, I reflected as I looked up at him, Winchester might have remained the throne of government and its cathedral taken the place of Canterbury as the seat of England's primate. "Never forget," a Winchester citizen remarked to me, "that this was the capital of England when London was just a small, muddy port!"

I turned from Alfred and followed his gaze up the straight sweep of the High Street, past the Butter Cross, toward the 13th-century Westgate, one of two gates surviving out of the original five that pierced the city wall. I realized that Winchester's

MODERN LIFE *roils round Alfred the Great in Winchester, hub of his Wessex realm. He faces High Street, "main street" since Roman times. America's bushel measure and the yard (said to match Henry I's arm) originated here.*

GEORGE F. MOBLEY, NATIONAL GEOGRAPHIC PHOTOGRAPHER

SOUTHERN COUNTIES

sightseers owe most of their delights to the conquering Normans, builders of the great cathedral, the ancient walls, and the castle which guarded the city.

Winchester Cathedral stretches 556 feet, making it the longest medieval cathedral. Below the East Window hang the colors of the Hampshire Regiment, the "Royal Tigers," recalling battles ranging from India and China in the 18th and 19th centuries to North Africa and Europe in World War II.

But history is more than battles. In a side chapel a stained-glass window commemorates Izaak Walton. Fishermen from many lands donated it in 1914. Jane Austen, that miniaturist in words and lover of domestic perfection, also lies in the cathedral.

William of Wykeham, a 14th-century bishop, was largely responsible for building the magnificent Perpendicular nave. His effigy lies in a chantry chapel in the south aisle, and at his feet sit three small tonsured figures probably representing his secretaries. When Roundheads looted the cathedral in 1642 and stabled their horses inside, they would have defaced the bishop's image, but one of their own number stopped them. He had been a pupil at Winchester College, England's oldest public school, which Wykeham founded in 1382.

BEYOND THE CATHEDRAL CLOSE I saw dozens of boys bicycling in straw hats: Wykehamists – students of Winchester College. They barely tolerate the claims of later schools like Eton and Harrow. "*They* get the publicity. *They* provide prime ministers," one remarked. "But Winchester produces the heads of the civil service – the people who really run the country."

A footpath from the college led me past the old city wall to the River Itchen. Jade-green lawns and flowerbeds riotous with color follow the banks where Izaak Walton loved to fish. Typical of Hampshire's many trout streams, the Itchen ripples, crystal clear, over a pebbled bottom.

In small alleys and broad avenues I explored the city. The High Street with its row of colonnaded shops, its Guildhall clock projecting on an arm high over the street, evokes the Middle Ages. Yet the city pulses

GEORGE F. MOBLEY, NATIONAL GEOGRAPHIC PHOTOGRAPHER (ALSO RIGHT)

with modern life. A television set flickered through the window of a 15th-century house. An old man in corduroy trousers lighting his pipe in front of the Godbegot House might have stepped out of Tudor times. But then he jumped on a motor scooter and put-putted away. I was hardly surprised, when I paused outside a baker's

"**ROWNDE TABLE OF KYNG ARTHUR**" *(below left) has hung in Winchester's Great Hall for at least 600 years. Historians doubt that the Arthurian knights whose names adorn its rim ever sat around it. Vestige of a Norman castle, the hall housed early parliaments. A tube in one wall—the "king's ear"—let monarchs eavesdrop, tradition says. Here Sir Walter Raleigh (left) heard his death sentence in 1603, fulfilled 15 years later in London (page 67). Townsmen pelted England's first pipe smoker with clay pipes en route to his trial for treason. Winchester Cathedral (Bishop Wykeham's west front, opposite) enshrines the bones of Saxon kings, St. Swithun, and King Canute.*

SIR WALTER RALEIGH BY NICHOLAS HILLIARD, C. 1605, NATIONAL PORTRAIT GALLERY, LONDON

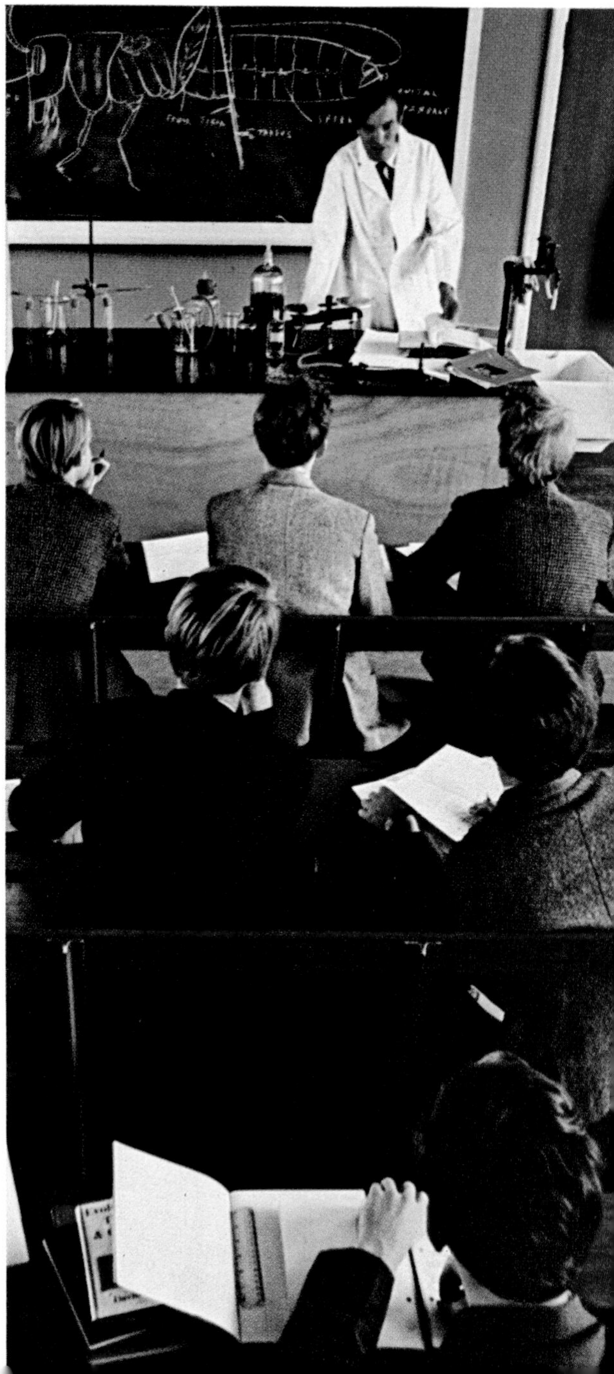

RIGHT: JOHN MARMARAS, THE DAILY TELEGRAPH

LESSON IN LIFE *absorbs a biology class (right) at Winchester College, now in its sixth century. Henry VI modeled Eton after it. "Manners Makyth Man," was its founder's motto. Flogging helped; a Latin wall inscription warns "Learn, leave, or be licked." Novelist Anthony Trollope endured five scourgings in one day. Scholars still live in Chamber Court where the first 70 dwelt. Many go on to Oxford, but one tomb says, "He went to heaven instead of to Oxford."*

shop to sniff the scent of freshly baked bread, to see the Bishop of Winchester in full robes walking down the street. Housewives, workmen, and farmers paid no more attention than if he had been a postman.

In the City Museum, treasures recall the distant past when this was a pre-Roman village. The Romans called their town Venta Belgarum. And William the Conqueror confirmed both Winchester and London as his joint capitals. Though the locus of power finally shifted to London, Winchester prospered on the wool trade and remained her chief rival as late as the 13th century.

At the top of the High Street stands the Westgate, to which Charles I was brought as a prisoner in 1648. Loyal city officials greeted him with traditional honors.

The museum in the Westgate displays tools of torture, and an iron cage in which a victim was hung up till he died of hunger and thirst. Debtors jailed here used to stick a collection box through the bars in hopes that passersby would drop in coins.

Nearby I visited the Great Hall, relic of a castle dating back to the Conqueror's day. In this castle Henry III was born, and here Henry V parleyed with French diplomats before launching the campaign that led to Agincourt in 1415. I admired the lofty roof of the hall, and then an immense roundel of wood caught my eye.

"The Round Table," said my guide. "But only a copy, the experts claim."

King Arthur's Round Table! Boyhood visions of jousts and heroic deeds welled up, veiling the cold fact that the table probably dates eight centuries too late for Arthur.

WAYFARER'S DOLE, *free beer and bread, greets the visitor at St. Cross Hospital, England's oldest house of charity. In 1136 Bishop Henry of Blois founded an order for 13 poor men on the banks of the Itchen near Winchester. Their successors wear black robes and silver crosses (below).*

Claret-colored gowns and cardinal's-hat badges mark Brothers of Noble Poverty, established by Cardinal Beaufort in 1446 for those who once "had everything handsome about them." Cross or badge passes from each pensioner to his successor. Brethren live in these tall-chimneyed 15th-century houses and worship in their Norman church.

PATRICK THURSTON

In this history-haunted hall nothing seemed more authentic.

I could not leave Winchester without a look at the Thetcher tombstone, which stands beside the avenue of limes leading from the City Museum to the cathedral. Raised to the memory of a young soldier, who "fell" in 1764, it reads:

Here sleeps in peace a Hampshire Grenadier,
Who caught his death by drinking cold small Beer.
Soldiers be wise from his untimely fall
And when yere hot drink Strong or none at all.

As a sort of postscript, a couplet was later added:

An honest Soldier never is forgot
Whether he die by Musket or by Pot.

SOUTHWARD from Winchester the Downs begin – those rolling hills of chalk which culminate in Portsdown behind the harbor at Portsmouth, and then sweep eastward to end in Beachy Head and the famous white cliffs. West of the Downs, Hampshire slips toward the Channel through the strange and beautiful New Forest. "New" means only that William the Conqueror made it his royal forest and hunting preserve shortly after 1066. Since then "the Forest" – which means here no more than an uncultivated area – has preserved a life of its own. It is now one of the largest national parks and nature reserves in Britain, covering some 92,000 acres.

New Forest verderers, or law officers, still hold their ancient court, the Swainmote, in the "capital" village of Lyndhurst to try offenses against the "laws and customs" of the preserve. Foresters – those who live in the villages here, or whose land abuts the region – may graze animals, gather wood, or cut peat in it. Thick-coated New Forest ponies have roamed here for centuries. Arab stallions have recently improved the strain, and the sturdy, good-tempered ponies are admirable for children. Many are exported to the United States.

I spent happy hours exploring the Forest's small roads – some little more than dirt tracks – which bear off through oak groves or across heather and gorse-entangled plains and lead to remote hamlets. Fritham, typically, contains about two dozen houses and has been the home of foresters since long before the Norman Conquest.

In its public house, the Royal Oak, I found a log fire burning in a vast open fireplace. In the corner a side of bacon was curing in the woodsmoke. Outside, ponies cropped the grass and pigs rooted for acorns.

From the Rufus Stone, where King William Rufus, son of the Conqueror, was slain by an arrow, to Fordingbridge with its seven-arched medieval bridge over the Avon, the New Forest has hardly changed since

SOUTHAMPTON'S *busy fingers touch a third of a million passengers each year. Beyond, the River Itchen*

the Conqueror's day. The only newcomers, black Galloway cattle put out during World War II, are now as native to the landscape as the deer that roam its shady woods, the otters that fish its streams, and the hawks that hover in the updrafts of its furzy ridges.

Two miles from Fordingbridge I came to the hamlet of Breamore ("Bremmer"). Here pagans buried their dead in a long barrow called "Giant's Grave." Romans worshiped at a shrine to Apollo; I found a charming Saxon church. Beside it, in a beautiful park, stands Breamore House, E-shaped to honor Elizabeth I. The studded door swung ponderously in wide welcome as Sir Westrow Hulse, the ninth baronet, showed me the treasures of his "quiet country house, never fortified or fought over." Portraits gazed at us from the walls, where tapestries muted the dark sheen of ancient paneling.

In Beaulieu (pronounced "Bewley") on the southeast edge of the New Forest I toured Palace House, home of Lord Montagu. Visitors may roam the residence, the

eaches toward Winchester.

GIANT OAKS, *centuries old, dwarf campers amid Hampshire's New Forest.*

GEORGE F. MOBLEY AND (LEFT) DEAN CONGER, NATIONAL GEOGRAPHIC PHOTOGRAPHERS

NE VILE FANO
Ladies

ALAN VILLIERS. OVERLEAF: DEAN CONGER, NATIONAL GEOGRAPHIC PHOTOGRAPHER. OPPOSITE UPPER: NELSON BY L. F. ABBOT, NATIONAL PORTRAIT GALLERY, LONDON

ALE AND HEARTY LAUGHTER *buoy spirits in Southampton's Red Lion Inn. Here Henry V tried his cousin, the Earl of Cambridge, and two allies for treason. "Get you hence, Poor miserable wretches, to your death," says Shakespeare's Henry. Next day he sailed with 30,000 men for France—and Agincourt. Two centuries later the Pilgrims embarked here for America.*

HORATIO NELSON *crushed Napoleon's invasion hopes off Cape Trafalgar in 1805. He led his captains through a battle line of French and Spanish ships. In his triumph Nelson fell, hit by a musket ball fired by a sharpshooter aboard* Redoutable *(below, soon to surrender). His body went home in a cask of spirits which his thirsty tars had few qualms about tapping—"broaching the Admiral." He lies in St. Paul's; his* Victory *lives on in Portsmouth (opposite).*

beautiful ruins of a Cistercian abbey founded by King John in 1204, and the Montagu Motor Museum with its vintage autos.

THE AGE OF SAIL comes alive in Buckler's Hard, two miles down the tidal Beaulieu River. Nelson himself seemed to stroll beside me along its one broad street lined with neat 18th-century houses. Here many of England's famous "wooden walls" were built from giant Forest oaks. After the ships were launched, sailors heaving on oars towed them to Portsmouth to be fitted out with masts, spars, sails, and guns.

I found it hard to believe that Lymington once eclipsed Portsmouth and gave twice as many men and ships to Edward III's fleet which invaded France in 1346. Between gracious Georgian houses stretches the main street, broad and straight so boats, masts, and spars could be carried right down to the water. Dinghies, ocean racers, and family cruisers nod at moorings where bluff-bowed, square-rigged ships awaited a favoring wind to take them down-Channel.

A ferry leaves from here for the Isle of Wight, and I joined holidaymakers for the five-mile trip across the Solent. Cutters and catamarans dropped astern as we made for Yarmouth. West of us I could make out the Needles, pinnacle rocks off the island's tip.

PAINTING BY A. MAYER, MUSÉE DE LA MARINE, PARIS

Near them in 1851 Queen Victoria watched the schooner *America* trounce a fleet of British yachts to win the ornate silver trophy now famed as the *America*'s Cup. The story goes that Victoria asked a signalman aboard the royal yacht, "Which is second?"

"Madam," he said, "there is no second."

Victoria and Albert built a small palace on the island at Osborne, and their son, Edward VII, made nearby Cowes a fashionable resort. During the regattas of Cowes Week in August, the Solent gleams with the varnished hulls of yachts from all over the world. I remember taking the helm of the yawl *Kay* for the start of the 1963 Fastnet Race and counting the flags of ten nations among the yachts that jockeyed for position.

"Sacred Cowes," some call the town, for it harbors the ultraformal Royal Yacht Squadron, Britain's premier yacht club. But its charm lies in its air of faded Edwardian splendor, its neat, small houses, and its clubs and taverns seething with the sailing set – yachtsmen in yellow foul-weather jackets, roll-neck jerseys, and blue jeans, and starlets and models in fashionable "sailing clothes."

The island, with its rolling chalk hills, intensive agriculture, and popular seaside resorts, reminds one of mainland Hampshire. A sign on the road to the east coast of the island surprised me: Godshill. My home is in another Godshill on the edge of the New Forest. I learned that folk from this pretty island village supposedly colonized my Godshill in the fifth century.

Locals call Portsmouth "Pompey." I have never found out why, though I was based there in 1940 in the Royal Navy. Only a few of the waterfront landmarks that I knew remain, for Portsmouth was one of the cities hardest hit in the Blitz.

PATRICK THURSTON. RIGHT: 1857 PHOTOGRAPH, ROYAL LIBRARY, WINDSOR CASTLE

VICTORIA AND ALBERT *pose with the royal children at Osborne House, the villa he designed on the Isle of Wight. Here they breakfasted to bagpipes and gardened. Here she died in 1901, 40 years a widow. On the grounds visitors see the Queen's "bathing machine," a curtained cabana wheeled to the seaside for royal dips. Victorian bathers boomed resorts like Bournemouth (above), where paths scrawl East Cliff.*

Nelson's *Victory* survived, though a German bomb holed her. Restored and rerigged, she remains technically the flagship of the Commander in Chief, Portsmouth Area. Open daily, England's most famous warship lies in her own dry dock just inside Portsmouth dockyard. Launched in 1765, H.M.S. *Victory* fought in most major sea battles of the Napoleonic Wars. On her quarterdeck Nelson led the British fleet at Trafalgar and was fatally wounded. A brass plate gleamed in the sun as I bent to read: "Here Nelson Fell—21st October 1805."

The crowds making a pilgrimage to this shrine brought to mind Thackeray's words: "The bones of the *Victory* ought to be sacred relics for Englishmen to worship. . . ."

ACROSS THE SUSSEX border stands one of Britain's oldest Christian shrines. On a Saxon foundation the Normans built the cathedral of Chichester. Once a Roman port, Chichester retains parts of its medieval walls now turned into quiet elm-shaded walks, an ornate market cross, and streets of stately Georgian houses.

I roamed the banks of a long tongue of water that licks inland from Chichester Harbour. Picturesque villages like Bosham, Chidham, and Itchenor line this inlet, one of Britain's most popular sailing grounds. Shortly after the Second World War, I lived aboard a sailboat at Birdham Pool, a little harbor locked off from the tidal waters. Few yachts were in commission in those days.

Twenty years later I asked for a mooring at Itchenor Yacht Club. "There's a seven-year waiting list, at least," I was told.

Ten miles east of Chichester stands Arundel Castle, the family home of the Duke of Norfolk. Why his home should be in Sussex puzzles visitors. In 1397 Thomas Mowbray,

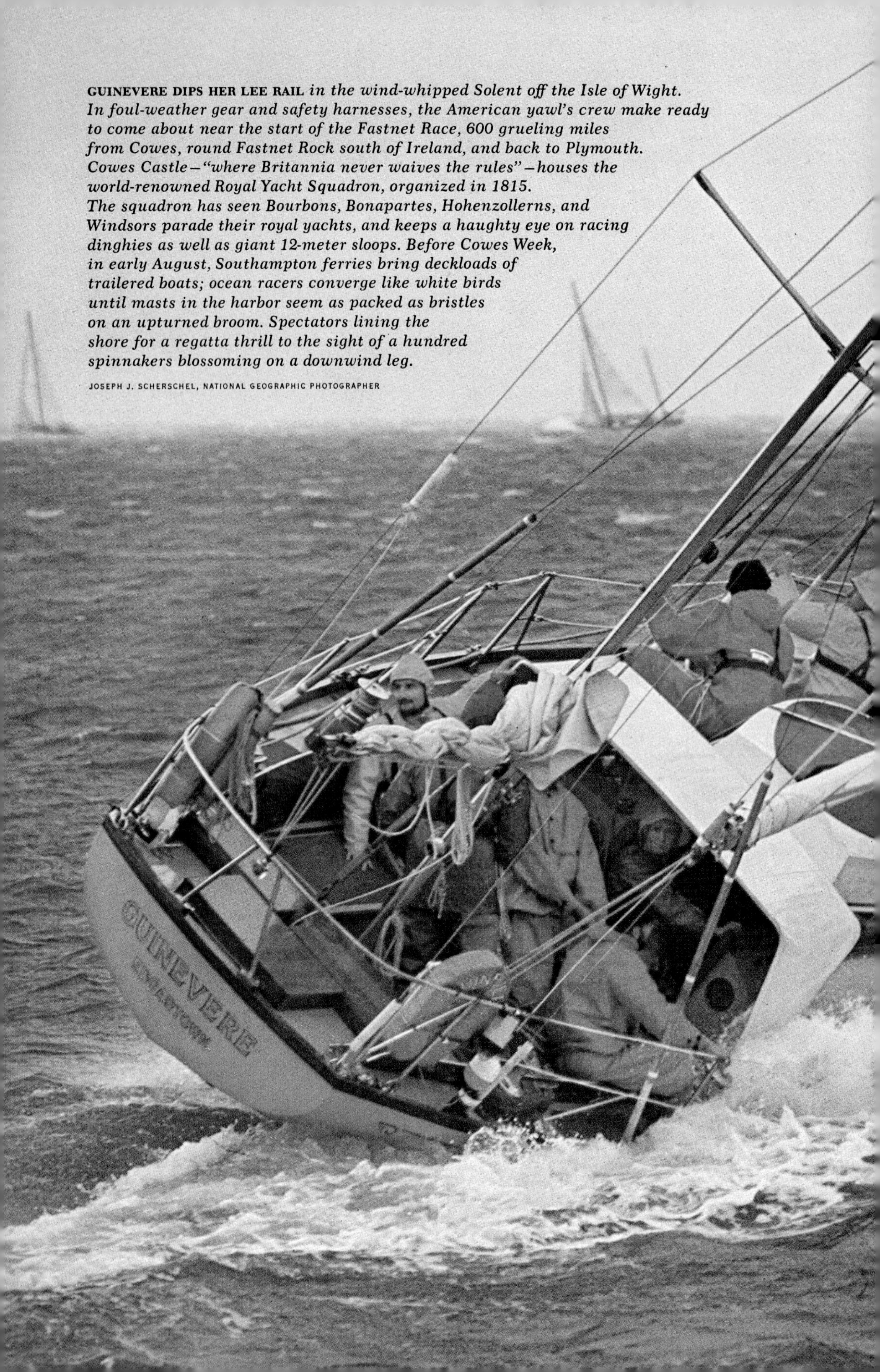

GUINEVERE DIPS HER LEE RAIL *in the wind-whipped Solent off the Isle of Wight. In foul-weather gear and safety harnesses, the American yawl's crew make ready to come about near the start of the Fastnet Race, 600 grueling miles from Cowes, round Fastnet Rock south of Ireland, and back to Plymouth. Cowes Castle—"where Britannia never waives the rules"—houses the world-renowned Royal Yacht Squadron, organized in 1815. The squadron has seen Bourbons, Bonapartes, Hohenzollerns, and Windsors parade their royal yachts, and keeps a haughty eye on racing dinghies as well as giant 12-meter sloops. Before Cowes Week, in early August, Southampton ferries bring deckloads of trailered boats; ocean racers converge like white birds until masts in the harbor seem as packed as bristles on an upturned broom. Spectators lining the shore for a regatta thrill to the sight of a hundred spinnakers blossoming on a downwind leg.*

JOSEPH J. SCHERSCHEL, NATIONAL GEOGRAPHIC PHOTOGRAPHER

Earl Marshal of England, helped crush Richard II's enemies. The grateful king made him Duke of Norfolk and gave him lands of the beheaded Earl of Arundel and Surrey. Soon Mowbray fell and the lands reverted. In 1555 a descendant of Mowbray, Thomas Howard, married Lady Mary Fitzalan, daughter of the 12th Earl of Arundel, thus uniting the families, with Arundel Castle the seat.

Henry I and King Stephen besieged the fortress in the 12th century; Parliamentary cannon pounded it during the Civil War. Today you can drive into the peaceful park and visit the castle itself – walking under the spiked portcullis, past the Norman keep on its man-made mound, or motte, into the high-beamed Barons' Hall. Though much restored, Arundel evokes the power and majesty of an earlier age.

BEGINNING in the late 18th century, resorts sprang up along the south coast to meet a craze for the newfangled sea bathing which a certain Dr. Russell of Lewes advocated. But behind today's seaside sprawl rise the unspoiled Sussex Downs. Even at the height of the holiday season, I walked for miles over their springy turf and saw hardly a dozen people in a day.

The slow, muddy brooks of Sussex cannot match the sparkling trout streams of Hampshire. But authors Rudyard Kipling, G. K. Chesterton, and Hilaire Belloc, and painters like Duncan Grant, Paul Nash, and Vanessa Bell found inspiration in the rolling downs through which the brooks run. "Notice the extraordinary clarity of the light," said Sir Henry Rushbury, former Keeper of Britain's Royal Academy. "There's an almost pearly quality about it over this stretch of coast."

At Midhurst, on the northwestern edge of the Downs, I lunched in the Angel, one of the town's old coaching inns, rich in their Pickwickian comfort – though autos squat in yards where horses once waited. I admired the town's timber-framed houses, elegant Georgian porticoes, and tall windows in high-ceilinged rooms.

I hiked a causeway leading to the ruins of Cowdray House, haunted by a curse. When Henry VIII gave famous Battle Abbey to his Master of the Horse, the last departing monk swore the family would end by fire and water. In 1793 the house burned to the ground. A week later its owner drowned.

I motored to Piddinghoe on the Ouse, seeing from afar the "begilded dolphin" of its church spire which Kipling describes in his poem "Sussex." The church is built of local flint, used in this area ever since neolithic men made weapons from it and built forts on the shoulders of the Downs.

The pubkeeper regaled me as I lunched on his Dover sole. "This was a great place for smugglers, like all the Channel coast. The boys would run to France for silks and satins and rum – especially rum." He spoke as if it were yesterday, not 200 years ago.

"I suppose they brought the contraband up the river?" I asked.

"Aye, that they did – up here and then on to Lewes for London. There's an old saying around here – dates from the time when Pidd'n'oo men hid their rum in chalk pits: 'At Pidd'n'oo they dig for moonshine!'"

Lewes made a fine center for my Sussex tour. From my window in the White Hart I could see the Downs rise and fall to the Channel nine miles away. The Normans carved Sussex into six "rapes," or great fiefs. Each rape included a strip of coastline, a river, some cropland, downland for grazing, and a northern fringe of forest for hunting and swineherding. Castles at Lewes, Pevensey, Hastings, Bramber, Chichester, and Arundel dominated each.

I climbed atop Lewes's ruined Norman castle, mute witness to the ragged flight of Henry III's army after the Battle of Lewes in 1264. Hard on their heels swept Simon de Montfort, who cornered the king in the priory here, forced his surrender, and soon

ELIZABETHAN BED *in Hampshire's Breamore House reflects the massive style of its age. Craftsmen to the wealthy used oak, often imported from Denmark, and carved every inch; few signed or dated their work. Though richly wrought, furniture was sparse. The King's Chamber at Arundel Castle held only a bed, table, and chair. Heavy linens went unwashed for months. While gentry burrowed in feather beds, curtained to tame cruel drafts, commoners made do with straw and boards.*

MERLE SEVERY, NATIONAL GEOGRAPHIC STAFF

convened the prototype of Parliament.

I climbed Cliffe Hill. The sound of traffic faded as I mounted the windy slopes, and I heard only the crickets and honeybees among the wild flowers that enameled the hill. Thick-fleeced Southdown sheep gazed incuriously at me. Their wool, and the cloth made from it, brought wealth to medieval towns of the South. A circular earthwork crowns the hill. Like nearby Chanctonbury Ring, it protected prehistoric Sussex folk. From it they commanded a view of the whole valley down to the Channel.

Behind me to the east lay Glyndebourne, an estate famous for its summer opera season, where one can listen to Mozart in a setting that truly complements the civilized elegance of *Figaro*.

The southwest wind blew up-Channel off the Atlantic—the wind that once boosted sailing ships home to London. In the lee of Beachy Head, some 12 miles from where I stood, hundreds of ships used to drop anchor until this wind had gone round to the east, thus giving them an easy passage down-Channel en route to America.

IN STANMER PARK, west of Lewes, the University of Sussex opened its doors in 1961—the first of seven universities England planned for the 1960's. Its varied courses of study contrast with the single-subject approach of most older institutions. An art center links study with practice in music, painting, sculpture, poetry, and drama. I discovered that most Sussex students live at the seaside instead of on the campus.

I followed their example, driving on to Britain's most fashionable seaside city, Brighton. Earlier called Brighthelmston, it was still only a village in the 18th century.

PATRICK THURSTON (ALSO OPPOSITE). BELOW: BRITISH TRAVEL ASSOCIATION

OCTAGONAL MARKET CROSS, *one of England's finest (upper), rose about 1500 to shelter Chichester vendors. Festival Theatre, opened in 1962 with Sir Laurence Olivier directing, draws summer playgoers to its apron stage.*

SAVIOR IN STONE *adorns Chichester's Norman cathedral in this superb detail from the Raising of Lazarus. Mystery shrouds its origin. This and a second panel, Christ at the Gate of Bethany, may have come from a vanished Saxon cathedral which tradition sites a mile off Selsey's shifting shore.*

To ease the load on Chichester's central tower, a detached belfry, unique in English cathedrals today, rose north of the nave in the 15th century. But the tower collapsed in 1861. Quickly rebuilt, it soars 277 feet—an inspiring sight from sea.

JANE AUSTEN *dwelt in Hampshire, Rudyard Kipling (right) in Sussex. Her world was the drawing room; his the British Empire. Miss Austen's social subtleties sparkle like champagne: "... they were neither of them quite enough in love to think that three hundred and fifty pounds a year would supply them with the comforts of life." "'Ere's a beggar with a bullet through 'is spleen," trumpets Kipling, in cadences that march to a drumbeat. Born in the rectory at Steventon in 1775, the shy Miss Austen spent the last eight of her 42 years in Chawton House, on the London-Winchester Road near Alton. Here you may see the parlor where she polished* Pride and Prejudice *and her five other novels, hiding them under needlework when the creaking door warned of visitors. Kipling, born in India, wed to an American, was world famed when he set eyes on Bateman's, a Jacobean ironmaster's home near Burwash. "That's her! Make an honest woman of her— quick!" he exulted. And here he dwelt till death took him from his "working tools" at 71 in 1936.*

PATRICK THURSTON (ALSO UPPER). OPPOSITE: JANE AUSTEN MEMORIAL TRUST

The Duke of Norfolk, at Arundel Castle, heads the illustrious ranks of Britain's peers

RISING ABOVE the River Arun, this rebuilt Norman fortress, open to tourists, is the home of Bernard Marmaduke Fitzalan-Howard, Earl of Arundel and Surrey, Baron Fitzalan, Clun, Oswaldestre, and Maltravers, 16th Duke of Norfolk, Earl Marshal and Chief Butler of England.

He organized Queen Elizabeth's coronation and Sir Winston Churchill's funeral, and heads the College of Arms (see box, page 91). His pay, £20 ($56) a year, has not been raised since the 15th century. But he doesn't feel the pinch. As premier peer of the realm he epitomizes "the tightest, richest, and most exalted blue-blood fraternity in the world."

Today there are 26 nonroyal dukes. If you meet one or his duchess, address either as "Your Grace." Next in rank come marquesses (about 40 of them), earls (about 200), viscounts (about 150), and barons (more than 500). Their wives are marchioness, countess (an earl's wife), viscountess, and baroness. "My Lord" and "My Lady" are proper.

Feudal power under the Norman kings centered in earls and barons; other ranks came later. As the military nobles evolved into the parliamentary peerage, their knights and esquires became gentry.

Estates and titles went to eldest sons, forcing other sons into the army, church, commerce, or obscurity. "New men" arose after the Wars of the Roses lopped the tallest family trees. James I sold baronies for £10,000. Peerages went to heroes like Marlborough and Wellington; also to the poet laureate Tennyson and the banker Rothschild. Churchill rejected a dukedom, preferring power in the House of Commons. The last nonroyal duke to be created was Westminster, in 1874, scion of the old Norman family of Grosvenor.

Barons are on the increase, for the Government can now elevate "life peers" to the House of Lords "without being burdened with their offspring." Peers have glamor in British as well as American eyes. Businesses like to display lords' names on letterheads. They get no salary while serving in Parliament, but can claim daily expenses of 4½ guineas ($13.20). They escape jury duty and never had to fear debtor's prison. Once it was their privilege to be beheaded rather than hanged like highwaymen. Later, when hanged, they could choose a silken cord. They can demand speech with the sovereign and on the way bag two royal deer.

Baronets and knights rank below peers. ("Sir" and "Lady" are correct address.) But they make it into *Burke's Peerage* and into *Debrett's Peerage, Baronetage, Knightage, and Companionage,* the bible of the pedigreed since 1675. Knights receive the accolade in Buckingham Palace, kneeling on a red cushion while the Queen taps them on each shoulder with a sword.

Then the Prince of Wales, later George IV, found it a good place to escape his London creditors and relax with his mistress, Mrs. Fitzherbert, and favorites like Beau Brummell. The Prince had architect John Nash design the crescents and squares that face the seafront, also the pavilion, that Indian-Chinese blend of onion domes and eastern spires. Some call it "the first example of surrealism," others "an oriental nightmare." Admirers see something of Coleridge's Xanadu, "A stately pleasure dome." But once past its façade, even its critics are struck by the exuberance of its furniture, including fabulous "Chinese Chippendale" chairs and tables and a Dolphin suite made to celebrate Nelson's victories.

One day I drove down the Cuckmere Valley to lunch at the Star Inn with its quaint Tudor carvings at Alfriston. This choice spot—on a riverbank with a protective hillock to one side—has felt man's tread for countless centuries. The medieval church stands on a pagan mound. "On no part of the South Downs," writes a historian, "is there more exquisite entertainment for the antiquary." But I did not have to be one to enjoy Alfriston's charm, or the excellent lunch of roast Surrey chicken, draft beer from the wood, and apple pie and cream.

That put me in the right frame of mind for an afternoon walk. I set off across the cliffs to Beachy Head. But the land flows up and down like a relaxed concertina, and ten miles on the map becomes a great deal more to a hiker plunging down each long slope and toiling up the far side!

The Downs rise toward the sea, their chalk cliffs dropping sheer into the Channel. Romans appropriately called the land

Albion, "white island." Here the Armada veered across the Channel to Calais, whence English fire ships drove the Spaniards out to destruction in the North Sea.

After three hours of walking this lovely coastline – now held by the National Trust – I crested the rise beyond Birling Gap, once a haunt of smugglers, where the wind swoops in full of the salty Channel air. Before me Beachy Head plunged 534 feet to the sea. The chalk headland was a graveyard of sailing ships lost in the fog. A clergyman had a cave cut at the foot of the cliff and a passage to the top so shipwrecked sailors could climb to safety. Seamen called it "Parson Darby's Hole."

OPERA LOVERS *picnic 'tween acts at Glyndebourne, where in 1934 John Christie opened an 800-seat theater beside his ancestral home. Blue bloods vie for tickets to the two-month festival; black-tied and jeweled, they ride the train from London to savor Mozart arias, to dine and wine from wicker baskets while the orchestra plays croquet under the eyes of Sussex cows.*

Sussex University (right) is pacesetter in England's new university explosion.

The new Yvonne Arnaud Theatre draws playgoers to Guildford, Surrey's bustling county town (below), whose Guildhall clock has kept time since 1683.

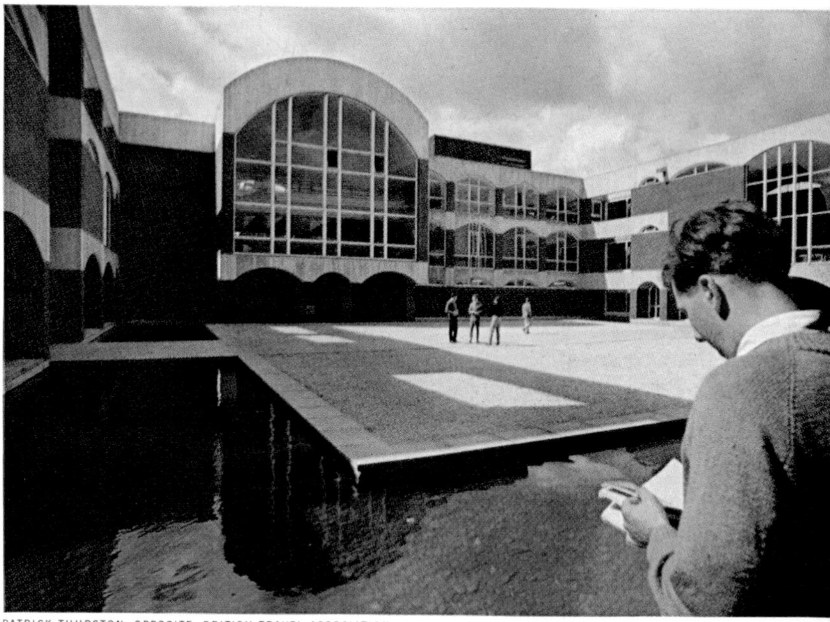

PATRICK THURSTON. OPPOSITE: BRITISH TRAVEL ASSOCIATION

It's "Brighton or bust" as dowager autos take their annual fling

BIG ANTIQUE CYLINDERS thump and gasp. Hand horns groan. Drivers grip wooden steering wheels, and the heady smell of exhaust drifts through London's Hyde Park. Thus some 250 elegant horseless carriages start the annual Commemoration Run to Brighton. Far from a race, the event celebrates "Emancipation Day" when, in 1896, a law that motor vehicles had to be preceded by a pedestrian with a red flag was repealed and the speed limit boosted from 4 to 14 miles an hour. Only cars built before 1905 may take part.

The first run was held in 1927. The Royal Automobile Club and the Veteran Car Club now organize it, and spectators by the thousands line the roads to watch one of the most colorful events of England's chill and misty autumn.

Early antique-car enthusiasts found their entries draped in rotting sheets in dusty stables or being used as roosts for farmyard hens. Some splendid old cars contained nesting rats; some had trees growing through them. One priceless 1902 Wolseley had been taken apart, bit by bit, by a country cleric who hadn't a clue how to put the thing together again. For such treasures car buffs used to pay as little as ten shillings and seldom more than five pounds!

Beautifully restored, their fresh paint and polished brass gleaming, entries wheeze over Westminster Bridge and head for Lambeth, Croydon, and points south. Cyclists ride escort. A daredevil on an ancient "penny-farthing" (left) joins the run.

What makes are the cars? A 1903 Renault landaulette gets away at the start (opposite, above). Same year is the pink Tony Huber above. Huffing toward the finish on Brighton's Madeira Drive are, from left below: 1904 Peugeot tonneau, 1904 Vauxhall tonneau, 1903 Humbrette two-seater, 1904 Minerva two-seater, 1901 Renault tonneau, and (below) a 1904 Peugeot two-seater.

Some cars are "sociables," "dogcarts," and "surreys," names inherited from the horse age. All are subject to breakdowns – which provide passengers a chance to climb down, stretch, and pass around the Thermos. Some tinkering under the bonnet (hood), and off they chug.

JAMES P. BLAIR, NATIONAL GEOGRAPHIC PHOTOGRAPHER

East of Beachy Head and six miles inland from seaside Hastings lies the town of Battle, near the actual site of the Battle of Hastings between William the Norman and Harold the Saxon in 1066. I went there on a cold, bright day when the wind blew from the sea and drove the woolly clouds over the great gatehouse of Battle Abbey. Founded by William to hallow "the very spot where God granted him the conquest of England," the abbey once ranked among the country's richest. Part is now a school for girls; the rest is open to the public every day.

I stood on the height where Harold drew up his troops, a long ridge commanding the route to London. I looked down the winding road to Hastings, where the Normans had moved after landing unopposed at Pevensey. William, stumbling as he disembarked, is said to have clutched a handful of English earth – a good omen, he told his men, for seizing the whole country.

King Harold, ringed by housecarls with battle-axes, watched the enemy approach. Each side mustered some 7,000 men.

The Normans charged up the hillside. But

the wall of shields held. Fighting raged. A Norman wing reeled back, Saxon warriors in hot pursuit. William rallied his forces and slashed at the pursuers.

As the day wore on, the Normans twice feigned retreat; each time their cavalry wheeled and cut down Saxons who broke ranks (page 14). William ordered his archers to shoot into the air so their arrows would rain into the mass of Englishmen instead of striking the outer shield ring. Though the English fought to the end, their morale broke when Harold thudded to the ground.

I gazed at a stone that marks where the last Saxon king of England died. The high altar of the vanished Abbey Church once stood here. I walked out into the streets of Battle, past merchants' houses centuries old. I sipped coffee in the Pilgrim's Rest where pilgrims to the abbey once lodged. The wind was strengthening off the sea, and it sounded like the whistle of arrows.

HASTINGS was one of the Cinque Ports that guarded the "Narrow Seas" of the Channel. The original five (page 168) were later joined by Winchelsea and Rye. All came under attack during the medieval Anglo-French wars. Winchelsea suffered heavily in these raids, and the sea has since receded so far from the town that I found it hard to believe that this was ever one of England's premier ports.

Across the valley, Rye's old houses caught the evening light as the town sat serenely on the brow of its hill. I wandered its cobbled streets and alleys, winding among gabled houses whose red roofs distinguish the town. Dominating all else was massive Ypres Tower, turreted at each corner. Nearby stands the lovely Norman church, from whose belfry on a fair day one can see the blue shores of France. Lookouts manned it when France was the enemy, and again in

PATRICK THURSTON

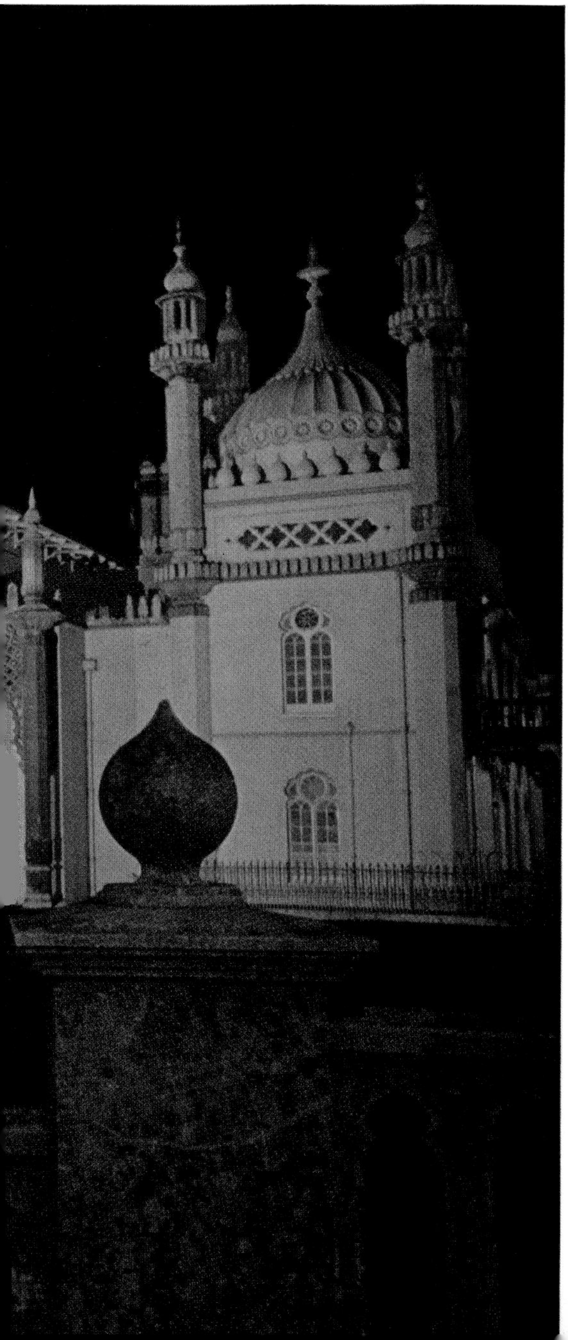

ARABIAN NIGHTS IN SUSSEX, *Brighton's Royal Pavilion embodies the most extravagant flight of Regency fancy. To Brighton in 1783 came young Prince George and a band of gay blades. With no one to say them nay, they galloped and raced their phaetons over seaside lawns, ogled bathing girls through telescopes, gluttonized, gambled, wenched, pranked—a resident might answer the door to find an upended coffin.*

When the Prince became Regent in 1811, a regal income enabled him to create his "pleasure dome." Guests in Beau Brummell garb, coming to gargantuan feasts in the Banqueting Room and to hear the Prince's baritone in the "Chinese Gothic" Music Room, gaped at writhing silver dragons, iron palms, and a one-ton chandelier hissing with the new gaslights. Seeing the onion domes atop the pavilion, one wag quipped that "the dome of St. Paul's must have come down to Brighton and pupped."

As the middle class flocked to "London by the Sea" ("brisk, gay, and gaudy, like a harlequin's jacket," in Thackeray's words), royalty left. Victoria found the pavilion too public; now the town displays it.

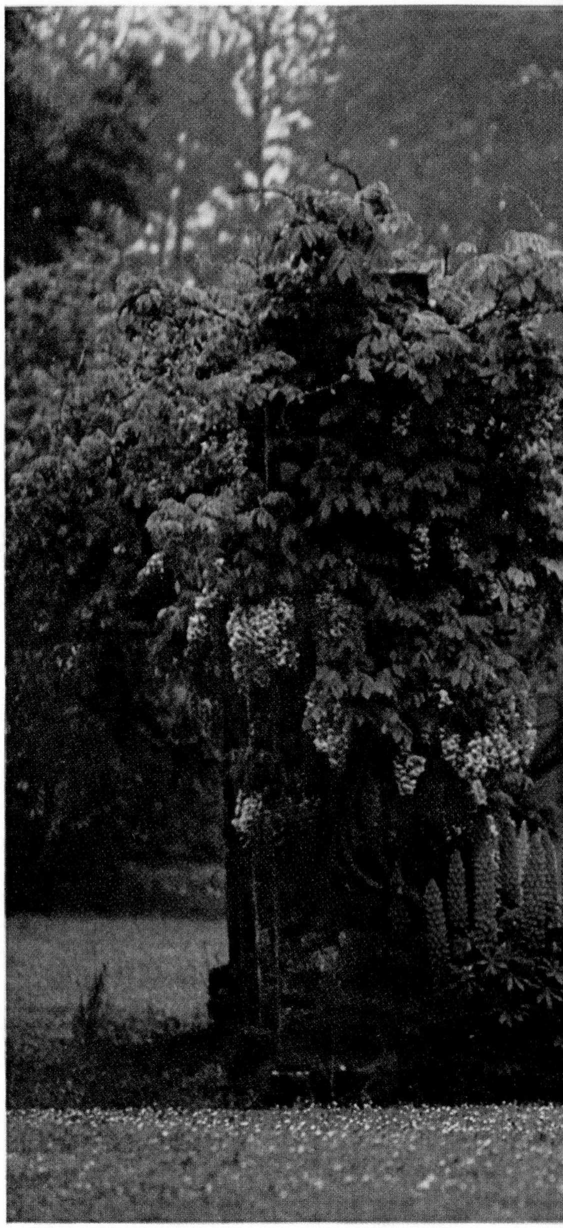

RED FLOWERS *spike the stone that marks where Harold of England, in the Battle of Hastings, fell in a field drenched with Saxon blood. It stands amid the ruins of Battle Abbey, whose carvings bespeak the mortality of man.*

The Bayeux Tapestry presents the Norman version of the Conquest. Below, knights charge the tight-packed English shield wall. Earlier Harold is shown pledging support of William of Normandy's claim as heir to Edward the Confessor, then taking the crown himself.

Gathering a host of land-hungry adventurers, William lands at Pevensey, September 28, 1066.

Harold, victorious over the King of Norway invading Yorkshire, rushes his army to London, 200 miles in a week. He gathers levies, marches on, 60 miles in three days. On October 13 his weary soldiers line the height of Senlac.

Next day the battle almost goes to the English when the Normans fear William slain and begin to flee. He lifts his helm: "Look at me well. I am still alive. By the grace of God I shall yet prove victor!" His men rally and win.

GEORGE F. MOBLEY, NATIONAL GEOGRAPHIC PHOTOGRAPHER (ALSO UPPER)

BELOW: SEGMENT OF THE BAYEUX TAPESTRY, AN 11TH-CENTURY EMBROIDERY ON LINEN; COMBIER, COURTESY MUNICIPALITÉ DE BAYEUX

MERLE SEVERY AND (OPPOSITE) W. E. ROSCHER, NATIONAL GEOGRAPHIC STAFF

World War II to spot German bombers. Along the quay, where the River Rother winds down to the sea, fishing boats were coming in. I headed for the Mermaid and a dinner of lobsters fresh from the Channel.

That night I reflected that Robert Louis Stevenson might well have had Rye in mind while writing the opening chapters of *Treasure Island*. Thackeray described Peacocke's School in his *Denis Duval*, and Henry James lived here in Lamb House the last 18 years of his life. It draws Jamesian pilgrims from all over the world.

Next day I drove to Bodiam Castle. Visit it as I did on a late summer day, its gray walls shining across its lily-starred moat, and you will see "one of the noblest façades of medieval military architecture in Britain." With its rectangular plan and its towers rising above gatehouse and corners, Bodiam looks like a film-maker's excuse for an epic. Grim barbs bristle from its portcullis; through openings in the stone above, boiling oil and lead could be poured on attackers.

On the Surrey border, where ancient Ashdown Forest forms a natural boundary, I visited Sheffield Park with its superb display of trees and flowering shrubs. Small lakes descending one into another seem to make the landscape recede and the garden look three times as large as it is. Nothing but the splashing fountains distracted me from the stateliness of the garden. Historian Edward Gibbon was a frequent visitor; perhaps here he found something of that "sober melancholy" with which he told of the fall of Rome.

MOONGLOW SOFTENS *stark cliffs of Beachy Head (opposite), whose lighthouse winks a warning 16 miles. No beach rims its toe; name comes from the Norman* beau chef, *beautiful headland. Bodies of tiny sea creatures—half a million to a teaspoon—built the chalk cliffs and downs.*

Ancients cut horses and men in downland turf, exposing the chalk. Long Man of Wilmington (upper), near the resort of Eastbourne, extends some 230 feet—probably the world's largest human figure. Date and purpose puzzle experts.

Bodiam Castle (left) broods over six centuries of peace. Erected against French invaders, who sacked Winchelsea and Rye in the 14th century, it was besieged but once, and fell without a fight when its rebel holders bowed to Richard III.

For centuries the rich and important have maintained country homes in Surrey. London was a few hours away by horse; now it's within easy commuting distance. Indeed, much of Surrey has been swallowed by "the Great Wen." Yet this corner of ancient Wessex retains some of the South's most attractive landscape – typically, a tamed and domesticated landscape.

Motoring through with friends from Ohio, I gazed at Surrey with new eyes. In towns like Godalming not a cottage is too small to have a garden. Clematis climbs on the half-timbered houses of Shere, and gardens form a patchwork of flowers.

I had not seen Guildford, Surrey's capital, since I was a boy before World War II. I was surprised to find it so little changed. The steep, cobbled High Street still climbs from the valley of the River Wey past gabled houses and old inns.

Guildford's brick cathedral, built this century, seems solid and practical from outside, but inside lofty aisles and plain glass give a noble impression of light and space. When I told a taxi driver I came from Hampshire, he said: "Then you'll prefer Winchester Cathedral to ours – just because it's older!"

All the modern folk of Wessex share this passion for their churches. In Rye locals

told me the church was "really the cathedral of East Sussex"; in Winchester people assured me that Canterbury and Westminster paled beside theirs. At Chichester they told me: "Ours is a Saxon foundation—nothing so late as the Normans!"

Near Dorking, I climbed Box Hill, a Surrey beauty spot which Keats visited while writing *Endymion*. Full of the peace of that countryside, I came down again to the Burford Bridge Hotel. Here Nelson spent some of his last hours ashore before boarding the *Victory* at Portsmouth for the Battle of Trafalgar. In the entrance hall I stopped to look at a picture of England's greatest admiral.

"And if it wasn't for him," growled a voice behind me, "you'd be living under General de Gaulle!" The growl belonged to an old naval friend I hadn't seen since 1945! In Surrey, as at Piccadilly Circus, you seem certain to meet someone you know.

On another hill nearby I ended my odyssey. Leith Hill soars nearly a thousand feet above the sea. From its crown I saw parts of six counties; on a clearer day I would have glimpsed the Channel beyond the Downs.

Wherever you go in Wessex, you are never far from the sea. And Alfred the Great and William the Conqueror seem to have been there just the day before.

PATRICK THURSTON

"**PAVED WITH BOULDERS,** *hard ends up," runs a wry comment on Henry James's "compact little pyramid of Rye," once lapped by the sea. Footsore folk on cobbled Mermaid Street (above) agree. Yarns that smugglers stored loot in cellars of the Mermaid (left) and escaped the law up a giant fireplace rang true when restorers of the 15th-century inn found booty.*

THE WEST COUNTRY

SOFT HILLS AND SPRAY-SWEPT SHORES

THE SORCERESS SEA once held this realm in thrall. She withdrew from the land, but her embrace lingers in the English Channel and the "Severn Sea." Her warm, moist breath awakens daffodils to an early spring, and nurtures a fruitful husbandry with its bounty of Devon cream, Cheddar cheese, Hereford cider, golden Wiltshire grain.

This is a gentle land, where "Melodious birds sing madrigals" and ponies frisk in moorland heather. This is a stern land, where winter seas snarl at towering cliffs and grim castles speak of border wars. This is a mysterious land, where Stonehenge broods on rites beyond our fathoming and sea mists waft a veil of myth over history's shards: Tintagel, Camelot, the Isle of Avalon – magic names of Arthurian legend. The lost land of Lyonnesse, where Tristram and Iseult knew the sweets and bitterness of their great romance. Glastonbury of the Grail.

The sea in Phoenician days brought traders seeking tin from Cornish veins. Romans came to mine Mendip lead, smelt iron in the Forest of Dean, bask in Bath's waters. They withdrew, turning a deaf ear to their Celtic citizens' cry: "The barbarians push us into the sea, the sea pushes us back to the barbarians!" The Saxon wave engulfed the land, swept the Celts into Cornwall's citadel, where they have held firm to this day. Sea dogs of Devon and bold Bristol mariners heeded the siren call to "golde, spices, aromatikes, and pretiose stones" and turned the barricading sea into a highroad to lands beyond. Today travelers from distant shores recross the sea to explore this green peninsula glazed with golden legend.

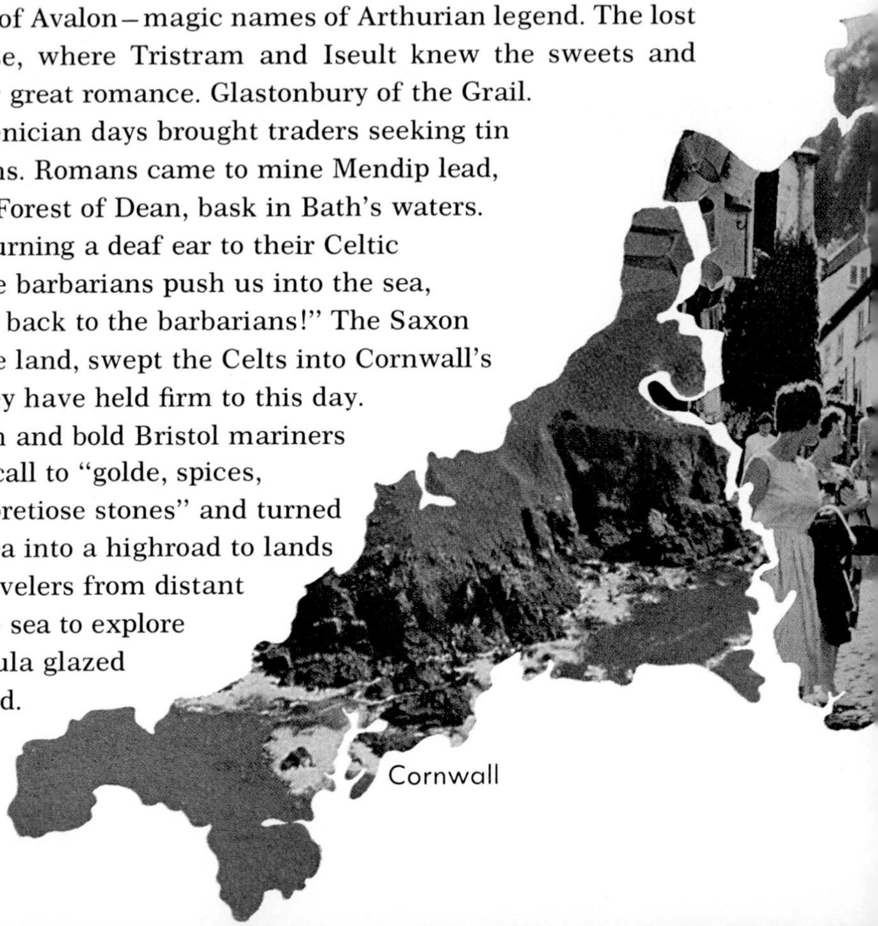

Herefordshire
London
Gloucestershire
Monmouthshire
Somerset
Wiltshire
CADBURY'S
milk flake
Dorset
Devon

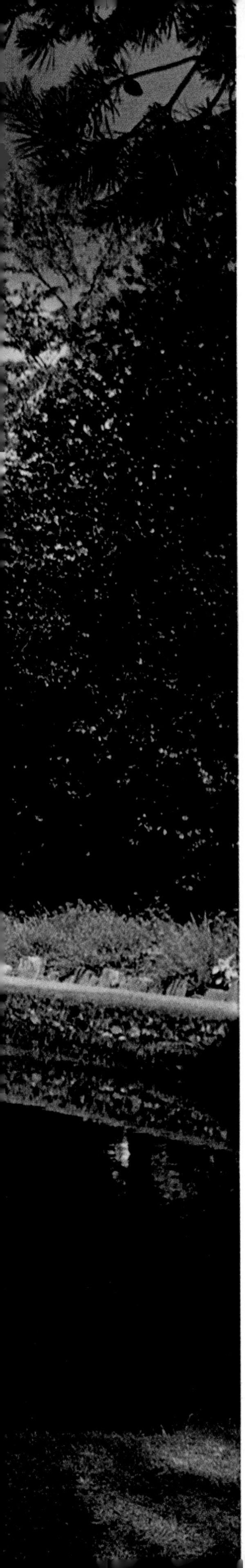

SOMERSET AND SISTER SHIRES

From a thatched home in England's "Middle West" Merle Severy discovers enchanted vales, the warmth of country life, the glory of great cathedrals

THE RAIN HAS STOPPED. I look past the thatched eaves and the rose garden, the handwrought iron gate and the lane that sees but a dozen cars a day. Cows file into the lower pasture. Mist rises from hedgerowed fields that march up the slopes. Leaves of the copper beech gleam outside my window. The gardener, Mr. Hardwell, tends the flower beds amid close-clipped lawns, trailed by his four-year-old son.

Days have ripened, and I feel the first tingle of autumn. I have seen evening shadows caress these gentle Somerset hills, moonlight bathe the meadows, morning haze, pelting showers, and sunset glow remold the scene. The play of light and shadow would exalt a Constable – and madden a photographer.

Downstairs, beyond the beamed dining room with its yawning fireplace, Mrs. Leslie, lady of the house, sits in her oak-paneled library. Upstairs with me in our wing are my wife Patricia and our two small children. This is Discove, a rambling house, 17th century mostly, with a scattering of outbuildings.

On earlier English journeys, we skipped from inn to inn. This time we sought a center from which to explore England's "Middle West," a home where we could share country life, seeing it from the inside as the hasty stranger seldom does. We wanted to be near Wells, our favorite medieval city. And Glastonbury, "holyest earthe in England," enriched by Arthurian legend. And Bath, handsomest of spas, haunted by Roman memories and Georgian ghosts. We would revisit Hardy country in Dorset, and at Stonehenge in Wiltshire we wanted as Henry James did "to put a hundred questions to these rough-hewn giants as they bend in grim contemplation of their fallen companions."

And what a feast of great houses! Longleat, "Treasure house of the West," Wilton, Stourhead, Montacute, and Mompesson, that Georgian gem in a necklace of houses round Salisbury's close. What a magnificent variety of cathedrals! Salisbury, lean, austere as the Salisbury Plain, thrusting its proud spire above the Avon meadows. Wells, warm, intimate, cupped in green hills. Gloucester,

SUMMER SETS A GREEN GARLAND *round Wells Cathedral, Somerset shrine three centuries abuilding. England's smallest episcopal city nestles beyond its close. Abundant springs that gave Wells its name still water the Bishop's Palace moat, relic of tiffs between bishop and burghers.*

MERLE SEVERY, NATIONAL GEOGRAPHIC STAFF

half stern Norman, half soaring Gothic. Hereford, earthy in its red sandstone, conservative as its rural diocese.

We placed a notice for a house in the *Times* and the *Western Morning News* and settled in a fine old inn to explore Wells while waiting for replies. Patricia poked into shops along the lovely curved High Street. Little Randall was entranced by the sparkling streams that gurgled down its gutters – water from the wells.

"*Hoc fonte derivata copia*–'from this source derives abundance.' " Mrs. Johnson, wife of the city engineer, read it from her embroidery of Wells's arms (page 9). "Actually there are seven wells beyond the cathedral's east end, not three as on the shield. The building floats on gravel, cushioned against tremors. Like a baby in the womb."

"Wells has only about 7,000 people, but the cathedral makes it a city," explained C. Wyndham Harris, Solicitor, in his office on Market Place. He chuckled as he recalled an American visitor who asked to see early diocesan records. A clerk was back in a moment with weighty ledgers. The American marveled. "You produce 14th-century records at the drop of a hat. In my office they can hardly find last week's letters!"

The bustle of High Street faded as I entered the cathedral close. Walled off from the town's distractions, I could savor the broad west front adorned by more than 300 noble figures. Inside, as spare as the façade is ornate, the pointed Early English nave looks like an upturned boat – nave comes from *navis*, ship.

I never knew stone could be so beautiful: limestone lacing the chantry chapels, a forest of delicate stone in the retrochoir. Beyond a curving flight of steps worn by the feet of centuries, the central pillar of the chapter house fans into a canopy of ribs.

Time and again I returned to explore "dim nooks of holiness," to glory in the singing color of the windows, to watch knights joust in the noon tournament above the 600-year-old clock. I'm convinced a Gothic cathedral should be sipped like fine wine, not gulped. It is not frozen for eternity like a Greek temple. It is a living organism, evolving over the centuries, expressing the faith of its people in a medley of once-fashionable styles.

As we awaited replies to our ad we watched the round of life continue: Wells masons replacing their forefathers' stones ("You don't wear the same suit forever, do you?"). Tousled lads scampering in to become transformed by the magic of white surplices into the angelic voices of evensong. A burst of joyous pealing when a bride in flowing white and her groom emerge at the west door. In the Middle Ages the wedding itself would take place outside so the populace could stand witness. "Housbondes at chirche-dore I have had fyve," said Chaucer's Wife of Bath.

Hasten through and you miss the earthy motifs of capitals overhead – men robbing an orchard, a man in the agony of toothache. Medieval craftsmen would lavish exquisite care on ceiling bosses that God alone could see. (Wells is small; here you too can see.) The unhurried eye delights in the tennis racket, cards, dice, and guitar in the memorial brass of a kneeling cavalier.

At Bath Abbey craftsmen provided ladders up buttresses for angels to climb. In a dim aisle at Gloucester you find a plaque to the composer of the tune later used for the *Star-Spangled Banner*. And outside Bristol's St. Mary Redcliffe, which Queen Bess and I consider "the fairest, the goodliest, and most famous parish church in England," is a monument to the church cat.

TALES OF A WITCH lured me into the water-gouged Mendip Hills. At Wookey Hole I saw a brooding stalagmite – "the witch a monk had turned to stone" – and hyena bones that spoke of a warmer prehistoric age. I pressed on to Cheddar Gorge, a gash in the limestone tableland thronged

BISHOP'S EYE, *gateway to his palace, casts stony stare on hawkers in Wells Market Place. Here Judge Jeffreys staged one of his Bloody Assizes, a judicial mopping up after Monmouth's rebellion against James II collapsed. Hundreds of West Countrymen were hanged or banished. In Penniless Porch at the plaza's far angle beggars once coaxed alms from churchgoers.*

Lower: Hedgerows seam a quilted tump beyond a rain-glazed country lane near Wells.

MERLE SEVERY, NATIONAL GEOGRAPHIC STAFF

with excursionists. The skeleton of Cheddar Man gazed at me from 12,000-year-old eye sockets as I studied flint tools in the museum at Gough's Caves.

From the top of the chasm I walked down between cliff walls that steadily grew more dramatic. Cheddar Gorge isn't Grand Canyon. But England isn't Arizona. In a tight little isle where nature's gradations are subtle, one miniaturizes his expectations. The gorge became unexpectedly grand.

I have known the name Cheddar for as long as I have chewed cheese – and I never tasted better cheddar than that made on Woodford Farm, near Wells. Its operator, Edward Harding, proudly showed me about his broad acres grazed by Friesian herds. "When I wur a bwoy I had nothing," he said in a broad Somerset accent. "My feyther lost a leg on the railway. I worked on a varm for 30 bob a week. Now I pay my men 17 quid and none o' they work near zo long as I done. Zhall us go hround the back?"

I learned later that Somerset dialect reflects the court language of King Alfred – Anglo-Saxon. Somerset folk avoid Latin roots. "I bin looken out var 'ee" one will say, instead of "I've been expecting you."

Harding hefted a cheese from a shelf and presented it. When Patricia and I cut into it, our smiles spoke as eloquently as the prizes that hung in farmer Harding's shed.

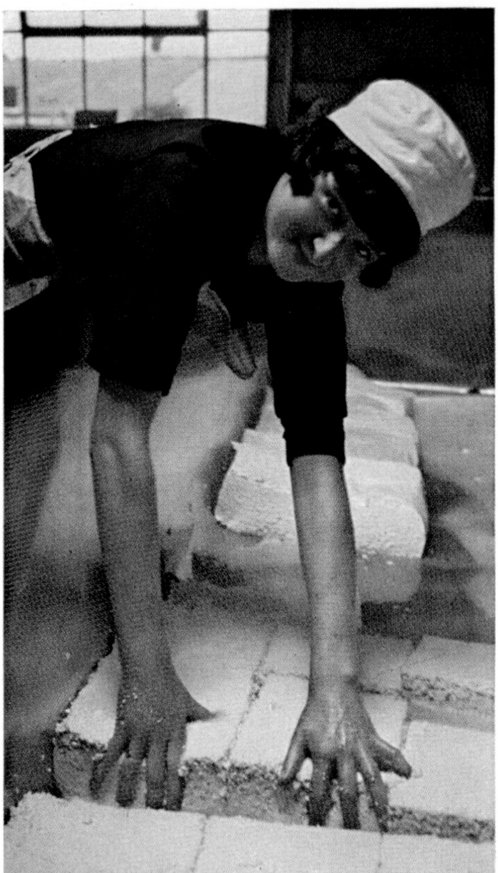

MERLE SEVERY, NATIONAL GEOGRAPHIC STAFF

DRIVING along the ancient Vale of Avalon, I watched Glastonbury Tor rise like a beacon from the peat moors. Here prehistoric lake dwellers once built islands and raised villages of conical huts. Medieval monks drained the marshes, but winter floods still wash over them. When morning mists drift across the vale, one can imagine a white-clad arm rising from the water, brandishing the great sword Excalibur, and see the dark barge bringing King Arthur to the Isle of Avalon for burial.

Glastonbury fascinates me. Each time I walk through the abbey ruins I feel a sense of wonder that goes beyond the legends of Joseph of Arimathea, the Chalice Well, the Holy Grail, noble Arthur and radiant Guinevere. One day I strolled toward the abbot's kitchen – intact despite the Reformation's misguided zeal – and heard singing, the pure tone of Latin polyphony. I expected to see black-robed monks as I entered the lofty vaulted chamber. But here, standing between great corner fireplaces, looking up at walls that resounded *Dona nobis pacem* – "Give us peace" – was a group of German boys in knapsacks and shorts. They had burst into spontaneous song.

The George and Pilgrims Inn had sheltered pilgrims to this abbey, venerated above all others in England. The innkeeper took me up to a timbered room, flung open the windows: "Henry VIII stood here in 1539 and watched the abbey's destruction."

CHASM AND CHEESE *earn Cheddar its fame. Mendip cliffs tower 430 feet over hikers in Cheddar Gorge (right). Nearby Burrington Combe inspired a famous hymn. Sheltering from a storm, an 18th-century clergyman wrote: "Rock of ages, cleft for me, Let me hide myself in thee."*

Cheese lovers gorge on cheddar, born in the 1600's when locals tried stacking curd mats (left) – "cheddaring" – to expel whey. Aging sets flavor: months for mild, years for sharp.

EAGER SPADES *delve into Arthurian legend and early Christianity in Somerset. Site of fabled Camelot? Almost certainly at Cadbury Castle, an Iron Age hill fort near Sparkford, declared archeologist Sir Mortimer Wheeler after diggers turned up imported sixth-century pottery there.*

Trenches atop 521-foot Glastonbury Tor (left), 12 miles away, yielded similar wares, which only a rich chieftain like Arthur could afford. Here a lake once lapped the Isle of Avalon; gaunt ruins of great Glastonbury Abbey (below) guard "King Arthur's tomb." Here too, tradition tells us, Joseph of Arimathea came with the Holy Grail, built a wattle church, and planted his thorn staff. Glastonbury thorns still bloom at Christmastide, "mindful of our Lord."

MERLE SEVERY, NATIONAL GEOGRAPHIC STAFF

SOMERSET GUILD *of Craftsmen, whose work adorns many a church, keeps old skills alive. Its Master, Lt. Col. J. A. Garton, here shapes iron at his Pylle Manor forge. The Guild's directory lists carvers, wheelwrights, organ builders, a dog-hair spinner, and the printers who publish it. In Taunton visitors may see the Guildhall, furnished wholly by members' hands.*

Hearsay rather than history, I realized. Yet I felt the massive presence of Henry, spread-legged, eyes like ice in a face grown gross, such animal magnetism that men he ordered hanged unjustly still shouted their loyalty to him from the scaffold. Then I remembered Glastonbury's beloved old Abbot Whiting, hanged, drawn, and quartered on the Tor; I saw great pillars standing empty-armed against the sky, exquisitely carved doorways leading to nothing. What a monument to lust and greed!

Back in Wells I visited Dr. Reid, member of the archeological group which had excavated for ten years at Glastonbury. Fresh dirt showed on his trouser knees. "I just returned from our excavations at Witham," the retired schoolmaster explained. "First Carthusian monastery in England. Henry II founded it in penance for Becket's murder at Canterbury.

"What people call 'Witham Priory' is probably the lay brethren's dormitory," he went on. "The priory church is a mile away. We spotted it in this aerial photograph. See that oblong in the field? That's it."

Much of England's history, written on the land, has been read from the skies: tracks

across the downs where men dragged monoliths for Stonehenge, Roman roads and camps, the sites of fishponds, salt pans, mills, iron mines, and marlpits "auunciently digged in fields." Flying cameras reveal square Celtic fields and long strips plowed by Saxon serfs. A dry spell browns the grass on the former ridges, but the furrows stay green. The length of the medieval furrow—the distance an ox team would pull before tiring—gave us our furlong, 220 yards.

The "changeless" landscape we see today mainly reflects the 18th-century hand of man, enclosing with hedgerows fields that ran endlessly to the eye.

Patricia and I still sought our niche in this countryside, but though responses to our ad made pleasant reading none quite filled the bill. Then, one day, a lady's voice came on the phone: "It may not be what you're looking for, but I have a historic home. My children have grown up and gone, so I have lots of room—it's the longest thatched house in England. John Steinbeck found it a nice place to write. Perhaps. . . ."

Discove. It was love at first sight.

THOUGH FOUR OUT OF FIVE English live in cities, their hearts are in the countryside, as in Tudor days when folk looked not to London but to the manor house. "Fate has but little Distinction set Betwixt the Counter and the Coronet," said Daniel Defoe, noting that 18th-century townsmen, enriched by trade, bought estates and married their daughters into insolvent but titled families. Today's long weekend offers the solace of sylvan acres. The midweek Londoner of tight-furled umbrella, bowler hat, and folded *Times* becomes the weekend squire in houndstooth jacket, baggy flannels, and smelly pipe. He putters in his garden, perhaps shoots some pheasant. Thus does he nourish his spirit.

The countryside nourishes more than the spirit. Medieval kings moved from castle to castle, since it was easier to bring the king to the food than the food to the king. The entire court would eat its way through the land like locusts.

Discove's owner, Mrs. Leslie, designs ceramics in Chelsea and shuttles to the estate, where she grows barley. Her Home Farm in nearby Wincanton supplies cows, pigs, chickens, and vegetables. Her neighbor, Henry Peregrine Rennie Hoare, of Hoare's Bank in London ("Twenty-two years older than the Bank of England," he says with a twinkle), is never happier than when overseeing ancestral acres at Stourhead.

Discove days rolled by pleasantly. The little red truck arrived in the cobbled back court with the postman, who made change for stamp money laid on the entry table or brought it on the morrow. Mrs. Martin, the housekeeper, hummed in the kitchen, one eye on the children. At tea, she'd press on us crumpets hot from the oven, streaming with Somerset butter. "You've got to eat them directly or they go all queer." She responded to my feeblest jokes with rumbling convulsions of laughter: "My, Mr. Severy, but you're switched on!" Or "Ooo now, all your circuits are working!"

Mrs. Rice, joined by her children, came to do laundry and cleaning, riding the two miles from Bruton with Mr. Green ("Coach and Car Hire, Quaperlake House"). He ran out of petrol in the driveway one day, borrowed some from Mr. Hardwell's mower, and his passengers piled out to push.

EXMOOR MISTS *and hoofbeats on heathered Winsford Hill evoke a scene from* Lorna Doone: *John Ridd pursuing evil Carver Doone. After a titanic struggle, Ridd flings his foe into a black bog, which sucks him in "like the thirsty lips of death." Then the yeoman gallops back to Lorna, a highborn maiden the Doones had held captive. R. D. Blackmore based his 1869 novel on an outlaw clan along the Devon border.*

Dunster's octagonal Yarn Market (below) recalls the wool trade. Luttrells have lived in the castle since 1376. Storybook villages in the region delight visitors. Selworthy's avalanche of thatch faces 1,705-foot Dunkery Beacon, where signals once flamed.

MERLE SEVERY, NATIONAL GEOGRAPHIC STAFF

The eldest Rice children, Anne, 11, and Colin, 9, offered to guide me around Bruton. They began by sprinting up a ruin-crowned hill to show me a view Anne promised was "smashing." It was. The stone-built town of some 1,700 souls nestled in the Brue valley, its noble 15th-century church rising against a backdrop of meadows and groves. Bruton Parish Church—it had a familiar ring. Then I recalled the church in Colonial Williamsburg and an early Virginia governor, Sir William Berkeley of Bruton.

We crossed a humpbacked bridge used by packhorses when Bruton thrived as a cloth center. Anne proudly showed me the grammar school where she would start in fall. She had passed her "11-plus" exams and qualified for the university preparatory course. Had she failed, she would have entered the secondary modern in Wincanton, perhaps to learn a trade. In some areas, comprehensive schools erase the distinction between grammar and secondary modern.

"Mum signed a paper that I'd stay in school five years or she'd pay back my tuition. Of course I can stay until I'm 18. If I pass my A-level exams and find a place, the state will pay for my university."

Daily I explored the countryside, driving on the left as Englishmen do because their ancestors on horses felt safer passing on the sword-arm side. At times I sped arrow-straight along Fosse Way, where the Roman engineer's stern hand still guides today's traffic. More often I followed vagabond lanes which squires of Tom Jones's day right-angled around their newly hedged fields. Henry Fielding's book and the rollicking movie came to life here. Born near Glastonbury, the author based Squire Western and Squire Allworthy on Bath acquaintances. I recognized stage sets when I poked into the Dorset village of Cerne Abbas.

We took Anne and Colin to Weston super Mare, where thronged piers stride into the Bristol Channel. Welsh excursionists flock here. On a scenic tour through the Vale of Taunton we found, as did Elizabethan William Camden, that it "wonderfully contenteth the eyes of the beholders."

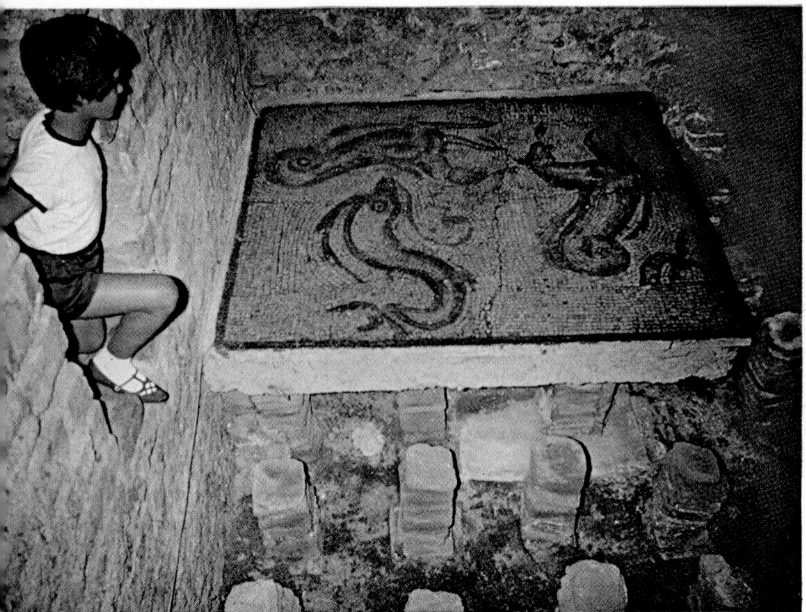

MERLE SEVERY, NATIONAL GEOGRAPHIC STAFF

BATH, *famed Somerset spa, was born of hot springs gushing amid seven hills. Men from another seven-hilled city came to this sacred spot and called it Aquae Sulis, for a native deity. They built a great bath, lining it with Mendip lead, and piped in 120° water 1,900 years ago.*

For three centuries Romans bathed, built, worshiped their goddess Minerva. Centurions and fat merchants plunged into radioactive waters now framed by Victorian statues and the pinnacles of Bath Abbey (opposite).

Roman hypocaust (left) carried furnace air under tiled floors to heat baths and villas. In modern Britain, Churchill rued, "a smaller proportion of the whole population dwells in centrally heated houses."

I noticed that Somerset resembles a green lake with three islands—the Mendip Hills near Wells, the Quantocks near Taunton, and the Brendon Hills rising to the purple uplands of Exmoor.

At Nether Stowey, below the Quantocks, we visited the room where Coleridge wrote *The Ancient Mariner*, inspired by a Bristol sailor who had sought the Northwest Passage. We wandered Exmoor lanes, dipping into a steep valley to follow Badgworthy Water through the haunts of the Doones.

OUR CIRCLE of acquaintances broadened. We met Mrs. Leslie's friends, and they invited us to their country homes. For Randall's birthday she gave a party, and neighbors flocked in with their children. The youngster of a countess romped with the gardener's child.

I admired Mrs. Leslie's wrought iron gate. "Archie Garton made that," she told me. "He's a justice of the peace, president of our big agricultural show at Shepton Mallet, and an authority on Somerset dialect and crafts."

Soon I was talking to Colonel Garton in the 17th-century manor house at Pylle. How did a military man come to learn rural crafts? His sister died when he was a boy, and the lonely child found companionship among craftsmen on the estate. He watched the wheelwright, the blacksmith, the cooper at work and hesitatingly tried their tools. He learned the thrill of the bite of the plane, the creative joy of seeing red-hot iron take shape under his blows. He learned the dialect, the mellow country philosophy.

He became master of Pylle Manor and master of the Somerset Guild of Craftsmen.

I watched him at his anvil, blows ringing, his strong face showing the wisdom of 74 years. He led me into the manor church which he had beautified, carving figures on the oaken pulpit, fashioning chandeliers that hung from the beams. We climbed to its tower and looked over the verdant fields where oaks and beeches stood like islands of serenity. He told me of feeling at one with God's work, and I understood.

Browsing Mrs. Leslie's library filled Patricia and me with images of 18th-century Bath. We joined the traffic heading for the famed "spaw," as Dr. Johnson spelled it. "One would think that the English were ducks," grumbled Horace Walpole, "they are forever waddling to the waters."

In the heart of the stately city, which rises in terraces and crescents above the Avon, our imaginations washed the soot from Georgian façades so they glowed once more with creamy Bath stone. Tires on tarmac became stagecoach wheels clattering on cobbles as our steaming horses jingled along the High Street. Now the Abbey bells ring; a band strikes up. A stout, officious man in plum-colored waistcoat opens the coach door, sweeps off his white tricorn, and bows low. Beau Nash, "King of Bath!"

BARE FEET TREAD *where elegance once promenaded; shopping bags blossom where Defoe saw beauty that "dazzles the eyes." But Bath, the city Swinburne called "a Queen enchanted," still charms those who stroll its flower-decked streets.*

At Parade Gardens by the Avon a Punch and Judy show enthralls young fans of an old art. Punch was Pulcinella of Italy when Pepys applauded him in Covent Garden in 1662. But he shed Continental manners and name and donned the rowdy, cudgel-swinging character that fits him like the glove he is. Punch took a wife, Judy, who tamed him somewhat. Fox and others joined his troupe. In the magic hands of roving puppeteers, he became immortal. In 1841 Punch gave his name to a magazine as cheeky as he.

MERLE SEVERY, NATIONAL GEOGRAPHIC STAFF

In our pleasant fantasy, he leads us through Bath Street's arcades among strollers in farthingales, knee breeches, and powdered wigs. On the North Parade we see him again, mounting a chariot hauled by six grays, his lace-clad lackeys bearing gleaming post horns.

Resplendent but penniless when he arrived here, Beau soon put winnings at the gaming tables into Hoare's Bank. Glibly he assumed the role of Bath's Master of Ceremonies, abruptly vacated by a losing duelist. Prudently he banished swords from public places. As "arbiter of elegance," he once tore a lace apron off a duchess, declaring she looked like her servant.

We picture him presiding over the Assembly Rooms under glittering chandeliers. ("The ball opens with a minuet danced by two people of the highest rank present," Oliver Goldsmith reminds us helpfully.) As musicians begin the stately measures and the floor shimmers with silks and embroidery, a lady refuses to dance. "Damn you, Madam!" blazes Nash. "What business have you here if you do not dance?" At the stroke of eleven, Beau orders an end. Princess Amelia begs for one more dance. But no. Not even for the daughter of George II.

In fanciful disregard of time, I turn to Jane Austen, magically at my side. "I hope you have had an agreeable ball?"

"Very agreeable indeed," Miss Austen replies, vainly endeavoring to hide a great yawn.

The magic of Bath continues. We stroll down Milsom Street among ladies of fashion, dandies, mountebanks. Liveried lackeys hand their mistresses into sedan chairs, tops up to accommodate towering headdresses. We see Tobias Smollett mulling his vitriolic words: "Every upstart of fortune, harnessed in the trappings of the mode, presents himself at Bath.... Even the wives and daughters of low tradesmen, who, like shovel-nosed sharks, prey upon the blubber of those uncouth whales of fortune, are infected with the same rage of displaying their importance."

We join the ostentatious parade, clopping across Pulteney Bridge in a gilded coach, peering at the Florentine shops over the foaming Avon, traversing Great Pulteney Street, where I tip

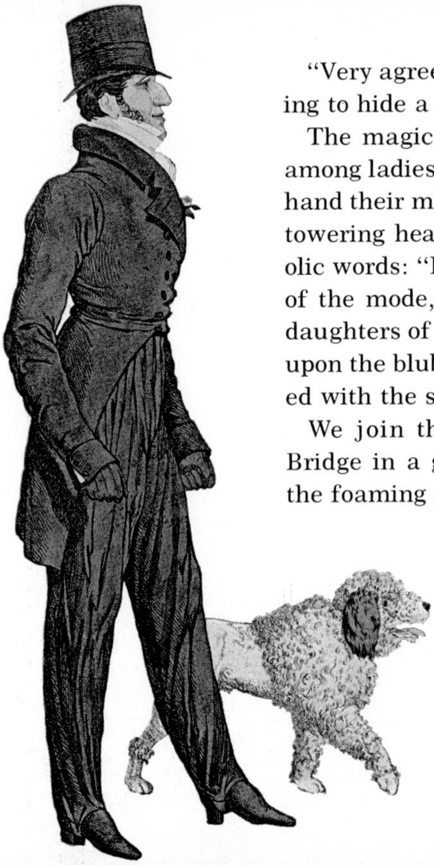

RESPLENDENT STAGE *for Georgian beauty and Regency beau, Bath mirrored in its warm stone the fashions of each age. Sarah Siddons, "queen of tears," began her reign here, in a theater that dispensed handkerchiefs for its weeping patrons. Gainsborough, also of Bath, exclaimed when he painted her (left): "Damn your nose, Madam, there's no end to it!"*

"MRS. SIDDONS" BY THOMAS GAINSBOROUGH, 1784; NATIONAL GALLERY, LONDON
UPPER: DUKE OF BEAUFORT BY R. DIGHTON, 1817
RIGHT: MERLE SEVERY, NATIONAL GEOGRAPHIC STAFF

my hat to passing carriages. We drive past Queen Square and round the Circus, built by the John Woods, father and son, like the Colosseum "turned inside out."

Time's doors open, and we greet William Pitt the Elder and his fellow resident James Wolfe, whom he will order to a hero's death at Quebec. We see Gainsborough—in 16 years his fees for a portrait jump from five to forty guineas. We nod to Clive of India, Wordsworth, Scott, Thackeray, and David Livingstone, back from Africa. Dr. Johnson, "blowing out his breath like a whale," exclaims that mixed bathing is a "barbarity that he believed could not be paralleled in any part of the world."

Herschel, organist at the Octagon, rushes out to tell us he has discovered a new planet with the telescope he built. Uranus, we muse—its discoverer another of England's magnificent amateurs.

Here Richard Sheridan finds inspiration for *The Rivals*—and the girl, Elizabeth Linley, over whom he fights two duels. A nurse for her family, Emma Hart, will become Lady Hamilton—and on the same street is the house where Horatio Nelson takes the curing waters.

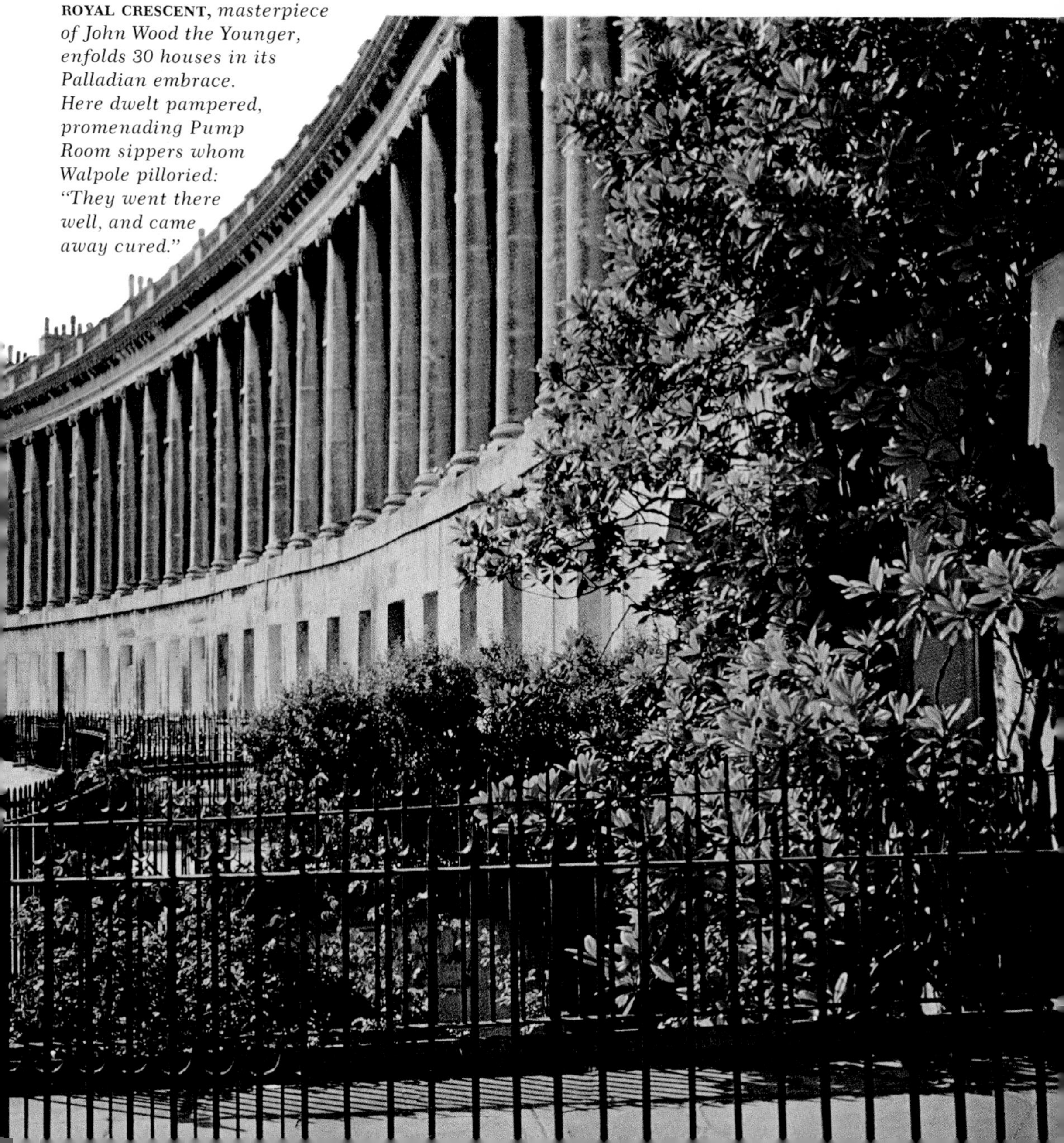

ROYAL CRESCENT, *masterpiece of John Wood the Younger, enfolds 30 houses in its Palladian embrace. Here dwelt pampered, promenading Pump Room sippers whom Walpole pilloried: "They went there well, and came away cured."*

Now, near the Royal Crescent, we meet Mr. Pickwick puffing uphill. He has had a quarter of a pint of the waters and "declared, in the most solemn and emphatic terms, that he felt a great deal better." And we, remembering our Dickens, are much delighted, though we "had not been previously aware that there was anything the matter with him."

We must pay respects to Ralph Allen, who discovered the beauty of Bath stone, and promoted the building of the Georgian city while reforming England's postal system. Dissatisfied with the view from his town house, he has built on a facing hill a Sham Castle. We survey it with respect, for not every man can execute a ruin. And we ride up the hills to see his Palladian mansion, Prior Park, designed "not only to see all Bath but for all Bath to see."

We return to the Pump Room, finding there the ghostly whisper of the gossip that flows with tea: "And at each Sip a Lady's Honour dies." But we overhear, as we slip back into 20th-century reality, the echo of a wistful feminine voice, "Farewell, dear Bath, nowhere so much scandal, nowhere so little sin."

MERLE SEVERY, NATIONAL GEOGRAPHIC STAFF

WE HAD our little dramas at Discove. Our daughter Karen, teething, loved to taste the English countryside. Into her mouth she popped a bee. It did what any unjustly treated English bee would do. It stung.

Worried by possible allergic reaction, the Bruton doctor let Karen "jump the queue" in his waiting room for her antihistamine injection. No charge. Randall ran up a 104° temperature. A doctor called at Discove, gave penicillin, and returned daily until the toddler was back on his feet. No charge.

"This is a holiday for me," said 28-year-old Dr. Leonard, down from Birmingham to fill in for one of Bruton's two doctors. He liked the West Country so much he was soon to join a Wiltshire clinic – after checking that the territory would provide him at least 1,500 patients. (The National Health Service stipulates this minimum to keep doctors from flocking to some areas, leaving others under-doctored.) "Of course we are free to take private patients on the side."

I remembered the private doctor who had prescribed a sedative for Randall in London. Charge: three guineas ($9.00).

Dr. Leonard estimated he'd make £4,000 ($11,200) a year. "Not as much as barristers or architects, but I have few complaints. The state paid my way from primary school through medical school. I owe something in return. Certainly, some patients come in with minor illnesses, and I could use secretarial help. But I'm for National Health – it gives people a sense of security."

Each time I drove eastward from Discove I saw a great tower on the horizon. "King Alfred's Tower," Mrs. Leslie told me. "One of Rennie Hoare's ancestors built it in Stourhead Park in the 18th century." It marks the traditional site on Kingsettle (king's seat) Hill where Alfred raised his standard in 878 to repel Danish invaders.

CASTLE COMBE *snuggles in a Wiltshire valley. Trees above the church hide the ruined castle of Sir John Fastolf, model, some say, for Shakespeare's Falstaff – but in girth not gusto. Fastolf let a town pub open only one day a week.*

Saxon church in Bradford on Avon (left) has changed little in a thousand years. Nearby stands a 14th-century tithe barn where vicars stored their tenth of worshipers' produce.

That year had begun darkly. The Danes had swept into Wessex, and men despaired that England was lost. Gone were the royal manors at Chippenham and Wilton, where the log fire leapt on the hearth, and torches cast shadows in the great hall as king and warriors quaffed mead from their horns.

With a small band of thanes, Alfred hid in the marshes along Somerset's River Parrett. They sallied out to strike foraging Danes, to scout their movements, and to spread word to loyal men of Wessex where to assemble when Alfred called for battle.

In May the host gathered on Kingsettle Hill and marched northeast. At Edington, near Westbury, they met the Danes. Alfred "closed his ranks, shield locked with shield, and fought fiercely against the entire heathen host," a chronicler records. "At last by God's will he won his victory. . . ."

I retraced Alfred's steps from the now drained marshes of Athelney to bustling Chippenham, where he captured the Danish base, and to Wedmore whose church window recalls his treaty with the heathen king he baptized. At sunset I drove up Westbury Hill. Lovers strolled hand in hand to look at the great chalk horse carved in the turf. The dying sun reddened the plain where Alfred freed Wessex from the Dane.

Kingsettle Hill, watershed of history, is also a dividing line in geography. To the west lie Somerset valleys tucked in a green quilt. To the east roll the chalk uplands of Wiltshire, spare and sparsely populated. On

ELEGANT GLOW *of 18th-century Bristol rekindles in the Georgian House, sumptuous symbol of the era when ships dropped with the tide down the Avon on triangular trade: to Africa for slaves, borne in holds of horror to auction blocks in America and the West Indies; then home laden with tobacco or sugar. From those imports evolved chocolate and cigarette industries. Slaving was outlawed in 1807.*

A wine port since Bordeaux flowed in with the Normans, Bristol bottles and re-exports wines. In the ancient cellars of Harveys of Bristol, its restaurant offers a 1,000-wine list. There an expert (right) decants a fine vintage Burgundy in a solemn rite. Watching for sediment silhouetted by a candle's flame, he pours off clear wine.

DEAN CONGER AND (UPPER LEFT) MERLE SEVERY, BOTH NATIONAL GEOGRAPHIC STAFF

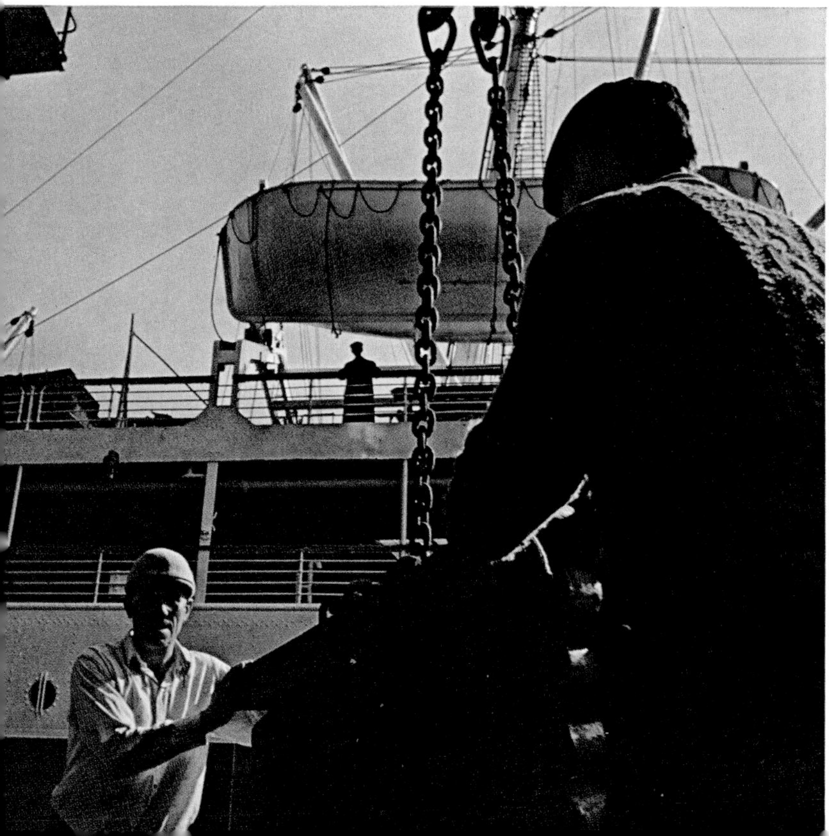

TRAFFIC *laces Bristol, towered by its University. Dockers heft cargo on a waterfront that looks west. Henry VII, who "could not endure to see trade sick," in 1497 sent John Cabot "ploughing the unknown seas." Cabot, courting Cathay's riches, found cod off Cape Breton. Henry gave him £10 for discovering the "new found land." Spurred by writings of Richard Hakluyt, prebend of Bristol Cathedral, bold mariners and merchants put Bristol in the van of New World trade.*

Nazi bombs missed the first Methodist chapel, founded here by John Wesley in 1739. Traveling by horse 5,000 miles a year, Wesley brought evangelical hope to the oppressed in an age when a child could be hanged for stealing a handkerchief.

this watershed is born the Stour, and here that infant river waters Stourhead's garden, the most beautiful landscaping Patricia and I have ever seen.

Rennie Hoare himself showed us about the Palladian mansion at Stourhead, first introducing us to some of his ancestors in the pedimented entrance hall. "That's Sir Richard, the goldsmith who founded Hoare's Bank. Lord Mayor of London in 1713. This is Good Henry, his son, who bought the estate in 1720. He pulled down the old house and built this one."

Good Henry looked full of philanthropy.

"His older brother is known as Naughty Richard. Trading ventures went awry and

WILTON HOUSE SPLENDOR *surrounds Charles I's children—one of the Van Dycks in a palatial state room designed by Inigo Jones. Royalty came in person too, as did Shakespeare's players, Ben Jonson, Spenser, Marlowe, Donne, and Sir Philip Sidney, who wrote* Arcadia *here.*

Upper: Furnishings reflect the magnificence of Elizabethan Montacute House in Somerset.

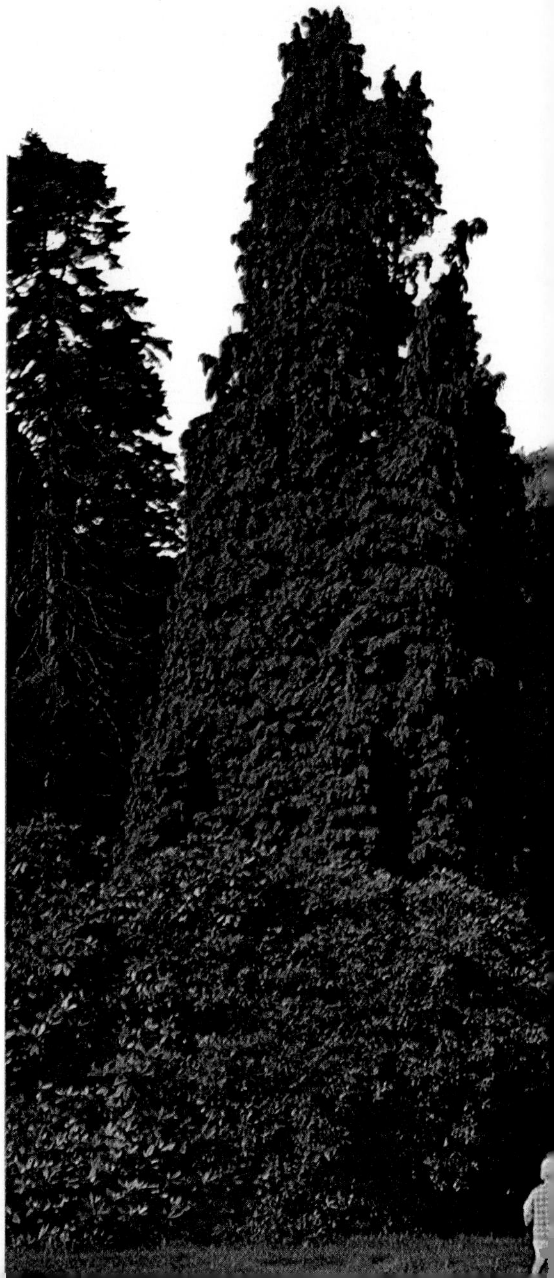

MERLE SEVERY, NATIONAL GEOGRAPHIC STAFF

STOURHEAD, *England's first landscape garden, was created by an amateur. In 1741, banker Henry Hoare conceived this sylvan lake with Roman bridge, Pantheon, and river god (above) in a grotto. Today's Henry (Rennie) Hoare peruses the library treasures.*

he ran up an overdraft of £62,000. And here's Sir Henry Ainslie Hoare, the Black Sheep. He gambled so much the family paid him not to be in the bank.

"This is Henry the Magnificent on a white horse. He created the gardens."

In the light, spacious library of another ancestor, Richard the Historian, I thought of Chaucer's Clerk of Oxenford, who yearned to possess "twenty bokes, clad in blak or reed"—lofty ambition in a day when scribes would "stoupe and stare upon the shepes skyne." I recalled William Caxton's proud announcement in his first printed volume: "It is not wreton with penne and ynke as other bokes ben," for all the copies "thus enpryntid... were begonne in oon day, and also fynysshid in oon day." And as I gazed at row upon row of Richard's books, leather backs shielding "the wisdom and learned folly" of the ages, I yearned to break the bonds of time and read through this English gentleman's library.

Rennie opened French doors onto a garden. A pair of Labrador retrievers frisked at his side as we walked down a luxuriantly wooded path to the pleasure grounds. We came to a crossing. Patricia and I started left. "No, you must circle the lake to the right," he gently directed. "That is the way Henry the Magnificent planned—so you behold each scene to best advantage."

Before Stourhead's day English gardens aped the rigid formality of Versailles. Partisans of geometric planting agreed with the clergyman who rued irregularity in the Creator's stars: "What a beautiful hemisphere they could have made if they had been placed in rank and order . . . according to the rules and acts of symmetry."

At Stourhead, man joined nature to fashion a freer beauty. A series of idyllic views unfolded before us, surprise adding zest to expectation. One view across the 20-acre lake led our eyes to the Pantheon; another to the Temple of the Sun, half-hidden on a

MERLE SEVERY, NATIONAL GEOGRAPHIC STAFF. LEFT: ADAM WOOLFITT

GOLD OF WILTSHIRE *ripples on its grainfields. Combine reaps behind Col. Godfrey Jeans (at left), "barley baron" of Broad Chalke, near Salisbury. He farms 2,200 acres, turning barley into beef.*

leafy slope. Ahead, unearthly light inside the Grotto revealed a river god emptying an urn from which flows a spring that feeds the Stour. Another gushes from the watery couch of a reclining nymph.

As I walked enthralled, the voice of Henry Rennie Hoare faded, and Henry the Magnificent strode beside me. I could hear the creak of carts as shouting workmen sculptured the barren slopes, dammed the tiny river to create a three-armed lake, built temples and a five-arched bridge. I shared Henry's vision as he planted firs and beeches that would grow tall and spread their limbs. A hundred years would pass before the gardens reached their prime, but he could see it all. Time did not matter. Stourhead and the family would always be there.

ENGLAND'S TIMELESSNESS struck me most forcibly at Stonehenge. It was harvest time, and fields of golden grain bent to the breeze. Combines chewed swaths on the plateau's gentle bosom, and grain spouted into trucks that pulled alongside.

The land dwarfs the monument when you first glimpse it. Only when you stand in the shadow of those mighty monoliths do you feel awe. Man's muscle, not machines, hewed and dragged and erected them.

Primitive man still haunts these southern uplands, which he crisscrossed with trackways when forests and swamps choked the valleys. Archaeologists have sunk shafts into Silbury Hill—Europe's largest man-made mound, rising 130 feet beside the highway near Marlborough—and found only chalk rubble. The Romans swerved their road from Bath around it—the only clue we have to its age. And at nearby Avebury stands a mysterious ring much larger round than Stonehenge, though of smaller stones. A computer to study stars and predict eclipses? Perhaps.

But as I stood in the somber circle at Stonehenge, I sensed that this was holy

STONEHENGE, *huddling on Salisbury Plain, answers "when" and "how," but guards its "wh Men 3,500 years ago dragged its monoliths 24 miles from Marlborough Downs. There they levered up 50-ton sarsens, shaped them with fire, water, heavy blows. These linteled giants encircle earlier Welsh bluestones, lugged some 250 miles over land and water.*

A dagger carving evokes ancient Mycenae. Greek architect's mark? Perhaps the final stage in a work that spanned four centuries. Built for Druid sacrifices? Far too early. Observatory? A Harvard astronomer put Stonehenge through a computer and concludes Solar and lunar alignments marked a calendar by which men planted and harvested. The oute ring of 56 holes enabled priests to predict eclipses. They could assemble the people at this awesome shrine for a terrifying spectacle, then by ritual bring back the life-giving sun!

ground. It seemed that only a force as strong as ritualized belief could impel men to labor so long on such a monument.

Or to build Salisbury's spire.

"At fifteen miles off," wrote John Constable, it "darted up into the sky like a needle." Now, across Salisbury Plain, the needle drew me to the scene that had inspired Constable's brush.

Standing on the river meadows, gazing at that 404-foot prayer in stone, I tried to visualize the cathedral when it was consecrated in 1258. It had taken form swiftly after the first stones were laid in 1220—England's only medieval cathedral built in a single style in one generation. But Salisbury's builders had left their queen uncrowned. Only a stub of a tower protruded.

In 1334, militant, dwarflike Bishop Wyvil and master mason Richard of Farleigh began a work of decades that would transform a vision into Britain's highest spire.

My mind's eye sees Farleigh direct his army of workmen. I hear clinking chisels shape the limestone, singing ropes hoist the blocks high. As masons build first one, then a second tall-windowed stage in the tower, men mutter at resting so great a load on a spongy bed. Farleigh presses ahead.

He raises an octagonal spire atop the tower. Here on high, men tread inside a giant oaken wheel to winch great timbers up through the crossing. They lash these into a mighty scaffold. Masons encase it in

KATHLEEN REVIS JUDGE. OPPOSITE UPPER: PAINTING BY BRIAN HOPE-TAYLOR. LOWER: W. E. ROSCHER, NATIONAL GEOGRAPHIC STAFF

GEORGE F. MOBLEY AND (BELOW AND OPPOSITE) MERLE SEVERY, BOTH NATIONAL GEOGRAPHIC STAFF

stone–two feet thick for 20 feet; nine inches thick for the final 175 feet.

To the creaking of the treadwheel, the spire thrusts heavenward, each foot a miracle–sometimes a tragedy. A worker missteps and plunges screaming to his death.

More than beams and stones are carried to its top: In the capstone men place a lead box containing what they believe to be a remnant of the Virgin Mary's robe.

My eyes moved up the spire. It was bent!

Inside the cathedral I leaned my cheek against a tortured root of the spire–a cool, smooth cluster of Purbeck marble pillars. I sighted up to the vaulting. The column was bowed! For six centuries this and three other columns have borne the off-balanced burden of 6,400 tons.

From the first, anxious eyes scanned the supporting piers. Stone girders were erected between them; inverted arches eased the straining walls. In 1668, Christopher Wren urged "the bracing ye Spire toward ye Top with Iron," and it was done. Bronze ties were added in 1939. In the 1950's the top 30 feet were rebuilt. Acoustical engineers tested vibrations from the great organ and restricted use of big pipes. Jet pilots are forbidden to crack the sound barrier nearby–a sonic boom might topple this stone hymn to man's faith and skill.

A JET from the naval air station near Ilchester whistled overhead as I headed south from Discove into Dorset. But in Sherborne, with its stone almshouses and

SALISBURY'S SUBLIME SPIRE *rises over meadows of the Avon and the Nadder. Izaak Walton, who fished with the bishop of Salisbury, wrote: "God never did make a more calm, quiet, innocent recreation than angling."*

When exemplars (originals) of Magna Carta were sent to key castles and cathedrals in 1215, one was promulgated at Old Sarum, today a ruin. In New Sarum–Salisbury–that document (upper) still tells "free men of... liberties, to be had and held... forever." Three other exemplars survive, on at Lincoln Cathedral, two in the British Museum.

William Longespée (left), Earl of Salisbury, was first to be buried in the new cathedral. Son of Henry II and "Fair Rosamund" (to whom irate Queen Eleanor gave the option of a dagger or bowl of poison), he stood witness as his half brothe King John sealed Magna Carta at Runnymede.

LONGLEAT HOUSE BY JAN SIBERECHTS, 1676, BY PERMISSION OF THE MARQUESS OF BATH

Sunday at Longleat House

FROM "HEAVEN'S GATE" you can see cupolas rise amid parkland and picture a paradise of prancing palfreys, regal carriages, lords and ladies.

An ungodly roar hits you: Racing cars snarl up the hairpin drive in a hill climb! You find the Wiltshire estate a beehive of picnics, donkey rides, gleeful children swinging, sliding, gaping at the lions. You survey the house's treasures, then stroll the landscaped grounds. Anglers fish lakes created from a long leat, or watercourse, in the late 1750's by Lancelot "Capability" Brown, capable of making "Woods vanish, hills subside and valleys rise."

Sir John Thynne picked up the estate, a monastic windfall in Reformation storms, for a trifling £53 in 1540. In an age that saw churches tumble and mansions grow, he boldly built England's first classical country house, parading symmetrical bays of radiant mullioned windows. Sculpture and rich hangings adorned it. Outdone rivals muttered that Sir John must have "met with *Treasure Trove*."

In 1574 Elizabeth herself came rumbling in with a train of wagons on a summer progress by which she aired her palaces, eased her purse, and saw her people. "Her entertainment in ye West parts" cost Sir John a fortune. He had sought to forgo the "honor," but could no more keep Gloriana away than stop the sun's rising.

Today his descendant, the Marquess of Bath, enhances his income by throwing a daily party for hundreds of commoner guests.

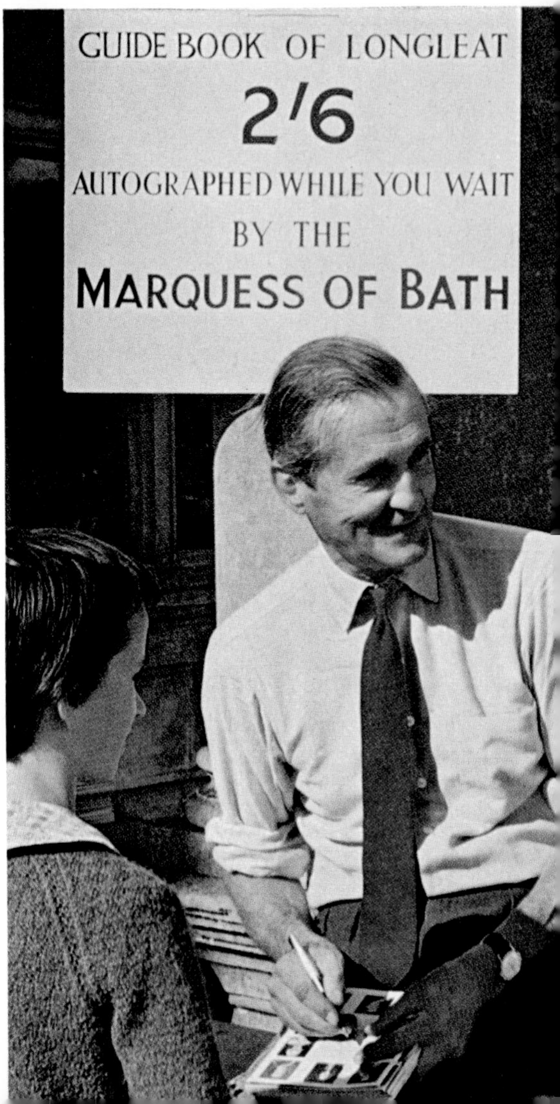
GUIDE BOOK OF LONGLEAT
2/6
AUTOGRAPHED WHILE YOU WAIT
BY THE
MARQUESS OF BATH

MERLE SEVERY, NATIONAL GEOGRAPHIC STAFF

THOMAS HARDY, *somber realist amid Victorian romancers, portrayed his native Dorset so vividly that visitors recognize his scenes today. They see his birthplace (below) at Higher Bockhampton. At Shaftesbury (right), where Gold Hill tumbles to the Vale of Blackmoor, they behold the quaint Shaston he described in* Jude the Obscure. *Its abbey shrine of King Edward the Martyr, murdered at Corfe Castle, drew medieval pilgrims.*

magnificent abbey church, I was back in the 15th century. In the boys' school I learned that two-year-old Randall was already too late to be registered. "Some parents even enroll an unborn child, hoping it will be a boy and have a place at Sherborne 14 years later," a master told me as we stood in a hall with a beamed ceiling and heraldic windows. Here masters sit at a raised head table; the boys dine "below the salt."

I was soon in the 19th century, bumping up to a thatched cottage in Higher Bockhampton. Here in 1840 a midwife revived a babe thought to be stillborn. Frailty delayed the child's schooling, but he taught himself Greek in his teens and won archi-

MERLE SEVERY, NATIONAL GEOGRAPHIC STAFF. UPPER: DORSET COUNTY MUSEUM

tectural prizes in his twenties. He limned in poetry his rustic birthplace, whose "high beeches, bending, hang a veil of boughs, And sweep against the roof."

To Thomas Hardy, author of *The Return of the Native*, Dorset and its people were the heart of his fictional Wessex.

Late in Hardy's life a Dorchester friend named Evans staged one of his novels, and Evans's son saw his first play. The lad became a famous actor – Maurice Evans. His sister Evelyn Evans lives in Hardy's birthplace. She showed me the bedroom where Hardy penned *Far From the Madding Crowd*, the ladder under which Grandfather Hardy hid smuggled brandy kegs, the "squint window" where he watched for excisemen. Behind the house extends the Egdon Heath, "mysterious in its swarthy monotony," which backdrops several Hardy tales. Now an atomic plant gleams on its "lonely face."

I crossed two bridges into Dorchester, Hardy's beloved "Casterbridge." There stands the "grizzled church" of St. Peter's; there the Bow, rounded street corner where a bride shivered while her man roistered inside; there the Hangman's Cottage where young Hardy, on the eve of a public execution, spied the placid hangman at dinner.

In the Dorset County Museum I saw Hardy's study, its contents gathered from Max Gate, the home he designed outside the town. There Hardy, once thought too

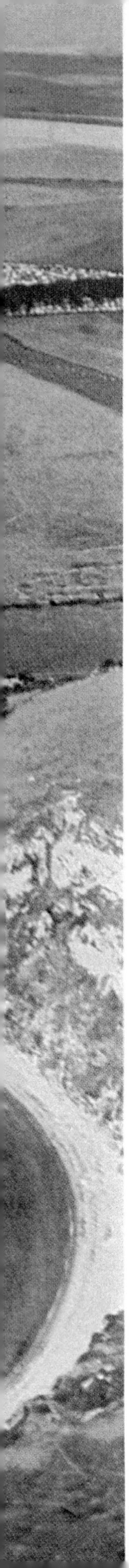

frail to go to school, lived half his 88 years.

The grim ruins of Corfe Castle, with its "windy corridors and mildewed dungeons," reflect Hardy's pessimism. It stands on a gunsight knob in the only notch in the Purbeck Hills. Treachery taints that tor. Here in 978, while drinking from a goblet offered by his stepmother Elfrida, young King Edward was stabbed in the back. Thus did she clear the throne for her son Ethelred. King John, who stayed in Corfe, flung 22 French nobles into its dungeons to starve. In 1643, Lady Mary Bankes and a tiny garrison held it against Roundhead artillery. It fell three years later – betrayed by a turncoat.

Leaving Hardy's doleful "Corvesgate," I explored the wave-gnawed Dorset coast. At Lulworth Cove I feasted on lobster fresh from that perfect basin, and on the Isle of Portland, Hardy's "Gibraltar of Wessex," peered into quarries where Wren got the Portland stone for his London buildings. From 14-foot-thick battlements Henry VIII raised against invasion from France, I looked over the harbor where in 1944 a mighty force set out to invade France.

On Weymouth's esplanade George III looks benignly upon the resort he made popular. When first trundled across the sands in a bathing machine, "he had no sooner popped his royal head under water than a band of music concealed in a neighbouring machine struck up God Save the King." I threaded the throngs to the old harbor, whence John Endecott sailed with Salem settlers; yachts lined it three deep.

THE YOUNG PEOPLE were all wild to see Lyme," wrote Jane Austen. They still are. With them, I descended its principal street "almost hurrying into the water."

Rather than Miss Austen, I sought a "prim, pedantic, vinegar-looking, thin female, shrewd, and rather satirical" – Mary Anning, the "fossil woman."

From cliffs near Lyme Regis, Mary, while still a girl, chipped a nearly perfect skeleton of an ichthyosaur, a paddle-footed sea reptile, bought by the lord of the manor for £23. Pecking deeper into time's layer cake, she mined a long-necked plesiosaur, then a giant gliding pterodactyl.

PATIENT SEA, *"distilled by the sun, kneaded by the moon," nibbles the Dorset coast and stamps a turquoise thumbprint at Lulworth Cove (left). Rock buttresses that stood firm while waves chewed the clays behind them once hid revenue cutters that pounced on smugglers running French brandy.*

At Lyme Regis (below), sand bastions recall that townsmen fought Prince Maurice from makeshift forts in 1644. "Breakfast work," sneered Royalists; some vowed not to dine until Lyme fell. Two months later they retired in defeat.

Yachts now nod behind the Cobb, a breakwater where Monmouth landed in 1685. Proclaimed king in Taunton, he was defeated at nearby Sedgemoor – last battle fought on England's soil.

MERLE SEVERY, NATIONAL GEOGRAPHIC STAFF. LEFT: ROBERT B. GOODMAN

CORFE CASTLE *crowns the Dorset village that bears its name; many homes wear its Norman stones. Outside the Greyhound, Mr. Battrick (to right) yarns of his nine decades. "Life is sweet," he says. Abbotsbury Swannery (left), England's oldest, thrives amid monastery ruins.*

When she died in 1847, paleontology was flourishing. Earth's periods were given English names: Cambrian from an old name for Wales, Ordovician and Silurian from early Celtic tribes, Devonian from Devon.

At the famed Abbotsbury Swannery I learned about Chesil Beach, an 18-mile bank that gives the swannery its lagoon. Smugglers used to rendezvous with boatmen here, swanherd Cecil Lexster told me as he rained grain on hundreds of swans.

How did boatmen find their way in the dark? They landed and picked up pebbles! The currents that build this beach grade its stones. "Smugglers could tell where they were by the size. The stones get bigger as you go toward Portland," said Cecil, knee-deep in a ballet of dipping necks.

THE BALLET was the same but the necks were pink when I watched flamingos feed several days later at the Severn Wild-

MERLE SEVERY, NATIONAL GEOGRAPHIC STAFF

fowl Trust in Gloucestershire. Director Peter Scott has gathered the world's largest and most varied collection of wildfowl—more than 2,000 birds of 160 species and races. As I strolled the landscaped 40 acres, Chinese spotbills, Australian shelducks, and Hottentot teal waddled up to look me over. I saw a mother and her young son share a picnic lunch with a quartet of nene, world's rarest goose.

I joined a stream of visitors to nearby Berkeley Castle. Most were so intent on viewing the chamber where one man died a horrible death that they passed without notice the home of a man who has saved the lives of millions: Edward Jenner.

In his day many dreaded smallpox even more than the plague—but not milkmaids who had caught cowpox, Jenner noted. For 23 years he doctored Berkeley's ills and experimented with cowpox lymph. In 1796

MERLE SEVERY AND (OPPOSITE) DEAN CONGER, BOTH NATIONAL GEOGRAPHIC STAFF

BERKELEY CASTLE, *with "a swagger of its own," rises round a Norman keep near the Severn, where a neighbor generates nuclear power. The Berkeley family, one of the few that can trace ancestry to Saxon days, has lived here 800 years. Its hunt wears yellow, not "pink," and once rode a territory extending all the way to London's Charing Cross. Death's-head (above) marks the murder room of Edward II.*

he vaccinated a young boy. Later he gave the lad smallpox – and found him immune! Jenner soon knew the world's acclaim.

I too went up the stone steps to the castle's Norman keep where Edward II, unwise in his favorites, unsuccessful in war, unlucky in his queen, was imprisoned in 1327. His jailers heaped rotting animal carcasses into the dungeon well so the pestilential stench would sicken him and he would die "by natural causes."

But Edward endured. His tormentors dared not cut the royal flesh. Their fiendish answer: red-hot irons inserted into the body. "The shrieks of death through Berkeley's roof that ring, Shrieks of an agonizing King," belied their claim of a natural death. But the "unmarked" corpse proved it.

Musing on the fates of kings, I followed a Roman road northward into Gloucester, where I checked into a room on the galleried courtyard of the half-timbered New Inn. "New," that is, in the 1400's.

In Gloucester, William the Conqueror ordered the Domesday survey of his realm. Today, industry holds sway in this bustling city, served by the 16-mile Gloucester and Berkeley Canal. In the medieval peace of the cathedral close, I looked up at the majestic edifice begun two years after the Conqueror's death. A white-haired canon, still robed from evensong, paused to explain the contrast between the cathedral's east and west ends.

Murdered King Edward was laid to rest here. Gradually reports of miracles transformed a weak king into a saintly figure. Pilgrims journeyed to Edward's shrine.

"Your inn was built to accommodate them," the canon said, "and their gifts glorified this church. The monks began by raising a choir nearly 90 feet high – so far above the nave that the choir has a west window, a novel feature. This new architecture, with stone paneling, soaring mullions, and gleaming walls of glass, became England's passion – the Perpendicular style."

AT TEWKESBURY *a glass-armored sentinel guards the abbey he founded ten centuries ago. Wide-eyed Robert FitzHamon witnessed the slaughter of Lancastrians seeking sanctuary here after the Battle of Tewkesbury in 1471. The Yorkist desecration closed the abbey a month—the only break in its worship to this day.*

"Butchers and villains, bloody cannibals," Shakespeare called the victors in Henry VI Part III. *Among those "mow'd down" like "autumn corn" was Henry's "sweet young prince," Edward. A brass beneath the Norman tower—England's largest—marks his grave.*

TINTERN ABBEY, *carpeted in green, roofed with sky, once knew the muffled tread of Cistercian monks and their litany of cloistered days.*

The midnight bell tolls, and down the night stairs they file, cowled white shadows gliding in gloom behind a taper's thin gleam. They enter the dark chancel to sing their praise of God. Two hours later, they mutely climb to pallets of straw.

Day breaks to the sleepless bell that summons them to prayers, to frugal meals, to the chapter house where errant brothers bow tonsured heads before the abbot and kneel, backs bared, for the lash. They munch a meatless supper to droning homilies. Their toil amid sheep or scripture ended, the last office chanted, they ascend to dim chambers. Then, "when sleep was sweetest," the bell calls them to a selfsame day.

TETHERED TREASURES *in Hereford Cathedral's world-famed Chained Library evoke medieval days when books were leashed, not lent. A canon displays Gratian's* Decretals, *an illuminated collection of church laws dating to 1150. The nearly 1,500 volumes include the 15th-century Cider Bible, whose warning in Luke 1:15 about "strong drink" is localized into "cidir."*

MERLE SEVERY AND (OPPOSITE) DEAN CONGER, BOTH NATIONAL GEOGRAPHIC STAFF

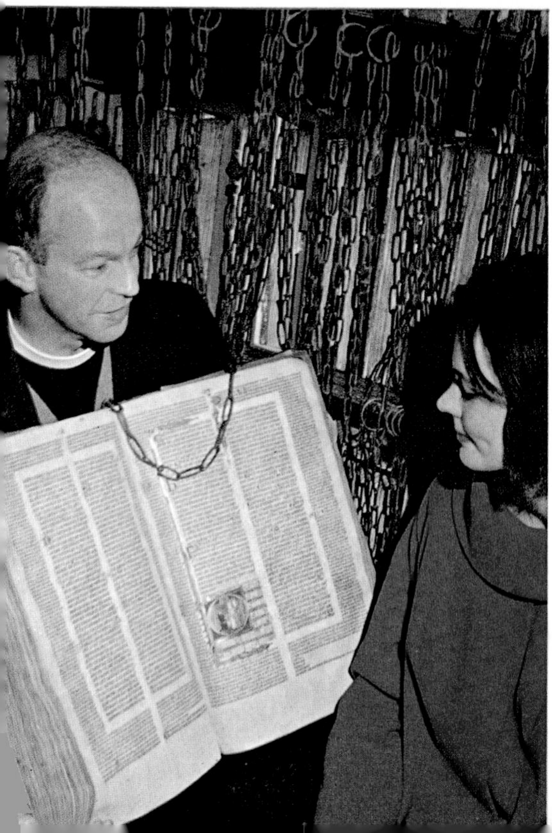

I gazed upon the alabaster features of Edward, serene despite his final agony. What a contrast between the massive Norman arches of the aisle and the lofty lightness of the choir, where angels play delicate stone instruments high over the altar and the entire east end glows with color—the first such window wall in the kingdom!

PILGRIMS of another age were pouring into Gloucester, for this was the week of the Three Choirs Festival, world's oldest annual music festival, held in rotation in Hereford, Worcester, and Gloucester cathedrals.

How different the trumpets, tympani, and fortissimo choruses of William Walton's *Belshazzar's Feast* from chanted plainsong! Yet the intent is the same—in the words of composer Thomas Morley—"to draw the hearer in chains of gold by the ears to the consideration of holy things."

During festival week I seized the chance

to revisit scenes warm in memory from earlier journeys. I sped up the broad Severn Valley toward Worcester, pausing at black-and-white timbered Tewkesbury. In the abbey I mounted the massive Norman tower and looked south upon the "Bloody Meadow." Imagination made it glint with armor and filled the air with shouts and the clang of steel. Yorkists drove Lancastrians against the river, then slaughtered their remnants in the town.

A verger opened the sacristy to show me the door the monks had plated with armor stripped from the slain.

Queen Elizabeth entered Worcester cathedral in 1575 "with GRETT and SOLOMPE singing and musick, with cornetts and sackbutts, with a CANAPY BOREN over her and so up into the chancell, where she diligently viewed the tomb of King John . . . all RYCHELEY and BEWTYFULLY adorned."

I recall softer sounds, for Patricia and I had heard a Three Choirs performance here of *The Dream of Gerontius* by Sir Edward Elgar, born in nearby Broadheath.

There was a nice nip in the air as I drove through resort villages along the wooded flanks of the Malvern Hills. Great Malvern's Festival Theatre brought to mind the tweedy figure of George Bernard Shaw, impish eyes twinkling above his gray beard, who premiered some of his plays here and provoked outrage and laughter with such sallies as: "My dear Tavy, your pious English habit of regarding the world as a moral gymnasium built expressly to strengthen your character in, occasionally leads you to think about your own confounded principles when you should be thinking about other people's necessities."

The day was so lovely that I hiked up Worcestershire Beacon to survey a dozen counties—eastward beyond the orchards of Evesham and the Regency spa of Cheltenham to the Cotswolds; westward to the Black Mountains of Wales.

SYMOND'S YAT, *a 473-foot cliff, overlooks the serpentine Wye. At Ledbury (right) half-timbered houses undulate along Church Lane. Castles studded the hard-to-tame Welsh Marches; Herefordshire alone shows 32 Norman motte-and-bailey earthworks. While other Royalist fortresses fell in the Civil War, Raglan Castle in Monmouthshire (below), "like winter fruit, hung long on."*

In Hereford's sturdy cathedral I saw the great parchment *mappa mundi* with Jerusalem at the center of the 14th-century world and Paradise at the top.

I love this countryside – white-faced Herefords red against lush meadows; hop fields, cider apples, rich red soil. I love that view at Wynd Cliff in Monmouthshire where the Wye writhes through rock to join the wide Severn – two rivers so different in aspect and course, yet born but a mile apart on a Welsh mountain.

Peaceful scenes – but you need only visit the grim keep at Goodrich, beetling Raglan Castle, and Chepstow's great fortress to realize that this border country was once bitterly contested. Or ask in a pub whether Monmouthshire is Welsh or English and hear the slow voices quicken.

MERLE SEVERY AND (RIGHT) BATES LITTLEHALES, NATIONAL GEOGRAPHIC STAFF

A "heaven-directed spire" led me to Ross on Wye, perched on a bluff. Several miles downstream, I wound up a steep hill and over a woodland path to another of my favorite viewpoints – Symond's Yat. Here the river, looping four miles, doubles back on the opposite side of the promontory, only a few hundred yards away.

I roved the country, savoring its delights by day and commuting to Gloucester for evening performances of the festival. Under glowering skies I headed down the sylvan Wye, past "the tall rock, the mountain, and the deep and gloomy wood." Soon the clouds broke; sunlight drenched the meadows. It gleamed on the gaunt gables of Tintern Abbey, looming larger than I had remembered it on my first visit here.

Now I could say with Wordsworth, "Five years have passed; five summers with the length of five long winters" since I had

DAN McCOY, BLACK STAR. OPPOSITE: MERLE SEVERY, NATIONAL GEOGRAPHIC STAFF

IN SONG AND STONE, *three cathedrals – Hereford, Gloucester, and Worcester – glorify God. Before the living wall of massed choristers, "musical salt of the earth," clergy file down Gloucester's Norman nave in the opening service of the Three Choirs Festival, held annually since 1724.*

King John (above) lies in Worcester, the cathedral he helped rebuild. At his feet a lion nibbles at his sword – as the barons' bite at Runnymede blunted his power.

heard the "soft inland murmur" of these waters. I had come upon a ghostly abbey at dusk, like a ship sailing in solitude through purple haze. Now tourists thronged it; sun routed the eerie mists. I strolled in the shadow of the great piers and still found the roofless ruin magnificent.

HIGH POINT of the festival was Benjamin Britten's *War Requiem,* written for the dedication of Coventry Cathedral, resurrected from the rubble of World War II.

Solemn phrases of the Latin Mass for the Dead alternate with searing poems by Wilfred Owen, a young English officer of the first World War. "All a poet can do today is warn," he wrote – and was killed just seven days before the Armistice.

Following the tolling of *Requiem aeternam,* the tenor bursts in with a bitter "What passing-bells for these who die as cattle? Only the monstrous anger of the guns."

The chorus *Quam olim Abrahae promisisti* introduces the Old Testament story wrenched into a parable on the readiness of elders to send their young off to slaughter.

"Father, behold the preparations, fire and iron. But where the lamb for this burnt-offering?" asks Isaac, the firstborn.

"Then Abram bound the youth with belts and straps, And builded parapets and trenches there, And stretched forth the knife to slay his son."

An angel stays him, urging him to offer the Ram of Pride instead. But the old man, unheeding, "slew his son – And half the seed of Europe, one by one."

I recalled the banners hanging in a hundred dim-lit aisles, the names inscribed on endless rolls of honor. And as a dead soldier and the enemy he had killed rued the "undone years" and quietly sang, "Let us sleep now," I looked down the stern march of Gloucester's piers that bespeak the Norman Conquest, and beyond the massed choirs to the soaring East Window that honors the fallen at Crécy.

In the shocked silence after the last pianissimo chord had died away, I felt that this stone and glass was England's blood.

ANNE REVIS GROSVENOR. RIGHT: ROBERT B. GOODMAN

CHANNEL CRUISE TO DEVON AND CORNWALL

Step aboard Tectona with Alan Villiers to brave the Lizard's jagged teeth and probe time-misted inlets whence sea dogs sailed forth for Spanish gold

AWAY TO WINDWARD great banks of summer clouds piled the horizon like a thousand sails. Up-Channel we swept toward the big breakwater at Plymouth. Along this old sea road have passed the ships of history—Venetian trading galleys, the little *Mayflower* of 1620, Drake's riches-heavy *Golden Hind*.

And it was here one July day in 1588 that the Spanish Armada sailed by. Rolling and creaking came those glorious galleons, ablaze with banners, guns run out tier upon tier, trumpets blaring on decks packed with troops. On they went, brave, magnificent, futile—missing forever their chance to bottle up the English fleet in Plymouth harbor.

Now the sun came out and shone on the Sound. Our crew swung the 83-ton

HEADSAILS FRAME *St. Michael's Mount, haunted*

ketch *Tectona* gracefully round Drake's Island, checking off the channel by its buoys. "Down sail! Let go the anchor!" We fetched up almost underneath the Hoe.

Upon that famous green atop the rugged cliffs we found a large group of bowlers. Not a one was less than 60.

"Well done, Veronica!" shouted one old gentleman. His teammate was skillfully curving the ball along the table-flat turf.

Here, the story goes, Sir Francis Drake was at his game of bowls as the Armada approached. Finding the English admirals on the green, the captain of a scouting ship shouted, "The Spaniards are coming!"

"Let them wait their turn," Drake replied in sum. "There's time for this and to beat the Spaniard afterwards."

So saying, he bent again to bowl.

Gutted by bombing raids in World War II, Plymouth rebounded with new buildings rising from a right-angled layout of wide, garden-filled streets along the fine sweep of Armada Way. Arcades link whole squares of stores to shelter shoppers from the rain. Big double-deck buses flow with the fast, smooth traffic. Beside the port at Sutton Harbour, whence Grenville, Frobisher, Hawkins, Raleigh, Drake, and the Pilgrim Fathers sailed, several ancient buildings have been restored.

Plymouth was a perfect portal into Devon, England's third largest county in area. We left *Tectona* berthed near the Hoe and set off to explore the countryside by car.

Those narrow Devon lanes sink low, where the rains of centuries and the iron-shod wheels of a thousand drays have worn

by a thousand years of prayer and strife. Sir Francis Drake (opposite) looks out from Plymouth Hoe.

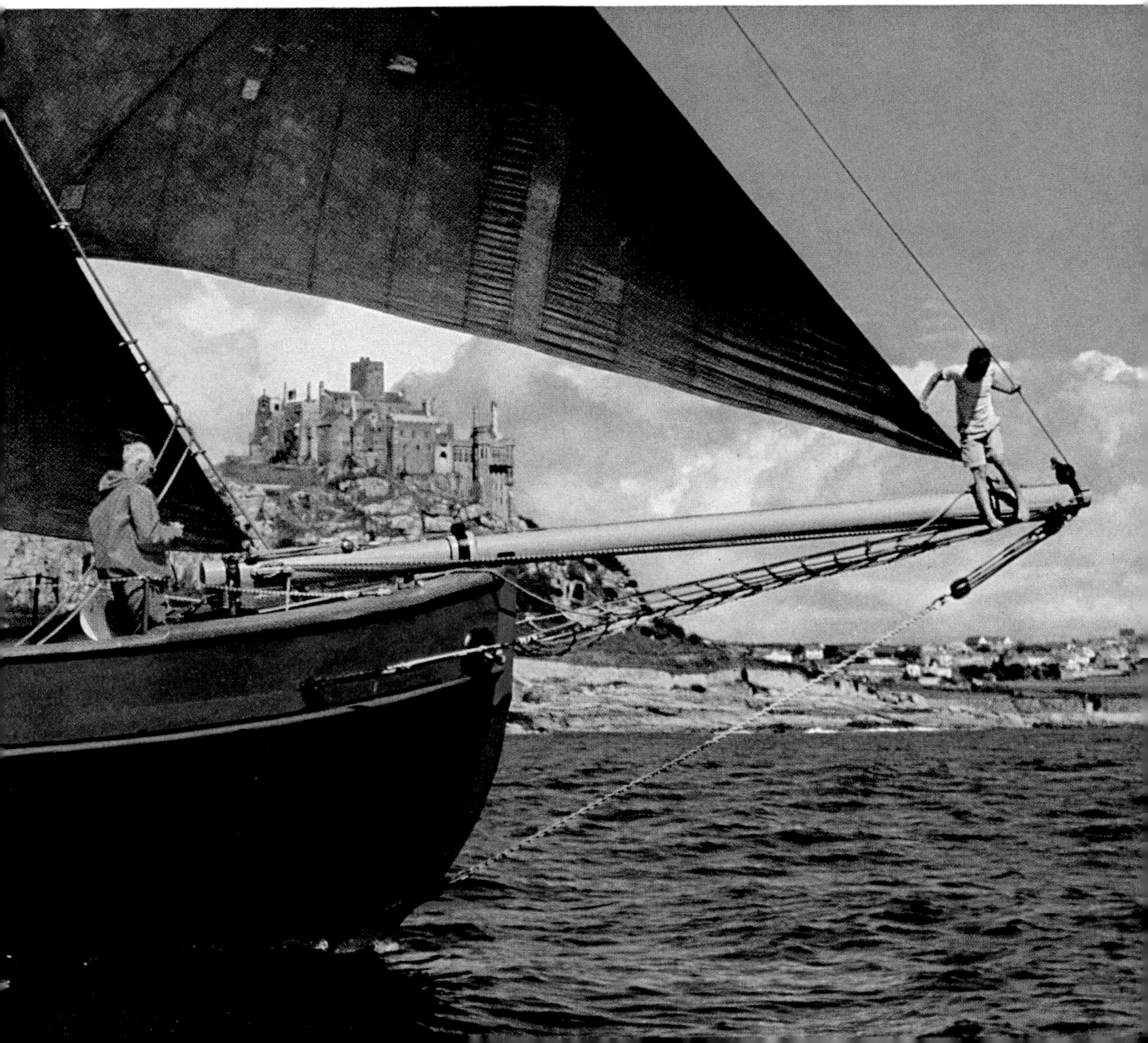

BOWLERS "THROW WOODS" *on the Hoe, where Drake, mayor of Plymouth after his 1577-80 voyage round the world, played out a famous game. Here the Pilgrims bade a last farewell to England in 1620. Behind this esplanade (opposite) Plymouth's modern buildings cover the scars of World War II. Drake's home, nearby Buckland Abbey, is now a museum.*

ANNE REVIS GROSVENOR. OPPOSITE: BATES LITTLEHALES, NATIONAL GEOGRAPHIC PHOTOGRAPHER

away the roadbed. Hawthorn, ferns, blackberries—ripe and lush and wonderfully tasty—all sorts of vegetation flourishes, often over car-top height.

"Three inches on this side!" Melville Bell Grosvenor, President and Editor of the National Geographic Society, issued this "sounding." A member of our *Tectona* crew, he was now spotting for our car driver. For the tenth time that morning we had reached an impasse with an oncoming car and had to back cautiously down a steep gradient to a wider passing place.

Just as we approached one wide spot a herd of red cows came calmly round the corner, heavy-uddered, orderly, unconcerned. We just had to stop until they plodded by. It was their road and they knew it.

Not far from Plymouth the well-tilled fields suddenly dropped behind. All around was open ground, hilly and treeless, rolling away for miles. It began to rain as we followed the tortuous road past granite outcrops springing rough and defiant from the furze and heather and peaty bogs. This, we knew, was Dartmoor, sinister, windswept, mysterious, a perfect setting for the prison built there during the Napoleonic Wars.

From that somber structure, successful escape across the eerie and often mist-shrouded moor is almost unknown. Many have lost their way here, and many have disappeared in its fastness. Stone cairns and remnants of Bronze Age huts dot the moor. Early Celts built forts on its fringes, and the remains of cremated bones have been discovered in stone-slab graves.

In the mist and rain the moor looked old, hostile, frightening. "Even the animals seem afraid of it sometimes," we were told.

"You hear the ponies whinny, see them trembling, and the dogs' hair bristles. Yet you see nothing—only feel."

ALONG DARTMOOR's fertile fringes villages and homes and flower gardens began to appear again. We stopped at an old thatched inn, the George, at Hatherleigh. In a dining room beamed with oak blackened by centuries of fireplace smoke, we regaled ourselves with roast beef and beer sauce. The talk turned to the bygone days of stagecoach travel.

"Those old coachmen were colorful characters," a villager observed. One driver, he said, pretended to find a broken kingpin underneath his coach every time he had a load of strangers. A defective kingpin could wreck the coach. So the grateful passengers would whip out half crowns for the coachman. The kingpin was perfectly all right, of course. He kept a bad one in his big coat pocket for use at the right time.

"The same old rascal used a ruse to lighten his coach before going up steep hills," the villager said. "He'd just say loudly what a wonderful thing it would be if all the *young* women would get down and walk, to help the poor 'osses. Every woman aboard unfailingly got off."

Later, as we left for Clovelly, I almost expected to hear the rattle of a coach rushing in, horns blowing, ironshod hoofs striking the cobblestones.

Clovelly clings to the side of a north Devon cliff. Its one main street tumbles

ROBERT B. GOODMAN. RIGHT: BATES LITTLEHALES, NATIONAL GEOGRAPHIC PHOTOGRAPHER. BELOW: ALAN VILLIERS

ROOFED WITH STRAW *and cloaked in foliage, snug houses hug a rain-washed lane near Dartmouth. Thatcher balances on a tine-anchored tool; his new roof may last 25 years. Devon lanes, made for man and mount or at most a one-horse dray, accommodate a horseless buggy between the hedgerows—if nothing comes the other way.*

down to the sea so steeply that no wheeled vehicle can use it. Boy-drawn sleds, sliding down the smooth cobbles, make deliveries. The picturesque harbor has an old stone pier with upended iron cannon for mooring posts.

We took a run along Hobby Drive, a toll road that skirts the clifftops east of Clovelly. A young woman carrying a baby opened the gate for us. Three shillings—42 cents—was the charge. "It is only fourpence if you like to walk," she added.

Driving on this rough road, we had glorious views of Clovelly's harbor and of the Bristol Channel coast as far away as Westward Ho! All along the beach at this curiously named village, forever linked with

BATES LITTLEHALES, NATIONAL GEOGRAPHIC PHOTOGRAPHER

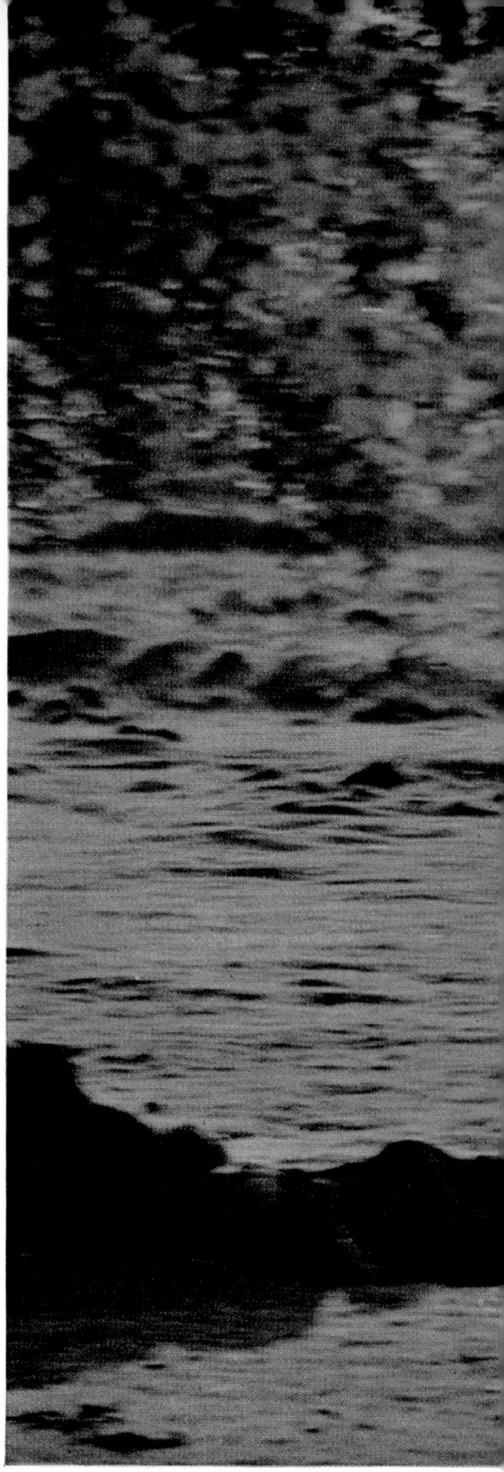

A FOAL PRANCES *in evening gold on Devon's Dartmoor. Once used to haul coal from mines, the famed moor ponies now roam free, paying little heed to the law that forbids roadside handouts. Tourists enjoy the gorges, swift streams, lofty granite tors, and bracing air of the heathery 365-square-mile plateau. But when mists descend or wild gales shriek, they apprehensively recall the "melancholy moor" in Sir Arthur Conan Doyle's* The Hound of the Baskervilles.

the novel by Charles Kingsley, the rollers came thundering in.

When we arrived at Barnstaple the famous fall fair was in full swing. The town says its festive event dates back to the time of the Saxon King Athelstan, ruler of all England, who died in the year 940. While I watched by the Guildhall, the mayor, his mace-bearer, and beadles marched by in their colorful robes.

One beadle later complained to me about a move that would widen the beautiful old arched bridge. "Spoil our bridge!" he grumbled. "Just to bring in more cars quickly, to knock more of us down...."

After Ilfracombe, a coastal tourist center to the north, comes the little port of Lynmouth. The poet Shelley loved this place and had a cottage here. Racing seas curl white along the cliffs. The steep, tumbling East and West Lyn rivers meet the Bristol Channel. Beyond slumber the blue mountains of Wales.

The name Lyn is well taken; it is thought to be from the Anglo-Saxon *hlynn*, meaning torrent. I talked to some boatmen about the terrible flood of 1952 which swept suddenly down on Lynmouth on a summer night. Two weeks of rain had soaked the ground, they said, so that the big bog lakes on nearby Exmoor could not store those waters bursting out of a freak cloud. The flood-control measures were not adequate then, as they are today. So the water roared

through the chasms in the hills which are the beds of the Lyn rivers. It swept like a mad and unpredicted tidal bore, undermining the banks of the village, bringing with it trees that knocked down cottages.

"It was night and the place was full of visitors," one of the boatmen said. "The poor little town didn't have a chance. Forty-three people died."

By automobile, we headed inland along a winding road beside the East Lyn to poetically named Water's Meet. Here Hoaroak Water meets the East Lyn at a wooded junction. In freshet the waters smash over rocks, throwing fine clouds of spray and spume halfway up the tall trees. The peaty water swished like churning ale below the little wooden bridges spanning the streams. A

ATHWART *the Bristol Channel shipping lanes lies a weather-beaten block of granite with a history as roaring as the breakers that pound it. For centuries it earned notoriety as a pirate pesthole and citadel of overlords who defied England's kings.*

Enduring fame came not from plunder and conquest but from the clouds of gaudy-beaked sea birds swarming about the heather-strewn rock. Viking rovers named it lunde ey, *"puffin island." Puffins and other sea birds, far outnumbering the 40 or so human residents, still nest on Lundy; their pictures adorn stamps—familiar to collectors as "Lundy locals"—issued by the island's private owner, who provides mail service to the Devon mainland 12 miles away. The bustling puffinries attract boatloads of visitors.*

"**TO LANDWARD,** *all richness, softness, and peace; to seaward, a waste and howling wilderness of rock and roller," wrote Charles Kingsley of the bays of north Devon. Wordsworth and Coleridge felt the region's enchantment. And to Lynmouth (right) came the angry young Shelley, sent down in disgrace from Oxford for advocating atheism. Here he penned radical tracts, crammed them into bottles, and flung them into the sea. The main street of tourist-filled Clovelly (below) cascades down a cliffside to Barnstaple Bay. "A village like a waterfall," a poet called it.*

BATES LITTLEHALES, NATIONAL GEOGRAPHIC PHOTOGRAPHER. UPPER LEFT: SMITHSONIAN INSTITUTION. ABOVE RIGHT: KATHLEEN REVIS JUDGE

silvery scene in sunlight—yet I would hate to be caught there in flood.

Beckoning from beyond the East Lyn's wild waters was Exmoor, Devon's other famed moor. I wanted to learn at least something of Exmoor stag hunting, although this was not the season for it. So we crossed over into Somerset and stopped for lunch at an inn in Simonsbath. It was set in a deep, sheltered ravine by the banks of the River Barle. A green lawn and flowers led to the welcoming door, and the gurgling of the Barle followed us into the hall. A stag's head stared at us from one wall.

"Stags?" said the host, tweed-clad and stockinged to the knee, as he dispensed a stimulant or two. "Whenever the hounds bring one this way, it empties my house in a flash. The last time the hounds rushed by, out went my 12 diners right away. Out went my bar full. Off went my waitresses."

"Yezzur," chimed in a customer over his ale and bread and cheese. "We take our hunting seriously here. It's been going on since around the year 1200."

I chatted with the waitress in the dining room—a pretty Devon girl, dark hair and black eyes set off by a pale magnolia skin. We talked whenever she was not staggering in with dishes of rich roast pork, mashed potatoes, and Brussels sprouts out of the garden, or lashings of batter pudding with Devonshire cream, or fritters made wonderfully around slices of Devon apple.

This 18-year-old lass was an ardent follower of the hunt, and I wondered why. The death of the stag can be unpleasant.

"It's the excitement," she cried, her dark eyes lighting up. "You know, when the hounds dash through the village with the huntsmen after them on their horses, all the men gay in their pink coats, their black

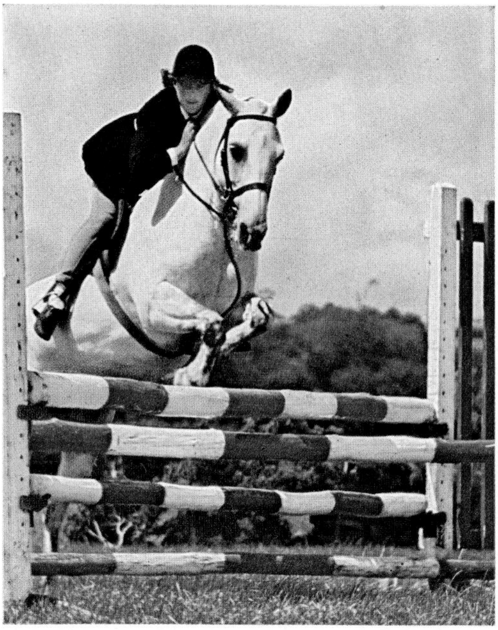

"DEVON IS FULL *of little girls on fat ponies," reports Alan Villiers. Here a teen-ager and her mount leap a hogsback at Ashburton.*

Ring guard (opposite), elegant in "pink" (a huntsman's scarlet coat) and topper, stands ready to relay judges' commands with his horn at the horse show in Honiton, a "neat and shewy town" famed for its lace. Medals show service in India and both World Wars.

Horsemen and baying hounds follow a stag across hilly, heathery Exmoor in an 1807 aquatint (below). Red deer, hunted here by Saxon kings, can run riders ragged. A stag may flit into bog-bordered hideouts, slip down in deep bracken where his horns look like old twigs, or swim straight out to sea for miles.

caps, and their riding gear—why, you wouldn't stay in here, would you?"

BELOW EXMOOR the Barle flows into the Exe. We drove through the river valley as far as Devon's county town of Exeter. This city has been in turn Roman, Saxon, Norman, and still has traces of them all. We gazed on the remains of Saxon walls built there by King Athelstan. At the renowned cathedral we saw the Exeter Book, chief anthology of early Anglo-Saxon poetry. We visited the Guildhall, one of England's oldest, and Mol's Coffee House, haunt of Elizabethan sea captains.

From Exeter our road led back across Dartmoor toward Plymouth. In Widecombe we stopped at the imposing village church known as the "Cathedral of Dartmoor." A tablet on the wall honors the memory of several worshipers killed when a stone pinnacle from the 120-foot tower crashed down through the roof, and "a great fiery ball" passed through the structure. This tragedy of 1638—barely yesterday in that area—is attributed to lightning.

But the locals give another version. They say the stones were hurled down by the devil, who came riding to Widecombe through that thunderstorm in quest of a worshiper known for sleeping through sermons. That very afternoon a stranger had called at a nearby tavern and tossed back a pint of ale. As the liquor passed through his

PRINT AFTER SAMUEL HOWITT, COURTESY PAUL MELLON COLLECTION. UPPER: BATES LITTLEHALES, NATIONAL GEOGRAPHIC PHOTOGRAPHER. OPPOSITE: ROBERT B. GOODMAN

Hunters (Ridden)

throat, the tavern mistress heard it sizzling like water poured on hot iron.

RETURNING TO PLYMOUTH, we soon had *Tectona* running with the west winds along South Devon's smiling coast. At Hope Cove, the wind freshened and we stormed along at nine knots. Mel Grosvenor took the wheel. And his young son Edwin clambered out on the bowsprit to enjoy the spectacle.

We hadn't noticed just how much the wind had gotten up till we rounded rocky Bolt Head to cross the Salcombe bar. By then we were fighting a moderate gale.

"Keep her up! Head into wind!" Shouts—and the rolling sea—brought Eddie in from his perch. A road of white water indicated the bar, and we pitched and wallowed past it in a wild heaving of waters.

"This is where Tennyson wrote 'Crossing the Bar,'" shouted Ike Marsh, the wry bos'n, "but I guess he was inside when he did!"

Salcombe, whose homes cling to the hillsides like limpets to a rock, is one of the fairest ports along this lovely coast. The splayed fingers of the Salcombe estuary

SUNLIGHT SHAFTING *through storm clouds brightens verdant hills of the well-watered "Garden of Dev*

offer hospitable harbor to hundreds of yachts, and some stay for years with whole families living aboard. Clipper schooners once slid down the ways here; the sweet smell of their cargoes, Azorean pineapples and oranges, rose on the balmy Devon air.

After a short stay we set sail again. Lollopy seas picked up the round rump of our ketch and hurried her along past Start Point and on to the safe haven of Dartmouth, at the mouth of the River Dart. The sheltered channel wound between high wooded hills and past a pair of "Strong and myghtye and defensyve" towers built on opposite shores in the 15th century. The Royal Naval College, Britain's Annapolis, dominated the town's hillside. A flock of swans made way for us, and we secured alongside in Bayard's Cove, one of Dartmouth's snug harbors.

We took a trip up the Dart in a little paddle steamer that looked at least 50 years old. A guide pointed out places of interest like Greenway, where they say Raleigh smoked the first pipe in England—and was doused with a jug of beer by a servant who thought his whiskers were afire.

near Totnes, whose colonnaded houses sweep down to the River Dart under a frowning Norman keep.

ROBERT B. GOODMAN

GEORGE F. MOBLEY AND (OPPOSITE) BATES LITTLEHALES, NATIONAL GEOGRAPHIC PHOTOGRAPHERS

EXETER CATHEDRAL, *pride of Devon, has endured centuries of strife. More than 1,000 years ago Saxons worshiped in a minster here. Destroyed by Danes, it was rebuilt by King Canute.*

When the Normans came, they reared a cathedral whose twin towers stand today, flanking the nave rather than rising out of it. From one of them a curfew bell nightly rings out the Norman injunction couvre feu, *"cover the fire," which warned Saxon peasants to put out their fires and go to bed.*

"Building bishops" of the 13th and 14th centuries shaped Exeter's core, laying out the longest unbroken stretch of Gothic vaulting in the world—more than 300 feet. With the sun streaming in through the windows and the ribs arching intricately overhead, the great nave seems "like a forest in springtime." Reformation upheavals damaged the cathedral, as did Nazi bombs. Devoted hands restored its splendors.

In the exquisite Lady Chapel (left) the Dean of Exeter browses the Exon Domesday Book, dating from 1086. Behind lies the painted stone effigy of Lady Dorothy Doderidge in Jacobean lace, her fingers touching the symbol of death.

At Torquay the streets rose from the waterside on elegant terraces of fuchsias, mimosas, and flowering palms. Villas here had been built during the Napoleonic Wars for families of Channel fleet officers.

Torquay today may be Devon's No. 1 holiday haven, but many thousand years ago it was something else—a domain of prehistoric beasts. Fossil remains of the woolly rhinoceros, cave bear, and mammoth have been found in a remarkable cave here, along with skeletons of ancient man.

All that south coast is fascinating. At the fishing village of Beer the red rock cliffs—which tradition claims were stained by the blood of Devon men and Danes who died fighting during the Viking raids—become mixed with white chalk. Here we ended our splendid tour of Devonshire and headed for the crag-girt county of Cornwall.

EIGHT BELLS!" shouted Ike, as *Tectona*'s big blue hull bucked down-Channel. "Rise and shine for the Black Ball Line!"

As we bounced into a morning southwesterly, half a gale on our nose, Ike was calling the other watch, down below: "Show a leg there, show a leg!"

What a tradition, this call of the sailing-ship watch! In the old days women were permitted in the 'tween decks of England's fighting ships in port. There was excuse from watch at hammocks from which a shapely leg was exhibited on demand.

Shapely? None of ours! Rise and shine! *Tectona*'s tanned sails were thrashing now, sprays belting halfway up the jib.

It was rough sailing that day. Merchantmen bound west in ballast bashed hard into the short Channel seas. But the weather improved, so we sailed on for Falmouth.

Night was falling on the deadly Eddystone Rocks as we rolled past Plymouth. Nearby rose the tower of Eddystone Light, the sea washing fretfully at its base.

"The first lighthouse on Eddystone was built by a joker," said Ike.

"It doesn't look like a good place for jokes," piped up Eddie.

Our best seaman, cook, and font of sailing lore, Ike told the old story of Henry Winstanley. A famous inventor and practical joker of the 17th century, Winstanley turned his home in Essex into a fun fair. He installed a turnstile and coined money from sightseers who flocked to see his trick chairs, mirrors, and booby traps.

The eccentric prankster eventually became a shipowner. When two of his ships were wrecked on the Eddystone Rocks, he demanded: "Why aren't they marked?"

No architect would attempt the job; Winstanley determined to do it himself. At first, waves washed over his work at every high tide; but he stuck to it for three summers. Finally, in 1698, he had his "mark" up—a bunch of candles burning in a lantern atop a wooden tower. It looked queer, but not a ship foundered there for five years.

Proud of his tower, Winstanley bragged that it would stand the roughest storm and that he'd be happy to stay there with it. His chance came in 1703. During a lull in weeks of gales, he went to repair the tower. That night a ripsnorter of a storm blew up.

"In the morning nothing was left," said Ike, "and no sign of the joker or his tower was ever seen again."

"But he showed it could be done," said Eddie. Indeed he did. We watched the present light, fourth on the site, grow tinier in the long twilight of summer.

MORNING BROUGHT FOG and we lay becalmed off Falmouth, so close that we could hear farmyard dogs barking. "Sailors round here in the old days knew the barks of all the dogs," said Ike. "That's one way they could tell where they were."

SPLAYED FINGERS *of Salcombe harbor (left) invite craft of every kind, from swift two-masted dinghies called Salcombe yawls to ocean cruisers. Would-be yachtsmen flock here for schooling in the sailor's art. Villas drowse on shaded slopes, laved by soft breezes that give the Devon port a gentle climate the year round.*

BATES LITTLEHALES, NATIONAL GEOGRAPHIC PHOTOGRAPHER

DEFT FINGERS *tie a clove hitch under the eyes of Malayan, English, African, and Pakistani cadets (above) at Dartmouth, cradle of the Royal Navy. Three of Britain's kings, along with a host of embryo admirals aged 13 and up, learned seamanship here at the Royal Naval College or its predecessor, the training ship* Britannia.

History drips from waterside stones along the River Dart. Knights embarked here for the Crusades; in 1944, 480 ships crowded with U. S. invasion forces sailed for the Normandy beaches.

At home in Compton Castle near Torquay, Comdr. Walter Raleigh Gilbert (left) stands beside a model of the Squirrel, *on which his ancestor, Sir Humphrey Gilbert, was lost at sea in 1583 after establishing on Newfoundland England's first North American colony. Sir Humphrey was half brother of Sir Walter Raleigh. The family's manor house, begun in the 1300's, welcomes visitors.*

Suddenly the mist lifted. Before us was the lighthouse on St. Anthony Head, and beyond it Pendennis Castle at the entrance to Falmouth's inner bay. A breeze came rippling across the sea with the morning sun. Now a regatta began, for this was Falmouth Week. Soon the entire estuary was splashed with the bright spinnakers of the yachts, oyster boats, and dinghies.

As we anchored, a picturesque oysterman rushed by under an enormous press of sail, a jerseyed Cornish seafarer holding the end of a tree-bough spinnaker boom in one great brown hand and half the sheet in the

TERRACES OF TORQUAY, *caressed by a Riviera-like clime, shield pleasure fleets. Town life, long focused*

other. "Ahoy, Cap'n!" he yelled. It was Jimmy Quintrell, an old sailing friend.

When we met him ashore, Jimmy confided the sea fishing was not so good just then. Cornish waters have long been famed for pilchard, herring, mackerel, and other homely fish. "I've seen shoals of pilchard that made the sea one mass of fish," Jimmy said. "They don't come like that now."

Maybe the boys would have to take to smuggling again, or even looting wrecks, I suggested with a smile. Cornishmen – allegedly – once excelled at these activities. "Our smugglers were all good men, honest

on Torre Abbey, founded in 1196, quickened when naval families flocked here in the Napoleonic Wars.

BATES LITTLEHALES, NATIONAL GEOGRAPHIC PHOTOGRAPHER

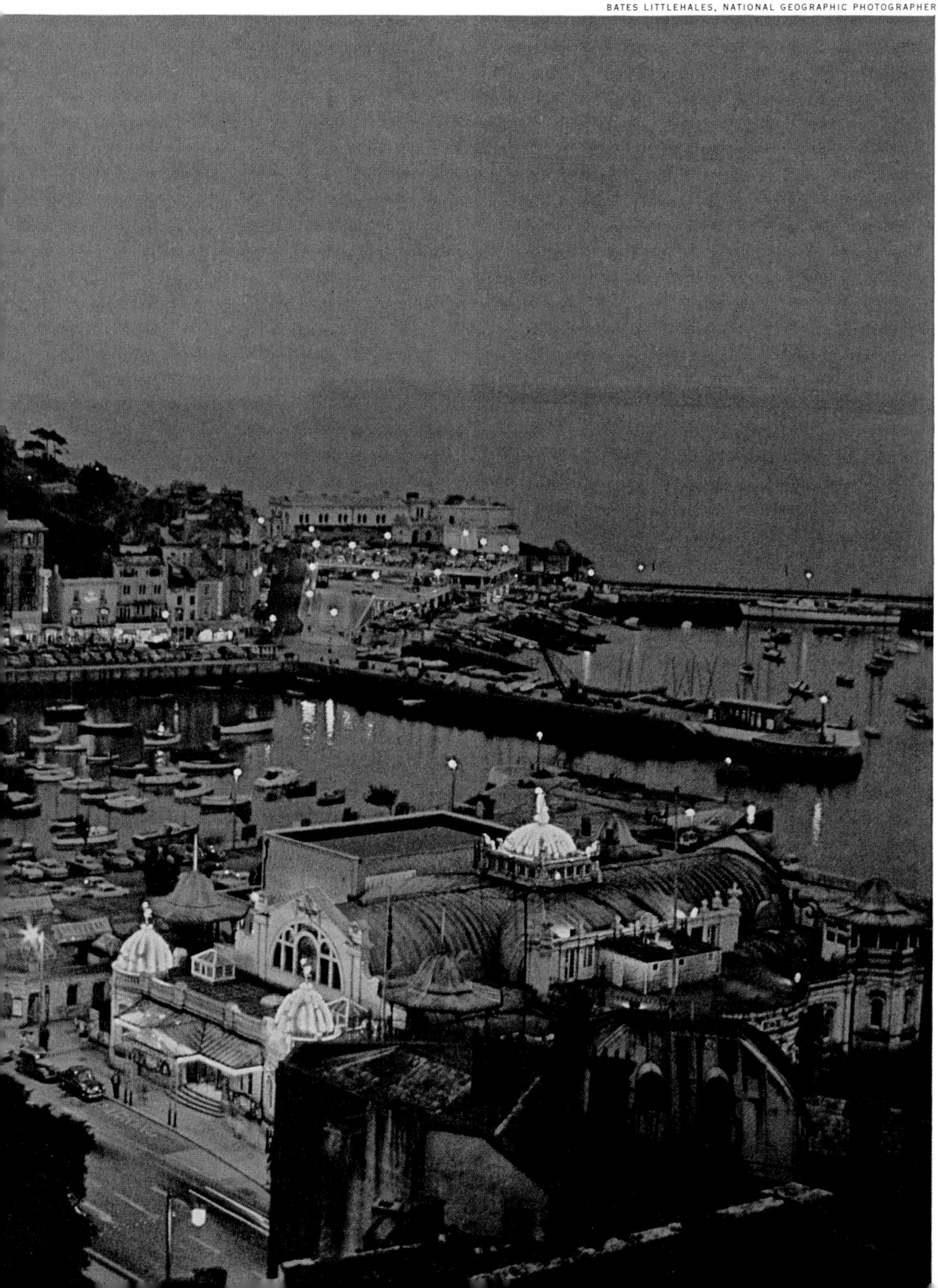

CORNISH BEAUTY *casts a spell—with the glance of a "fair-eyed, brown-tressed" maid, or a splendid sweep of seacoast. Blue-winged dinghies skimming across Falmouth harbor (right) in a Falmouth Week regatta follow the wake of a long parade of ships. Tradition tells of Romans coming here for grain, Greeks for hides, Phoenicians and Bretons for tin. World War II convoys clustered in this big Channel port nearest Land's End.*

Ferry on daylong shuttle (lower) nudges its ramp at steep-streeted Fowey, where freighters load china clay used all over the world.

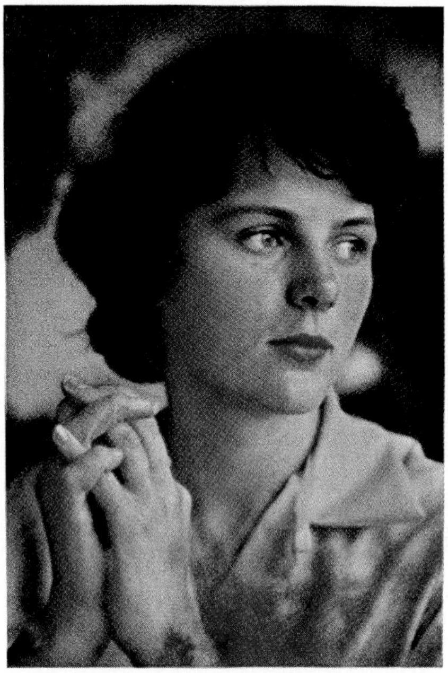

ROBERT B. GOODMAN. RIGHT: ALAN VILLIERS

in their own way," retorted Jimmy. He reminisced about Honest John Carter, who broke into a customs house. Honest John took back his contraband which the King's men had seized while he was away; he needed it to deliver to his customers. "He'd promised 'em, and he had to keep his word!"

Old Jimmy became more serious as he spoke of wrecking. "If Cornishmen ever did that, they've more than made up for it with the lives our lifeboats have saved from wrecks these past hundred years."

And indeed it took nerve to go out in one of those boats, launching them down runways into the turbulent, rock-strewn sea.

Volunteers, I learned, make up regular lifeboat crews. But in an emergency, any fisherman goes. He takes his chances on getting back. In churning seas even the best boat might roll over, as the St. Ives boat did years ago. There was one survivor.

"It was bad, watching the men go," an old fisherman's wife in Cadgwith told me. "They used to cry out through the village, 'Wreck! Wreck!' The men rushed off, but a wild fear struck the women's hearts. Now they explode maroons – loud fireworks. We hate to hear them too."

Cadgwith's whitewashed cottages straggle up the steep street. Their large chimneys often carry the smoke from driftwood cast up from wrecks or washed in on the ocean current from anywhere on earth. Up many a side, clear to the eaves, pile sweet roses, jasmine, honeysuckle.

Balmy Cornish air, blown in from the warm North Atlantic Current, and Cornish soil are kind to flowers. Thick golden gorse scents this upland plateau. Daffodils and sweet narcissus bloom weeks before they

JAGGED ROCKS *hole the doomed* Cromdale *off the Lizard in 1913. In a trough of foam her port rail shows one of the dummy gunports painted on to fool pirates. Calm and fog fooled the old steel skys'l-yarder, last of the famed wool clippers in the Australian trade. Loaded with nitrates from Chile on this run, she rammed the rocks and began to break up. Cadgwith lifeboatmen saved her crew in the nick of time.*

Such deeds outweigh the grim tales of plunder in bygone years. When Sir John Killigrew built the first primitive lighthouse on the Lizard in 1619, locals complained he was depriving them of God's grace—meaning there would be fewer wrecks for them to pillage!

ROBERT B. GOODMAN (ALSO RIGHT). UPPER: F. E. GIBSON

SMACK! LIZARD LIFEBOAT *furrows a placid sea on a practice run. On call day and night, crews often brave howling gales and mountainous waves. England's lifeboat service has saved more than 83,000 lives. Visitors at Mullion Cove (right) heave-ho to free a mired yacht-towing tractor. The sailboat* Wingoes*, stranded by storm, lies on greased planks awaiting a pull into the water. At neighboring Poldhu in 1901, Guglielmo Marconi's station flashed to Newfoundland the first transatlantic radio signal.*

are ready elsewhere in England. Subtropical plants and palm trees flourish in this mild climate. Small wonder the coast here is called the Cornish Riviera.

From Falmouth we sailed south to round the Lizard, dread heel of Cornwall's boot and southernmost reach of the English mainland. We passed scarcely a reef or point of land which hadn't claimed some famous wreck. Though the wind was gentle, we tossed and tumbled in the turbulent seas.

From here the granite shoreline winds west to St. Michael's Mount. As I gazed upon that sea-girt crag, the mist parted and the sun shafted down like a spotlight. Gleaming white on the perfect plinth of its pyramidal hill stood a fairy-tale castle. St. Michael's Mount from seaward ranks as one of the finest sights in all England.

I had been invited to this fantastic 21-acre island by Lord St. Levan, head of the family of St. Aubyn and last in a long line of St. Aubyns to own the Mount. He and his lady still lived there, though in 1954 he gave it to the National Trust.

I WALKED the causeway, above water only at low tide, which links the island with the Cornish shore at Marazion. A retainer in seaman's garb led me past the Mount's tidy little harbor, the stone-built village, and up the hill. Up and up we climbed the cobbled track, steep and stepped, to the ancient stone outworks, the military lookouts and the batteries, where cannon had stood guard for centuries.

At last the path brought us to a great 13th-century doorway. Inside, an elevator carried me up the last few feet, and I was grateful for that. Lord St. Levan showed me around the airy and well-lighted apartments. Despite walls of massive masonry,

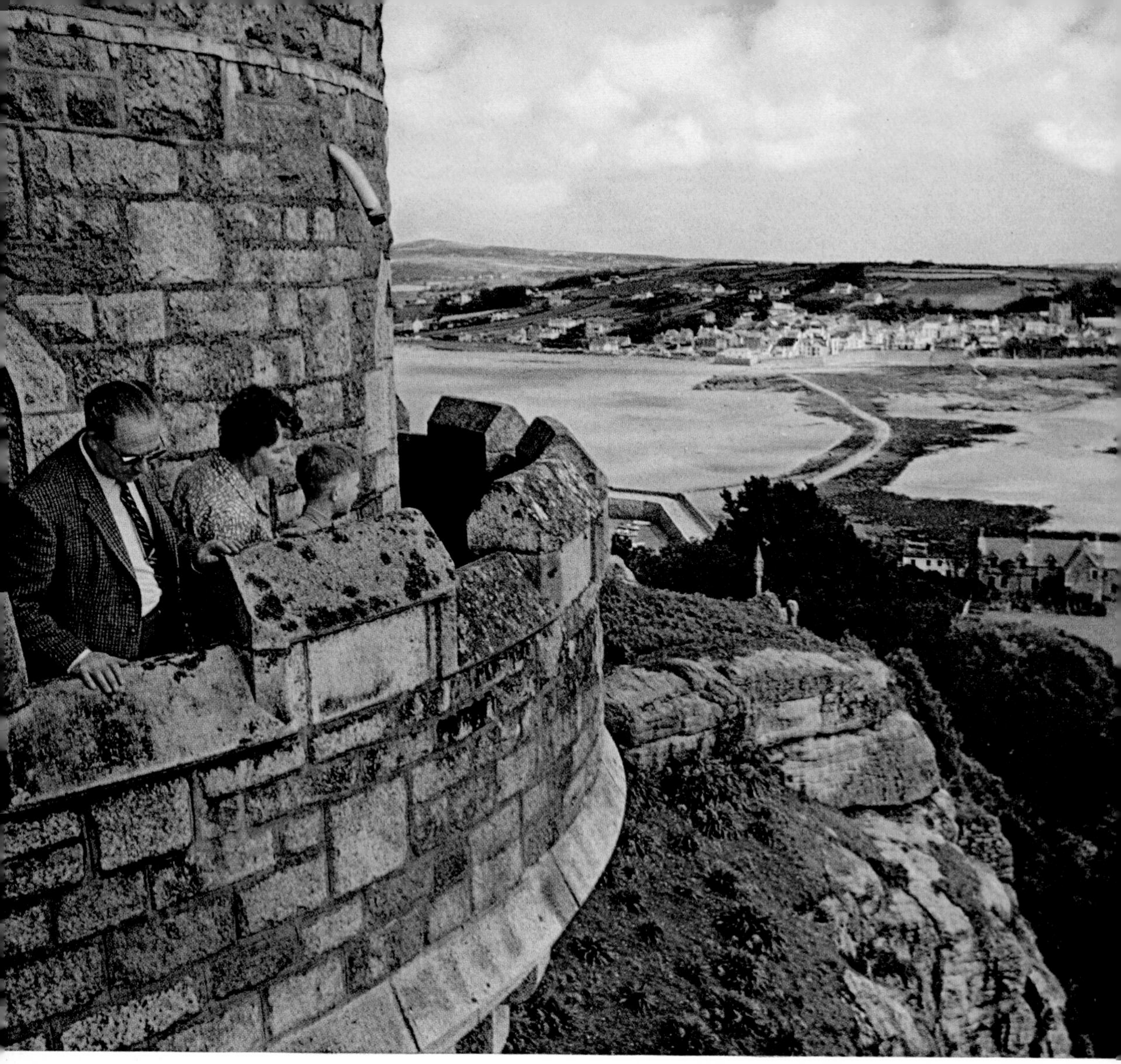

there was no feeling of medieval gloom. Sunlight streamed in windows. We visited the armory with its weapons, the library lined with huge old books, and the drawing room built in a former chapel.

We lingered in the Chevy Chase Room, named for its plaster frieze depicting a "chase" in full cry after stags, bulls, and wild boars. The term means noisy hunt and probably derives from the nature of hunts in the Cheviot Hills of northern England. Monks once dined in this old, vaulted hall.

The archangel St. Michael, related my host as we strolled along, is said to have appeared on the islet in the fifth century. As the story spread, the faithful flocked to St. Michael's Mount. In the 11th century King Edward the Confessor presented the island to the Benedictine Order. For some 400 years the Mount and its sister island across the Channel, Mont St. Michel, were united through the Order.

The Mount became an almost impregnable bastion. It has its own springs of water; it could be supplied by sea or land. But during the Wars of the Roses, John de Vere, the 13th Earl of Oxford, took it by dressing his men as pilgrims.

Lord St. Levan pointed to a group of visitors peering up at the relic on the chapel tower called St. Michael's Chair.

"I hope they don't start trying to climb into it," he remarked. "There is an old yarn that if a newly married couple comes here, whichever of them climbs into it first will be the head of the household for life."

BATTLEMENTED TOWER *of St. Michael's Mount (opposite) overlooks the bay—and a sprite flitting in the shallows (right). Though ebb tides bare the half-mile causeway, the sea still hides a forest drowned about 1700* B.C. *and, Cornish legends say, the lost land of Lyonnesse. St. Michael in stained glass spears a devil in the castle's chapel; reports of the archangel's visit in* A.D. *495 brought pilgrims to the island.*

ROBERT B. GOODMAN. OPPOSITE: BATES LITTLEHALES, NATIONAL GEOGRAPHIC PHOTOGRAPHER

I had heard of a wife who was so keen to be first into the chair that it killed her. She did not even wait for the bells in the tower to stop pealing, and their reverberations shook her out of her lofty perch.

When I left, the causeway was underwater. Lord St. Levan and I walked down steps Queen Victoria had once climbed. A motorboat took me to the stone pier at Marazion. As I glanced back at the Mount, a gull cried in the gathering gloom, and a cold, bone-searching wind rose.

Lights winked from Penzance across the bay. Spanish seamen pillaged and burned here seven years after the defeat of their Armada. I thought of the Pirates of Penzance, those cheerful imaginary figures of Gilbert and Sullivan—imaginary indeed! Many a local family engaged in the trade.

Cornwall's coast contorts past Mousehole to Porthcurno. Near here, surrounded by the roar of breakers and the screech of gulls, we peered over a cliff and found a fascinating open-air theater on rocks above the sea. Here groups from Cambridge, Oxford, and Cornwall stage plays in summer.

In full swing was *The Taming of the Shrew*—good, gusty Shakespeare for that gusty setting. Playgoers sat on earth seats cut in semicircular rows. Players with stout

STONE WALLS *ring a bathtub harbor in tiny Polperro; cobbled lanes lace the hillside. Author Villiers (below) explores the fishing village with its flowered walks and pastel-painted shops. West Cornish harbor hamlets like Cadgwith and Mousehole—locals say "Muzzle"—echo the flavor of this exquisite up-Channel miniature.*

MELVILLE BELL GROSVENOR

ROBERT B. GOODMAN

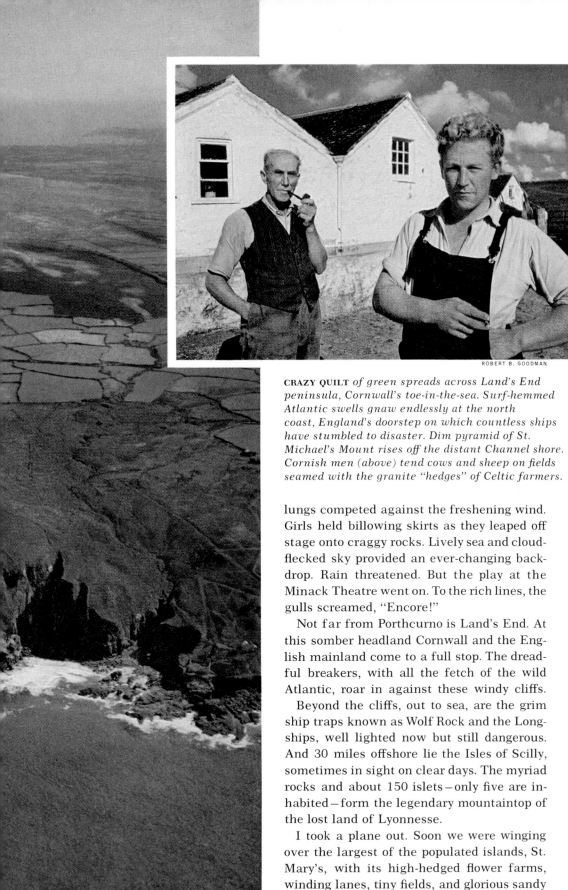

CRAZY QUILT *of green spreads across Land's End peninsula, Cornwall's toe-in-the-sea. Surf-hemmed Atlantic swells gnaw endlessly at the north coast, England's doorstep on which countless ships have stumbled to disaster. Dim pyramid of St. Michael's Mount rises off the distant Channel shore. Cornish men (above) tend cows and sheep on fields seamed with the granite "hedges" of Celtic farmers.*

lungs competed against the freshening wind. Girls held billowing skirts as they leaped off stage onto craggy rocks. Lively sea and cloud-flecked sky provided an ever-changing backdrop. Rain threatened. But the play at the Minack Theatre went on. To the rich lines, the gulls screamed, "Encore!"

Not far from Porthcurno is Land's End. At this somber headland Cornwall and the English mainland come to a full stop. The dreadful breakers, with all the fetch of the wild Atlantic, roar in against these windy cliffs.

Beyond the cliffs, out to sea, are the grim ship traps known as Wolf Rock and the Longships, well lighted now but still dangerous. And 30 miles offshore lie the Isles of Scilly, sometimes in sight on clear days. The myriad rocks and about 150 islets – only five are inhabited – form the legendary mountaintop of the lost land of Lyonnesse.

I took a plane out. Soon we were winging over the largest of the populated islands, St. Mary's, with its high-hedged flower farms, winding lanes, tiny fields, and glorious sandy beaches interspersed by rugged headlands – a

continuation of the Cornish backbone. Here the blue of the Atlantic turned to a lacy foam round the rocks.

"There is evidence that people have lived here for thousands of years," said banker Cyril Short as we tramped the gorse- and bracken-covered hills of St. Mary's. "We've got three times as many known ancient burial places as all the rest of Cornwall—more than a hundred."

We strolled to look at them through purple heather as thick as in the Highlands of Scotland. A beautifully clear artists' light covered the island. We visited several monuments, and Mr. Short told me animatedly of still another. On the small deserted island of Nornour a recent heavy gale and high sea had washed away part of the beach, exposing a series of upright stones.

"Further excavation revealed a two-room building," said Mr. Short, "with hearths and small furnaces, crucibles, and such. There were also over 250 brooches, mostly Roman, and more than 70 Roman coins. The place was a regular Roman jeweler's store! But the archeologists found it was

much older than that. It had been originally a Bronze Age dwelling."

Jewelry may have once dominated Scillonian trade. But for most of the past century spring flowers have been the staple. The Riviera-like climate produces tons of daffodils, narcissus, and iris each season.

Seafaring and, some say, highly organized smuggling also played a part in the islands' past. The rocks became a death trap for sailing ships. Legends hold that the islanders were not above profiting from wrecks, or perhaps even causing them. There was a prayer offered regularly in the St. Mary's parish church in the 18th century: "We pray

SEA SETS THE RHYTHM *of life in the Scilly Isles. Hardy boatman (right) ferries tourists; another tends lobster pots that sometimes net an errant conger eel (below). Warm currents bring early bloom to daffodils (opposite) that cheer chilled Londoners; when World War II shut off truck and rail shipments, bicycle teams pedaled the fragile cargoes 280 miles from Penzance to the capital. Relics of the sea's darker mood—figureheads from wrecks (lower)—adorn Tresco Abbey Gardens.*

BATES LITTLEHALES, NATIONAL GEOGRAPHIC PHOTOGRAPHER

ROBERT B. GOODMAN

STARK SENTINELS *of stone guard the ruins of a tin mine at Botallack (above). Gorse and briar tug at roofless buildings; sea winds moan through gaping windows. In one shaft here miners worked beneath the sea and could hear the water rolling boulders on the ocean floor overhead.*

Cornwall traded tin as early as Phoenician days. Most was shipped by Bretons to Gaul, thence overland to the Mediterranean, where it was blended with copper from Cyprus to make bronze. In later centuries hundreds of pits were working. But depressions often closed them. Miners scattered; some joined the Gold Rush to California. "Where a hole is dug in the ground," a 19th-century observer noted, "no matter in what corner of the globe, you will be sure to find a Cornishman at the bottom of it, searching for metal." In the 1920's destitute miners roamed the land in choirs, singing instead of digging for their supper.

Most mines stand abandoned today. But men still sweat and pick deep in the bowels of the earth at Camborne's South Crofty mine (left). Water oozing from rocks seems hot enough for tea.

Thee, O Lord, not that wrecks should happen, but that if any . . . happen, Thou wilt guide them into the Scilly Isles for the benefit of the inhabitants."

Back in Hugh Town, the pint-size, bustling harbor which is the capital of the archipelago, the 800-ton motor ship *Scillonian* was coming in on her daily trip from Penzance, crowded with passengers.

Long queues were forming at the stone steps leading to the open launches that serve the islands. Young women in shorts hurried along the quay leading their children. The menfolk toted picnic baskets jam-packed with provender to last a week.

CORNWALL'S MAINLAND abounds in relics of early man – remains of his forts, his villages, his industries. Tin has been mined here in one way or another as far back as the Bronze Age. Copper, tungsten, arsenic, kaolin, zinc, silver, and lead also exist on the boot-shaped Cornish peninsula.

Leonard Thomas, manager of South Crofty, one of the few tinneries still worked in Cornwall, took us proudly about the works. Above ground, ore moved on conveyors into grinding machines and ended as brown sludge in large vats. The great wheels of the hauling machinery led down into the shafts. In that tin-veined inferno 2,000 feet below, most of the 200 miners toiled in temperatures that range above 100° F. But these were Cornishmen. And Cornishmen are miners.

All along the brooding north coast, savage cliffs fell to a sea littered with fang-toothed rocks and shallow reefs. Yet on the

"**THE OPEN COLISEUM** *of each little cove . . . the unending presence of the sea breathing ceaselessly over the shoulder of each hill. . . ." Thus does the Cornish coast inspire artists, who flourish amid the charm of St. Ives (above). Here sculptor Barbara Hepworth (left) prepares*

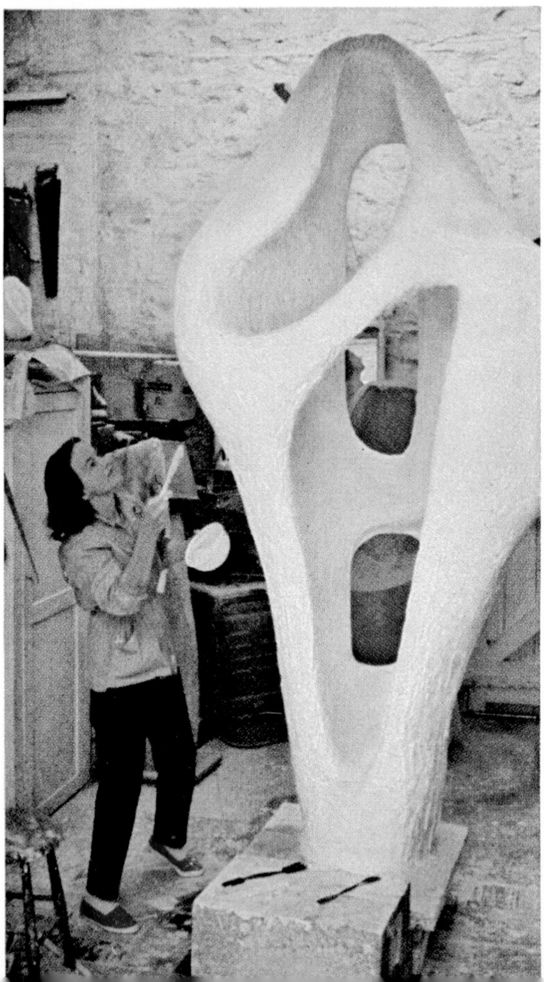

ROBERT B. GOODMAN

a model for her nine-foot "Figure for Landscape." Color in stained glass intrigues painter Peter Lanyon, who roams beach, cliff, abandoned mine, translating what he sees into nonobjective works. Potter Bernard Leach sees his work as the "counter-revolution, the refusal of the slavery of the machine."

Colin Wilson (below), one of England's "Angry Young Men" and author of The Outsider, *lives at Gorran Haven. Daphne du Maurier writes in solitude at Menabilly (top left). "Every book is a purge," she says. "At the end of it one is empty . . . like a dry shell on the beach, waiting for the tide to come in."*

THE CLOISTERS COLLECTION, METROPOLITAN MUSEUM OF ART
RIGHT: ANNE REVIS GROSVENOR

ATOP TINTAGEL'S *sea-sundered headland stand castle ruins long linked in fancy with the sixth-century court of King Arthur. A Celtic chieftain who, after the Romans left Britain, led his countrymen against invading Saxons, Arthur became enshrined in legend. Chroniclers and troubadours wove enchanted tales of his knights of the Round Table. This 14th-century French tapestry, an early portrayal of chivalry's paragon, enthrones him in a cathedral as the perfect Christian king.*

land side we found charming places everywhere. I particularly liked St. Ives.

This old town around its ancient harbor is picturesque, its history romantic, its climate soft. Its name? St. Ia, according to legend, came floating in from Ireland on a large leaf. The leaf, however, was possibly a coracle, a seagoing wicker basket that some Irish and Welsh fishermen still use.

The brilliant light, the sparkling blue waters, the splendor of cliffs and sand and sun have long lured artists to St. Ives. Among them came James Abbott McNeill Whistler, the onetime West Point cadet who became a great painter and etcher in Europe during the 19th century.

Bernard Leach, the renowned potter, was at work when I visited him. He had kilns downstairs and a workshop above. He talked little about himself, but he *did* talk about the arts. "The machine takes the heart out of labor. The craftsman is almost the only worker left who has the privilege and the satisfaction of employing his hand, heart, and head in balance."

IF NO KING named Arthur ever lived, then he should have. And Cornwall was the right place for him and his chivalrous knights of

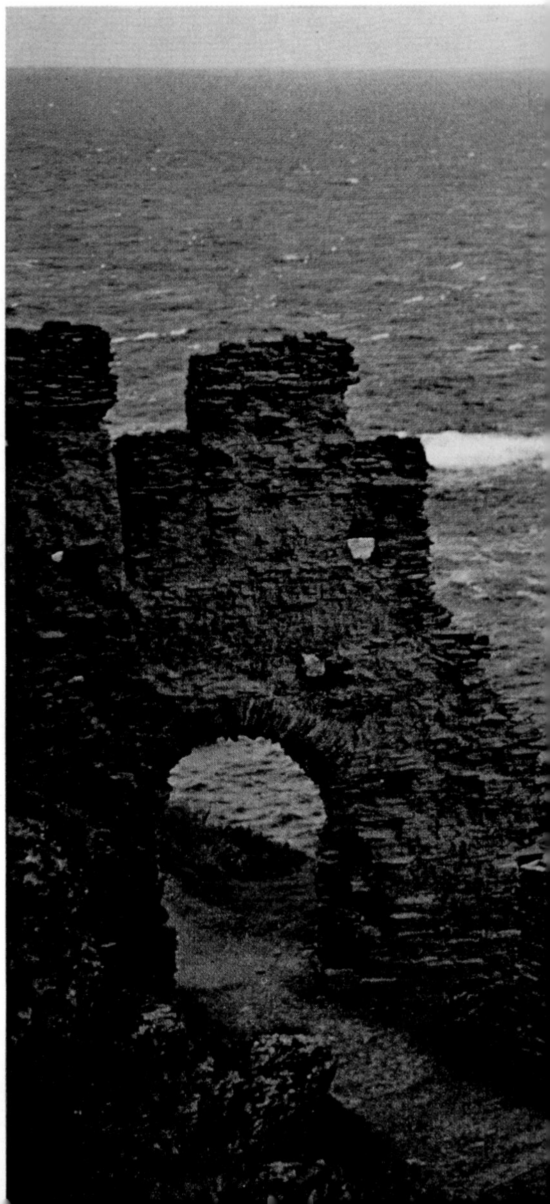

the Round Table. Some scholars are skeptical. But even the most skeptical admit that once a great chieftain in Cornwall fought off the Saxon invaders.

Many places claim connection with King Arthur. But nowhere is belief in the legend stronger than on the headland called Tintagel on Cornwall's northern coast. Beyond the rolling fields with the dark clouds racing in from the sea, I found a venerable and romantic ruin upon a sea-torn cliff, a gaunt wraith of a castle, split in two where the sea has cut the whole headland.

A government treatise on ancient monuments denies that Tintagel has "any authentic connection with Arthur." It says the castle "was, in fact, first built by Reginald, Earl of Cornwall," and the "visible remains were mostly built between 1236 and 1272." But who knows? Under these stones are the traces of a Celtic monastery dating from the sixth century, and of what else before that no man now can say.

At Tintagel I forgot the scholars. As I looked upon this mystic, eerie scene of wildness and beauty, I voted for Lord Tennyson and his *Idylls of the King*. I was prepared to go along with the romantic Sir Thomas Malory, who lived when Columbus was a youth and whose fame rests on his stories of Arthur's deeds.

Crumbling walls overlook the cove where a legendary wave, bright with flame, once swept a naked babe destined to be King

Arthur into the arms of the magician Merlin. Springy green turf floors the spot where the famed Round Table may have stood. The crash of thundering seas, the crying of the gulls, and the sighing of the wind have long replaced the harp of Guinevere. But in Cornwall the legends are real, and at Tintagel the ghosts remain.

RETURNING to *Tectona* in Falmouth harbor, we glanced aloft with horror. At the masthead, 60 feet above the deck with precious little to hold to, sat young Eddie Grosvenor, calmly surveying the countryside!

Eddie was impatient to move off to sea again. We all were. So we hove up and headed up-Channel before a gentle west wind.

The wheel's kick was quiet and the wind's song low as we wandered along, staying close in by the land. South Cornish fields looked parklike from seaward. Rain squalls hung languidly about, but none caught up with us. We were bound for Fowey, that 15th-century hotbed of pirates. "Gallants of Fowey," they called themselves, and they bossed the whole Channel in their day. Yet no Gallants did we see as we sailed into Readymoney Cove. Instead, around that peaceful harbor were vacationers' trailer towns and yachts and bathing children.

"Fowey children learn to pull a boat soon after they can walk," Daphne du Maurier, the famed novelist, told us at her home at nearby Menabilly. The local color and romantic background of several of her books came vividly to life for us in Cornwall.

Sir Arthur Quiller-Couch, Leo Walmsley, and Colin Wilson have added to the region's literary luster. Fowey and Falmouth were haunts of Kenneth Grahame; immortal Mr. Rat and Mr. Mole in *The Wind in the Willows* may have a bit of local blood.

Here, and everywhere we went in Cornwall, we found a vivid sense of the long past. Secure in their hilly fastnesses, the ancient Cornish people had remained cut

BOATS STRANDED *at ebb tide before hillside hamlets like Mevagissey; a young smile reflecting the old*

off from England. They liked it that way. Roman occupation meant little to them. Even the Norman Conquest took time to penetrate, and then not too deeply. The Cornishman used his own language down to the 18th century. He has remained a true son of his native land, far more than the people in other parts of England.

"This isn't England, you know!" I was told. "This is Cornwall."

Aboard *Tectona* once more, we watched a lively yachting race. As we sat on deck for one final meal of Cornish pasties, a trio of heeling dinghies swept by. Then a family of swans came alongside. With great reluctance I gave the order to heave up the anchor. Our wonderful tour of Devon and Cornwall was ending.

Eddie loosed the jib. The men stretched the main and the mizzen. The sails filled nicely with the soft warm breeze, and we were off. But as we passed out to sea, we all looked back for a long, long time.

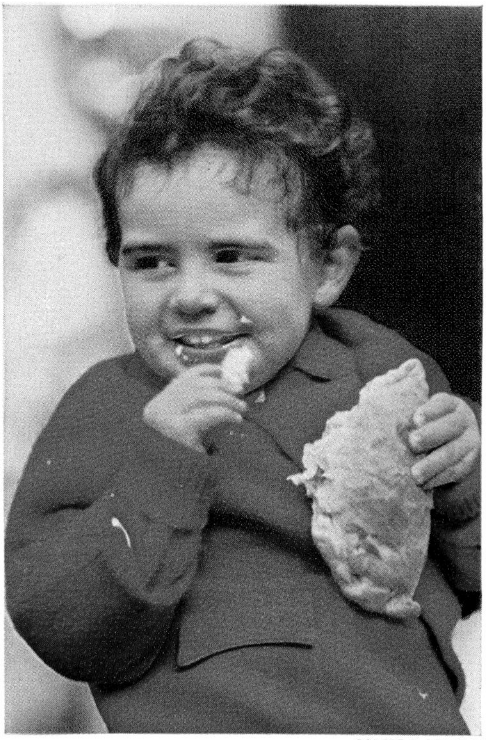

ROBERT B. GOODMAN

delight in a hearty Cornish pasty—with scenes like these Cornwall marks the memories of her guests.

THE MIDLANDS

INDUSTRIAL MUSCLE

IN A GREEN AND PLEASANT LAND

THE SAXON KINGDOM of Mercia swept from Welsh hills to East Anglian fens, its fields and wooded vales unbroken save by scattered villages. Birmingham was one, valued at 20 shillings by conquering Normans in their Domesday Book. Chester's walls soon rose atop Roman stones; castles and abbeys thrust up towers. Yet Sherwood Forest could still cloak Robin Hood's Merrie Men.

When Tudor peace ended feudal war's "dire division," men richer in purse than in pedigree trumpeted their status with lavish country houses. The plowman stood aside, cap in hand, as squire and gentry galloped past, hounds chorusing. Clay underlay the farmer's soil; coal and ironstone edged the heath where the fox hid. What mattered coal and iron in a world of maypole dancing?

Hargreaves' and Crompton's spinning machines, Cartwright's power loom, and Watt's steam engine changed that world. Lombe's silk mill at Derby, rising five stories, light glowing from 468 windows as workers toiled into the night, inspired Arkwright, a barber. He invented a spinning frame, built cotton mills, and advertised: "Children of all Ages, above seven years old, may have constant Employment." Josiah Wedgwood, "Vase Maker General to the Universe," sought to "ASTONISH THE WORLD ALL AT ONCE, for I hate piddleing...." He put the plowman to work in the Potteries, turning clay into teacups and living by the clock instead of the sun. At Coalbrookdale in Shropshire, the Abraham Darbys, father and son, learned to smelt iron with coke instead of charcoal. Coal and ore were ripped from the soil. Country lads swelled man-eating Birmingham, where Bessemer converters would redden the night sky.

"And was Jerusalem builded here," cried William Blake, "among these dark Satanic mills?" Skies purer, scars healing, the "Black Country" gleams with new-built cities. Prospering workers breathe the free air of parks, and plowland returned to pasture spreads a grass carpet for huntsmen riding in the mists of morning.

BRITAIN'S PROSPEROUS MIDRIFF

Amid the ringing of anvils National Geographic's Stuart E. Jones hears the hunting horn echo over Midland meadows

NEAR NORMANTON LE HEATH, in Leicestershire, we followed a winding road between fields blessed with a very special, very English kind of summer beauty. On all sides stretched a rolling countryside of extravagant greenness touched here and there with golden blazes of flowering mustard. Fat cattle stolidly cropped the lush grass, and lambs frisked about their black-faced mothers. Honeysuckle and new-mown hay perfumed the soft June air.

All that this picture of rural England lacked was the sight of the Quorn Hunt streaming past with yelping hounds and halloing riders in "pinks." That would come later, on frosty autumn mornings.

We pulled into a lay-by, one of the roadside rest areas that motorists in Britain find every few miles. My host, Ronald Harley, served up bread, cheese, and beer. Lounging under a giant beech, we basked in a tranquillity that I thought had gone from this world. From the village, unseen beyond the hills, a faint pealing of church bells floated like a silvery benediction.

We had driven north from London, and this was my introduction to Britain's industrial Midlands, a region usually described as smoky, grimy, and grim.

"We have smoke and grime here, right enough," Ron said, "and perhaps there's grimness too. But you can't very well have heavy industry without a certain amount of dirt. Midlanders are realistic people. They have a saying, 'Where there's muck there's brass'—brass meaning money."

My tour would cover the counties of Warwickshire, Northamptonshire, Leicestershire, Rutland, Nottinghamshire, Derbyshire, Worcestershire, Shropshire, and Cheshire, as well as parts of other shires. Roughly the size of Massachusetts, this populous area spreads over nearly one-sixth of England.

Ron Harley lives near the heart of the Midlands in a pleasant Leicestershire market town whose name makes me think of a man drinking coffee through a drooping moustache: Ashby de la Zouch. It honors the de la Zuches, a Norman family.

From their living room window the Harleys look across a green to the tower of ruined Ashby Castle. Mary Queen of Scots stayed there briefly during her long imprisonment that ended with a blow from the headsman's ax at Fotheringhay Castle, now just a mound in Northamptonshire. Sir Walter Scott, reconstructing English history for his *Ivanhoe*, made Ashby de la Zouch the scene of a tournament in which his hero jousts with Richard the Lionheart.

Already Ron had taught me to avoid high-speed motorways like M-1 and M-5 and take secondary roads through the Midlands. I poked about obscure villages with names that might have been invented by P. G. Wodehouse: Long Itchington, Upton Snodsbury, North Piddle, Sheepy Magna, Barton in the Beans.

Ron helped himself to more Leicestershire Stilton and sighed contentedly. "You know, England seems to be tidying itself up a bit. It has discovered that it can do its job

STEAMING MOUNTS, *milling hounds—the famed Quorn Hunt readies for brisk January sport near Loughborough. Though factory chimneys thrust into Midland skies, miles of field and hedge beckon in the Shires: "Unmarred is our sport—undiminished our fame . . . For 'Hunting and Les'tershire' still mean the same."*

BATES LITTLEHALES, NATIONAL GEOGRAPHIC PHOTOGRAPHER

without permanently defiling the countryside. Not many years ago this very spot was a raw wound for open-cast coal mining—what you Americans call strip mining. Hundreds of acres were torn up. A ghastly sight. But after the miners exhausted the deposit, the National Coal Board made them fill the holes and replant grass, trees, and shrubs."

IN CROWDED, bustling Birmingham, second largest city in the British Isles, manufacturers, merchants, craftsmen, and shoppers go about their affairs today amid vast difficulties. On all sides the word is "Tear it down and build it anew." Many buildings were crumbling before World War II. Hitler destroyed or damaged more than 155,000 dwellings, factories, and other buildings. Almost the entire red-brick core of the city

BATES LITTLEHALES, NATIONAL GEOGRAPHIC PHOTOGRAPHER

BIRMINGHAM'S *new Bull Ring Centre stands in the old market plaza where dogs ripped bulls and cockfights drew clamorous crowds. Stalls with bright awnings recall days when young Samuel Johnson watched his father hawk books. When John Wesley preached here, church bells dinned to drown him out. A nobleman who tried to build on the market place gave up when townsfolk tore down the day's work each night.*

A mustachioed merchant's mannequin (far left) struts Christmas styles while produce rides to booths on a cart (below). A "good market towne" even in Tudor times, its economy "mayntayned by smithes," Birmingham was humbly born, probably as the Saxon "homestead of Beornmund's people." It counted only nine tenants in Norman days. The Industrial Revolution blighted the city with dark mills and workers' hovels. Hitler's bombs razed them; from the rubble the citizens rebounded with gleaming buildings.

disappeared. In its place rose dozens of new structures. At its heart Birmingham now has the ultramodern Bull Ring shopping center, spreading out for many blocks from a site where sports fans of an earlier age once enjoyed bullbaiting.

Automation grows apace in Birmingham. I noticed that barmen in the plush new Hotel Savoy no longer had to "pull up" pints of beer, ale, or stout with hand pumps. Instead, they flipped microswitches, and exact measures, complete with snowy collars, filled glasses. The beverages flowed through color-coded nylon pipes from kegs in some hidden central storeroom.

The spectacle appeared to unnerve a tweedy gentleman standing next to me. Upon tasting his beer, he was even more upset. "Good heavens!" he exclaimed. "It's been chilled!" He set his glass down with a thump. "India, Suez, a Labour government – and now cold beer! What next?"

Birmingham's reputation as one of the world's foremost manufacturing centers lies deeply rooted in the past. In 1586 the historian Camden described it as a town

PATIENT PAINTERS *ply an ancient art at John Hardman Studios in Birmingham. Stained-glass windows for the Houses of Parliament and for churches as far afield as Australia took shape here. Guided by a colored drawing, an artist adds detail to pre-cut, solid-color panes held to his easel with wax. Lead-laced mosaics shed a blessing (right) as skilled hands fit them to a new Birmingham Catholic church.*

BATES LITTLEHALES, NATIONAL GEOGRAPHIC PHOTOGRAPHER

"resounding with hammers and anvils." Toward the end of the 17th century William III, fearing invasion, ordered the city's gunsmiths to supply 200 flintlocks a month "at seventeen shillings per piece ready money."

Thus was born the association of gunsmiths which in 1861 became the Birmingham Small Arms Company Ltd., one of the best known industries in the Midlands. During World War II, BSA produced nearly half a million Browning machine guns, the weapon that put the sting in the Royal Air Force's Spitfires and Hurricanes.

BSA first ventured away from munitions in 1880. An inventor, E. C. F. Otto, turned up with a strange bicycle with a large wheel on either side of the rider. He pedaled it up

and down the boardroom table; impressed, the directors went into production. Otto's cycle never quite caught on, but it pushed BSA toward becoming one of the world's largest makers of bicycles, and later of motorcycles and scooters. Around 1900 the company broke into the infant auto industry by buying Britain's oldest car firm, Daimler, whose name appears on limousines, sports cars, and on many of England's big red double-deck buses. A few years ago BSA sold Daimler to Jaguar of Coventry.

In addition to its diversified heavy industries, Birmingham has more than 10,000 firms that employ fewer than 30 workers. Take the goldsmiths and silversmiths of Vyse Street, for example. To jewelers the world over, Vyse Street means what Wall Street means to financiers. I spent a morning touring workshops, watching graying craftsmen fashion rings, brooches, necklaces, bracelets, and earrings.

Many of these baubles, I was told, would wind up on department-store bargain counters or in Oriental bazaars. But others are so finely wrought, so cunningly set with rare gems, that they find their ultimate owners in Cartier's and Tiffany's.

Birmingham's booming factories have made heavy use of the immigrants who poured into Britain in recent years from opposite sides of the earth. I saw scores of them standing in movie queues or gazing into shop windows. West Indians seemed to be longing for their sunny islands. East Indians and Pakistanis, mackintoshes covering their saris and pantaloons, looked sadly displaced. In the drab red-brick houses of suburban Smethwick, where the newcomers have concentrated, the familiar aroma of boiled Brussels sprouts still predominated. But I could also pick out the heady odors of curry and roast kid.

I MADE my headquarters in Coventry, 16 miles away. From there I planned to drive to Birmingham whenever necessary. But one car trip was enough. Thereafter I rode on the comfortable top deck of the "Midland Red" and let the bus driver fight traffic.

Sometimes my own struggles with traffic yielded pleasant rewards. This happened to

MIDLANDS MUSCLE *flexes in the "workshop to the world." Coventry's Jaguars (lower right) growl down distant roads; jet engines from Rolls Royce in Derby (below) scrawl contrails across global skies. "Rolls" rolls its plush cars from a Cheshire plant; Rover and British Motor assemble at Birmingham. Cadbury's pleases many a sweet tooth with chocolates from a garden suburb that bans pubs. Sausage skins, handcuffs—you name it, the Midlands makes it.*

Birmingham hammered out 15,000 swords for Roundheads, but snubbed Charles I's orders. Townsfolk even hijacked his baggage as he trekked to Banbury in 1642. Enraged, Prince Rupert fired houses and levied taxes to buy boots for his troops. Making shoe buckles once busied 20,000 here. Idled by newfangled laces, some switched to counterfeiting coins.

As city mills feed world trade, so Birmingham University feeds minds from many lands (right). "Oxbridge" traditionally breeds scholars and statesmen; "Redbricks" like this, sired by factory towns as trade schools, today produce engineers, actuaries, industrial managers. Courses range from cybernetics to brewing, and campuses often mix Victorian halls with skyscraper dormitories and shiny new labs.

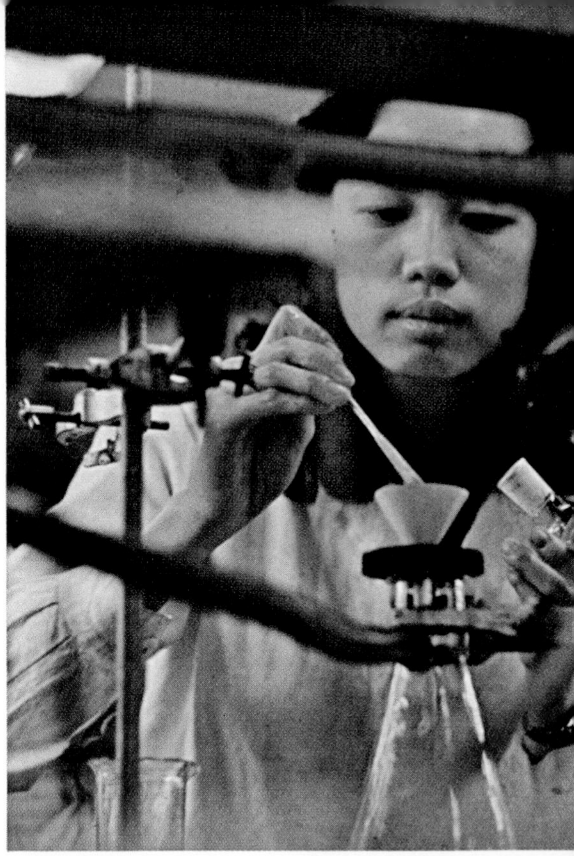

BATES LITTLEHALES, NATIONAL GEOGRAPHIC PHOTOGRAPHER

me in Worcester, the ancient city on the southwestern edge of the Midlands.

Serene amid Worcester's tumultuous urban renewal stands the Gothic cathedral, its pinnacled tower and buttresses mirrored in the placid Severn. Tourists come to view the effigied tomb of King John (page 259), the rich carvings, the Norman crypt. Other quiet havens include the Commandery, founded in 1085 as a hospice, and a cluster of black-and-white timbered houses in Friar Street, one dating from 1480.

A serpentine route with many detours led me to the famed Worcester Royal Porcelain Company. I toured the factory that turns out some of England's finest bone china—so-called because it contains bone ash. This ingredient gives the china its special finish, translucency, and strength. In the studio I watched artist Ronald van Ruyckevelt put finishing touches on sketches of tropical fish. From his drawings come plasticine models. Finally, after repeated kiln firings and painting by experts, emerge lifelike porcelain fish in realistic settings of coral and sea fans.

Rows of locked cabinets contained whole aviaries of birds looking as if they might take wing any moment. These were created in porcelain by the late Dorothy Doughty, whose figurines command big prices among collectors all over the world.

Trying to find my way out of Worcester's tangled streets, I braked to avoid a truck entering a factory. The name beside the gate rang a bell: Lea & Perrins Ltd. . . . Worcestershire sauce, of course! Here I was at the home of the orange-labeled bottles whose piquant dark-brown contents had mystified me since boyhood.

I parked, presented myself to a receptionist, and shortly was welcomed by General Manager Julian E. Lea—no relation to John Wheeley Lea who, with William Perrins, launched the firm in 1837. Messrs. Lea and Perrins had opened a chemists' shop, or

BATES LITTLEHALES, NATIONAL GEOGRAPHIC PHOTOGRAPHER

pharmacy, in 1822. One day a distinguished customer, Lord Sandys, brought a recipe for a condiment he had enjoyed in India. Could Lea and Perrins duplicate it?

The chemists went to work with mortars and pestles, flasks and beakers, and a variety of ingredients. Several days later they asked Lord Sandys to taste the result. He sipped, frowned, took another cautious taste, and frowned again. "Interesting, but not quite what I had in Bombay. Pity."

Disappointed, the partners tasted their product and agreed they had added little to the joys of gastronomy. They poured the stuff into a barrel, banished it to a cellar, and went back to prescriptions. Months later one of them stumbled upon the forgotten barrel. He opened it, took a taste, and then another, in growing excitement. Time had worked a miracle. Lord Sandys was notified and arrived posthaste. He sipped the brew, and a joyful light came into his eyes.

"Gentlemen," he said emotionally, "this is excellent – precisely what I had in mind. I salute you as benefactors of mankind. Make up another batch immediately. We shall call it Worcestershire sauce."

Lea and Perrins made up another batch and, as the word spread, another and another . . . until the chemists' shop was forgotten and the batches came to be measured in hundreds of gallons.

"Many Americans," I said to Mr. Lea, "believe that Worcestershire sauce contains a secret ingredient. If I promise not to print it, will you tell me what it is?"

He laughed. "There is no secret ingredient. Anyone can mix the same materials and call the result Worcestershire sauce. In fact, our competitors in the United States do just that. But ours is the 'original and genuine,' as we say on the label."

Mr. Lea unstoppered a bottle and treated himself to a sniff. "Really, it's rather good stuff, you know," he said. "It makes a tired cut of beef get up and dance."

I crossed the Worcester and Birmingham Canal, and resolved to explore, someday, the waterways that lace the Midlands. In 1759 the Duke of Bridgewater, seeking an efficient way to move coal to Manchester from his mines at Worsely, commissioned James Brindley to build a canal. Brindley made a "ricconitoring" and decided to lift his "cut" across the River Irwell on an aqueduct – an engineering marvel. In 1761 boats began making the 10½-mile voyage. Coal prices in Manchester dropped 50 percent.

Brindley envisioned more than 260 miles of canals linking Severn, Mersey, Thames, and Trent, and lived to see much of the work completed. Others carried on. Gaily painted barges slipped along an estimated 4,100 miles of British inland waterways.

Horses, mules, or men towed a boat. Hand-operated locks usually lifted it over hills. In tunnels bargemen would lie on outthrust boards and "leg" the boat along, pushing against dank walls. Families lived aboard, raising children to the proud lore of the canals, wearing their own dress – gypsylike earrings often adorning the men.

The great canal era lasted some 80 years. About half the network remains, much of it navigable only for pleasure boats.

I FOUND COVENTRY, second city of Warwickshire, a busy, fascinating place. Among its complex of factories, at least three rank with the world's leaders in their fields: Courtaulds Ltd. in spinning rayon and nylon; the Coventry plant of Massey-Ferguson Ltd., a Canadian firm, in producing tractors, reapers, and other equipment used where

COSTUMED DANCERS *(opposite) evoke the Regency heyday of Leamington. A doctor's endorsement of its waters in 1794 brought three duchesses in one season. Victoria's 1838 visit made the Warwickshire spa "Royal." John Ruskin arrived ill, stayed and sipped, and left exulting, "I have gone back to brown potatoes and cherry pie!" Visitors still take the waters in the Pump Room, and stroll the illuminated gardens on the banks of the Leam.*

Canal life means paint, polish, and a bit of gossip for Mum as her floating home waits its turn at Braunston Locks, Northamptonshire. "Narrowboat," 70 feet long with 7-foot beam, carries 40 tons of cargo on Midland waterways.

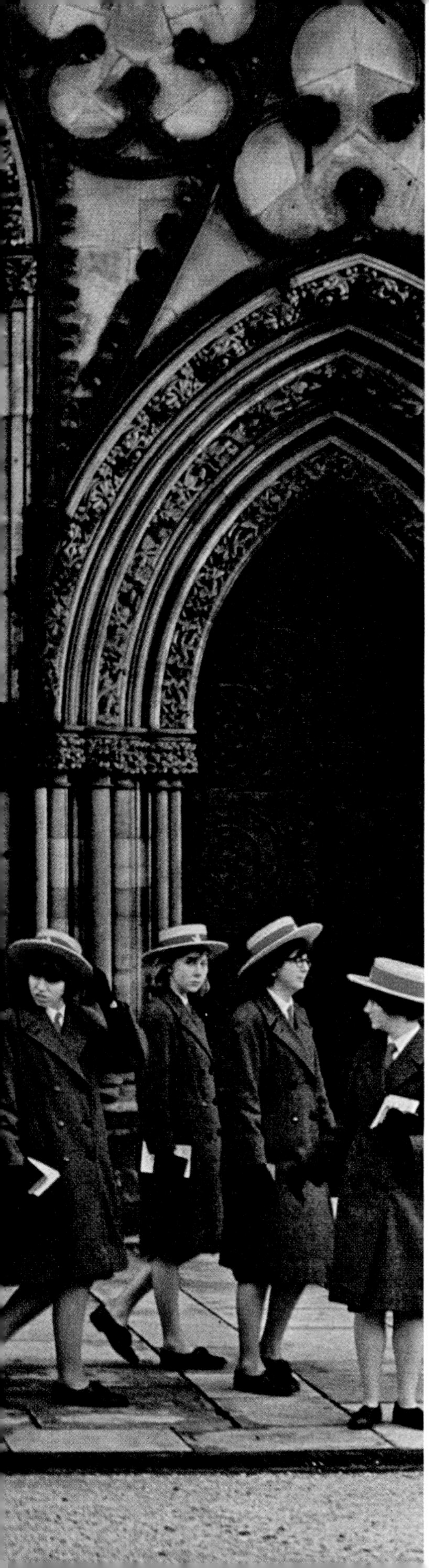

earth must be moved or crops cultivated; and Alfred Herbert Ltd. in making machine tools. The glamour product of Coventry is, of course, the sleek Jaguar sports car.

Coventry began life toward the end of the seventh century as a crossroads hamlet. A Saxon convent here was destroyed in 1016 by Danish invaders led by King Canute. From this and later religious houses the medieval village may have taken its name, though some trace the source to "Cofa's tree"—a famous tree owned by an early resident.

By 1226 the town had become an important wool center. The expression "as true as Coventry blue" survives as a tribute to the skill of the city's dyers. No one can date the expression to "send one to Coventry," meaning to banish. One possible derivation is that during the Civil War Birmingham sent Royalist prisoners to Coventry.

This old insult may explain why many Coventry citizens derisively refer to Birmingham as "Brummagem" and its natives as "Brummies." Both derive from the old pronunciation of the larger city's name and recall days when it made shoddy goods and counterfeit money. Birmingham's football team, incidentally, is known as "the Brums."

THE NIGHT of November 14, 1940, was one that George J. G. Collier and his fellow citizens of Coventry will never forget. Mr. Collier locked his midtown bookshop and set out through a blackout made largely ineffective by a full moon—a bomber's moon. Air raid sirens were wailing before he reached home.

"I had been through a number of raids," Mr. Collier recalled to me 25 years later. "In fact, my earlier shop had been destroyed and I had moved to another. Something told me this night we were in for a really bad one—a blitz.

UNDER THE STONY GAZE OF SAINTS, *schoolgirls gather before Lichfield Cathedral, whose three spires thrusting heavenward are unique in England. Samuel Johnson, born here in 1709, set up a school nearby that drew three pupils—one of them the great actor David Garrick. Dr. Johnson said his townsmen were "the most sober, decent people in England... and spoke the purest English." But a century earlier George Fox, founder of the Society of Friends, had walked the streets barefoot, crying, "Woe to the bloody city of Lichfield!"*

BATES LITTLEHALES, NATIONAL GEOGRAPHIC PHOTOGRAPHER

"I got my wife and we went to Rugby, to stay with friends. As we left the city, the first flames were aglow, high-explosive bombs crashed among the factories, machine guns chattered, the anti-aircraft barrage thundered, and searchlights swept the sky.

"All that night, until dawn, I stood on a hilltop at Rugby and watched the lurid glare in the sky that was Coventry burning.

"I made my way back and managed to enter the city. My bookshop had vanished. So had my home. But the greatest shock was finding that our beautiful medieval Cathedral Church of St. Michael was gone."

Coventry Cathedral lay open to the sky, its timbers smoking, its pillars, arcades, clerestories of the nave, chancel, and aisles in long, broken piles. Melted lead from the roof had splashed the tumbled stones.

Standing amid the ruins, the Very Rev. R. T. Howard, Coventry's provost, felt a "deep certainty that as the cathedral had been crucified with Christ, so it would rise again with Him. How or when, we could not tell; nor did it matter. *The cathedral would rise again....*"

Rise it did. In May, 1962, the new Coventry Cathedral was consecrated. This vast structure, marvelously combining glittering modernity with the deepest and sincerest traditions of the Church, rises beside the ruins. Architect Sir Basil Spence refrained from disturbing the bombed-out relic except to form a junction between old and new—a bridge from past to present.

I joined the thousands who troop daily through the cathedral. A blaze of sunlight struck an enormous bank of stained glass

LADY GODIVA *in bronze still rides in Coventry, "clothed on with chastity," says Tennyson's prim phrase on the pedestal. Old accounts say the 11th-century countess rode the streets naked to persuade her husband Leofric, the Saxon Earl of Mercia, to free the town from "heavy bondage." Legend later added Peeping Tom, who peeked and went blind. Exotic dress of Indian and Pakistani workers enlivens today's streets, where shops tempt young and old.*

BATES LITTLEHALES, NATIONAL GEOGRAPHIC PHOTOGRAPHER

and turned the nave golden. And beyond the altar the vast tapestry of Graham Sutherland's Christ seemed to vibrate in the light. That tapestry, the world's largest, weighs nearly a ton; 40 men carried it in when it arrived from the French looms that wove it. The effect is overpowering.

The ruined cathedral outside also reaches deeply into human emotions. The open floor, washed by the rains between the roofless walls, is still used for services on Easter and Whit Sundays. A crude altar, fashioned from fallen stones, stands beneath the tracery of the Gothic apse. Here rises a cross of charred beams that was put together after the destruction. Behind it, carved on the wall, are the words, "Father Forgive."

THE TOWN OF RUGBY, 12 miles east of Coventry, encloses within its busy streets an island of tree-shaded grass and mellow brick, Rugby School. Here is the scene of that boyhood classic, *Tom Brown's Schooldays*. Its author, Thomas Hughes, stands in sculptured dignity outside one of the Tudor-style school buildings.

A grocer, Lawrence Sheriff, founded Rugby in 1567 to give free education to local lads. It gained imperishable fame after Dr. Thomas Arnold took over as headmaster in 1828. For 14 years England's greatest public-school reformer infused Rugby with moral purpose, inspiring his boys to develop a code of "fair play" and "good form."

Under Dr. Arnold the younger boys continued to "fag" (do menial chores) for the older ones, but the ritual gained meaning as a character-building discipline. Under Arnold the masters continued to flog, but with righteous justice instead of helpless rage.

RISING IN THE SHADOW *of shattered ruins, Coventry's new cathedral symbolizes the city's rebirth from the ashes of war, when the work and beauty of centuries were destroyed in a single evil night. Angels and saints by John Hutton etch the West Front; its glass panels reflect gaping windows and roofless walls of the Gothic cathedral founded on the site of Leofric and Godiva's abbey church. Spectators in the porch linking the two cathedrals watch men of the Warwickshire Regiment rehearse a ceremony.*

BATES LITTLEHALES, NATIONAL GEOGRAPHIC PHOTOGRAPHER

Five years before Arnold arrived, a young player invented Rugby football. Instead of booting the ball downfield, he grabbed it and scampered off "with a fine disregard for the rules of football as played in his time."

"Somewhere, surely afar ... is practised that strength, Zealous, beneficent, firm!" So wrote poet Matthew Arnold, memorializing his father in "Rugby Chapel." Certainly Dr. Arnold's strength was practiced here on earth. England's public schools followed Rugby's example in giving their boys a Victorian sense of manliness and decency.

I walked the quiet lanes that wind through the old school and watched sixth-form boys hurrying to class. They looked a good deal more pleasant–tall youths in varicolored house caps–than the loutish bullies who "roasted" the hero before a fire in my illustrated edition of *Tom Brown*.

Britain's public schools have been heavily criticized for being based on caste. "Eton, Harrow . . . and their cheaper and more pernicious imitators should be razed to the ground and their foundations sown with salt," wrote one of the more vituperative critics–George Bernard Shaw. Midlands visitors may not agree with him, but they drop by his home, "Shaw's Corner," at Ayot St. Lawrence, Hertfordshire.

Not far away stands Hatfield House. Of the stately homes that abound within the loosely defined area of my story, Hatfield is nearest London. I had stopped on my way north to marvel at its brick façade, topped by a cupola that reminds one of New England. I walked its broad grounds, both well kept and well used, and had tea in the remnant of the Old Palace.

Cardinal Morton built the original in 1497, and Queen Elizabeth I lived here in virtual imprisonment in her younger years. She was sitting under a great oak on the grounds, tradition tells us, when she received word that Mary Tudor, her Protestant-burning half sister, had died and that she was queen. I saw what is supposed to be the tree–a gnarled and rotting old stump.

Robert Cecil, son of Lord Burghley, Elizabeth's chief minister, acquired the Old Palace from James I. He pulled down all but the Great Hall and used the bricks to build

Hatfield House. Cecil, also an adviser to royalty, became the first Earl of Salisbury, and since 1612, when Hatfield was finished, it has been the family seat.

The third Marquess of Salisbury, Victoria's last Prime Minister, loved science. He installed a telephone in 1877 and electric lights in 1881. His crude wiring often fizzed and sparked, to the alarm of his guests, and small fires would break out which the Marquess smothered with sofa cushions.

Another branch of Lord Burghley's kin still lives at Burghley House, Northamptonshire, built on the ruins of a 12th-century monastery. Completed in 1589, Burghley exemplifies the most lavish Tudor style. Verrio's paintings in the Heaven Room amused me with their lush gods and goddesses and fat-limbed cherubs.

Tombs of Lord Burghley and other Cecils are in nearby St. Martin's Church. In the adjacent cemetery lies Daniel Lambert, who died in 1809. His claim to fame was his bulk. He weighed 52 stone 11 pounds – at 14 pounds per stone, a total of 739 pounds!

IN MANY of England's stately homes the titled owner remains in residence, keeping his property in repair with the help of the National Trust. Usually he lives in a secluded apartment in a wing of the big house, out of sight of the paying visitors.

Hugh Edward Conway Seymour, eighth Marquess of Hertford, has a different view. He likes visitors. Master of Ragley Hall, near Alcester, Warwickshire, His Lordship shares his 17th-century mansion and 8,000 parklike acres with the Marchioness, three children, a Great Dane, a beagle, assorted livestock, and about 50,000 visitors a year.

Lord Hertford asks only that his guests keep out of the grainfields and away from the cattle. Otherwise, they may do as they please. On fine days they deploy all over the estate with picnic hampers and beach chairs. Most weekends are enlivened by sports-car races, field-dog trials, antique-car rallies, sailing, or waterskiing.

Five days of the week the Marquess spends in London, running a public relations business. During weekend visiting hours he stations himself behind a desk

Rebirth of Coventry Cathedral quickens the arts

"I SHALL NEVER FORGET the moments of ecstasy," wrote Sir Basil Spence of the 12 years in which Coventry Cathedral grew from a dream to breathtaking reality.

Britain's top architect today, noted for fresh statements of traditional forms, such as university quadrangles in arched concrete and glass (page 203), Spence was shocked by the Coventry blitz. Later, dug in near a Normandy beach, he watched British tanks blast snipers out of two fine old churches. He vowed that someday he would build a cathedral.

He entered the Coventry competition in 1950 with faint hope, but a visit to the cathedral moved him deeply. "I am the sacrifice," the stones seemed to say, "Build now for the future, the resurrection." In those moments the idea of the design was planted. The box of pink sandstone with sawtooth walls focusing the light of lofty stained-glass panels onto a great tapestry embodies his vision of "a plain jewel casket with many jewels inside: but the biggest and brightest jewel would be the altar."

LORD SNOWDON. UPPER: SIR BASIL SPENCE BY MICHAEL ROSENFIELD

SCULPTURES *shaped by the hands of Henry Moore and American-born Sir Jacob Epstein have brought world fame to British art. Just before his death, Epstein completed a monumental bronze—St. Michael conquering the Devil—that hangs dramatically against a stark outside wall of Coventry Cathedral, guarding its steps.*

Henry Moore (below) found the hearts of his nation with World War II sketches of life in London's bomb shelters—human vignettes of patience and courage. His sculpture evokes round womanhood, waterworn rock, the surge of mountains: "universal shapes to which everybody is subconsciously conditioned." His six-ton reclining bronze figure that adorns New York's Lincoln Center for the Performing Arts grew from his study of a bone. Holes through his figures, he says, make them "immediately more three-dimensional. A hole can have as much shape-meaning as a solid mass." Here human form emerges from a tree trunk at his Hertfordshire home.

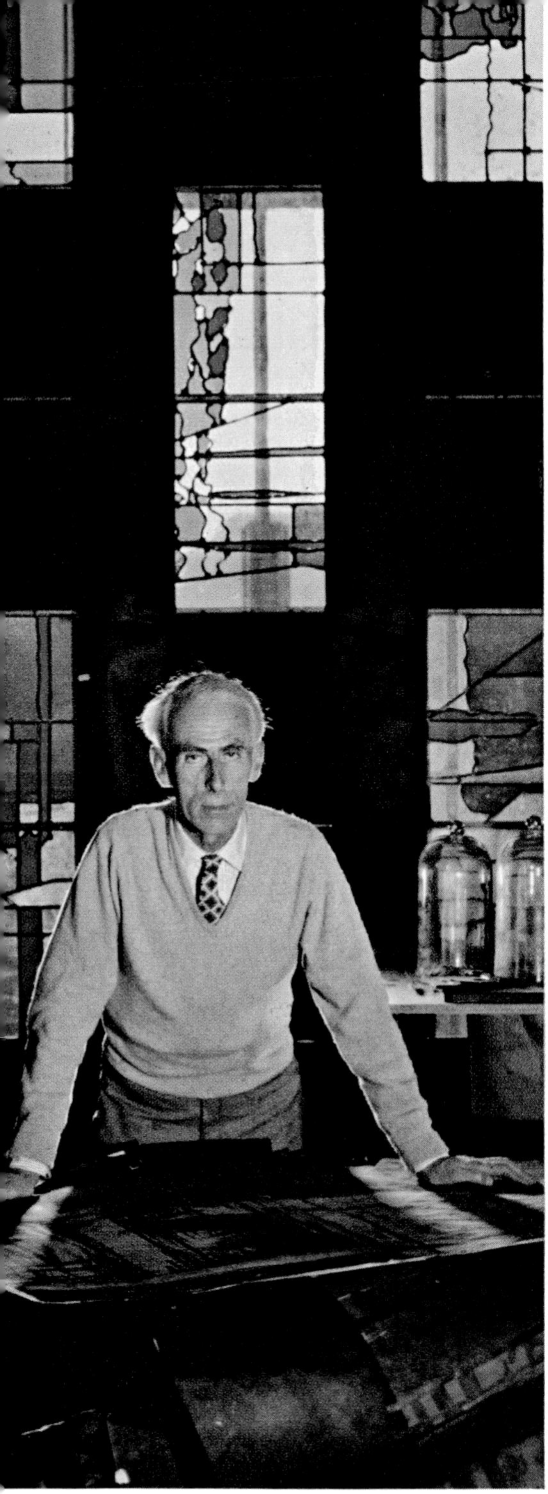

HUMILITY *marked Spence's approach to his Coventry triumph. He shared the glory of the work with Graham Sutherland (opposite), who designed the world's largest tapestry, Christ in His Majesty, which rises behind the altar. John Piper (above) created the great baptistry window; its curved stone honeycomb holds radiant rectangles whose colors converge in a sunburst of gold. Many artists cut fees; 16 German craftsmen contributed their services.*

BRITISH TRAVEL ASSOCIATION (ALSO LEFT)

DAN McCOY, BLACK STAR. BELOW: THE "ERMINE PORTRAIT" BY NICHOLAS HILLIARD, COURTESY MARQUESS OF SALISBURY; B.B.C. PHOTO

near Ragley Hall's entrance. Here he has a cheery word for all comers, while selling them half-crown guidebooks. He looks especially pleased when people tell him how much he resembles Danny Kaye.

"The house has 85 rooms in all," His Lordship told me between guidebook sales, "but we use only 15 as living quarters."

In the guidebook the peer writes that the Seymour line goes back to Guy St. Maur, who came over with the Conqueror. "With a little imagination," he adds, St. Maur's ancestry is traced to a seventh-century hermit who, in his turn, claimed descent from Solomon and the Queen of Sheba! The Marquess also notes that in 1757 a footman tidied a room "so thoroughly that nearly all the family archives got burnt. My secretary and I now eschew tidiness."

About the library: "Only room . . . that is really warm. From my 18th-century French writing table I have a wonderful view over

LORD BURGHLEY BY MARCUS GHEERAERTS, COURTESY MARQUESS OF EXETER

DAN McCOY, BLACK STAR (ALSO LOWER)

WILLIAM CECIL *steered Elizabeth I on a safe course between the might of Catholic Spain and overzealous Calvinism. Protestant at heart, he deemed "life well worth a Mass." She created him Lord Burghley, first commoner she ennobled. Near Stamford her chief minister built Burghley House (top right) on a lavish scale to honor his queen.*

Their 40-year partnership began at Hatfield, on her accession in 1558. Here Cecil's son Robert, chief minister for James I, would build Hatfield House. Elizabeth's portrait, ermine indicating royalty, hangs in the Marble Hall (opposite). Visitors see her stockings (first of silk in England), a parchment tracing her pedigree to Adam, and letters from Mary Queen of Scots, whom Burghley brought to the block.

Right: A ducal Disneyland keeps a regal roof over the Duke of Bedford's head at Woburn Abbey. While parents throng 18th-century rooms packed with art, children ride carousel, swings, paddleboats, coaches, or thread a maze in a park roamed by bison and 3,000 deer. Henry VIII dissolved the abbey here and hanged the abbot for speaking against his marital plans.

HEREFORDS *parade a ring at the "Royal." Honors ribbon brows. Health and heft belie descent from scrawny medieval forebears. Cattle then fed—and bred—on communal land. Owners wintered a few on dry leaves; the rest made salt beef. With Enclosure Acts in the 1700's, herdsmen fenced their cattle and bred for better stock. They found root crops like turnips could feed herds in winter. Weights tell the tale: 370 pounds for beef cattle at Smithfield Fair in 1710, about 800 in 1795. Herefords now reach 1,200 pounds.*

Piston-powered ponies prance at the Royal Agricultural Show

SNORTING STEEDS paw the ground with cleated "hooves." Crowds gape; lunching lads pause in mid-bite to savor the spectacle. Hearts quicken in bemedaled breasts as the Damsel in Distress tugs plaintively at her chain. For here comes the Dragon, a 60-foot, smoke-belching terror! Just as she is about to be eaten—or excavated, for such is the "dragon's" workaday role—up grinds St. George with his mount at full tilt to slay the British-built beast with a deft lance-jab to the carburetor. Sharp eyes may spot the damsel later as an onion or a wireworm when dancers enact the Battle of the Crops—and a sprayer lurches in to decide the issue.

When the "Royal," Britain's premier farm show, began in 1839, pioneers had already sparked an agricultural revolution: Viscount Townshend, dubbed "Turnip Townshend" for using turnips in crop rotation; Jethro Tull, whose machines seeded in rows for easier weeding; Robert Bakewell, who bettered herds by selective breeding; Arthur Young, whose books helped spread new methods.

Long a traveling show, the Royal now thrives at Stoneleigh Abbey, where the Royal Agricultural Society runs a national farming center. Model farms coax higher yields. Groves serve forestry studies; bees buzz in a showcase of beekeeping.

Invitations bring foreign buyers to the four-day Warwickshire gala in July. Tourists and city folk, drawn more by the hoopla than the hardware, elbow dairymen and tillers for a ringside view of beauty queens, antique coach parades, clay pigeon shoots, motorcycle races, skydivers, and visits of royalty, sometimes by helicopter. And behind the trappings, the farmer yarns with his fellows, dickers for a new spreader, then goes home to fill Britain's breadbasket.

GEORGE F. MOBLEY, NATIONAL GEOGRAPHIC PHOTOGRAPHER

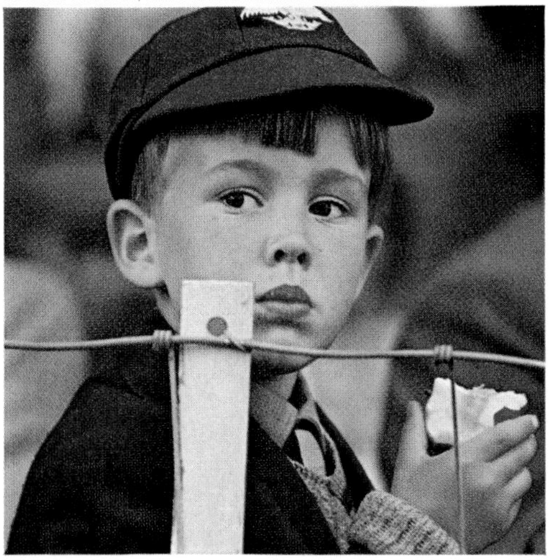

the lake to the Cotswold Hills." About the billiard room: "From the windows . . . notice a small castle. It is called Oversley Castle. It was built in the 1800's because the Prince Regent . . . remarked to his host: 'My dear Lord Hertford, your view would be improved by a castle.' So there it is."

The Marquess walked with me to this room, where four Seymour ancestors, painted by Sir Joshua Reynolds, looked down upon the most ornate billiard table I had ever seen. His Lordship sighted along a cue. "I do wish I could ask you to play. But I must get back to the desk. Another time, I hope."

SURELY, one of the most agreeable experiences of a summer's sojourn in England must be a trip through the fox-hunting country of Leicestershire to Loughborough,

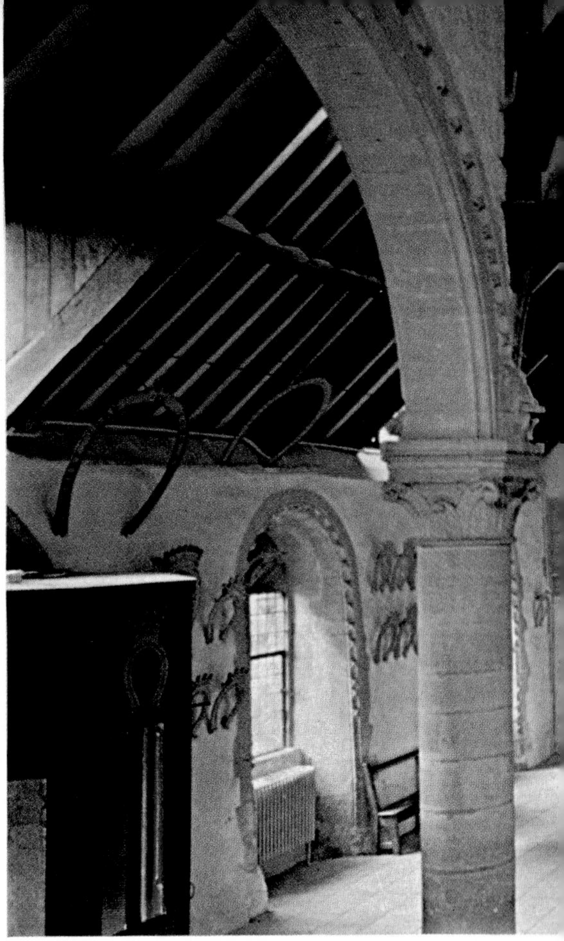

HORSESHOES, *some presented by royalty, deck Oakham Castle's banquet hall, where Normans roistered 800 years ago. Here in Rutland, England's smallest county, custom demands of each peer who enters the manor for the first time "a Shoe from the Horse whereon he rideth."*

Wars of the Roses end with a plea: "My kingdom for a horse!"

RICHARD III meets death on Bosworth Field in 1485. Victory of the future Henry VII, ending 30 years of slaughter, ushers in the Tudor age.

The close of the Hundred Years' War in 1453 had flooded England with jobless soldiery. War was their wont, plunder their pleasure; nobles with money found armies easy to raise. Yorkists chafed under the "usurped" rule of the red rose of Lancaster; they too descended from Edward III, and from an older son at that.

As Henry VI sank toward madness, the white rose of York struck at St. Albans in 1455. Battle followed battle as fortune's scythe swung to and fro. In the blood-red snows of Towton, Warwick made York's Edward IV king. Later the Kingmaker switched sides and propped that "crowned calf" Henry back on the throne.

Edward rebounded, slew Warwick at Barnet, saw to Henry's death in the Tower.

When Edward died, his brother Richard seized the crown. Murder of the Little Princes shook the realm, and from France came Lancastrian Henry Tudor to triumph at Bosworth. Marrying a Yorkist princess, he united the families that made "poor England weep in streams of blood."

Today visitors see King Richard's Well (right) where "Crookback" was said to sip his last.

DEAN CONGER, NATIONAL GEOGRAPHIC PHOTOGRAPHER. UPPER: DAN McCOY, BLACK STAR

PAINTING BY JOHANN HEINRICH RAMBERG, FROM THE FOLGER SHAKESPEARE LIBRARY

the "town of the bells," a community with a perpetual ringing in its ears. On a sunny Saturday I sat in Queen's Park and listened.

The golden sound came from a memorial tower which honors the 480 Loughborough men who fell in World War I. Below, white-flanneled cricketers moved through their stately ballet. On a neighboring rectangle of turf, two teams of older men in blazers and club ties competed at bowls.

During an intermission in the carillon recital, a man walking a terrier sat down next to me and we talked about bells. No sincere carillonneur, he said, regards his career as complete until he has climbed 90 steps to the clavier, or keyboard, of Loughborough tower and hammered out a hymn, a classic, a folk song, or perhaps "Get Me to the Church on Time," from *My Fair Lady.*

"It's no job for a weakling," he added. "When the carillonneur strikes a key, leverage moves the clapper so that it hits the

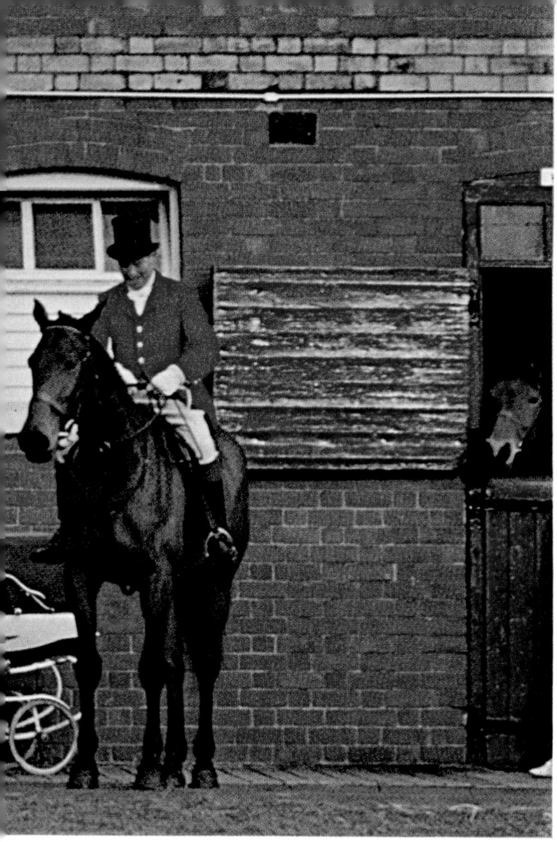

BATES LITTLEHALES, NATIONAL GEOGRAPHIC PHOTOGRAPHER

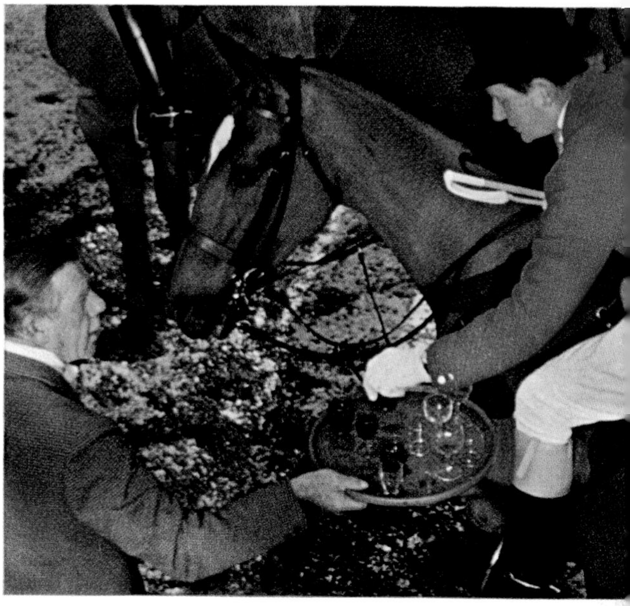

"CORN" AND "BEAVER"—*Quorn and Belvoir Hunts—give Midlands foxes a merry chase. Here the Quorn meets near Melton Mowbray, some riders in black, others wearing pink. A stirrup cup routs morning's chill. Huntsman and whippers-in, paid employees, work hounds; "Yoicks!" urges them on. Hounds—never "dogs"—are paired; one is "half a couple." Heads down, sterns high, they find a scent and give tongue. The field thunders over fence and pasture. Then it's "View halloo!" The huntsman's horn ta-tas.*

Workers have plugged dens, but Reynard finds one and "goes to ground." From a saddlebag comes a terrier to flush him. Cornered, he is slain by the pack. To deserving riders the Master of Foxhounds awards "mask, pads, and brush"—head, feet, and tail. Youngsters "in at the kill" for the first time are "blooded" on both cheeks. "Hopelessly English!" exulted a foreigner. But Oscar Wilde dubbed it "the unspeakable in full pursuit of the uneatable."

side of the bell. The tone depends upon the force he puts behind the blow. He strikes with his closed hand; some carillonneurs wear protective finger coverings.

"The clavier," he went on, "has rows of projecting levers corresponding to the black and white keys of an organ. The larger bells—those of the lowest octave and a half—are rung by foot pedals, so that music can be played in three or more parts. Thus, to play a carillon properly, a carillonneur must

ROBIN HOOD *aims a gray goose shaft outside Nottingham Castle, and a member of the Ancient Order of Foresters rouses ghosts of the merry men amid remnants of once vast Sherwood Forest. Foresters make an annual pilgrimage to honor the 13-foot grave of "Little John" at Hathersage, Derbyshire.*

KATHLEEN REVIS JUDGE. BELOW: ACE WILLIAMS
RIGHT: BATES LITTLEHALES, NATIONAL GEOGRAPHIC PHOTOGRAPHER

display physical strength as well as musical ability. As an authority on the subject once said, you 'must have good hands and feet and no gout.' "

My informant explained the difference between a carillon and a peal, or ring, of bells. "In a carillon," he said, "the bells are hung in fixed positions in a metal frame. Only the clappers move. In a peal, the bells swing in a full circle on headstocks, and are rung by pulling ropes" (page 122).

He suggested that I consult Paul Taylor, who carries on a family tradition as head of John Taylor & Company, makers of carillons, peals of bells, and chimes. The family has been casting bells since the 1780's.

The foundry produced 17-ton Great Paul, the largest bell ever cast in England, which sounds its mighty bronze voice daily at 1 p.m. from St. Paul's Cathedral in London. Other Taylor bells delight listeners at the Bok Tower near Lake Wales, Florida; at Harvard, Yale, Duke, and the University of Michigan; at the Luray Caverns, Virginia; at Niagara Falls, Ontario, and at Washington Cathedral in Washington, D. C.

"How lucky you are!" said Paul Taylor when I told him I lived in Washington, not too far from the cathedral. "You can hear the finest bells in the world."

The town of the bells has rung with discord. In the early 19th century, workers, rioting over low wages and high food prices, destroyed lace-making machinery in a local factory and drove the owner out of town.

The rioters were called "Luddites," after Ned Ludd of Anstey. Around 1779 his employer, a "stockinger," had Ludd whipped for laziness. In a rage, Ludd smashed his employer's stocking frames. He became a symbol of protest for decades. Masked Luddites roamed the Midlands, destroying machinery. In Nottingham, the city of Robin Hood, they wrecked factories and homes and burned the Norman castle.

Even in the 1590's workers were fighting automation. William Lee, a clergyman of Calverton, near Loughborough, invented the stocking frame that produced the first full-fashioned stocking (one that follows the curve of the female leg, without sag or wrinkle). Women – and men – may hail the clergyman's invention today, but in his day he was forced to find refuge in France.

THE PENNINE CHAIN, the series of rolling whalebacks and high moors that form a ridgepole for the North Country, begins on the northern edge of the Midlands. Here the land erupts in a tumble of hills and ravines called the Peak District, or simply the Peak.

I doubted the aptness of the word when I saw the region; the summits are rounded,

NOTTINGHAM'S FOREST OF ROOFS *stands in serried ranks on the site of Saxon Snotingaham. Center of power under the Danes, then the Normans, the city lives in legend as the seat of the sheriff (from shire reeve, royal overseer of a county) outfoxed by Robin Hood. In 1642, Charles I unfurled his banner here, marking the start of the Civil War.*

Nearby Wollaton Hall amid its deer park evokes Elizabethan elegance. Newstead Abbey, 12th-century priory with glorious gardens, was Lord Byron's home.

not jagged. Then I learned that the name derives from prehistoric inhabitants, the Peacs. Romans visited the hills to bathe in the warm springs at Buxton, which became a famous spa. Today the area serves as a "lung" for Birmingham workers.

In 1951 the Peak District became Britain's first national park—a playground and nature preserve that covers 542 square miles. Hikers strike off across the stone-walled moors. Climbers scale the cliffs to train for the rock faces of the Lake District, Scotland, and Wales. Spelunkers explore some of Britain's best limestone caverns.

DELICATE LACE *from massive machines: a Nottingham success story. Fortune smiled when Arkwright and Hargreaves set up their spinning inventions here on the banks of the River Trent around 1770. Famed for lace and hosiery, the city also produces Player's cigarettes and more than a million Raleigh bicycles each year.*

A tuner at the Taylor Bell Foundry in Loughborough (right) checks the A-flat bell for Yale University's carillon. An upright lathe spins the 4¾-ton bell, and bits of metal, sometimes "a gnat's eyebrow," are shaved off certain points inside to give precise pitch.

BATES LITTLEHALES, NATIONAL GEOGRAPHIC PHOTOGRAPHER (ALSO OPPOSITE). UPPER: ADAM WOOLFITT

Rolling a cheese or weighing a mayor, the English love odd customs

AT THE TICK of the New Year, front doors in Staffordshire and northern England burst open. In strides a man carrying a bit of coal or bread. He kisses the girls. He may be Dad, a son, or a neighbor, but "First-foot," bearing symbols of wealth, should have dark hair. Judas, they say, was a redhead, so such a man brings ill luck.

So starts a yearly cycle of customs rooted in pagan worship, medieval piety, and half-forgotten property rights. On a January night Carhampton, Somerset, wassails (drinks to) its apple trees. Folk leave an offering of cider-soaked toast, then fire guns through the branches to rout demons.

Shrove Tuesday is Pancake Day. Lent begins on the morrow, so wives make pancakes to use up butter and eggs, once banned as Lenten fare. In Olney, Buckinghamshire, women race to church flipping flapjacks in skillets. The winner gets the verger's kiss.

Eight centuries ago Lady Mabella Tichborne begged on her deathbed that land be set aside to grow crops for the poor. Her lord held aloft a torch and sneered that she could donate all she could crawl across before the flame snuffed out. Miraculously, she covered 23 acres, still called "The Crawls," and vowed that if ever their bounty was withheld the house of Tichborne would fall. The Hampshire villagers still get a dole of flour.

Eostre, a pagan goddess, gave her name to Easter, and the egg, symbol of fertility, found a role in Christian rites. Villeins often paid eggs to their lords at Eastertide – the first Easter eggs. Egg-rolling in England and Washington, D. C., may recall rolling the stone from Christ's tomb.

May's festivals include weighing the mayor of High Wycombe, Buckinghamshire, amid groaning if he's judged too heavy to do his job well and cheers if a year's loss confirms an active tenure. On Mayoring Day in Rye, Kent, the mayor tosses hot pennies, once fresh from a now-closed mint, to children. On Ascension Day some manors and parishes "beat the bounds." Officials pace boundary lines, sometimes upend a youngster and bump his head on a marker so he won't forget it.

Whitsuntide calls for cheese rolling at Cooper's Hill, Gloucestershire, traditionally to establish grazing rights. One Devonshire village roasts a deer, originally a ram, recalling sacrificial rites.

Quitrents to the Crown include a lamprey pie from Gloucester, 100 herring from Yarmouth, and a French tricolor on the anniversary of Waterloo from the Duke of Wellington for his Hampshire home, presented by the nation to the first duke.

Weeks before Guy Fawkes Day, November 5, tots beg "a penny for the guy" to buy fireworks. People build bonfires and burn in effigy the man who in 1605 tried to blow up Parliament. In Ashburton, Devonshire, ale-tasting is serious business. The portreeve, a Saxon rank, gives a sprig of greenery to each publican whose ale is not "wappy" (flat).

Limestone characterizes the southern part of the region. Streams sometimes dive into underground channels called "water swallows." Rock formations, worn and rounded, have a grayish look that explains why people call this the White Peak. North of the Hope Valley, limestone gives way to a dark sandstone that the British call gritstone. It edges the moors, provides building stone for farmhouses and walls, and gives the area its name, Dark Peak.

An Englishman's home remains his castle, even within park boundaries. People of the Peak continue to live there, though visitors may have access to parts of their land. Two of England's greatest homes, Chatsworth and Haddon Hall, lie within the Peak District National Park.

Haddon Hall lifts its crenellated walls above the River Wye with impressive grandeur. Yet the thing I like most about it is its simplicity. Its builders, from Norman times on, used the same limestone and gritstone that make up the Derbyshire Peak. When a 20th-century Duke of Rutland found he had to restore parts of the house, which his family had not lived in for two centuries, he avoided fakery and put in new beams that declared their youth as honestly as the ancient ones whisper their age.

Americans are fascinated by Chatsworth. I think the grounds help explain it. Hardly anywhere has man so sculptured the earth as around this huge Derbyshire house. A great lawn stretches southward, encompassing a fountain pool, then a 300-yard-long rectangle of water with Europe's second highest fountain (after Lake Geneva's) spouting 290 feet. On the east side the Great Cascade tumbles from a small temple in terraces of water. It was built in 1696, along with another astonishing hydraulic achievement – water closets.

Chatsworth was originally the Tudor mansion of Sir William Cavendish, second husband of Bess of Hardwick, one of the most ambitious ladies in English history. She inherited it and passed it on to her second son, who became the first Earl of Devonshire. His great-grandson rebuilt the old house, altering the aspect so that it faces west instead of east. Later, the fourth Duke

OFF TO THE BOTTLE-KICKING *march the men of Hallaton, Leicestershire, on Easter Monday. Their vicar has tossed scraps of hare pie to scrambling villagers in memory of a hare that distracted a charging bull and saved a parish lady. Now the men will vie with neighboring Medbourne in kicking, carrying, shoving casks, or "bottles," toward streams a mile apart. The free-for-all resembles Shrove Tuesday football between villages—"a bloody and murthering" fling before Lent. "If this be but playe," runs a 1588 comment, "I cold wishe the spaniardes were here to see our plaies. . . . Certes they would be in bodielye feare of our warre."*

BATES LITTLEHALES, NATIONAL GEOGRAPHIC PHOTOGRAPHER

MERLE SEVERY, NATIONAL GEOGRAPHIC STAFF. OPPOSITE: TRUSTEES OF THE CHATSWORTH SETTLEMENT. UPPER INSET: BESS OF HARDWICK BY AN UNKNOWN ARTIST, C. 1555, COURTESY NATIONAL TRUST. LOWER INSET: LOUIS H. FROHMAN

of Devonshire attacked the landscaping to give the house a proper vista. He straightened the River Derwent, rebuilt a bridge, replanted gardens, built new stables, and moved aside the village of Edensor so it would not sully the view. The sixth duke pushed Edensor even farther from the scene. Its houses cluster around a 19th-century church with a graceful spire.

FROM PASTORAL HILLSIDES to industrial valleys, from serene isolation to frantic traffic – abrupt contrasts in Midlands scenes sometimes left me gasping. It seemed I had no sooner left the wild, lovely moors of the Peak than I entered the veil of smoke that hangs over the Potteries. Green fields ended and red brick began. Memories of Chatsworth's gracious landscaping faded in the reality of Stoke on Trent's complex of commercial buildings and factories.

England's famous pottery industry centers here in what novelist Arnold Bennett called the Five Towns – Stoke, Burslem, Longton, Hanley, and Tunstall. These and another, Fenton, federated in 1910; all run

BESS OF HARDWICK *(opposite) parlayed four marriage into wealth second only to that of Queen Bess, and built the most prodigious house in the realm.*

Daughter of the indigent squire of Hardwick, Derbyshire, she married, at 12, a boy of 14 and was widowed in months with "a considerable property." At 27 she wed Sir William Cavendish and induced him to buy Chatsworth. She rebuilt it, was pleased, and produced three more houses – and six children.

Cavendish died, leaving every penny to his belovec despite claims of children by his former wives. Bess wed again, was again widowed, and further enrichec

At 48 Elizabeth enraptured the Earl of Shrewsbur He accepted her marriage terms – that two of his children wed two of hers the same day. Jealous of his custody of Mary Queen of Scots, she returned to Hardwick and built a manor round her old home.

The earl's death in 1590 gave her, at 70, the riches she craved for her masterwork, "Hardwick Hall, more glass than wall." Perpendicular mullions rose, tiers of windows "increasing in magnificence, like her marriages, as they mount upwards." She kept strict books. Under a column of Roman numerals itemizing payments for "This fortnighte work" in 1593, she totaled "Six ponds nyne shyllyngs 3d" and signed "E. Shrovesbury" as boldly as she put her "ES" atop Hardwick's four great towers.

Nearby Haddon Hall, England's finest medieval house, looks over terraced gardens and the River Wye from Tudor bays in its Long Gallery (above).

This fortnyghte worke begynnynge on monday the ... and endyd the ... of novembre ... 1593

[illegible]

John [illegible] — vs
Henrye [illegible] — vs
[illegible] — iiijs viijd
John [illegible] — iiijs
[illegible] — iiijs viijd
[illegible] — iiijs iiijd
[illegible] — [illegible]
[illegible] — xxijd
Thomas [illegible] — xxd
Wm [illegible] — xxijd
John [illegible] — xxijd
[illegible] — iiijs iiijd
[illegible] — viijd
[illegible] — xxijd
[illegible] — ijs

[illegible] — xxxjs viijd

[illegible] — xxxs

[illegible] for iiij [illegible] nayls [illegible] bede ... and so he is payd for ... — xxs iiijd

Some is ... iiijd

xxx pounde nyne shyllynge iiijd

E Shrouesbury

together and produce much the same thing – the fine chinaware of Wedgwood, Spode, Doulton, and Minton, and other ceramics.

The Romans made pottery from the good red clay of northern Staffordshire, and 13th-century kilns have been found. But medieval crocks and mugs were a far cry from the elegant earthenware that began coming from the kilns in the 18th century.

"The tea habit started the demand for good chinaware," my guide explained as he took me through the Wedgwood factory in Stoke. "Tea became a fashionable drink in the 18th century, and the squire and his lady wanted proper cups and saucers and teapots to serve it with."

When Josiah Wedgwood of Burslem set up shop, the area's fame spread. Young Josiah was apprenticed to his brother at the age of 14 to learn "the Art, Mistery, Occupation or Imployment of Throwing and Handleing." A knee infection from smallpox left him too lame to pedal the potter's wheel on which the "thrower" shapes clay. He learned the family business, and in 1754 joined a leading potter as partner.

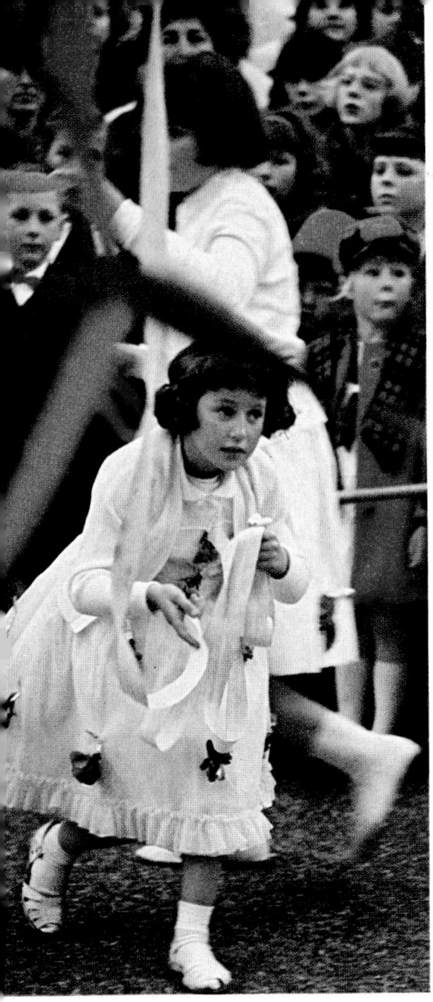

GARLAND DAY *at Castleton honors Charles II's Restoration in 1660. Enveloped in a garland, the "king" (below) and his "queen" in Cavalier garb parade through the Derbyshire town. Elsewhere May 29 is Oak Apple Day, recalling when Charles hid in an oak to escape the Roundheads after his defeat at Worcester in 1651. At the Royal Hospital, Chelsea, which Charles founded, old soldiers wear oak sprigs. Wishford villagers in Wiltshire assert ancient rights in Grovely Forest by chanting over oak branches at an altar: "Grovely! Grovely! And all Grovely!"*

Maypole dancing caps the ceremonies here and at Castleton. Puritans gnashed their teeth to see folk "daunce . . . like the heathen" round a "stinkyng Ydol" in this age-old fertility rite. Charles II restored the revels, and white-frocked girls adorned with posies carry miniature maypoles to a dance of innocence.

BATES LITTLEHALES, NATIONAL GEOGRAPHIC PHOTOGRAPHER

DERBYSHIRE SAYS THANKS *for its wells with flowers. At Tissington (left) villagers outline drawings with seeds or cones in clay-smeared wooden trays. Bark, lichens, moss go in next; then a bright mosaic of blossoms and petals, many hands putting last touches at midnight before Ascension Day. Morning brings clergy in procession to bless wells where the Bible now blooms.*

Linked with ancient sacrifices to the gods of springs, this rite may date from the Black Death (1348-49), when the villagers ascribed their deliverance to the pure water.

Eyam, another Peak District village that dresses wells, is famed for heroism in 1665-66. Its tailor opened a shipment of cloth from London, where the Great Plague was raging. Pestilence struck him down and put terror in the villagers' hearts. But the rector stayed their flight: The plague must not spread. Sealing itself off from the world, Eyam buried the rector's wife and three-fourths of its 350 souls—but the Midlands and North were spared.

Wedgwood's stained, unglazed jasperware, green glaze, and black basalts are unique and beautiful. But the man should be remembered also as a leader of the Industrial Revolution. He used an early James Watt steam engine to drive his clay mixers and stone grinders. To speed mass shipments of his wares to Liverpool and Hull for export, he pushed through completion of the 93-mile-long Trent and Mersey Canal.

There is more to the Potteries than just pottery. Modern industries range from ironworks to chemicals. Moreover, parks and recreation grounds now ease the clutter of dingy industrial sections.

The urban complex ends suddenly—the way Midlands cities do—and gives way to pleasant fields and grazing cattle. As I drove southwestward, the thatch on village cottages seemed to grow thicker, the roads narrower, and when I pulled into a lay-by and shut off my engine to check a road map, birdsong flooded through the car window. I had been told that Shropshire ranked as one of the least-spoiled counties in England. Sure enough, I was well inside it.

"When smoke stood up from Ludlow, And mist blew off from Teme...." The lines went through my mind, for I was bound for Ludlow on the River Teme, the land of A. E. Housman's *A Shropshire Lad.*

Ludlow, when I arrived, showed me little smoke but displayed the huge castle that

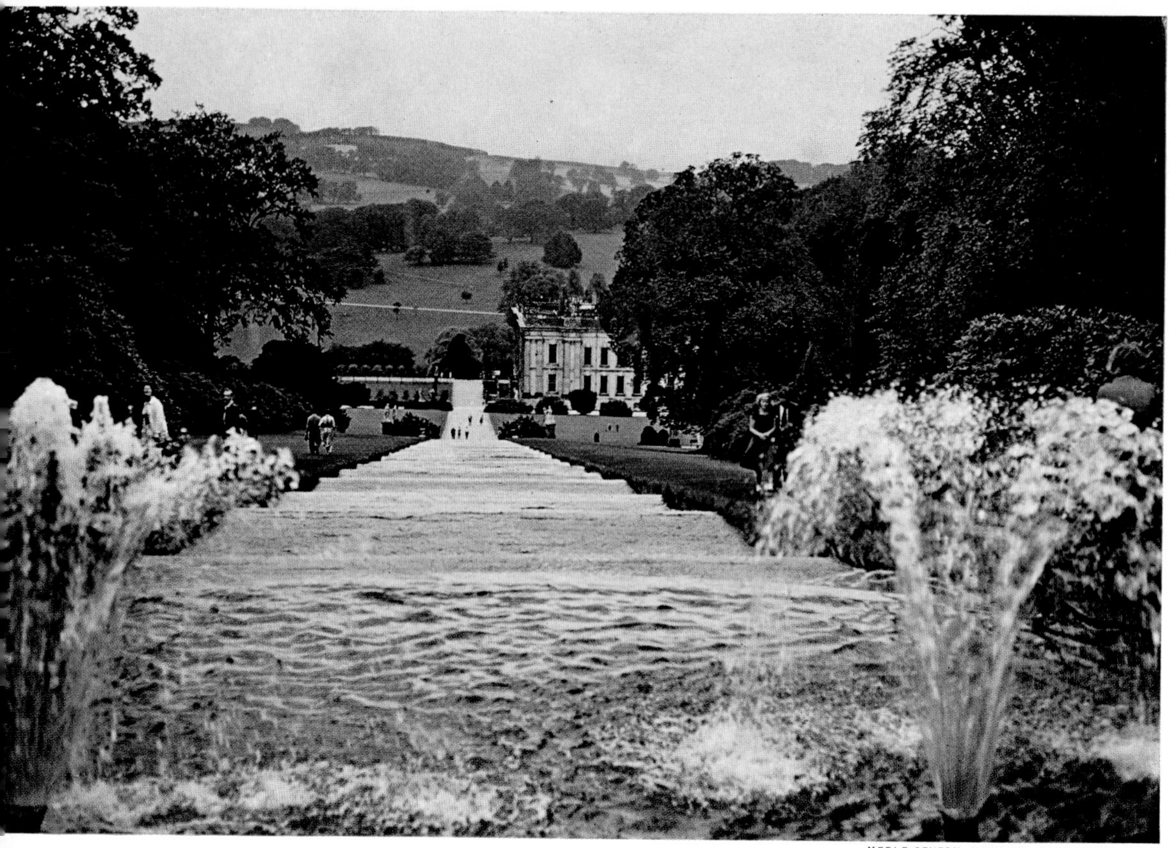

MERLE SEVERY, NATIONAL GEOGRAPHIC STAFF

LIQUID STAIRS *march down a Derbyshire slope to Chatsworth, Palladian "Palace of the Peak." The Great Cascade was created by the first Duke of Devonshire. Bitten by the building bug, as well as addicted to horse-racing, he replaced, wing by wing, the four-story Elizabethan mansion built by his great-great-grandmother, Bess of Hardwick. Mary Queen of Scots had stayed there in decorous detention in the custody of Bess's fourth husband, the Earl of Shrewsbury.*

Lavish murals and ceilings, carved paneling, statuary, and a notable library adorn Chatsworth. Marble paves the Painted Hall (opposite). Buried on the estate are the son of the 10th duke, killed in World War II, and his wife Kathleen, sister of the late President Kennedy.

Nearby Kedleston Hall, with its famed Marble Hall of the 1760's, is a classic Robert Adam design.

ART AND INDUSTRY *unite in the Midlands. Derbyshire power surges from snowy serenity (opposite), and Wedgwood, Minton, and Copeland (Spode) "throw" clay in Staffordshire potteries at Stoke on Trent. Classical forms still adorn jasper (upper), an unglazed stoneware perfected by Josiah Wedgwood in 1774. His skill still guides the hand modeling Canada's arms (center). From such models come molds for pieces like the Kennedy candy dish in satinlike "Wedgwood blue." At Derby (below) an artist decorates Royal Crown Derby bone china.*

BATES LITTLEHALES, NATIONAL GEOGRAPHIC PHOTOGRAPHER

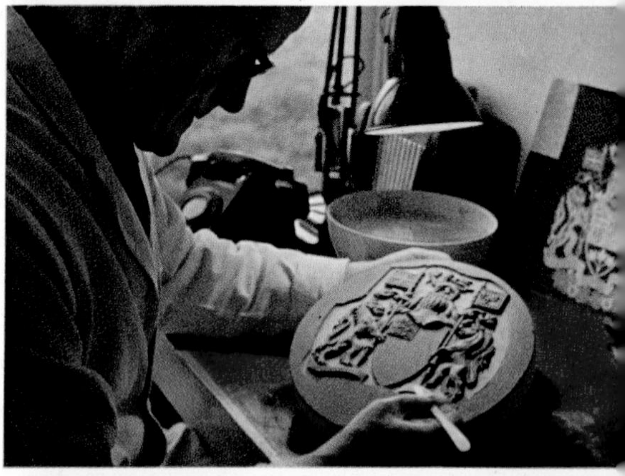

Josiah Wedgwood's brave new world

THIRTEENTH CHILD of a poor potter, thrust to work at nine, crippled, self-educated, Josiah Wedgwood raised earthenware to classic heights of beauty and pushed to the van of his confident era.

"Everything yields to experiment," maintained this man of uncommon clay. He fired more than 10,000 pieces before he perfected jasper. Earlier, his cream-colored Queensware had caught the eye of Russia's Catherine the Great; she commissioned a set with 1,244 hand-painted English scenes.

Inspired by discoveries of "Etruscan" pottery, he founded the model village of Etruria. Seeking "to make such machines of the men as cannot err," he stumped about on a wooden leg, smashing with his cane any piece that failed to meet his standards.

The "Queen's Potter" joined James Watt of steam engine fame, Joseph Priestley, who discovered oxygen, printer John Baskerville, canal engineer James Brindley, artist George Stubbs, and others in the Lunar Society. This met when a full moon lit their travel. The "Lunatics" promoted turnpikes, canals, Parliamentary reform. They thundered against slavery, cheered the American Revolution. Wedgwood made medallions of Washington, Franklin, John Paul Jones.

His closest friend was Dr. Erasmus Darwin, "that large mass of genius and sarcasm," who supervised the amputation of Wedgwood's leg (without anesthetic) and rhapsodized on an Arkwright mill ("Then fly the spoles, the rapid axles glow..."). Darwin's son married Wedgwood's daughter; their son Charles shook the world with his *Origin of Species.*

dominates the town and long defended the border against Wales. Norman in part, Ludlow was once owned by the de Lacy family. In the anarchistic 12th-century reign of King Stephen, they lost it, then tried to win it back. A page, Fulk Fitzwarine, saw the castle lord set upon by de Lacys and sprang into the fray. He slew two knights, captured two, and won his spurs—and the lord's daughter. But one of the captives whiled away his time by wooing a ward of the castle. She helped him escape, then sent for him on a dark and lonely night.

He came, left the way open for the de Lacys, and only the cries of the garrison being slaughtered roused the damsel from

her lover's arms. Realizing the treachery, she ran him through with his sword and leaped from a window to her death. Thus did the de Lacys take back the castle.

Ludlow in time went to the Mortimers, lords of the Welsh marches and ancestors of kings. Roger Mortimer, in the 1320's, took as his mistress Edward II's queen, and with her help arranged the King's deposition and subsequent murder at Berkeley Castle (page 253). Mortimer practically ruled England for three years, then young Edward III had him hanged and drawn, and Ludlow Castle went to the Crown. No wonder history so haunts this splendid pile.

Stokesay Castle is reputedly England's oldest fortified manor. Parts date back to the 13th century. John Leland, the 16th-century antiquarian, noted that it was "buildid like a castel V miles out of Ludlo"—and thus I found it. It guarded against Welsh raiders who came over the western hills—Wenlock Edge, a sharp spur, and the Long Mynd where glider pilots now chase air currents. Eastward rises the 1,335-foot Wrekin, a landmark for miles.

Welsh raiders also worried the traders of Shrewsbury. They crammed their town inside a loop in the River Severn, and goods crossed this natural moat over the English Bridge or the well-fortified Welsh Bridge. Half-timbered houses still huddle together in this peninsula, and traffic jams now give Shrewsbury more trouble than the Welsh.

In Liverpool's heyday as a passenger port, travelers hustled from ships to the London train and never looked around until they were whipping through Cheshire's pastoral plain. "How green England is!" they'd exclaim. I saw why as I drove north from Shropshire. Cheshire's fields with grazing cattle seemed designed as postcards.

So also seemed Little Moreton Hall, a half-timbered Elizabethan manor with a top-story gallery whose mullioned windows sag with charming antiquity.

BALUSTRADES *mark the famed Rows of Chester (right), "little caverns of traffic" that link whole blocks of upstairs shops. Quaint names—Pepper Alley, Broken-Shin Row—amuse sheltered strollers; one Row takes them through a church tower. Antiquarians, noting that the Rows flank four intersecting streets of Deva, legionary fortress on the River Dee, speculate that medieval merchants built some stalls atop Roman ruins, others in front; later builders overhung the setback story with dwellings. Thus "medieval England sits bravely under the gables" of this bustling little cathedral city girdled in stone.*

Pitch-blackened timbers, white plaster, and pane-patterned windows make jeweled quilts of the half-timbered façades in Cheshire and Shropshire. Carvings enrich the Feathers (below), a Ludlow inn built in 1603. Whittlers' whims, like the tapster (opposite), adorn 15th-century misericords—seatlike supports for standing clerics—in the choir of Ludlow's parish church.

BATES LITTLEHALES AND (FAR RIGHT) MERLE SEVERY, BOTH NATIONAL GEOGRAPHIC STAFF

Nearby Capesthorne, another fine manor house, was rebuilt in the 1800's. From its park you can see the radio telescopes of Jodrell Bank – parabolic discs operated by the University of Manchester. One, 250 feet across, is the world's largest fully steerable disc. They gather radio waves generated, for example, by colliding galaxies, and they track satellites like bloodhounds. Director Sir Bernard Lovell was spared a probe of the observatory's mounting costs in 1957 when his big dish picked up the peep of Sputnik. In 1966, Jodrell intercepted Russian signals and produced moon pictures, to the annoyance of the secretive Soviets.

HENRY JAMES wrote that an American used to straight lines and right angles finds in ancient Chester "a perfect feast of crookedness – of those random corners, projections and recesses" which give "a wholly novel zest to the use of his eyes."

I agree. I was charmed by the unconcern of half-timbered shops, pubs, and offices shouldering each other and giving glimpses of enticing courts. The cathedral stands rooted in history, and around strides the medieval wall – two miles of it – the best preserved city wall in England.

I paced its top, past once-fortified gates, past King Charles' Tower where, in 1645, he watched his Royalists beaten at Rowton, past the Grosvenor Museum with relics of Roman legionaries once garrisoned here.

Meanwhile my car was serviced in a streamlined garage. That mixture of old and new, of charm and efficiency, summed up for me the whole spirit of the Midlands.

EAST ANGLIA AND THE FENS

LAND OF LONG HORIZONS

ALONG ENGLAND'S BROAD SHOULDER, so the legend goes, seamen nearing port can hear, tolling beneath their ships, the bells of drowned churches. For centuries, street by street, home by home, the North Sea devoured villages, towns, even the great medieval city of Dunwich, which took 400 years to die. But the men of East Anglia learned to dike the sea and channel the rivers that deluged their fields.

Men who looked beyond their time sprang from this low-lying land. No single generation could wrest the soil from the thralldom of rivers and sea. In epic labors that spanned centuries, men waded into the Fens and drained broad swamps. Romans cut canals through the watery maze. Where Saxon monks had found refuge on an isle amid marshes that teemed with eels, Normans boldly built magnificent Ely Cathedral, bringing in every stone, every timber by boat.

Slowly, like a bewitched realm emerging from an ancient spell, a fertile land arose. Corn and oats sprouted from black soil. Cows and sheep grew fat grazing where floods had swept away whole herds. The once desolate kingdom of the East Angles bountifully yielded apples and plums, potatoes and peas. Growing rich with their land, men built flint churches that immortalized their prosperity. Here flourished "more good things than man could have the conscience to ask of God."

Sunniest place in all England, the East Anglian coast long has lured holidayers, who throng havens of fishing fleets. The sea has fed native and visitor here since legionaries first savored the Colchester oyster.

Inland, where Stone Age men mined flint and Newton saw the apple fall, Cambridge's radio telescope scans the stars. In Huntingdonshire the same school taught "perfidious Cromwell" and Samuel Pepys, who lived to see the Lord Protector's head on a pike. Here with pen and palette, Tennyson and Constable portrayed the beauty in "A league of grass, wash'd by a slow broad stream." And here, at the first Boston, Pilgrim Fathers envisioned the freedom they would find on another eastern shore.

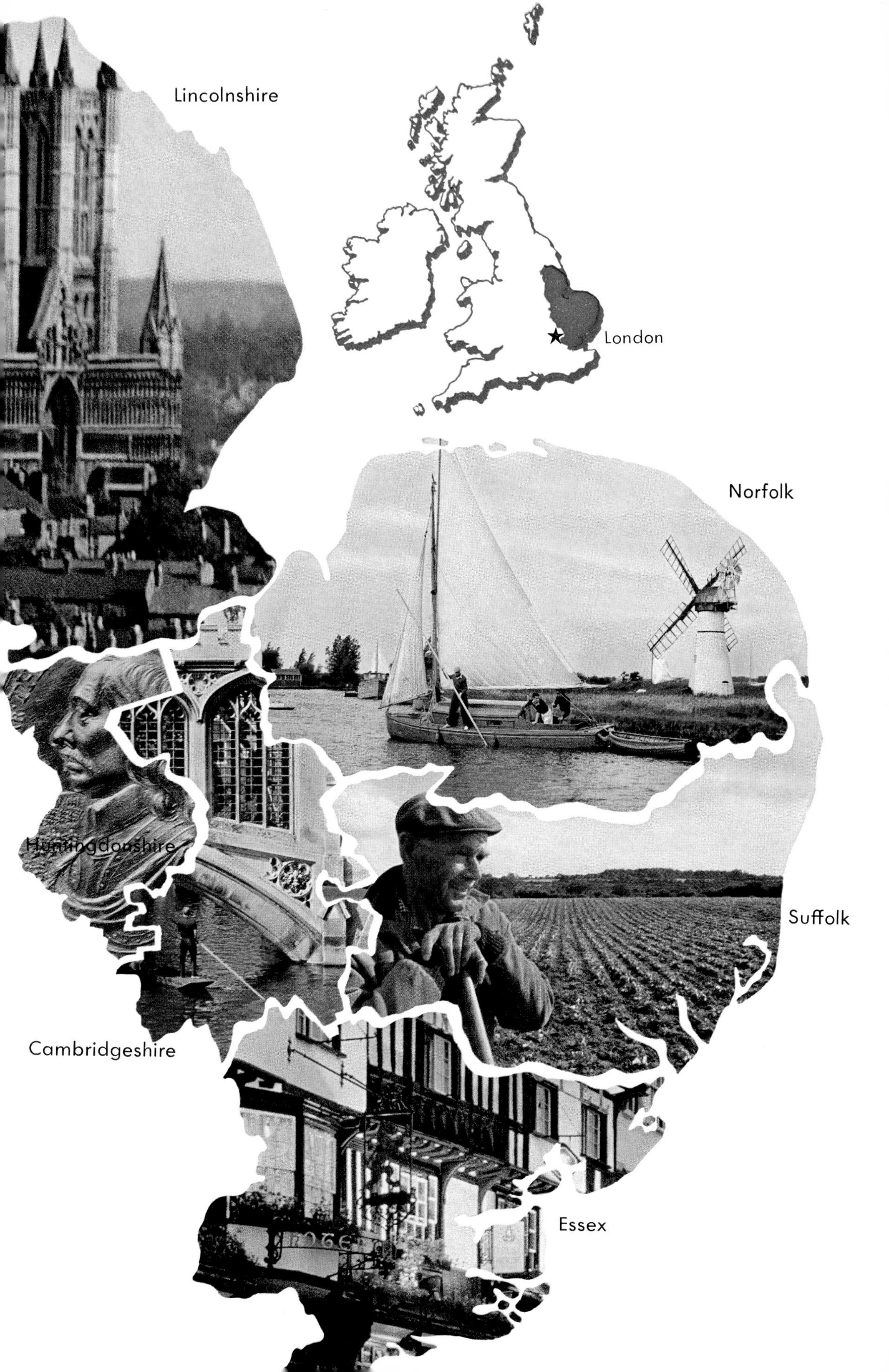
Lincolnshire
London
Norfolk
Huntingdonshire
Suffolk
Cambridgeshire
Essex

INLAND

I WOULD NEVER have seen the sign had not my friend Henry Saward called my attention to it on the end of the house away from the street. We stood in that unkempt garden in the corner of the churchyard at Scrooby, Nottinghamshire, and read, "William Brewster lived here. . . ."

"You can live here yourself if you like," Henry said. "The cottage is empty. The last tenants moved to a modern place."

I peered through the small Tudor windows at the beams inside, the tiled floor, the minute rooms. I looked in vain for modern conveniences, but the place was neat and orderly, the roof sound. A little capital would make it into a grand little home. And vacant? The old home of Elder Brewster of Plymouth Colony fame *looking* for a tenant?

"There has been nobody in it for a month or so," said Henry. "All you have to do is look after it and show visitors around. Sometimes they come by the busload."

Scrooby is still a village, though traffic roars along a main road at the top of the rise, and the railroad from London to Scotland passes nearby. In this hamlet leaders of the Pilgrims lived and worshiped at the beginning of the 17th century. In this house William Brewster, William Bradford, and their small group listened to Pastor Richard Clyfton. Here they organized their escape from England, which eventually led to the *Mayflower* voyage.

Like many visitors, I had resolved to seek out the early American shrines that abound in the eastern counties. Here in Nottinghamshire I began a tour that would take me through the Fens and Broads, the bustling fishing ports, and the ancient towns of neighboring East Anglia.

I have had a special interest in the Separatists since the days when I sailed the *Mayflower* replica to America in 1957. She was crowded enough with only her professional crew. How the Pilgrim Fathers, their womenfolk, and their children must have

STALKING BEAUTY *from a blind of billowing green, artists invade the heart of "Constable Country." Among quiet fields of Suffolk and Essex, where winds the gentle Stour, John Constable grew up. These scenes, he said, "made me a painter."*

WINFIELD PARKS, NATIONAL GEOGRAPHIC PHOTOGRAPHER

CRUISE OF THE EASTERN COUNTIES

Captain Villiers sails the Fens and Broads of East Anglia and traces Pilgrim roots in this fertile land

suffered, cramped in their tossing tiny ship!

Their courage and determination had been born amid these rolling farmlands where the counties of Lincolnshire, Nottinghamshire, and Yorkshire join. I turned from the cottage and entered the church. A plaque by the porch, put up by the American General Society of Mayflower Descendants, noted William Brewster's association, but nothing else indicated that this ever had been the Pilgrims' church.

"We don't need memorials," said Henry Saward. "Everybody in Scrooby knows the Pilgrims' story, and we're only too happy to point out the sights. Scrooby was a great place long before the Pilgrim Fathers."

He swept an arm toward the old manor house, or what remains of it, across a small field where Shropshire sheep grazed.

"Here was the Archbishop of York's palace, or one of them," he said. "Kings and queens and noblemen came there, and the Pilgrim Fathers met there too."

As I sat in the Brewster pew in the little

WINFIELD PARKS, NATIONAL GEOGRAPHIC PHOTOGRAPHER

SUN-GOLDENED FLEECE *glows in the soft light of a summer morn near Louth in Lincolnshire, where Capt. John Smith and Tennyson went to school. The golden trade in wool built ports, ships, and market towns, entwining wool and weavers in England's history and language. "Spinster" and "spinning a yarn" enriched the King's English; wool merchants' taxes enriched his treasury. Britain still leads the world in wool textiles.*

Near King's Lynn a Norfolk woman harvests potatoes on fenland. Before large-scale draining began in the 1600's, fever stalked marshes here, and fenmen of "brutish unciviliz'd tempers" slogged on stilts, eking out livings by shepherding, fishing, and fowling. Windmills and sluices reclaimed an area 80 miles long and 10 to 30 miles broad.

church, I read the name Sandys on a stone in the floor. Sir Edwin Sandys, son of the archbishop and onetime joint manager of the Virginia Colony, had lived at Scrooby's manor house. His brother George dwelt in Virginia from 1621 to 1628 while the Pilgrims were slowly establishing themselves in the harsher climate farther north.

William Bradford lived in the small village of Austerfield about a mile north of Scrooby. His house there is now a private dwelling. He and Brewster used to walk the country road to the church at Babworth, that other famous Pilgrim village some ten miles to the south. There Clyfton preached until his superiors removed him because of his unorthodox views.

I walked part of the way from Scrooby along the modern road to Babworth. I did not walk the whole way, as Bradford and Brewster did regularly.

"People had time to walk ten miles then," said Mr. Saward. I needed his directions to Bab'orth, as he called it, for the beautiful little church hides in a clump of sycamores, cedars, beeches, and horse-chestnut trees.

The main road left it in peace many years ago. Inside, a photograph of *Mayflower II* hung by the font. A Society of Mayflower Descendants plaque on the porch honored Richard Clyfton and the pioneers who worshiped here "until the Separatists moved to Scrooby in 1606, to Amsterdam in the Netherlands in 1608, to Leyden, 1609, and to Plymouth in New England, 1620."

And from there into the fabric of history.

THE PURITANS who settled Boston in 1630 and founded the Massachusetts Bay Colony came mainly from East Anglia. John Winthrop, first governor of Massachusetts, was born in Suffolk, and John Harvard, for whom the college was named, came from Cambridge. Samuel Lincoln, ancestor of Abraham, left Hingham, Norfolk, landed in Salem, Massachusetts, then moved to Hingham, just south of Boston. Virginia's John Smith was a Lincolnshire man. John Rolfe, who married Pocahontas, came from Norfolk.

I took the sea route to the ancient port of Boston, Lincolnshire, chugging up the River Witham in a shrimp dragger. I had bounced about in this little vessel in the Wash, that bite which the turbulent North Sea has taken in the eastern flank of England between Norfolk and Lincolnshire. Four rivers of East Anglia—Witham, Welland, Nene, and Great Ouse—spill their silt into the Wash as though to fill it in again. The tide roars over such sandbanks as the Blackguard and Roaring Middle. And whenever the tide runs out, seals appear by the hundred on the sandbars as though they had been waiting underwater for just this chance to catch a breath.

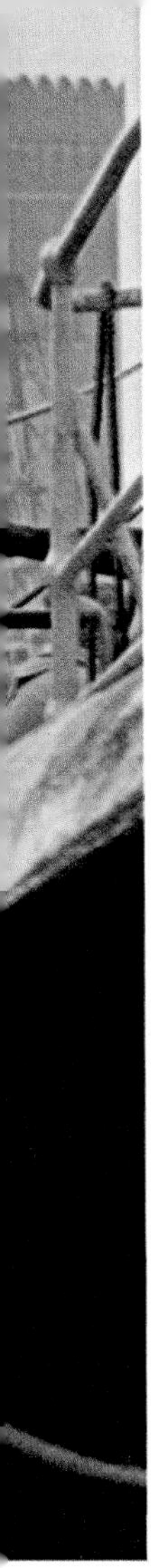

WINFIELD PARKS, NATIONAL GEOGRAPHIC PHOTOGRAPHER

The dragger's skipper gave the seals a sullen look. "If there ever were any fish hereabouts," he growled, "they would eat 'em."

I asked if he thought he might sometime net a piece of King John's treasure, supposedly lost in the Wash in 1216. The tide came in with a rush – as it still does – caught the King's baggage train and all his treasure out on the sands, and swirled and broke over them. The King narrowly escaped.

The skipper thought little of the story. He looked at me as if I were a seal.

"Do you think us would leave a treasure lying about all these years, in the Wash or anywhere else?" he asked. "If it was ever there. And if it was, it'd be far inland now, over to Sutton Bridge way. There's a silver cup called King John's in the Guildhall in King's Lynn. If the King ever drank out of that, I'll eat a bushel of mussels – aye, in

"A WILD, AMPHIBIOUS RACE," *poet George Crabbe called the seafarers of his native East Anglia. Fisherlads today – wrestling the bulging cod end of a net while the trawler stands on her beam-ends in freezing seas; rising before dawn and still gutting, sorting, icing the catch past midnight; living hard, spending freely at the end of a three-weeks' voyage – carry on salty traditions of "Fishermen Venturers" who sailed for Elizabeth I. To build up fisheries she sternly enforced "fish-daies" when her subjects had to eat fish. Uncoerced today, Britons eat or export enough to keep more than 20,000 men at their trawls.*

At Lowestoft (center), England's most easterly town, plaice, halibut, and other bottom fishes fill barrels on a dock where "lumpers" unload the catch. Grimsby (opposite), home of England's largest trawler fleet, also bristles with the masts of Scandinavian vessels – as does Hull across the Humber. Like other towns whose names end in by, *Grimsby was in the Danelaw, the northeastern region which the Vikings held by treaty with Alfred the Great. Norse links survive in the blood of the people as well. From a nearby creek in 1608 the Pilgrims left for Holland, their first voyage in search of freedom.*

their shells. They tell me it's a kind of cup that wasn't made until a hundred years after King John died."

By now we were pushing up the muddy Witham toward Boston. The 272-foot tower of St. Botolph's Church – one of the largest parish churches in England, said my shipmate with pride – had been in sight all day. Known as the Boston Stump, it towers over Boston, the river, and the docks.

Outside Boston are two small places called Bunker's Hill and New York. All East Anglia abounds with place names repeated in America: King's Lynn (Lynn), Lincoln, Groton, Dedham, Danbury, Ipswich, Cambridge, Sudbury, Medford, Bedford (*New* in New England) – these are only a few. The hamlet of New York looks far from new.

Not far from Boston, on a trip by car with my East Anglian friend Adam Eggett, I spotted a great thick tower. A high battle-

mented place of extraordinary solidity standing alone in a field, it frowned down on the flat countryside.

"Tattershall Castle," said Adam. "That nearly went to America too. William Randolph Hearst, I've been told, tried to buy it and ship it across." Only the castle keep had endured the centuries. It was restored and placed in the care of the National Trust. This was once the castle of the Earl of Lincoln, where John Smith stayed before he set out for Virginia.

Smith attended the King Edward VI grammar school at Louth. We sought directions from the cheerful constable on traffic duty near Louth's large church.

"Oh! Captain John Smith!" he said. "You'll find him up the road, in the old school." He

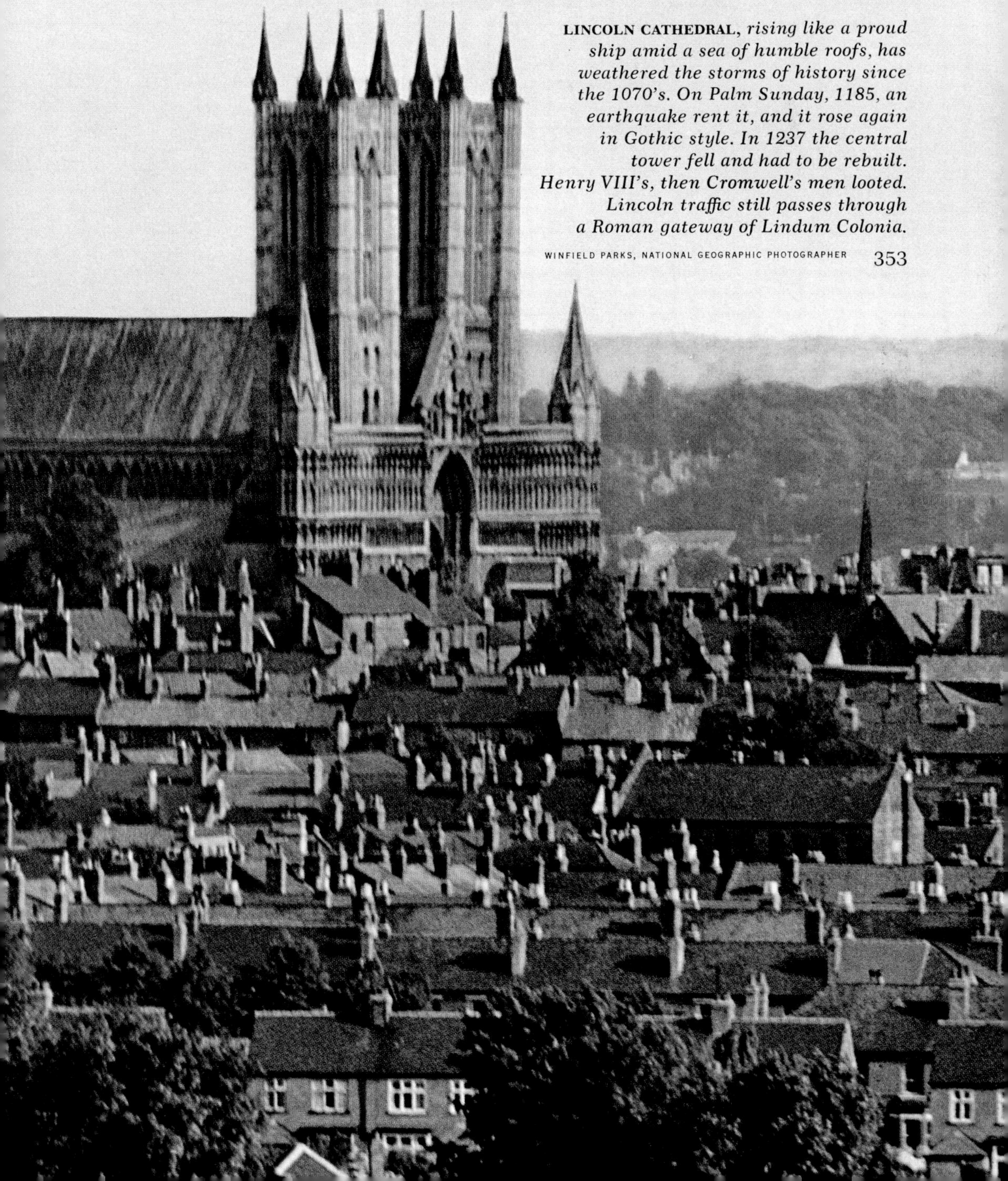

LINCOLN CATHEDRAL, *rising like a proud ship amid a sea of humble roofs, has weathered the storms of history since the 1070's. On Palm Sunday, 1185, an earthquake rent it, and it rose again in Gothic style. In 1237 the central tower fell and had to be rebuilt. Henry VIII's, then Cromwell's men looted. Lincoln traffic still passes through a Roman gateway of Lindum Colonia.*

WINFIELD PARKS, NATIONAL GEOGRAPHIC PHOTOGRAPHER

spoke as if the captain were an old friend and we were about to find him in person.

In the King Edward School a large mural shows a handsome Pocahontas pleading before her father Powhatan for John Smith's life. Tall, haughty braves, in feather headdresses and armed with spears, stand by.

North of Louth the great fishing port of Grimsby sprawls along the south bank of the River Humber. Its very name reveals Grimsby's Scandinavian origin: *by* is a Danish word-relic akin to "ville"; *Grim* was a fabled Danish fisherman.

The Lincolnshire port processes some 200,000 tons of fish a year. Trawlers and seiners sail in from fishing banks as far away as Iceland and the White Sea. The fish are sold in frenzied auctions and then sped to market in trucks and trains. Danes, Norwegians, Icelanders – fishermen all – mingle with East Anglians. Some linger only briefly while their ships take on ice, fuel, and stores for another voyage.

Just a few miles northwest of Grimsby the Pilgrims fled England for Amsterdam.

A SAILING MAN can get a good glimpse of Norfolk from the deck of a small boat in the waterways of the Fens and Broads. This, of course, I planned to do. But to see a bit more of this East Anglian county, I based myself for a while at the Duke's Head in King's Lynn.

The old hotel, with its oak stairs and banisters hewn by adz-wielding shipwrights, was built in 1685 to accommodate merchants. It stands in Tuesday Market Place, a large square so named to distinguish it from Saturday's market at the other end of town. Adam Eggett said townsfolk used to burn witches at Tuesday Market Place.

Lively old King's Lynn, sitting beside the straightened mouth of the Great Ouse, still offers vistas that its prosperous merchants knew in medieval days, when this was one of England's leading ports. The house of one Hanseatic merchant stands as it did when King's Lynn was a walled city.

Adam showed me the marks on the Church of St. Margaret which indicate the heights to which great floods have risen.

NOBLY RETIRED *to a Royal Air Force base at Scampton, near Lincoln, a Lancaster bomber which flew 100 missions over Germany in World War II stands watch over R.A.F. children. Liberators and Flying Fortresses of the U. S. 8th Air Force also roared from many an East Anglian field. Airmen, like mariners of old, sought the landmark of Boston Stump (below), 15th-century lantern tower of St. Botolph's Church on the River Witham.*

WINFIELD PARKS, NATIONAL GEOGRAPHIC PHOTOGRAPHER

BOSTON, *Lincolnshire, gave its name (from Botolph's Town, honoring a Saxon monk) to New World Boston. Five of its men became Massachusetts governors; John Cotton, vicar here, became "patriarch of New England."* Mayflower *model (left) recalls the Pilgrims, imprisoned in the Guildhall when a ship captain betrayed their 1607 attempt to flee England.*

SLEEPING BEAUTY *basks in the enchantment of sunny East Anglia. From the Cockney paradise of Southend on Sea north to charming Cromer and here on Yarmouth's golden sands, the coast abounds in beaches where holidayers make port. Literary pilgrims head inland to Boulge, near Woodbridge. There Edward FitzGerald lies neath a "Rose of Yesterday" descended from one at the Persian grave of Omar Khayyám, whose* Rubáiyát *he lovingly rendered into English.*

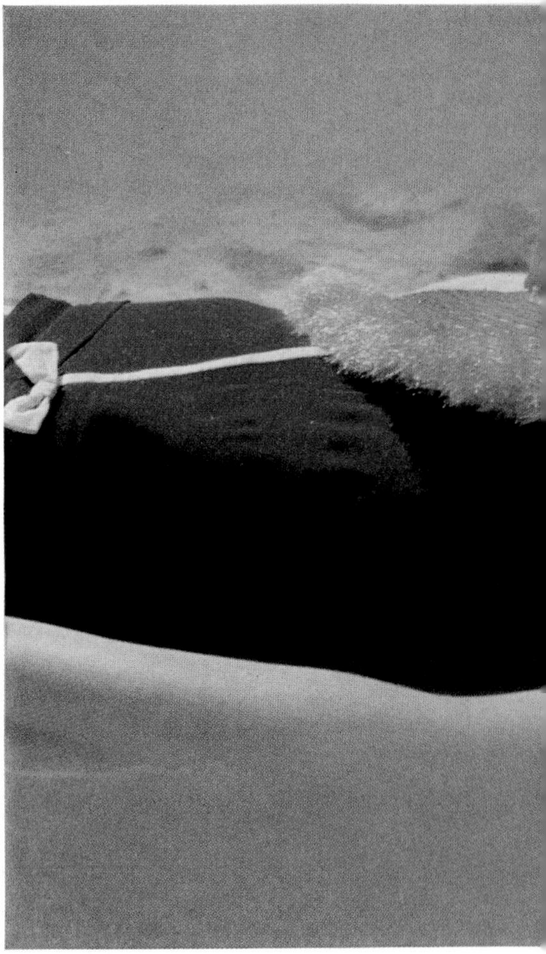

The worst one—waist-high even on raised ground—came in January, 1953.

"That was a flood, that was!" he declared. "A big storm and a giant tide came at us together—same hour, same day. Then the wind backed the tide up. Our defenses broke. A lot of people were drowned. A lot more would have been if it hadn't been for the American airmen stationed hereabouts. They came with their boats and took people from roofs, windows, and trees."

East Anglia's most famous son, Vice Admiral Horatio Nelson, was born in the vicarage at Burnham Thorpe. The son of the rector, young Horatio was a quiet, sickly boy. But he apparently struck everyone as ready, always, to give his best. I asked Adam to drive me to Nelson's birthplace.

"No use looking for the house," Adam said. "Some rich parson knocked it down before the Battle of Trafalgar."

Some distance from the roadside marker for the vicarage, we found the church, where battle-stained white ensigns trailed in the chancel. A cross and lectern were made from timbers of H.M.S. *Victory.* A sheet of her copper formed a plaque.

We continued on, making a wide, leisurely swing round north Norfolk. We entered one of those glorious avenues of great trees one finds at times along the roads of England. The gracious branches mingled their tracery of soft leaves overhead and, like stained-glass windows in a cathedral, softened the sunlight. A carpet of wild flowers danced in the breeze on the leaf mold of centuries. I wandered in this place called Wayland Wood for a while, not realizing that here, according to the early English ballad, the Babes in the Wood perished.

About 15 miles south of this beguiling wood lies the ancient town of Thetford, on the Little Ouse. It recently found new life as one of the "expanding towns" named to take the "overspill" from crowded London. Some 40 firms and 1,000 families have moved here from the capital, swelling the population to nearly 10,000.

Once the capital of the Iceni tribe and the seat of East Anglian kings, Thetford is better known today as the birthplace of Tom Paine. In 1964 Americans erected a gilded statue of the pamphleteer in Thetford. Though Paine had been dead since 1809, some townspeople opposed a statue honoring a man they still considered a traitor.

DURING THE ENGLISH SUMMER thousands of people take to the Broads for a holiday. This system of inland waterways—rivers, canals, lakes, and estuaries, some tidal, some not—threads the flat land that forms the hump of East Anglia.

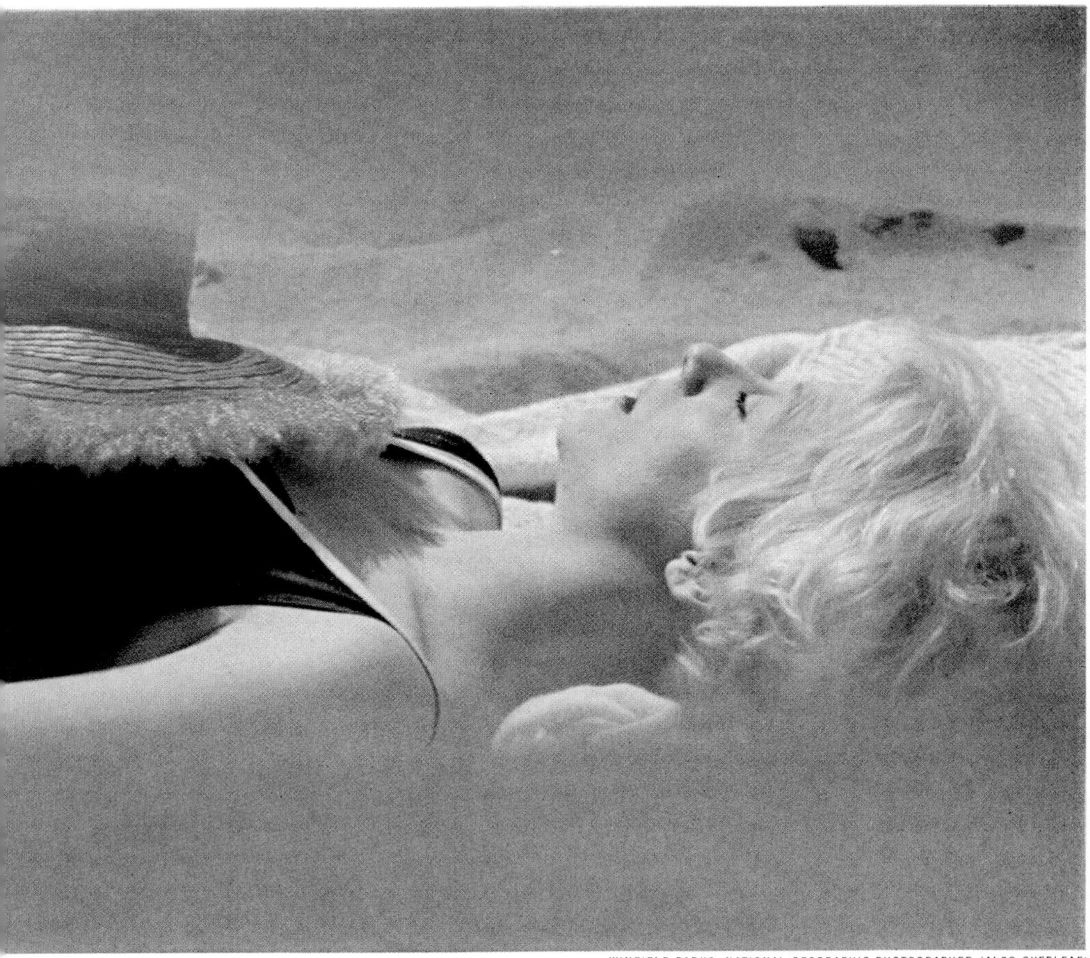

WINFIELD PARKS, NATIONAL GEOGRAPHIC PHOTOGRAPHER (ALSO OVERLEAF)

A "broad" is really a wide spot or lake along one of the reed-edged streams. Some were carved out by ancient peat cutters who dug up the fuel, then moved on. At the height of the season most broads are crammed with all manner of boats as well as swans, gulls, fish, anglers, and fat old sightseeing boats that suddenly charge through all the other vessels while their passengers sit silently and stare.

I had heard hair-raising stories of the Broads, and it was with some slight trepidation that I drove into Messrs. Collins' boatyard on Oulton Broad near Lowestoft with my wife Nance and our son Kit, just graduated from Oxford. We transferred our gear from our car to a hospital-clean and well-fitted launch named *Swan Lake*. After five minutes of briefing we were turned loose in the midst of all the congestion.

Within the first moments a small yacht appeared beneath our bows out of thin air. I stopped quickly and she drifted out of the way, guided by a young couple who stared happily at one another without a glance where they were going or, apparently, a clue how to get there. I expected to see collisions all around—hulls torn open, bodies spilled into the water. But craft would occasionally touch lightly and draw apart again, the helmsmen all smiles. Narrow escapes are part of the fun on the Broads.

As we cruised the winding streams we became used to seeing the masts, bridges, and upper works of coastal steamers moving incongruously across the flat land, their hulls obscured by a bend in the river. They were no problem on straight stretches: We kept on the right side, well over. They kept in the middle.

"Here comes a liner," said Nance suddenly as we neared the town of Reedham.

A NORFOLK WHERRY *more than a century old, gaff-rigged* Albion *gets under way on the crowded Broads near Wroxham. Smooth-water sailors exploring the 200 miles of navigable waterways in this triangular maze of lagoons, sluggish streams, and cow-dotted meadows between Norwich and the coast may wonder with David Copperfield "if the world were really as round as my geography book said, how any part of it came to be so flat." But they delight in charming inns and villages, fine old manor houses and round-towered flint churches. Windmills remind them that this countryside looks across the North Sea to the Netherlands. At Burgh Castle they find massive walls of the Saxon Shore, a Roman defense chain from Norfolk to the Isle of Wight.*

Ahead was a coaster, her enormous bow turning the brown stream to a creamy froth. She was probably about 600 tons, but on the Broads she looked more like 10,000.

The Reedham railway bridge swung slowly open for the big vessel. I stopped, well over on the right-hand side.

Then I saw the sailing yacht. She had also stopped, but not on the right side and not under control either. Her sails flapped uselessly because they were not set properly. Four young men aboard, obviously without the slightest notion of what to do, looked up and saw that they were right under the big ship's bows. The steamship, caught in her approach to clear the bridge, stopped engines and blew a loud blast. Two of the young men frantically tried to start the auxiliary engine, then grabbed whatever came to hand. One thrust a pole deep in the mud and promptly lost it; the other tried to paddle with a floorboard.

The steamship's bow wave lifted the yacht slightly and pushed her gently aside – but not far enough. Now the mainsail was trailing in the water. The youths threw themselves along the side and began to push the steamship off with hands and feet, for her wash – though she was going very slowly – was sucking the yacht towards her.

Soon the yacht drifted directly beneath the cooling water gushing from the steamer's engine room. "Yow!" yelled one young man. "Turn that stuff off! It's hot!"

Stopped dead, the steamer lurched into the bridge with a crash. The yacht slid from beneath the waterfall and, with her engine going at last, made a leap at full throttle for the bank – to moor, I supposed. She hit with a solid clout, bounced off, and came again. A youth in the bow swung a mooring line like a lasso, and leaped. He misjudged and fell in the water. He roared with laughter. So did his shipmates and, as far as I could see, half the waterfront of Reedham.

The steamship, meanwhile, remained stuck in the bridge, which was jammed open. No trains ran that night.

We repaired to a Reedham pub to hear some Norfolk accents and yarn with the locals. Here I found members of the famed tug-o'-war team, the Reedham Vikings. They travel all over the country, beating all comers, and train, they say, on Norfolk beer, large steaks, and long runs in heavy boots. Several times after that we passed husky youths pounding along the lanes in shorts and iron-shod boots.

In the morning, with an air of Sunday peace over Reedham (and the swing bridge restored to service), we passed upstream bound for Norwich. The pleasing city, with its famed cathedral, its castle, bridges, and large ships, loomed suddenly after we had

WINFIELD PARKS, NATIONAL GEOGRAPHIC PHOTOGRAPHER

NORWICH SKYLINE *spans centuries. The cathedral, a Norman jewel in a setting of 33 medieval churches, thrusts its 15th-century spire above today's towered city hall (center) and the castle's square keep (left) that spelled power in Henry I's day.*

Prospering with the influx of Flemish weavers, the Norfolk city sprawled second in size to Tudor London. Guests at the Maid's Head (right), near cobbled Elm Hill (above), relax in an inn already old when Elizabeth I slept here.

slipped past miles of quietly lovely rural England. At the flower-lined suburb of Thorpe St. Andrew we changed to my friend Philip Pank's launch *Califa*, which is fitted with an electric echo sounder reading in half inches. The Panks, an old Norfolk family, know their way round Norwich afloat and ashore.

"We'll go to the end of navigation," said Philip. "We need only 18 inches of water."

We started with six feet. We dodged under bridges, past Dutch coasters, timber yards, warehouses, breweries, a long quay jammed with craft like the *Swan Lake*, an ancient ruin called Cow Tower (once part of the city walls), lovely waterside houses with gardens down to the river's edge. Friends crossing above us on the bridges called greetings to the Panks. Fat pigeons looked out solemnly from holes in ancient brickwork among the foundations of historic buildings. We were given glimpses of the beautiful cathedral, begun in 1096 and one of the loveliest in England.

ROCKERS ROLL ALONG THE COAST, *adding a swinging new look to old towns David Copperfield first saw from a cart behind "the laziest horse in the world." Great Yarmouth (opposite) is awash with trippers at the high tide of summer holidays. From Michaelmas (September 29) to Martinmas (November 11) the principal guests are herring. One "blow," or smoking, transforms a plump herring into a Yarmouth bloater. The port preserves a Tudor house as the place where Cromwell decided Charles I's fate. A 144-foot monument to Nelson recalls the Norfolk-born hero's triumphant arrival after the Battle of the Nile. Administering the oath in the Freedom of the Borough ceremony, the clerk noted Nelson's left hand on the Bible: "Your right hand, my Lord." "That," said Nelson, "is at Tenerife."*

WINFIELD PARKS, NATIONAL GEOGRAPHIC PHOTOGRAPHER

We swung hard aport by a bridge near an Elizabethan hostelry with a large yard for coaches. The echo sounder clicked away.

"Eighteen inches," said Philip, stopping the engine. "This is it." He swung the launch around. The soundings slowly increased as we chugged downstream.

NORWICH was too fascinating to leave like that. Back in Thorpe St. Andrew we moored the *Swan Lake*, and Nance and I headed for a hotel in Norwich. A plaque noted that Elizabeth had lodged here, meaning the first Elizabeth. She would not find it greatly changed today, though the floor of her large room is now sagging. Norwich was old even then, for Romans and Saxons had lived here, and King Sweyn of Denmark "wasted and burned" the town in 1004.

Flemish weavers arrived in the 14th century and built up the city's wealth on woven cloth. The name "worsted" comes from the nearby Norfolk town of Worstead, where the woolen fabric originated.

When Norwich thrived as the center of England's cloth trade, much of its wealth flowed into the building of churches—and into the restoration of its magnificent cathedral. The graceful, 15th-century spire, soaring 313 feet, is surpassed in England only by Salisbury's 404-foot spire. Stone for the cathedral, shipped from France, arrived up the River Wensum. Seagoing ships still ply the Wensum and the River Yare.

I tried to visit Great Yarmouth—its name discloses its river-mouth location—by water. But we ran aground, following navigational signs. So we got there by car and found a city looking more like a resort than a fishing port. Great Yarmouth (often simply called Yarmouth) turns to fishing mainly after the summer visitors leave.

Dickens visited the town and used it as a setting in *David Copperfield*. Peggotty, a plump character in the novel, proudly calls herself a "Yarmouth Bloater." A bloater is a succulent, lightly smoked herring. I tried some and found them splendid.

"You mean Wind'am?" asked the elderly local on the road near Norwich. I had pronounced all three syllables when I asked the way to Wymondham. In East Anglia, as in many other parts of England, you must be prepared for often incomprehensible variations on the pronunciation of place names. The equally incomprehensible Norfolk accent, however, is fading before the general spread of education—and the standardizing influence of what has come to be called "the BBC accent."

Wymondham was the birthplace of Robert Kett, who in 1549 led a peasants' revolt against the enclosure of communal peasant lands for sheep-grazing. The uprising was quickly put down, and Kett was hanged at a spot now marked by a plaque on the 12th-century keep of Norwich Castle.

THE FENS beckoned next, and once more Nance and I were in a chartered launch, wandering in another waterland of East Anglia. The Fens cover 2,500 square miles of Norfolk, Cambridgeshire, Huntingdonshire, and Lincolnshire. Drainage converted this once tremendous, reedy swamp into rich farm land.

You don't really cruise the Fens. You paddle, sail, row, or chug along the series of rivers and large ditches which drain them. But this "ditch-crawling" reveals one of the

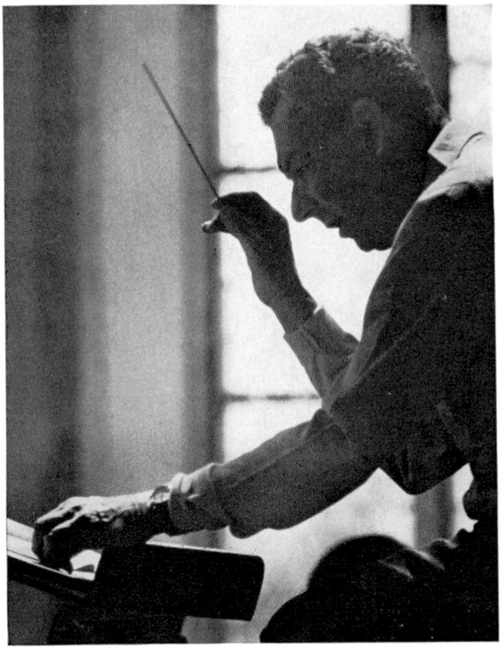

SYMPHONY OF LIGHT *from Ely's vaulting lantern tower bathes the octagonal chamber where Sadler's Wells musicians perform. Great oaken timbers support the engineering marvel built to replace the central tower that fell in 1322. The Norman cathedral, shrine of St. Etheldreda, began to rise on a fen island in the 1080's.*

BENJAMIN BRITTEN *rehearses in Blythburgh Church for his June festival. "I belong at home in Aldeburgh," the world-famed Suffolk composer said. "I have tried to bring music to it in the shape of our local festival, and all the music I write comes from it." He based his opera* Peter Grimes *on the harsh poetry of Aldeburgh's George Crabbe.*

GEORGE F. MOBLEY, NATIONAL GEOGRAPHIC PHOTOGRAPHER (ALSO OPPOSITE). UPPER: BRIAN SEED

most interesting large-scale navigable drainage systems in the world.

We went to Ely and boarded a 30-foot four-berth cruiser. Here on the "isle of eels" stands the great cruciform cathedral which grew on the site of a Benedictine abbey founded in 673 by St. Etheldreda, Queen of Northumbria. Danish raiders sacked the abbey two centuries later, as they did the Benedictine monastery at Peterborough across the Fens to the northwest. There, too, a Norman cathedral rose. Catherine of Aragon lies buried in it.

From the shadow of Ely's cathedral, we set off up the Ouse and the Cam, bound for Cambridge first, then for any point of interest in the 200 miles of Fen waterways.

"You'll find the Fens very different from the Broads," the boatman had told us at Ely. "They aren't crowded and they're quieter. On the Fens, it's said, only three things move – the water, the clouds, and the windmills. The windmills are stopped now."

We found this true enough. On some summery days even the clouds stood still. Surrounded by fresh air and tranquillity, we headed upstream toward Jesus Green in the university city of Cambridge. The River Ouse became the treelined River Cam, the perfect approach to Cambridge. The sun shone; we shared the river with ducks, swans, and cygnets. A big red bull at Baitsbite Lock also watched us from his vantage point on the bank. Nance eyed him warily. If he leaped for our launch we were sunk.

"He's friendly," said the lockkeeper.

We left our launch at the Jesus Green Lock and hired a punt to enjoy leisurely the famous Backs – that lovely riverside vista of stately colleges and close-cropped lawns rolling down to the Cam.

Punting looks graceful. But it is easy – and most undignified – to be left puntless, swinging for a precarious moment on the end of the pole stuck in the mud, then crashing into the water. I avoided such a fate by leaving the punting to Nance, an expert.

We landed at King's College to see the magnificence of its chapel, considered by many the finest example of English Perpendicular Gothic. As we approached, we heard the glorious King's College choir.

WINFIELD PARKS, NATIONAL GEOGRAPHIC PHOTOGRAPHER

SANDRINGHAM *(above), the Queen's Norfolk home, stretches 450 feet, a Tudor-style mansion built in the 1860's. Thick with game birds, the estate found special favor with George V, a fine shot.*

James I reputedly quipped that Audley End (opposite), built by the Earl of Suffolk while Lord High Treasurer, was too large for a king, though it might do for a king's treasurer. Charles II disagreed: He bought it for himself. In 1701 it reverted to the Howard family. In its cellar Samuel Pepys "drank most admirable drink [and] played on my flageolette, there being an excellent echo."

To diarist John Evelyn, the Essex mansion seemed "a mixt fabrick, twixt antiq and modern." The fame carved screen of 1605 bears figures, arches, and garlands that proclaim the Renaissance; scrollwork gallery above whispers of the Middle Ages.

ADAM WOOLFITT, COURTESY MINISTRY OF PUBLIC BUILDING AND WORKS

PATRICK THURSTON

WHERE TRAVELERS *of old threading between fen and forest found a crossing, and graceful arches now span the Cam, Cambridge spreads its lovely Backs (center above). Punters pole past Clare College and, to its right, the glory of Cambridge, King's College Chapel, rising tall-windowed and pinnacled in the epitome of Perpendicular style. Some two miles of delicate stone rib its fan vaulting; 11,000 square feet of stained glass suffuse it with Scriptural light. Henry VI founded King's in 1441, then enlarged it for scholars from Eton. In festive May Week—marking term end in June!—spectators (far right) throng the banks downstream for bumping races. Lacking room to race abreast, one crew overhauls another and eliminates it by a bump, thus taking its place in the next heat. In King's College boater and blazer, a coach (above) urges on his eight.*

BEDELLS BEARING MACES *lead a Whitsun procession from Senate House to university church. "Bulldogs," in top hats, are drawn from porters' ranks to help proctors make lively undergrads toe the line. Dons holding doctor's degrees wear scarlet gowns; among them marches a professor from Newnham, one of three women's colleges.*

Peterhouse, oldest of Cambridge's 29 colleges, was founded by the Bishop of Ely in 1284, 20 years after Merton's founding at Oxford. Queens' College sheltered Erasmus, famed scholar of the early 1500's, who taught Greek, worked on his New Testament edition, and complained, "I am beset with thieves, and the wine is no better than vinegar." Emmanuel, citadel of the Puritans, produced John Harvard, whose college rose at another Cambridge. Trinity, with more than 800 students, is the largest in Cambridge or Oxford.

At Christ's College, a porter pointed out Charles Darwin's rooms. At Magdalene College, we saw the library of Samuel Pepys, whose famous diaries lay open, showing his shorthand that long baffled decipherers. The list of famous Cambridge men seems endless: Newton, Francis Bacon, Tennyson, Milton, Pitt. And who is to come in the future? This I wondered as I looked at the new Churchill College, founded in 1960.

"We must go to Grantchester," Nance said. And so we went to the village near Cambridge that Rupert Brooke knew so well. Nance recited from Brooke's poems as we poled along, especially his lines on Grantchester and its vicarage gardens. It is still a quiet and lovely hamlet:

I only know that you may lie
Day long and watch the
Cambridge sky.
And, flower-lulled in sleepy grass,
Hear the cool lapse of hours pass,
Until the centuries blend and blur
In Grantchester, in Grantchester...

After Cambridge we sailed the Cam again, then turned upstream on the Old West and Great Ouse toward St. Ives, Godmanchester, and Huntingdon. A fine old man wandering along the highway near the upper reaches of the Ouse directed us to a pumping engine which, he said, James Watt built. The old fellow hadn't seen the engine for 60 years (for, though he was 91, there was so much to see in those parts) but he remembered where it was.

SPECTRUM *of Cambridge science compasses Newton's genius and the cosmic reach of radio astronomy.*

Born at Woolsthorpe Manor in Lincolnshire, Isaac Newton entered Cambridge in 1661 as an 18-year-old subsizar, a student earning his way by chores. At 23 he began the experiments that led to his discovery of the nature of light.

At Sturbridge, England's most famous fair, held near Cambridge, "I procured me a Triangular glass-Prisme," related Newton, "and made a small hole in my window-shuts, to let in... the Suns light." Having taken the rainbow out of sunlight and displayed it on the wall, Newton (left above) and a roommate turn it back to white light with a convex lens. Dust or smoke would make the light beam visible.

Newton's theories, set forth in his incomparable Principia, *unlocked the cosmos to science.*

Radio telescope of Cambridge's Cavendish Laboratory (right) looks out to the stars, feeding data to Sir Martin Ryle (left) for new concepts of the universe's shape and origin. The laboratory helped develop wartime radar.

ROBERT C. MAGIS, NATIONAL GEOGRAPHIC STAFF ARTIST. BELOW AND OPPOSITE: GEORGE F. MOBLEY, NATIONAL GEOGRAPHIC PHOTOGRAPHER

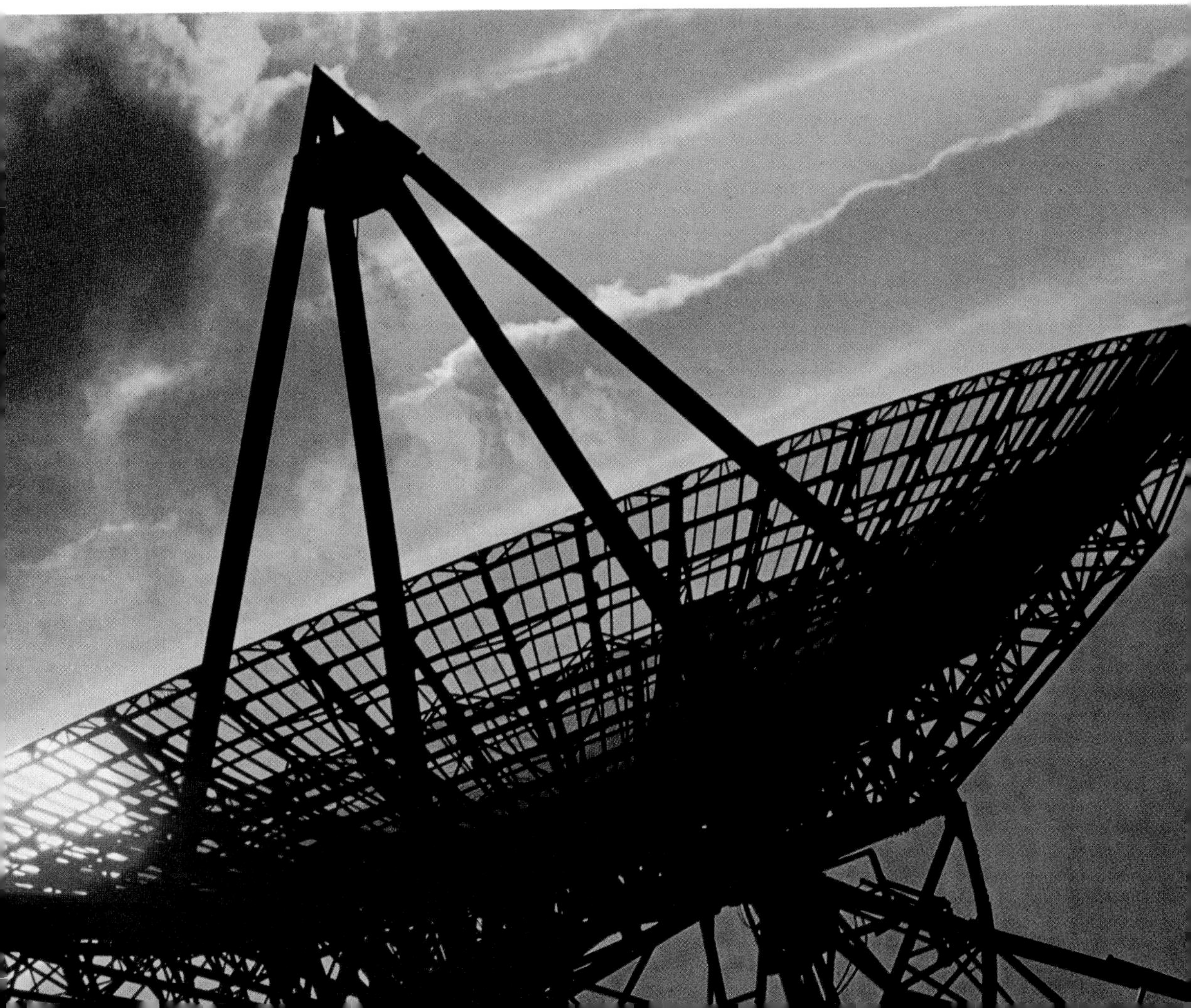

As we parted, he gave us his recipe for a long life: "Eat good, sleep sound, and don't go rushing about in them motorcars."

We tied up for the night in a pretty backwater on the Ouse, a berth right out of this world, though a road of sorts ran within a hundred yards of it. Ashore, a road sign caught Nance's eye. "Bluntisham," she read aloud. "Why, that's Dorothy Sayers' village! She was brought up in the vicarage there. The 'Nine Tailors'! They're a peal of church bells. She used them for the title of one of her best mysteries. I'm sure we'll find the bells in Bluntisham church."

Off we went to look. The church, large and imposing for so small a village, had bells, and a tablet on the wall listing the rectors back to the year 1217 mentioned the Rev. Henry Sayers, M.A., as vicar from 1897 to 1917. "Now we have to find the rectory where Dorothy lived," said Nance. "There is a door in it from Cromwell's old home, Slepe Hall at St. Ives."

The rectory, usually so easy to find, proved to be miles from the church. We found it a pleasant old country house in large gardens. The vicar amiably showed us the Cromwellian door, now preserved in his study. He spoke very rudely of Lord Protector Oliver Cromwell, who was born in Huntingdon, the county town of Huntingdonshire. He called him "Butcher" as if Cromwell's suppression of the Church of England had been quite recent.

A statue of Cromwell stood in the marketplace of St. Ives, which we reached later that day. We dined in the Cromwell room of an old coaching inn. The central carriageway, where the long-distance coaches used to drive in, now is roofed over to make an attractive lounge.

The inn had some paintings by a local artist who, the headwaiter said, had come to St. Ives under the odd impression that it was the other St. Ives in Cornwall – a seaport famous for its wonderful light and its artists' colony. But he liked this inland St. Ives, which also had good light and many subjects, and, said the waiter, he never bothered to move. I could understand why.

WINFIELD PARKS, NATIONAL GEOGRAPHIC PHOTOGRAPHER. AQUATINT BY R. HAVELL AFTER JAMES POLLARD, COURTESY R.H.C. NEVILLE, AUDLEY END

CHURNING THE TURF *at Newmarket, thoroughbreds charge down a straight course, unlike the American oval. Racing was born here in the reign of James I. Banned by Cromwell, it was restored to favor by Charles II, who rode several winners in a 1675 meet. In 1816 Sir Joshua, an eight-time winner here, beat Filo da Puta by a neck in a 1,000-guinea match. R.H.C. Neville, a descendant of Sir Joshua's owner, found this print in an attic of his ancestral home, Audley End.*

WINFIELD PARKS, NATIONAL GEOGRAPHIC PHOTOGRAPHER

LAVENHAM'S *half-timbered houses, nodding as if asleep 500 years, dream of woolmen who thronged the market place (left) before their splendid guildhall, attended the church faced with a hundred thousand flints, and relaxed in the Swan (above). Nearby, Jane Taylor, gazing out her window, immortalized a diamond in the sky: "Twinkle, twinkle, little star. . . ."*

"GOOD LORD! That swan is standing up!" shouted Nance, pointing just off our starboard bow. Indeed it *was* standing on its large webbed feet, and the river water was barely covering them. We'd been told the river had lots of islands just below the surface, but where the swan stood there could only be about four inches. We needed 18. I stopped, expecting to ground, but we didn't. The swan must have been on a very small personal island. Cautiously, I got under way again, carefully watching all the swans in case any suddenly stood up.

With a multitude of swans to do the sounding for us, we wandered slowly on past Houghton Mill, Hartford, and the pretty riverside villages of Offord Cluny and Offord D'Arcy, all at their best that morning. We worked the few locks ourselves, following the instructions in the little book which had been given us at Ely.

Soon we turned about and headed downstream to a place called Holywell, on the banks of the Ouse not far from St. Ives.

" 'There is a tradition that Hereward the Wake crossed the Ouse to the Ferry Boat Inn at Holywell when escaping from the Normans,' " read Nance from the book.

"It says the inn has been there since the tenth century—parts of it, anyway—and running the ferry all that time, until the other day. It has a ghost too, but it's a nice ghost and it's abroad only on St. Patrick's Day. Let's go there for lunch. Hereward is one of my heroes."

Hereward the Wake of Lincolnshire defied William the Conqueror and fought the Normans successfully for months in 1070-71, plundering Peterborough and defending the Isle of Ely. "Last of the English," he remains a symbol of 11th-century freedom fighters. The successor of any ferryman who had helped him, we decided, was well worth our patronage.

Hereward, we found, is a vague figure in the Ferry Boat Inn. But the ghost becomes vivid and real. "She lived hundreds of years ago; her name was Juliet Tewsley. The stone from her grave is here, partly under that settee in the lounge floor," the manager told us while we waited for our tasty roast duck. "She was in love with a local lad named Tom Zoul, but he loved ale. One St. Patrick's Day she died. Now each March 17 she appears from beneath the stone. She goes out and looks for Mr. Zoul."

"Anybody seen her recently?" I asked.

"She's a sort of shadowy image in the night mist," said the manager. "People say they've seen her. I don't know. I'm always pretty busy then."

"THE HAY WAIN" *captures fleeting sunlight and shadow near Flatford on the Stour. This 1821 painting by a miller's son, Constable, awed Delacroix; its play of light anticipated the Impressionists.*

Willy Lott's cottage, a favorite Constable subject, lures artists today to this land that earlier produced Thomas Gainsborough (far right), son of a Sudbury spinner. Famed for his portraits, he longed to "walk off to some sweet village where I can paint landskips."

"THE HAY WAIN" BY JOHN CONSTABLE, 1821, NATIONAL GALLERY, LONDON

WINFIELD PARKS, NATIONAL GEOGRAPHIC PHOTOGRAPHER

Kensitas
Fine cigarettes
SKETCH
IS HERE
SKETCH
SKETCH
Sale

IPSWICH, *county town of Suffolk (opposite), has long been a port of call for history. Romans, Angles, Danes fought for this sea gate to East Anglia. Edward III in 1340 sailed from the River Orwell with a mighty expeditionary force that destroyed the French fleet at Sluys.*

Prospering amid a land "fatte, fruteful, and full of profitable things," Ipswich bequeathed a rich Tudor heritage. The Ancient House (left), built by a fish merchant in 1567, displays exquisite pargeting beneath its mullioned bay windows. The sculptured plaster symbolizes Europe, Asia, Africa, and America. Australia was yet unknown. Royal arms of Charles II call to mind the story that he hid in a secret room here while Cromwell hunted him.

Cardinal Street and Wolsey's Gateway recall Henry VIII's Lord Chancellor, Thomas Wolsey, Oxford-educated son of an Ipswich butcher:
"Begot by butchers, but by beggars bred,
How high his honour holds his haughty head."

Ipswich was a center of the Puritans, who banned dancing and other frivolity. But the Morris dance lives on at the Aldeburgh Music Festival, where dancers jingle before the 16th-century Moot Hall.

WINFIELD PARKS, NATIONAL GEOGRAPHIC PHOTOGRAPHER

SUFFOLK AND ESSEX are counties I know and cherish. I had lived near Ipswich, and I had sailed in Thames barges from London docks up Essex creeks.

I renewed acquaintance with Suffolk by first walking the streets and docks of Ipswich, the port to which I had brought my full-rigged *Joseph Conrad*, back in 1934, to begin a two-and-a-half year voyage round the world. I visited again the haunts of Cardinal Wolsey, who was born here. Wolsey had hoped to make Ipswich as great a center of learning as Oxford, where he had founded Christ Church college in 1525. But as Shakespeare said in *Henry VIII*, the college at Ipswich "fell with him," and little more than its gateway survives. Gone, too, is the theater where David Garrick began his acting career in 1741. But the Great White Horse Hotel, to which Dickens brought literary fame, still stands.

I crossed by river ferry from Felixstowe, a fashionable resort once the site of a

TRAVIS

At Colchester, wild Britons dared the might of Imperial Rome

JAMES P. BLAIR AND (LEFT AND OPPOSITE) WINFIELD PARKS, NATIONAL GEOGRAPHIC PHOTOGRAPHERS. CENTER: ADAM WOOLFITT

ROMAN INVADERS *swept into East Anglia in* A.D. *43, establishing their first colony at Camulodunum—now Colchester, Britain's oldest recorded town. It almost died 18 years later when Queen Boudicca (Boadicea) led her Iceni tribesmen against the legions. Her monument on the Thames Embankment (above) reminds us, in Churchill's words, "of the harsh cry of liberty or death which has echoed down the ages."*

When the hordes of the chariot-driving queen sacked Camulodunum and slew its inhabitants, they desecrated the grave of a centurion. His tombstone (left), in a Colchester museum built on the remains of a Roman temple, shows him bearing a vitis *or staff of office. Atop the town hall stands St. Helena (opposite), mother of Constantine the Great and daughter of King Coel, traditionally the "Merry Old Soul." Actually, he lived centuries before pipes or fiddlers reached England.*

Boudicca also razed London and Verulamium, later named St. Albans for England's first Christian martyr. Museum visitors in the Hertfordshire town (left, above) inspect a model of the gateway to Verulamium. The Romans watched spectacles at a second-century theater, now excavated. St. Albans Cathedral was partially built with Roman brick.

Roman fort, to Harwich, where the Orwell joins the Stour. Harwich's harbor bustled with North Sea ferries, for Harwich is a main gateway from London to northwest Europe.

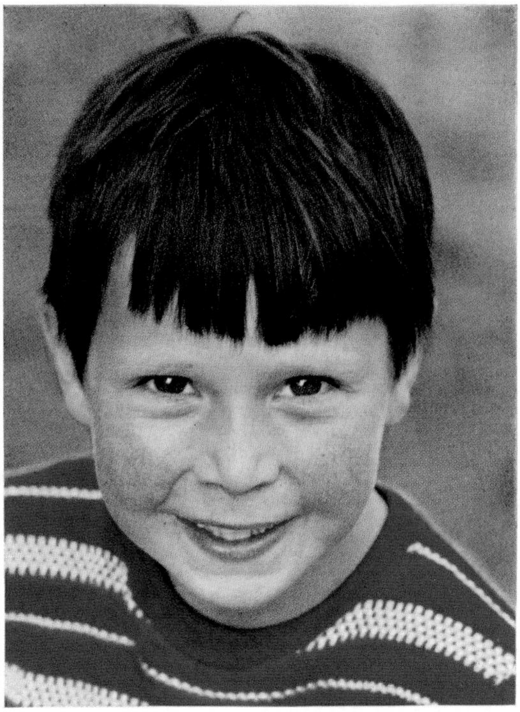

Up the coast of Suffolk I sipped tea in a tearoom near the beach at drowned Dunwich. I noticed that the tearoom's timbers had come from the wreck of a barge—fitting symbol of Dunwich's own fate. The seat of the first East Anglian bishopric in the seventh century, Dunwich was once a busy port. Now the sea and beach cover it. The North Sea has also claimed much of Aldeburgh to the south of Dunwich. But Aldeburgh, home of composer Benjamin Britten, thrives as the setting for the Aldeburgh Music Festival.

Charming villages adorn inland Suffolk. Lavenham still looks much as it did when it prospered as a cloth-making center. Its ancient Wool Hall has been incorporated into a comfortable hotel, the Swan. At Kersey, another ancient wool town, I cycled through the splash where a little stream, untamed, crosses the narrow road. At Long Melford, I walked the two-mile main street which gives the village its name.

Bury St. Edmunds bears a noble motto—"Shrine of the King, Cradle of the Law." The town is named for St. Edmund, the last king of East Anglia, whom the Danes murdered in 870. At the magnificent abbey church erected to enshrine his body, barons chafing under King John's rule assembled in 1214 to draw up the "Petition of the Barons," the basis for Magna Carta. I sat in a park that covers much of the site of the abbey, now a ruin. Across the road I could see the Angel Hotel, well known to Dickens—and Mr. Pickwick.

At Newmarket I saw stableboys—and stablegirls—riding thoroughbreds in from morning exercise. I asked if any of these pretty girls had yet risen above the status of stablegirl. "Not yet," my informant said. But someday, he feared, girls might ride in the races there.

Through Essex villages and byways we meandered to Southend, playground for holidayers—and the great funnel through which vessels reach London with all the world's goods. Southend engulfed me in memories. In the 1930's I flew from nearby Rochford field. In 1944 I waited off this shore for my landings in Normandy with troops of Britain's Eighth Army; Southend was the last of England many of those fine men were ever to see.

Centuries ago, Roman invaders used the Essex city of Colchester as a base for maintaining the *Pax Romana* in East Anglia. They wrested it from the Catuvellauni, who had made their capital here on the site of an earlier settlement. The port on the Colne rose from a forest that swept all the way to London. Epping Forest is a remnant.

In this oldest recorded town in Britain we ended our tour of East Anglia. It seemed fitting to return to Roman days to remind ourselves of how much history has washed against this eastern flank of Britain.

A SMILE AND A SHIMMER *greet the visitor to Kersey, where a ford mirrors sturdy old houses that long heard the whir of the spinning wheel and the clack of the loom. Just as neighboring Lindsey gave its name to linsey-woolsey, so did this Suffolk village find fame in its woolens. Shakespeare's "honest kersey" testifies to the cloth's Parliament-enforced quality. Inventions in the 18th century drove weaving from cottage to factory, whose hum was the hand weaver's knell.*

WINFIELD PARKS, NATIONAL GEOGRAPHIC PHOTOGRAPHER

THE NORTH COUNTRY

ROLLING MOORS, ROMAN GHOSTS, AND RUINED ABBEYS

Cumberland

THE BACKBONE OF ENGLAND, the Pennines, runs northward through this stark and storied land, tilting rivers toward the North and Irish Seas. Lakes fill craggy, glacier-scoured valleys. Heather blooms on high moors coarsened by sand.

Across this wild country Romans flung a great wall. They vanished, but it endures. In from the sea swept Vikings. They left legacies in the speech and in the blue eyes of fiercely independent North-countrymen. Norman knights carved fiefs but could not tame the Border. "And the bludd ran down like rain" at Chevy Chase, where Scots slaughtered English, and at Flodden, "Where shiver'd was fair Scotland's spear, And broken was her shield!" Brother slew brother, staining the roses of York and Lancaster. Meantime, white-robed monks jeweled the North with abbeys. Lovely ruins speak of the piety that raised them, the greed that pulled them down.

Beside mountain-shadowed tarns Wordsworth found his daffodils "Fluttering and dancing in the breeze." On "bluff, bold swells of heath" Emily Brontë beheld *Wuthering Heights*. And where a river meets the sea, folk sang joyously of the cliffs of old Tynemouth: "They're wild and they're sweet, And dear are the waters that roll at their feet."

Brassy Blackpool, cocky Manchester, rocking Liverpool, proud Sheffield—each city has its stamp. And beyond, curlews cry above Rome's northernmost frontier; winds mourn the long-fallen on the minstreled Border; waves claw at castles that grip the black basalt of Northumberland with the grim will of men who built them to last as long as the land.

Northumberland
London
Durham
Westmorland
Yorkshire
Lancashire

YORK AND THE NORTHERN COUNTIES

Tracking the legions, Leonard Cottrell meets zesty folk in moorland hamlets and storied cities

A TELEVISION DIRECTOR was spending a weekend at my home in Westmorland on his first visit to northwestern England. I took him to the local inn to talk to its landlord, Tom, whose rich accent I can barely understand. If Tom drops into the true Westmorland *dialect* I might as well be listening to Norwegian, for it descends from the Norse settlers who landed here from their longships more than 1,000 years ago. In World War II, Westmorland soldiers captured at Narvik found that the Norwegians still understood their dialect.

Tom, speaking merely with the accent, greeted my friend with a crunching handclasp: "Ah'm allus glad to meet a friend of Mr. Cottrell's, but as fur television, Ah think it's a slaw way o' driving ye mad."

SWIRLING TRAFFIC *besieges York's medieval Micklegate Bar, once the gory roost for foemen's heads.*

DEAN CONGER, NATIONAL GEOGRAPHIC PHOTOGRAPHER

Brutal candor is characteristic of the North Country. The people rarely mean to hurt, but verbal toughness is part of their makeup, inherited perhaps from stubborn ancestors and conditioned by harsh winters and a hard land. It is risky to generalize, however, about North-countrymen. Practically all they have in common is a genial contempt for the southern Englishman, whom they regard as "soft."

As a native Midlander who has made his home in the North Country, I usually escape censure. But I am still looked upon as an "off-comer," someone not of the North. I once overheard a remark in a Westmorland inn: "'E's a foony chap . . . 'e writes bukes. . . ." (Long pause.) "But 'e's all right."

I think it was the highest compliment I have ever been paid!

Folk memories of the Wars of the Roses survive in the rivalry between Yorkshire and Lancashire. Differences in character

DEAN CONGER, NATIONAL GEOGRAPHIC PHOTOGRAPHER

THE MIDDLE AGES *live on in York's streets. A butcher carries carcasses in the Shambles, an old word for slaughterhouse. Half-timbered houses press so closely that people in overhanging stories can shake hands across the narrow street. Whip-ma-Whop-ma-Gate, "street of punishment," often saw whippings. Spurriergate recalls spurmakers, "gate" stemming from the Danish for street. At aptly named Knavesmire outside the 13th-century walls highwayman Dick Turpin was hanged in 1739.*

and speech are as sharply defined as the Pennine hills which broadly divide the counties. Again, men of Cumberland are as different from those of County Durham as Texans are from Virginians. Yet all northern England – Yorkshire, Lancashire, Westmorland, Cumberland, County Durham, and Northumberland – could fit within the state of West Virginia.

The North beguiles visitors into byways leading to secret and rewarding places. Knowing of these Circean enchantments, I decided not to attempt one all-embracing tour, but to make forays like an old Border raider. For the first one I planned a sweep to York from my home in the Lake District.

I drove southeastward, climbing into the Pennines until a roadside sign announced Yorkshire. Here in England's largest county, North Country bluntness has become enshrined in a splendid repertoire of stories which Yorkshiremen tell on themselves. They recall, for example, a man returning to his Yorkshire village and learning that his best friend had suddenly died.

"It must have been a terrible shock," he said to the widow.

"It were a reet blow," she agreed. "Tom 'ad gone to the garden to cut some cabbage. As 'e bent down 'e 'ad an 'eart attack."

"What did you do?"

"What *could* I do?" replied the widow. "I jist 'ad to open a tin o' peas."

IN ROMAN TIMES York was called Eboracum. From this great legionary base, headquarters of the Ninth "Hispana" Legion, Petillius Cerialis, when governor, launched his first attack on the Brigantes, the rebellious warrior tribe of northern England. In this city Constantine the Great, founder of Constantinople, was proclaimed Roman emperor in A.D. 306.

From the Roman occupation to Hitler's air raids, the history of this county town of Yorkshire unfolds like a pageant. And the architecture bears the marks and scars of each act. Dig in the center of York and you find Roman foundations. Yorkshire Museum is a treasury of Roman brooches, or *fibulae*, military accoutrements, gravestones of the legionaries and their families.

The original legionary fortress has been

DEAN CONGER, NATIONAL GEOGRAPHIC PHOTOGRAPHER

buried under later buildings or incorporated in the city walls. But from knowledge of other Roman forts we can judge its size, shape, and the position of its bastions. The gate to the general's headquarters, or *praetorium*, would have straddled what is now St. Helen's Square. The lower part of the Multangular Tower, which overlooks the River Ouse, is Roman. And nearby stands a fragment of the original Roman wall, distinguished, as always, by courses of narrow bricks alternating with gray stonework.

Little remains from the Saxon period. The Saxons built mostly with wood, and the Danes who ravaged northern England repeatedly in the ninth and tenth centuries destroyed what buildings there were.

After the Norman Conquest York came into its glory. The superb cathedral, or minster, soars above the city, dominating the countryside for miles around.

This architectural jewel is England's largest medieval cathedral and boasts stained glass to rival that at Chartres. Volumes have been written about it, but *The Times* of London sums it up: "No temple made with hands has more power than York Minster to uplift men's hearts to heaven."

York is my favorite northern city. I love to walk the medieval walls that still encircle its oldest part—walls of yellow sandstone pierced at intervals by gateways. What names they bear: Micklegate Bar, Walmgate Bar, Fishergate Postern! And what gruesome images they conjure. From Micklegate Bar during the Wars of the Roses both sides displayed on poles the heads of their enemies. Among the victims was Edward IV's father, the Duke of York, who fell in the Battle of Wakefield in 1460. Covered with a mock crown, his head was impaled facing the city. In Shakespeare's *Henry VI Part III* Queen Margaret cries:

Off with his head and set it on
York gates!
So York may overlook the town of York.

Atop the walls one can walk for two and a half miles like the sentries who guarded the city 600 years or so ago. From the battlements I looked out toward Marston Moor where Oliver Cromwell defeated the Royalists in 1644 in one of the major battles of the Civil War. An unrepentant Cavalier

IN AGELESS GLORY *York Minster endures, sustained by generation after generation of faithful artisans. A mason (opposite) hews a stone to replace one shaped by a man of another age. About 1472, after some 250 years of labor, the Minster (Saxon for "large church") stood completed.*

No other English cathedral preserves as much medieval stained glass; the art of four centuries glows in more than 100 windows. A portrait of Edward the Confessor (right), only inches high, is one of scores of figures limned in the magnificent East Window, a 2,000-square-foot masterpiece.

In ruined St. Mary's Abbey (below) the famous York Cycle of Mystery Plays triennially depicts the story of mankind from Creation to Judgment—as Englishmen saw it when Chaucer was a boy. Revived in 1951, these pious, yet richly human pageants were first acted by guildsmen around 1350 and banned for heretical passages in 1572. Here St. Veronica displays the miraculous imprint of Christ's face left on the cloth with which she wiped His face as He bore the Cross.

© DEAN AND CHAPTER OF YORK MINSTER. BELOW: YORKSHIRE EVENING PRESS

myself, I could picture Prince Rupert, King Charles's dashing general, leading his troopers with his red cloak streaming as they made a last, furious charge against Cromwell's matchless cavalry, the Ironsides. I was told that musket balls can still be found in the trees of Wilstrop Wood.

From the plain of York I continued eastward toward the coast. At Stamford Bridge I stood on the field where Harold, last of the Saxon kings, defeated his brother Tostig and Tostig's ally, the Norwegian warrior king Harold Hardraada, on September 25 in the fateful year 1066. Less than three weeks later King Harold himself lay dead on the battlefield of Hastings, defeated by William the Conqueror.

Northward from Flamborough stretch

CROWNED BY A NORMAN CASTLE *and a Roman signal tower, both in ruins, Scarborough in 1966 marked the 1,000th anniversary of its founding by a Norse raider dubbed Skaroi, "the hare lip." Skaroi's burg, or Skaroaborg, became Scartheborc, Scareburgh, and finally the Scarborough whose fame as a spa dates from the discovery of a medicinal spring here in the 1600's. Explorer James Cook first went to sea from Whitby, to the north. On nearby Flamborough Head crowds watched John Paul Jones's* Bonhomme Richard *defeat the British frigate* Serapis.

DAN McCOY, BLACK STAR

ANCIENT ABBEYS, *ravaged by time and man, once stood as beacons of faith in a sea of barbarism. Whitby (near right) and Lindisfarne (far right) kindled Christianity in northern England in the seventh century. Destroyed by Danes in the ninth, they were refounded two centuries later by Benedictines. Caedmon, a Whitby lay brother, was England's first known poet. Cistercian monks founded Rievaulx (above) and Fountains (center) in the 12th century and pioneered Yorkshire's wool industry. At Bolton (lower) children skip on stepping-stones once trod by Augustinian monks.*

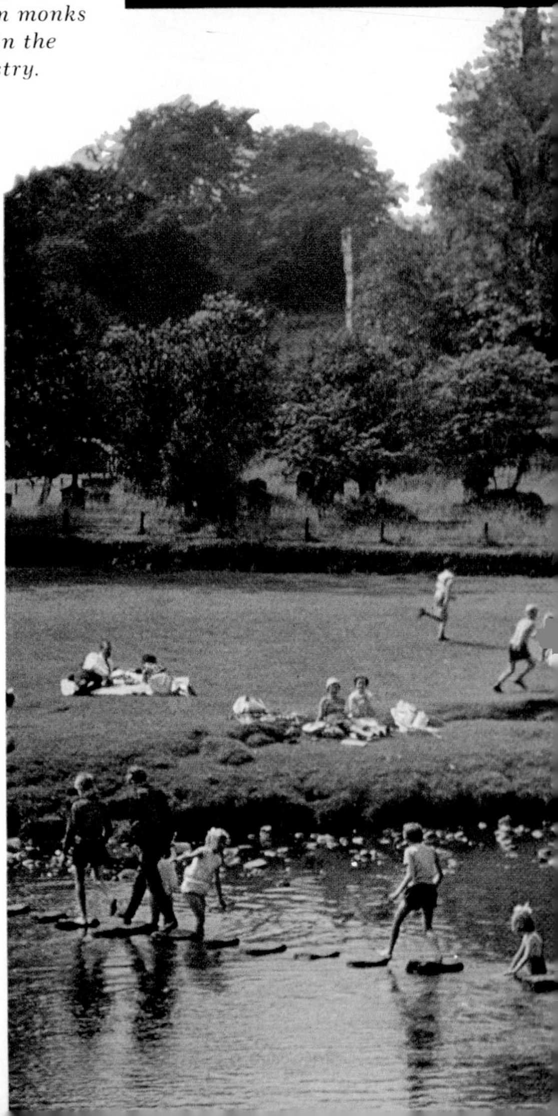

the chalk cliffs, beaches, fishing villages, and seaside towns beloved of Yorkshire folk and "off-comers" alike. Scarborough is the Brighton of Yorkshire. It offers holidayers great beaches, promenades, gardens, and breathtaking strolls along the clifftops. Its Norman castle, enclosing a keep with 12-foot-thick walls, still looms above the town. Cromwell besieged the castle during the Civil War, but the story that he bombarded it from another hill is tradition rather than truth. The hill bearing his name, Oliver's Mount, is a fine place to walk.

I turned inland, heading back to my Lake District home, and on the way came upon parties of sightseers exploring the dales of the North Yorkshire moors, lovely towns like Richmond and Ripon, and of course the numerous abbeys – Byland, Jervaulx, Rievaulx, and my favorite, Fountains.

A few miles southwest of Ripon, Fountains Abbey stands amid the serene parklands of Studley Royal, once the home of the Marquis of Ripon. Like Rievaulx, Jervaulx, Byland, and Kirkstall, Fountains was

MERLE SEVERY AND (BELOW) EDWARDS PARK, NATIONAL GEOGRAPHIC STAFF
OPPOSITE: JOHN LEWIS STAGE, PHOTO RESEARCHERS

founded by Cistercians, those white-robed monks who detested the comparative luxury of the Benedictine and Cluniac orders and built their monasteries in remote places. Their distrust of color and elaborate ornamentation and the simple purity of their architecture chime with the austere splendor of much of the northern landscape and with the character of its people.

In the 18th century the owner of Studley Royal used the ruins of Fountains, one of the best preserved of all English abbeys, as the centerpiece of his landscape garden. He engulfed it in acres of shaven turf adorned with garden ornaments, and he framed the approach with a long avenue of trees, now in glorious maturity, which belong to the age of reason, not the age of faith.

BILL BRANDT

NATIONAL PORTRAIT GALLERY, LONDON

"OH! THESE BLEAK WINDS *and bitter northern skies...."* Wuthering Heights *captured in its pages the mood of these wild Yorkshire moors near Haworth. In the parsonage there the Brontë sisters and their brother Branwell began writing as a childish game. The sisters, in tragically short lives, wrote classics: Emily's* Wuthering Heights, *Charlotte's* Jane Eyre, *Anne's* The Tenant of Wildfell Hall. *Branwell, a failure, effaced himself from his portrait of Anne (left), Emily, and Charlotte.*

The Cistercians, I am sure, would have disapproved of all this. Artificial beauty, save that devoted to the glory of God, would have affronted them.

Yet the monks have triumphed in the end. Their sublime buildings, which miraculously combine magnificence with simplicity, overwhelm the smug Georgian tidiness of the contrived landscape.

ANOTHER FORAY took me into the Pennine Chain. I passed through Skipton, a busy market town high in the hills, and suddenly the countryside changed. The broad green fields divided by stone walls, the avenues of ancient oaks, the cottages of warm sandstone, the timbered parklands surrounding many a gracious home—all this gave way to a landscape marked (some would say "marred") by the Industrial Revolution.

Stark and uncompromising against the valley sides rise woolen mills, with their chimneys of smoke-grimed brick. The mills and the rows of workers' cottages spoke unmistakably of the power which, from the late 18th century onward, drew men from their fields to serve strange machines. Yet obstinately, elements of rural life remain. Moors and woods are rarely out of sight in industrial Yorkshire.

After passing Keighley, an agglomeration of blackened houses and mills, I snaked through a maze of lanes for some eight miles to Haworth, home of the Brontë family, and recognizable to all who have read *Wuthering Heights* and *Jane Eyre* and expect the mood of a moorland village. Haworth's steep main street is still paved with stone blocks set like steps to prevent horses' hoofs from slipping.

At the Black Bull, where I parked my car, the unhappy Branwell Brontë used to carouse with his cronies. Farther up the hill rises Haworth parsonage, now the Brontë Museum. Here the Reverend Patrick Brontë raised his family, including the brilliantly talented Charlotte, Emily, and Anne. In his study still stands the piano which Emily played, and upstairs I visited the tiny room where the girls wrote in minute notebooks extraordinary romantic "novels" about the mythical Gondals. On one carefully preserved wall the plaster is marked with penciled drawings they may have made.

The parsonage overlooks a grim churchyard where, during my visit, the gravestones gleamed black and wet under the dripping trees. I climbed higher still along a narrow path which the Brontës must often have used, and came upon the moors that Emily so loved. The pure, fresh wind braced my mind and spirit. It swept down from rock-strewn, heathery heights that have not changed since Bronze Age people built stone circles and burial mounds here 3,000 years ago.

Leaving the land of the Brontës, I sped northwestward along the route of a Roman road through Lancaster, home of a new university, and on to Kendal where within

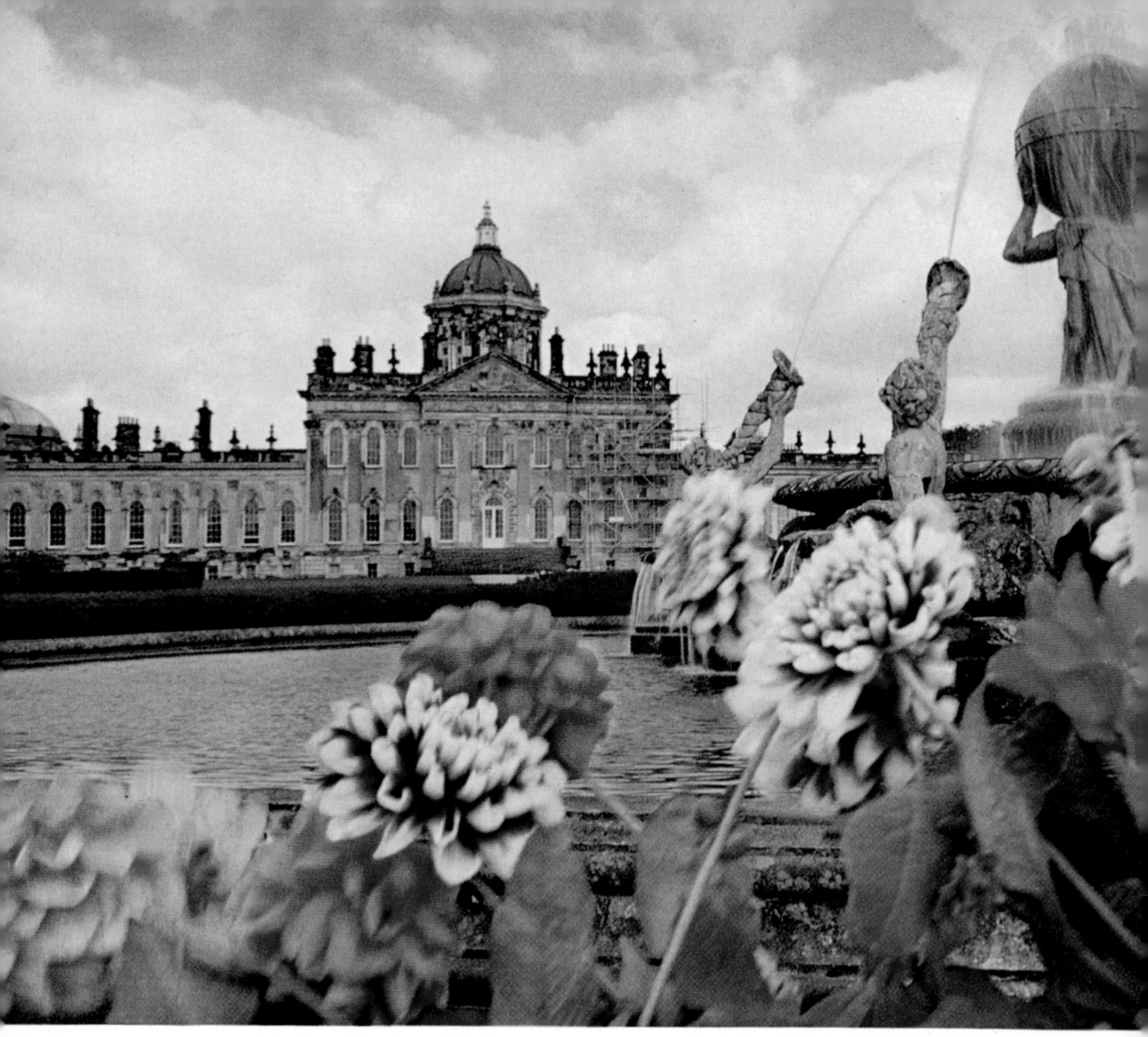

an elbow of the River Kent stand the remains of a Roman fort. A bracken-covered hill called Helm may have served as a lookout for the Roman garrison. Centuries later men lit a beacon here to signal the defeat of the Spanish Armada.

From this breezy height I looked upon the gray roofs of the town. Industry has hardly touched Kendal since the days when it made the worsted cloth mentioned by Shakespeare in *Henry IV Part I*. Falstaff tells how "three misbegotten knaves in Kendal green came at my back and let drive at me." Beyond I saw the tumultuous mountains of Westmorland and Cumberland. In early evening, ridged and hacked as if by a giant's sword, they seemed immense.

Soon I headed north. At Penrith, a Cumberland market town guarded by its ruined castle, I swung eastward and mounted that magnificent pass called Hartside. A high wind screamed down from the moorland heights and buffeted my little car at every exposed bend of the road.

Again my mind went back to Petillius Cerialis. I thought of the fierce Brigantes, who took refuge in these remote valleys, and of the Roman auxiliaries – cavalrymen from Spain, archers from the Balearic Islands in the Mediterranean – who fought them.

Then the Roman ghosts vanished, and those of the Middle Ages replaced them. For I had come to Alston, a Norman town climbing a steep hill. At the Turk's Head Inn the landlord told me the town was gradually losing population. Once-thriving lead mines are closed, and the large farms have given way to small sheep farms.

"You should go to Garrigill," he said. "There's a reet little poob there, George and Dragon, and if ye want to know about local history, ask for Len Wilkin; 'e's the man.

ITALIANATE PALACES *and graceful Chippendale mark citadels of Whig power in the age of elegance. Noblemen on Grand Tour collected art by the shipload and imported painters to fresco classical mansions rising amid landscaped parks. Castle Howard (left), first building by Vanbrugh, Blenheim's architect, crowns a Yorkshire hill. Domed hall (below), 70 feet high, has welcomed visitors for 250 years. The estate's mausoleum, said Horace Walpole, "would tempt one to be buried alive." Harewood House, near Leeds, treasures rooms by Robert Adam and Adam-designed furniture like the wine cooler (lower left) crafted by Thomas Chippendale, native of nearby Otley.*

DAN McCOY, BLACK STAR

And ask 'im to tell ye about wolf packs."

Wolf packs? I was snared. Away went the small-scale map of all northern England, and out came the large-scale one with every hill and tarn, hamlet and byway marked in fascinating detail. Night was falling as I climbed out of Alston and wound through narrow, stone-walled lanes. A signpost announced Garrigill, a tiny moorland hamlet of stone-built cottages surrounding a green sweep of turf high in the Pennines. A light above the inn sign welcomed me to the George and Dragon.

A ruddy-faced young man was holding forth at the bar, banging down his pint tankard for emphasis. I guessed correctly that he was Len Wilkin, and by the second pint I had established that a village called Milburn is built around a square and fortified not against human raiders but the wolves which, he said, roamed this part of England 600 years ago. "Ah've found wolf bones meself, in an old cave way oop above village. What's more," (hearing growls of skepticism) "a professor feller from London seen 'em and 'e says they *are* wolf bones."

DEAN CONGER, NATIONAL GEOGRAPHIC PHOTOGRAPHER

FIT FOR A KING *in nobler days, Middleham Castle was wrecked for building stone in 1646. Memories of the Wars of the Roses haunt the 12th-century Yorkshire ruin.*

Warwick, that proud "setter up and plucker down of kings," held Edward IV captive here in 1469. Two years later the Kingmaker was killed in the Battle of Barnet. The castle passed to Edward, who gave it to his brother, the future Richard III. Here died Richard's only son.

When Richard was slain at Bosworth Field, Henry VII got the castle.

In Henry VI Part III, *Warwick's dying words sound like an epitaph for Middleham: "Why, what is pomp, rule, reign, but earth and dust?"*

Left: Heather mantles a Yorkshire heath. In the 6,000 square miles of England's largest county a boy from industrial Leeds can find wide-open spaces not far from home.

Just then the landlord's charming wife broke in and told me I must see a village called Blanchland, built within the walls of a medieval monastery.

Milburn or Blanchland? It was a difficult choice, but next morning I set out for the latter and was richly rewarded. The journey took me through some of the wildest and

loneliest country in the whole of Britain. Mile after mile I rose and dipped over undulating moors and saw hardly another car. The words "overpopulated Britain" seemed a mockery. Occasionally I passed gray spoil heaps of lead mines, mostly overgrown. Sometimes clumps of conifers in the hollows broke the monotony of broad fields crisscrossed by stone walls. When I stopped by the roadside I heard only the wind singing in the telephone wires and the distant bleating of sheep.

Away to the northwest the line of the Cheviot Hills beckoned. Now on each side of the lonely road rose ten-foot wooden posts painted in alternate bands of black and white. When snow blankets the land these markers show snowplow drivers where the road is. I wondered how the Romans coped with the northern winter.

Suddenly the road dived toward a green valley. Below lay Blanchland, sometimes hidden, sometimes revealed as I snaked downward. Then I was upon it – an L-shaped arrangement of handsome dwellings built of golden sandstone; a high, medieval gateway, a noble church; a square with a market cross; an inn, the Lord Crewe Arms.

The name Blanchland probably originated in the white robes of Premonstratensian canons who founded their abbey here in 1165. After Henry VIII dissolved it, much of it was quarried for building stone. In the mid-18th century John Wesley, founder of Methodism, preached in the Blanchland churchyard to worshipers kneeling in the grass. Soon after, the choir of the church was rebuilt to give people a place to worship.

Lord Crewe, Bishop of Durham, directed the raising of the village's present charming houses on the site of the abbey's domestic buildings. His namesake inn uses a massive, barrel-vaulted 12th-century chamber as its principal bar – a not inappropriate fate, as it almost certainly formed part of the monastic wine cellars.

FROM BLANCHLAND I drove north again, crossing the line of Hadrian's Wall near Chollerford. I resisted the urge to explore it on this foray and held to my objective: the Northumbrian coast and its castles. Now I entered the region of the North Tyne, scene of bloody combat before the union of England and Scotland. In this borderland, according to one of many ballads:

There was never a time in the
North Countree
When the Douglas and the Percy met,
There was never a time but the
red blude ran
As rain doth in the street.

Border killings, feuds, and cattle stealing bred rough justice. One murderer, a man of some rank, escaped Bellingham's busy gallows but met with haunting retribution in his village church. The vicar buried the victim where the slayer would have to step over the tomb to get to his family pew.

North Tynesiders played hard too. At Kielder, when athletes met in the first "futba'" match between England and Scotland, "full time" was called only, so they say, when the last contestant was carried off the field. "Savages," noted both Sir Walter Scott and the historian Macaulay when they touched on the men of Kielder.

Wind-whipped breakers pound the dark basalt on which the frowning citadels stand: proud Warkworth, stern Bamburgh, lonely Dunstanburgh, built by kings and by feudal barons who were often more powerful than kings.

Scenes from *Henry IV Part I* ran through my head as I explored Warkworth. The Percys, dukes of Northumberland, owned it for 600 years. One ancestor was Harry Hotspur, the rebellious Border lord killed in the battle of Shrewsbury. His was one of those heads mounted on Micklegate Bar at York. In Shakespeare's play he is slain by Prince Hal, the future Henry V.

The present duke maintains a suite at Warkworth and presents free fishing rights each year to the person who catches the season's first salmon in the River Coquet. The custom sounds feudal, but nothing could be further from the truth. Northumberland folk are fiercely independent and democratic – often quick to disagree with the duke at meetings of the town council of Alnwick, his home. They are proud of the Percy family, however, and its traditions.

DAN McCOY, BLACK STAR

LIKE A GARDEN IN WONDERLAND, *sculptured yews and box hedges adorn Levens Hall in Westmorland. Such topiary work delighted ancient Rome, graced Renaissance Italy and France, and caught the fancy of 17th-century England. Then fashion's pendulum swung. Essayist Addison deplored "the mark of the scissors upon every plant and bush," and clipped creations fell under the ax to make way for "romantic" landscaping where a rose is a rose.*

A rare survivor, Levens Hall's topiary, originally created by James II's gardener, stands unmatched. The Elizabethan house, noted for Italian plasterwork ceilings, oak paneling, and candlelight musicales, peeks over the leafy labyrinth. A heart motif decorating its drainpipes recalls that in 1689 Sir James Grahme won the mansion at cards with an ace of hearts. His descendants still reside here.

John of Gaunt (left), "time-honoured Lancaster," guards the ancient capital of Lancashire. Born in Ghent (hence "Gaunt"), the son of Edward III, he sired the Lancastrian kings (Henry IV, V, and VI); his line runs through royalty from Tudor to Windsor. His title, Duke of Lancaster, is now the sovereign's.

Named for a Roman castrum above the River Lune, Lancaster grew in the shelter of its Norman castle, target of raiding Scots. In the castle witches were tried and malefactors branded with "M."

On the way to Dunstanburgh Castle I dipped down into the village of Craster, famous for herrings. They are caught from stubby little vessels called cobles, then smoked by a secret process involving oak chips, and exported to the United States and many other parts of the world.

I approached Dunstanburgh by a footpath across turf where sheep grazed. It looked like a Tennysonian dream—towering gateway, clean, hard lines of 14th-century masonry welded by iron-hard mortar. I stared up at it and listened to the deep, sucking roar of the sea washing into the Rumbling Churn, a crevice in the cliffs. This fortress once belonged to John of Gaunt, scion and sire of kings.

Westward from Dunstanburgh stands

CASTLES GUARD *grim memories on the northern border. Warkworth Castle (opposite) looms over tidal waters of the River Coquet. Northumberland fisherman reflects its peaceful mood today. But here and at Alnwick ("Annick") the Percy dynasty battled Scots, challenged kings, and earned immortality in Shakespeare's* Henry IV. *Hotspur's son built the barbican of Alnwick Castle (lower left), today manned by stone sentinels. Walls of Norham Castle (below) date from 1160's.*

DEAN CONGER (ALSO OPPOSITE) AND (LOWER) MERLE SEVERY, BOTH NATIONAL GEOGRAPHIC STAFF

BH 46

Roddam Hall, with lands still held by the family which received them ten centuries ago. King Athelstan's grant has been translated into the Northumbrian dialect:

I, King Athelstan, give unto thee
Pole Roddam,
From me and mine to thee and thine ...
and for a certen truth,
I bite this wax [seal] with my
gang [strong] tooth
So long as muir [moor] bears moss
and snout grows hair,
A Roddam of Roddam for ever mare.

Nearby, the houses of York and Lancaster fought the Battle of Hedgeley Moor in 1464. Two stones 27 feet apart marked the legendary leap made by Sir Ralph Percy when he was dealt a mortal blow.

"**HALF CHURCH OF GOD,** *half castle 'gainst the Scot" depicts the dual role of the "grey towers of Durham. The River Wear loops round the peninsula (below), stronghold of a buffer state set up by William the Conqueror. From his castle, now part of Durham University (behind the cathedral towers), powerful bishop-princes long ruled the wild Border country.*

Durham Cathedral, best preserved Norman church in England, was begun in 1093. A fugitive who grasped its sanctuary knocker (far right) won shelter for 37 days and safe-conduct to the coast.

When Danes raided Lindisfarne in 875, the monks fled with the body of St. Cuthbert, said to have been miraculously preserved. The holy burden was carried over northern England, finally coming to rest at Durham two centuries later. A stole (detail at right) found in the coffin is the earliest English embroidery. The monks also saved the Lindisfarne Gospels, inscribed in Latin about 700. "XP" on the page shown (Matthew 1:18) denotes "Christ." Northumbrian words interlined about 950 makes this the oldest extant English translation of the Gospels.

DAN McCOY, BLACK STAR

MERLE SEVERY AND (LEFT) GEORGE F. MOBLEY, NATIONAL GEOGRAPHIC STAFF. BELOW: BRITISH MUSEUM

ROME'S RAMPART in the north began to rise around A.D. 122 when the emperor Hadrian visited Britain. Sentry turrets and mile-castles placed a Roman mile (1,618 yards) apart bristled atop the squared-stone barrier, 4 to 5 feet thick and 12 to 14 feet high. Borcovicus, one of its 17 forts, held 1,000 men—ten centuries, each led by a centurion. A settlement nearby gave the site its present name, Housesteads. In 197, in 296, and in 367 tribes overran Hadrian's Wall. Around 383 it was abandoned, foreshadowing Rome's fifth-century withdrawal from Britain. The wall became building stone. Housesteads visitors see a partially restored strip (right and page 12) on Northumberland moors. In the museum Mars, god of war, guards his altar. Goose at his feet recalls sacrificial rituals. Geese symbolized watchfulness.

A FEW MILES SOUTH of Dunstanburgh I swung inland to Alnwick, seat of the Duke of Northumberland. Dominating a thriving little market town, Alnwick Castle is no ruin. Its massive Norman keep harbors an early 19th-century "gentleman's residence" full of marble statues, paintings, leather-bound books, and armor.

Looking up from the courtyard, I saw carved figures manning the battlements—a crossbowman, a soldier drinking from a horn. These 14th-century stone warriors may have fooled enemy archers.

Bamburgh Castle, farther north on the coast, rises sheer from a rocky spur. I walked toward it at dusk, stumbling among dunes which sweep to its mighty base. A few other visitors on the sands seemed tiny and helpless against the stark, dark mass of the walls rising at one place 200 feet above the rock. Then I saw a casement window open high above, and a light shone out, one small gleam in that black cliff of masonry. I felt relief; people lived here after all.

Centuries before the present castle was built, Saxon kings ruled from its site ancient Northumbria, the lands north of the River Humber. One of these kings, Oswald—later St. Oswald—set about converting all the north to Christianity. He fought and defeated pagan kings of Wales and the Midlands, then sent for a bishop from Iona, the island off the west coast of Scotland where Christian missionaries had established a center of learning. The first monk to arrive failed in his mission of conversion and went back. The second, Aidan, chose as his episcopal see the island of Lindisfarne within sight of Bamburgh.

I made my way there, crossing the moist sands at low tide. About 200 fishermen and farmers live on Holy Island, as Lindisfarne is now called, but summer brings hundreds of tourists. There is a village, a castle, and dunes where children romp. But visitors come to see the ruined Norman priory which stands on the site where St. Aidan built his wooden church more than 1,300 years ago.

DAN McCOY, BLACK STAR

St. Aidan's greatest successor, the fair-haired St. Cuthbert, loved animals. Wild ducks allowed him to stroke them while they sat on their nests. Today ducks and many other water birds enjoy a sanctuary on the Farne Islands, near Lindisfarne.

His name returned to me when I stood beneath the majestic vaulting of Durham Cathedral and saw at my feet a plain stone slab bearing the word CUTHBERTUS. Here once stood the sumptuously jeweled shrine that held the relics of the saint. Henry VIII's commissioners destroyed it.

I have seen the great French cathedrals and I say without hesitation that none excels Durham in splendor and majesty, and few equal it. The superb setting, on a cliff high above the River Wear; the huge nave supported by massive Norman columns, some deeply incised with spiral decorations; and the soaring Neville Screen, made in 1380 to frame the high altar—all these combine to overwhelm the spirit.

I gazed at a Latin inscription lit by tall candles beside a tomb slab, and I worked out the meaning: "In this grave are the bones of the Venerable Bede." The father of English history joined a monastery at nearby Jarrow late in the seventh century when he was nine and wrote most of his works there. He would hardly comprehend the throbbing industry that has nearly obliterated all memory of his monastery in today's smoke-blackened Jarrow.

If Bede could have joined me in my sports car as I sped westward in the moorlands of Northumberland, he might have seen familiar sights. He might even have been amused that the supply route which the Romans built south of Hadrian's Wall is still, after 1,800 years, called by the locals "t' Military Road." Bede might recognize in the Northumbrian dialect the Anglo-Saxon vowels of his own language.

I mounted to that exhilarating road which drives, straight and swift as a legionary's spear, toward Carlisle, and the high, shrill wind sang with the car. The urgent note of the exhaust seemed no blasphemy here, but in tune with the wild frontier of Roman days and its alert guardians.

Ahead lay the triple ramparts of banks and ditches flanking Hadrian's mighty wall, which stretched 73½ miles from the Tyne estuary past Newcastle and Carlisle to Solway Firth. Men from Spain and the Rhine and the Danube manned its forts—even archers from Syria, the famed Palmyrenes.

At Housesteads I halted and strolled across springy turf to Borcovicus, the best preserved fort on the wall. I entered the South Gate with its stone pavement deeply grooved by chariot wheels, and I marched—yes, marched—past the *praetorium*, the commandant's house, where no doubt a smart salute would have been required, past the *principia*, the headquarters where troops drew their pay, and so to the crest of the ridge. Beyond lay nothing save a steep slope, and beyond that miles of moors.

To right and left Hadrian's Wall undulated across the hills like a great stone snake, wide enough to take two men marching abreast. For nearly 300 years this was the northernmost frontier of an empire which extended southward to include all Egypt and eastward to the Euphrates.

Castles of the Middle Ages may impress the eye more. But in terms of military efficiency they were puny compared to the line of little forts, each manned by a garrison and linked by roads and signal stations, that spread through this turbulent land south of the wall. The defense system, which helped Rome hold its grip for four centuries, covered the countryside like a giant spider's web. One tug on the web, perhaps from some isolated garrison, could set the beacons blazing and might bring a legion out from its base at York or Chester.

And no British tribesmen could long withstand those 6,000 heavily armed infantry-

men, disciplined and battle-hardened. With their traditions and emblems, honors and promotion systems, they were the counterpart of a crack modern regiment.

The Twentieth Legion had for its emblem a winged horse. I thought of it as I rolled out of Chester, where the Twentieth had been based, on a Roman road which the legion had certainly used. Then I put the past firmly behind, left the Roman road, and followed the River Mersey to a city with few buildings older than the 19th century: thriving, noisy, bustling Liverpool.

The phrase "Mersey Sound" applies to the pop music associated with the ubiquitous Beatles. With originality and verve these four young Liverpudlians have carried round the world their city's qualities of vitality and salty humor born in dockland. In Liverpool mingle Irish, Scots, seafarers of many lands, and the native English amid the thunder of trains and trucks, the scream of cargo winches, the hooting of tugs, the groan of foghorns, and the cry of gulls.

Manchester, just east of Liverpool, is Lancashire's commercial capital and England's second largest metropolitan area. Some 4,500,000 people live within 20 miles of the city center. Manchester people call themselves "Mancunians" for the Roman name of the city, Mancunium.

For years the city was called "Cottonopolis" because of its cotton trade and industry. Today only three percent of the population works in textiles. The city provides banking, shipping, marketing, and other commercial facilities for most of northwestern England. Since the Manchester Ship Canal opened in 1894, giving the city a 35½-mile link with the Mersey, Manchester has been an international seaport.

The swing from industry to commerce, the use of smokeless fuels, and electrification of railways have outdated the stories about the city's grime. Still, one bears retelling: Two small, grimy Mancunian birds were perched on a telegraph wire. One turned to his silent companion in annoyance. "What's the matter with ye'? Can't one sparrer talk to another sparrer?" The second bird drew himself up haughtily. "I'm *not* a sparrer," he said, "I'm a robin!"

In 1538 a visitor called Manchester "the fairest, best-builded, quickest town in all Lancashire." Quickest is a good word. The people have always been in the forefront of

A SMASHING RACE, *the Grand National resounds with the thud of bodies as horses thunder over 30 hurdles and ditches. In 1961 animal lovers succeeded in easing sometimes fatal obstacles, reputedly set up by a man who vowed, "I'll get them all yet!" Even so, only 14 of 47 starters completed the 4½-mile course in 1965, 12 of 47 in 1966. The spring classic began in 1839 near Liverpool as a formal version of the steeplechase—a cross-country race toward a landmark, often a steeple.*

WIDE WORLD PHOTOS

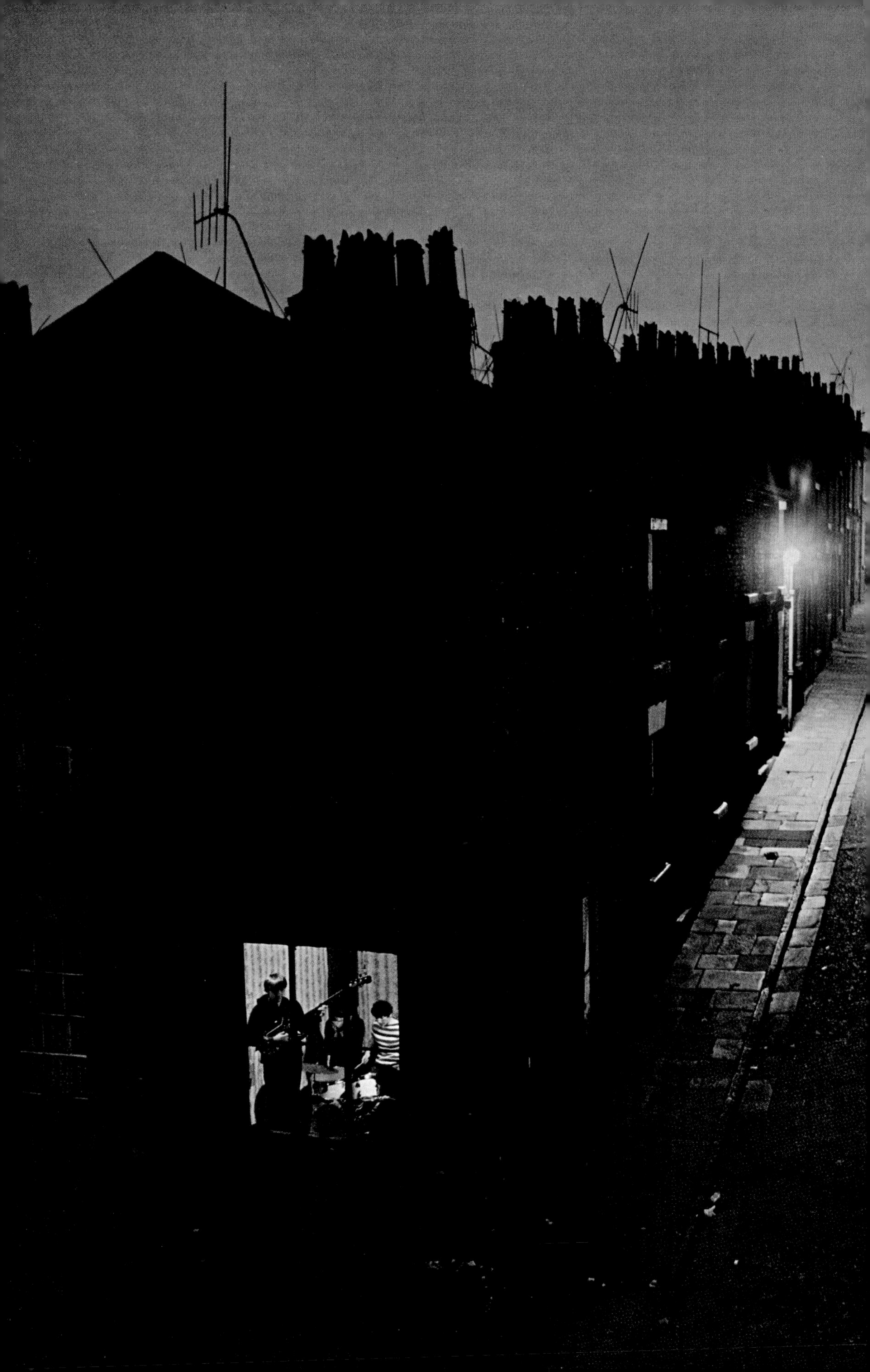

A LONELY STREET *in Liverpool throbs with the muffled beat of the "Mersey Sound." In cellar clubs, waterfront dens, and on a River Mersey ferry, disciples of the Beatles rock 'n' roll the city.*

Once the world's premier cotton port, Liverpool also was the gateway to America for thousands of emigrants. Liverpudlians watched the fantastic Great Eastern *lumber out to the Irish Sea in the 1860's, welcomed proud Cunard liners, mourned the Liverpool-bound* Lusitania. *Cunard headquarters remain here, though the majestic* Queens *today dock at Southampton, closer to London and the Continent. With seven miles of bustling docks, Liverpool still serves the mills of Lancashire and the Midlands. It ranks as England's second port and leading export outlet.*

JOHN LAUNOIS, BLACK STAR

progress. Theirs was one of the world's first steam-powered mills, the first canal network in Britain, the first main-line passenger railway—the Manchester-Liverpool line, opened in 1830.

Sheffield, across the Pennines, is one of Britain's most beautifully planned modern cities. Woods flank the valleys of five rivers—Don, Loxley, Rivelin, Porter, and Sheaf—that flow through or around Sheffield. No indiscriminate development mars the hillsides. Where building is necessary, 14- or 15-story apartments have risen. Belts of unspoiled country are preserved.

In Chaucer's *Canterbury Tales* the miller of Trumpington had a "Sheffeld thwitel" (a whittle, or knife). By Elizabethan days

MANCHESTER'S MAGNET, *a ship canal opened by Queen Victoria, draws shipping inland to busy docks (opposite). Home of the Hallé Orchestra and* The Guardian, *Manchester also takes pride in its John Rylands Library, memorial to a 19th-century merchant. This rich trove of manuscripts and more than 3,000 incunabula (volumes printed before 1501) displays a Gutenberg Bible from about 1456 (right), first book printed from movable type.*

Stainless-steel cutlery gleams in the glow of molten steel at Sheffield (below), whose name has been a proud trademark for 400 years.

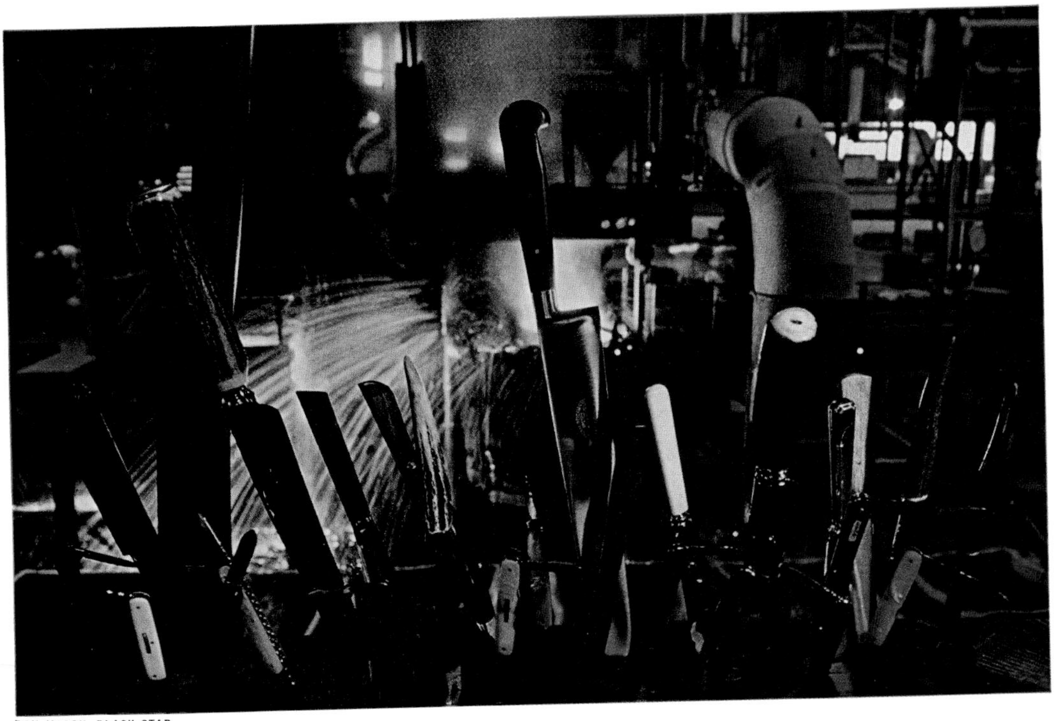

DAN McCOY, BLACK STAR

DAN McCOY, BLACK STAR

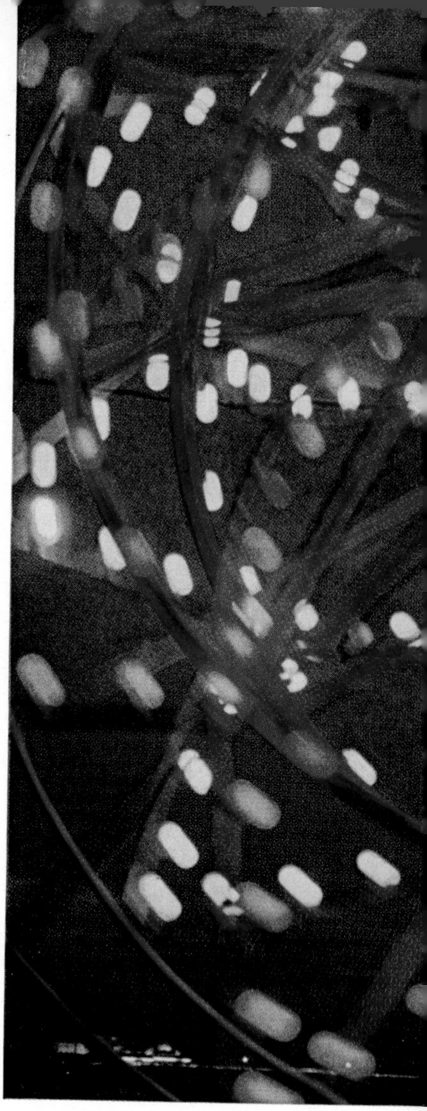

FUN AND GAMES *annually lure millions to Blackpool, friendly, glittering resort on the Irish Sea. Coney Island, Disneyland, Atlantic City, and the Iowa State Fair all packed into a strand of Lancashire coast, Blackpool offers electronic bingo (above) to the sedentary, a convention center to politicians. Day trippers and holidayers from 5,000 hotels and boardinghouses head for a promenade jammed with shooting galleries, dancing girls, tattoo parlors, palmists, and stands selling jellied eels. At night in September and October they oh and ah at the Illuminations—whirling wheels and tableaux conjured up by miles of lights. The resort's symbol, a 520-foot tower, straddles a zoo, a circus, and a gilded room where 5,500 can have a ball.*

Sheffield knives, sickles, scythes, and shears were famed all over England. Many a bowie knife carried by American frontiersmen was forged beside the Don. And Sheffield machetes still hack away in tropical forests. Today, "Sheffield cutlery" and "Sheffield plate" bring to mind elegant tableware, but the city also produces razor blades and scalpels, dentists' drills and granite saws.

BLACKPOOL, England's Coney Island, is pure North Country. In the 19th century, promoters turned this fishing port into a "pleasure beach" with sideshows like the "panoramic picture of Niagara Falls 80 feet wide and 60 feet high," and men who would extract your teeth to the sound of a brass band (to drown your cries).

Whole families from Lancashire cotton towns descended on Blackpool by train and wagonette. Though the average worker earned only about a pound a week, he saved his "brass" throughout the year for a week in Blackpool, leaving one small coin in an envelope suspended on a string behind the front door letter box. This sufficed to pay for the wagonette which brought him home from the railway station.

The descendants of the Victorian mill hands, better paid, dressed, fed, and educated, still crowd the resort and climb the Blackpool Tower that their grandparents probably knew. They also spend their brass on more sophisticated entertainment—swimming pools, golf, and night spots with top-ranking artists. Yet despite a generation of listening to BBC English, they retain their dialect—the blunt, honest speech of the North Country.

And long may they do so.

GHOST TRAIN
FRESH FRUIT

THE LAKE DISTRICT, POETS' CORNER OF ENGLAND

By meres and fells
H. V. Morton walks in Wordsworth's steps,
where "Heaven's pomp is spread"

A DAY OF SAVAGE RAIN was struggling into afternoon as I drove to Grasmere in the heart of England's Lake District. I had seen nothing but sullen mountains decapitated by mist, gray sheets of water, and dripping woodland. The road, bounded by stone walls that were museums of ferns and mosses, was enlivened by hundreds of hikers with backpacks. Sometimes a girl's face seen for a moment through the windscreen – a face glistening with raindrops and framed in a plastic hood of red or green – would linger in the memory like a verse by Wordsworth. Why was she battling wind and rain and carrying upon her slender shoulders a burden that would make a guardsman swoon?

This, I thought, is what visitors mean when they say we English take our pleasures sadly. Yet there was nothing sad about these hikers, except, perhaps, their saturated silhouettes.

When I arrived at Grasmere the rain had turned into a thin drizzle that somehow enhanced the beauty of this village of narrow winding streets. I made my way to my

WINDERMERE, *"like a vast river, stretching in the sun," as Wordsworth saw it, sparkles with sails.*

DAN McCOY, BLACK STAR

DAVID S. BOYER, NATIONAL GEOGRAPHIC STAFF

KESWICK, *like an enchanted village rising from the mists of time, shimmers in the vale that enfolds the pale beauty of Derwent Water. Nearby, with a poet's eye, Robert Southey saw the Falls of Lodore "gleaming and streaming and steaming and beaming." Rain or shine, hikers plot their courses in the land of the poets, where, as Wordsworth said, "One impulse from a vernal wood May teach you more of man . . . Than all the sages can."*

hotel beside the gray tower of Grasmere Church, whose encircling wall is washed by the glass-green waters of the Rothay.

From my window I looked across a lawn to the churchyard, where earnest young faces gazed upon the weathered headstone marking the grave of William Wordsworth.

I soon learned that Grasmere was marking the day of the annual rush-bearing. Beneath a tree the village band shielded its instruments from the rain. Choirboys, starched and surpliced, crowded in the vestry door. Children, wearing mackintoshes over their best clothes, carried bunches of flowers entwined with lake rushes.

The custom of rush-bearing goes back to a time when the floors of churches, castles, and halls were strewn with rushes. In summer hygienically minded Saxons changed these floor coverings. Though Grasmere's parishioners no longer use rushes to keep their feet warm, the old ceremony still takes place each year on the Saturday nearest to St. Oswald's Day, August 5.

"Early in the morning of rush-bearing day," the schoolmaster's wife told me, "we go down to Grasmere Lake to cut the rushes. When we have strewn the church floor, we make our 'bearings,' which are flowers and rushes shaped over wooden forms that have been handed down for generations.

"One represents Moses in the bulrushes, another is David's harp. But the most famous of all is the hand of St. Oswald, King of Northumbria and for centuries the patron saint of Grasmere's church."

As the sun peeped out church bells began to ring, the band played "The Rush-bearers' March," and the procession started through the village. Choirboys led the way, the first carrying a cross made of golden flowers. Another bore a reed standard shaped like a human hand. Spelled out in the rushes was the date of Oswald's death, A.D. 642, and the words, "May this hand never perish." A bishop bestowed the blessing, legend says, after Oswald interrupted his Easter feasting to hand food and gold plate to the starving poor outside.

Then came the other bearings, a men's choir, and the clergy. Next, six young maids

MEMORIES *of Lakeland laureates linger amid the brooding fells and rippling waters. A troubled William Wordsworth found peace at Dove Cottage in Grasmere, where his battered hat, cane, and coat evoke* An Evening Walk. *Beside his bust a guest book lies open, his spectacles on it. Samuel Taylor Coleridge sampled Grasmere's quiet charm, and Thomas De Quincey found it "the very Eden of English beauty." John Ruskin's search for beauty ended in Lakeland upon his "five acres of rock and moor and streamlet."*

OVERLEAF: THIRLMERE BY DAN McCOY, BLACK STAR

SAMUEL TAYLOR COLERIDGE BY J. NORTHCOTE,
COURTESY JESUS COLLEGE, CAMBRIDGE

THOMAS DE QUINCEY, AFTER A DRAWING BY JAMES ARCHER

JOHN RUSKIN, ENGRAVING AFTER A PAINTING BY J. E. MILLAIS

DOVE COTTAGE BY DAN McCOY, BLACK STAR

held a sheet strewn with flowers and rushes. Following the band came the villagers.

We crowded into the church, whose floor lay inches deep in lake rushes. The old building, with its roof beamed like a barn's, has changed little since Wordsworth's day. How strange it seemed to sit in this church at a service that recalled a Saxon king who lived 13 centuries ago! I went to bed that night with the feeling that I had taken a good clean plunge into Lakeland.

A CRUMPLED PATCH of misty green and silver 35 miles square, the Lake District lies in the three northern counties of Lancashire, Westmorland, and Cumberland. Windermere, ten miles long and a mile wide, is the largest of its 16 lakes. Around them stand mountains that give an unforgettable impression of majesty, though the highest, Scafell Pike, rises only 3,210 feet.

Since the 18th century the lakes have cast a spell over English writers. In 1799 William Wordsworth sought refuge in Lakeland from what he felt to be the ugliness of an industrialized and revolutionary world. The tall, rawboned young man explored on foot every inch of the land. His verse recalls its sights, sounds, colors, and its humble cottages. Here Wordsworth "wander'd lonely as a cloud" and "saw a crowd, a host, of golden daffodils."

Here, too, Thomas Gray found an "unsuspected paradise" where "all is peace." And in this land dwelled Robert Southey, Wordsworth's predecessor as poet laureate; Samuel Taylor Coleridge; and Thomas De Quincey, who took over Wordsworth's cottage at Grasmere. Alfred and Emily Tennyson spent their honeymoon at Coniston Water. Shelley stayed briefly in Keswick, and Keats once roamed Lakeland.

The shrine of "Wordsworthshire" is Dove Cottage in Grasmere. Thousands of tourists

come each year to this cottage of diamond-paned windows and rose-flecked, roughcast walls. The Reverend C. W. Wordsworth, the poet's great-grandson, accompanied me to Dove Cottage. Looking at him I marveled at how some families go onward stamped like coins with clearly defined personal characteristics. We climbed the narrow stairs to the sitting room above, where William Wordsworth wrote many of his early, and some think his best, poems. Later we went down into the little garden at the back. The syringa that William and his sister Dorothy planted still grows there.

In the village of Near Sawrey, by the small Esthwaite Water, stands Hill Top Farm, another Lakeland literary shrine. Here Beatrix Potter wrote of Peter Rabbit, Squirrel Nutkin, Mr. Jeremy Fisher, and Mrs. Tittlemouse. Hill Top, left just as it was when its mistress died in 1943, is worth seeing for itself as a typical northern farmhouse. And to Beatrix Potter fans it is a delight. Children run here and there, recognizing the staircase where Tabitha Twitchit mewed, the old oak dresser that Anna Maria passed with her plate of dough, and the clock from *The Tailor of Gloucester*. Upstairs is a dolls' house; in it readers of *The Tale of Two Bad Mice* can recognize "two red lobsters, and a ham, a fish, a pudding, and some pears and oranges."

Four miles from Near Sawrey is Coniston Water, where John Ruskin settled in 1871, when he was 52. A famous critic with a private fortune, Ruskin could have chosen to live anywhere in the world. The grandeur of Lakeland, however, had deep roots for him. "The first thing which I remember as an event in life," he once wrote, "was being taken by my nurse to the brow of Friar's Crag on Derwentwater."

From his windows Ruskin had a magnificent view extending across the lake to the green banks where fields rise to the swelling curve of Coniston Fells, whose highest point is called Coniston Old Man. Ruskin's beautifully precise watercolor sketches still fill the many rooms of the huge, gaunt house where he died at the age of 80.

I HAVE STUDIED Coniston Water, Ullswater, Derwent Water, Windermere, and Thirlmere—indeed, all the greater lakes—at various times and I am unable to say which I consider the most beautiful. But they each fulfill what I call the first essential of a lake: Delightfully narrow and compact, they are easily seen at a glance.

I remember standing one day at Bowness ferry when the clouds were low and Windermere was drenched in that kind of melancholy that is best expressed by solemn music. When I next passed that way the landscape sang with joy beneath the sun.

I have seen Derwent Water sheeted in a gray shroud of mist, cold and terrible, lying

GRASMERE *lies "within its mountain urn, smiling so tranquilly and set so deep," as Wordsworth wrote. Round the lake he rambled, and here his genius blossomed. In this vale that flames with rhododendrons he lived, first at Dove Cottage and then, beyond the meadow, at Allan Bank.*

DAVID S. BOYER, NATIONAL GEOGRAPHIC STAFF

in a stillness so awesome that I was grateful for the movement of a waterfowl as it skimmed the surface and vanished into the mist. I have seen it, too, on a morning when not a ripple broke the great sheet of water, when the lake lay in a hush whose spell encompassed hills and sky.

Perhaps only the walkers and the mountaineers know the true beauty of Lakeland. Having earned their view by strenuous hours on the fells, they slip the packs from their backs and look downward from a summit to smooth hills folded against one another to the sky, and to a spoonful of blue lake water cupped in a green valley.

LAKELAND ATTRACTS a great variety of roamers. Here are hikers and cyclists, caravanners and campers displaying their domesticity in a damp field, the girls washing nylons, the men shaving with mirror in a cleft stick. I once encountered a band of men and women from Algeria, of all places! Hostels, spaced generally a day's march apart, appear everywhere – in towns, villages, and on the fells.

Anywhere in the high fells of Lakeland you may come across rock-climbers clinging to the face of some overhanging pinnacle. Or you may enter an inn and find them, bearded, beer mugs in hand, looking for all the world like tough commandos. I saw such a group in an inn parlor in Langdale. One of the most menacing turned out to be a gentle teacher of typography from Kent; his savage-looking friend was an oculist. I liked the way they laughed off their achievements on the fells.

The fells breed rugged men, but few have matched the legend of John Peel who, at the age of nine, is said to have tracked foxes as much as 30 miles a day on foot! In 1832 he was immortalized in a ballad – "D'ye ken John Peel . . . With his hounds and his horn . . .?" When Peel's friend, John Woodcock Graves, wrote it, he jokingly remarked, "By Jove, Peel, you'll be sung of when we're both run to earth."

Today a worn path leads to John Peel's grave in Caldbeck. And John Peel's horn – the horn that so often awakened the Cumberland countryside – has passed down to a great-great-grandson of Peel. He lives in Ireby, a few miles from Peel's grave. The steep, wild fells of Lakeland yet echo the sound of horns like Peel's.

No worn path leads to Greta Hall, where Southey and Coleridge lived. Tourists pass it by in favor of nearby Keswick Museum, with its store of improbable objects: a lock of Wordsworth's soft, white hair; Southey's clogs, gloves, and flute; and Ruskin's court dress. Here also rest the manuscripts of a more recent Lakeland author, Sir Hugh Walpole, who wrote his "Herries" novels near Keswick. Among the Walpole letters I read one from Lawrence of Arabia. In it Lawrence describes his *The Seven Pillars of Wisdom* as "part ponderous, part hysterical, too long and very amateurish."

THE ROWANBERRIES had turned from green to crimson. The bracken now was gold, and the little cone-shaped hayricks, so like those of Scotland, stood in emerald fields, each wearing its waterproof cap. Apples ripened; dahlias and Michaelmas

BEHIND LAKELAND'S CHARMING FACE, *countryfolk follow antique ways. A shepherd drives his flock near Langdale (opposite); red daubs, or "smits," mark the animals like brands. At Hill Top Farm, home of Beatrix Potter, Peter Rabbit's creator, children pore over her stories (below). She raised Herdwick sheep, said to have been introduced by Norsemen. In the 15th-century farmhouse Hugh Walpole used as a setting for his novel* Judith Paris, *tarts are readied for the oven (left).*

DAVID S. BOYER AND (OPPOSITE) WALTER MEAYERS EDWARDS, BOTH NATIONAL GEOGRAPHIC STAFF

DAN McCOY, BLACK STAR (ALSO UPPER), WALTER MEAYERS EDWARDS (RIGHT) AND DAVID S. BOYER (FAR RIGHT), BOTH NATIONAL GEOGRAPHIC STAFF

daisies brightened the cottage gardens. On the menu of one hotel appeared jugged hare with red currant jelly.

In this ripe, autumnal moment posters appeared in town and village to herald the forthcoming Grasmere Sports, one of the grand events of the Lakeland year. Farmers and shepherds pour into the village. Wrestlers famed throughout Lakeland arrive with their entourages. Runners arrive

A CLIFF FOR A CLASSROOM, *an Outward Bound patrol acts out a rescue on Great Gable. Comrades at the top belay the "victim." The Outward Bound Trust runs sea and mountain schools to teach boys to be men.*

In summer Lakeland's fells lure vigorous holidayers. Campers' tents brighten Grasmere's shore. Hikers trek along the Band, a shoulder of Bow Fell; from its 2,960-foot summit the Isle of Man can be seen out in the Irish Sea. Pack of the cyclist pausing in Grasmere bears the symbol of the Youth Hostels Association, whose hostels include farmhouses and onetime shepherds' huts.

with half their villages to cheer them on. Tents and marquees sprout on the turf.

When I returned to Grasmere I found my hotel preparing for an invasion. My friend Charles the waiter, like some character out of Dickens, dashed about, pink and dictatorial, from kitchen to dining room, chatting with the regulars but contemptuous of casuals who, in his opinion, never knew what they wanted and grumbled when

they got it. Once, in one of his memorable asides, he handed me a menu and, pointing to the words *poulet roti,* remarked: "The French may be very good at cooking, sir, but I don't like their terms. Roast Chicken? They call it 'pulley rottey!' Nonsense!"

MY MEMORIES of the Grasmere Sports are of wet feet, of rain dripping down my neck, of the sweet smell of churned-up turf, of pork pie and a slice of gingerbread eaten in a damp marquee, of giant wrestlers in tights hugging one another like grizzly bears, and of undaunted spectators in gum boots sitting beneath umbrellas and enjoying every moment of it. This is, of course, the lesson of Lakeland: One never lets weather interfere with anything.

Now and again one may be surprised. In a day or two the sun shone. I glanced from my window astonished. Like a sobbing beauty who suddenly dries her tears and becomes radiant again, the day was sunny and smiling. Thrushes were singing.

"It's a grand day for the sheep-dog trials," everyone was saying. In a grassy valley ringed by hills, huntsmen stood about in pink coats, surrounded by foxhounds. Eager little white-and-tan beagles darted about with twinkling tails. Shepherds leaned upon their crooks. Some wore blue-serge Sunday suits, others breeches and woolen stockings.

But the heroes of the day were the little Lakeland sheep dogs. These small black-and-white collies hovered at their masters' heels, ready to obey a lifted finger or a whisper. The shepherd stands beside a pen made of hurdles, and his dog crouches beside him. A few hundred yards away four sheep stand about cropping the grass.

The shepherd tells his dog to fetch the sheep, and the dog streaks off until he is pulled up sharply by a whistle from his master. The dog drops as if shot, his eyes on the sheep. The shepherd then signals the dog to the left or right. Often the dog wriggles forward on his stomach through the tall grass. Now the slightest miscalculation will alarm and split the sheep, sending them off in all directions.

When the shepherd thinks he has maneuvered his dog into the right position he whistles to lift, or gather, the sheep. The dog must drive them through three sets of hurdles and pen them (page 32).

The whistles sound identical to a stranger's ear, but a dog can distinguish his master's signals from all others. A shepherd told me of an acquaintance who entered a young dog in some sheep-dog trials which were broadcast. At home the shepherd's family was listening to the trials when the mother of the dog suddenly awakened at the sound of her master's whistle on the radio. She jumped through a window in an attempt to answer his call.

The eight-mile hound trail tests nose, speed, and stamina. The hounds follow a scent laid down by a man dragging a rag soaked in aniseed and turpentine.

When the flag dropped, 40 hounds raced off in full cry. Half an hour later, far off and invisible to all save Lakelander eyes, a movement stirred the bracken. Then came the flicker of running hounds. I was astonished; at that fantastic distance the owners could distinguish their own hounds, even call them by name. "Cracker's in front!" "Here comes Nimrod!"

Seemingly as swift as the hounds were the young men who competed in the fell race. Across the sports ground they poured, through the bracken, and over boulders up the vast bulk of the fell. In minutes they came racing back, and the winner was there panting before us.

On that perfect afternoon, as the sun shone upon the green grass and golden hillsides, with the smell of bruised turf in the autumn air, I thought myself as near to the heart of Lakeland as I had ever been. Later I went back to lean over the old stone bridge where the trout laze in the Rothay and where, in a corner of the churchyard, lies the poet whose love for this countryside has encircled the earth.

"WALKING DOWN *by Sour Milk Ghyll . . . when the water is whiter than snow." Hikers near Borrowdale evoke Hugh Walpole's words. Old Norse nomenclature lives on in* gill *(ghyll), a ravine with a stream.* Beck *is* brook, force *a cascade,* wyke *a bay,* holme *an islet. Sheep follow* trods *and graze rounded* hows *amid tarns and lofty fells and pikes in this enchanted land.*

DAVID S. BOYER, NATIONAL GEOGRAPHIC STAFF

Text references are indicated in roman *type; illustrations and illustrated text in* **boldface**.

Index

SAXON BROOCH, *found near Kingston in Kent, now rests in the City of Liverpool Museums. Seventh-century smith adorned it with gold filigree, cuttlefish shell, garnets, and lapis lazuli.*

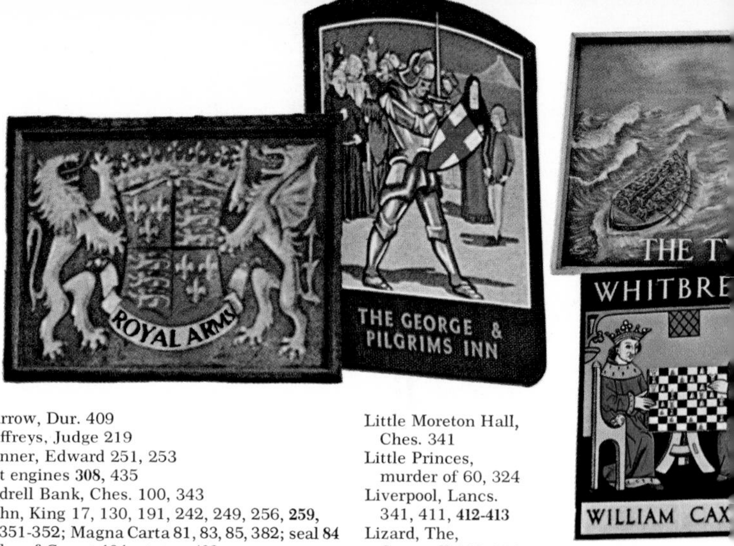
ROYAL ARMS
THE GEORGE &
PILGRIMS INN

Heraldry, history, humor hinge on the inn signs of England

WITH HEAVY HEART the landlady found her ducks sprawled lifelessly. With thrifty fingers she plucked one for her menu – until it quacked! A leaky beer keg had spiked the feed. The inn sign recalls the event: the Drunken Duck. Trivial or triumphal, England's snapshot album creaks from her inns. The Wooden Walls of Old England honors her warships. Ask about Cannards Grave, and the innkeeper will tell you of an 18th-century predecessor – "last sheep thief hanged in Somerset." Dickens immortalized the Leather Bottle.

English publicans once followed Roman custom, hanging out an ivy sprig, symbol of Bacchus. Chaucer noted jutting "alestakes" that held the "bush" overhead. So the Bush is patriarch of inn names – and butt of rival Bird-in-Hand signs that crow they are worth two in the Bush. Many signs blazon history. The Trip to Jerusalem hosted departing Crusaders; several Saracen's Heads mimic the device returning knights put on their arms. The White Hart was Richard II's badge; many a Royal Oak recalls where Charles II hid from the Roundheads after the Battle of Worcester. Nelson commands a fleet of inns; Wellington, Robin Hood, William Caxton – England's first printer – hold sway at others. The Pilt Down Man is no hoax to its "regulars"; the Ordinary Fellow lauds George V, who said as throngs cheered, "I can't understand it . . . I'm just an ordinary sort of fellow."

Adam and Eve hang in Paradise, Gloucestershire, and also in Norwich, where a former host was Cain Abel. In the Wars of the Roses, White Lions and White Boars turned red when Lancaster won. Henry VIII broke with Rome, and Pope's Head became King's Head. Elizabeth I ordered signboard portraits of her burned and gave artists kinder ones to copy. Artists often paid inn bills in signs. Hogarth's Man with the Load of Mischief shoulders monkey, bird, and tipsy wife. Some painters couldn't spell: Bacchanales became Bag O'Nails.

Steeped in history, or modern as the Jet and Whittle, honoring Sir Frank Whittle and his first jet engine, inns give a special welcome born of amber glasses, oak beams, and warm smiles. "There is nothing . . . by which so much happiness has been produced," said Samuel Johnson, "as by a good tavern or inn."

DELICATE FAN VAULTING *soars in Henry VII Chapel, Westminster Abbey, with the "airy security of a cobweb." Elizabeth I and Mary Queen of Scots, mortal rivals who never met in life, share the sepulchral peace in this masterwork of late Gothic, or Perpendicular, design, emblazoned with banners of Knights of the Bath. Succeeding Tudor, Elizabethan, and Palladian styles reflect the spreading Renaissance spirit.*

Major architectural styles

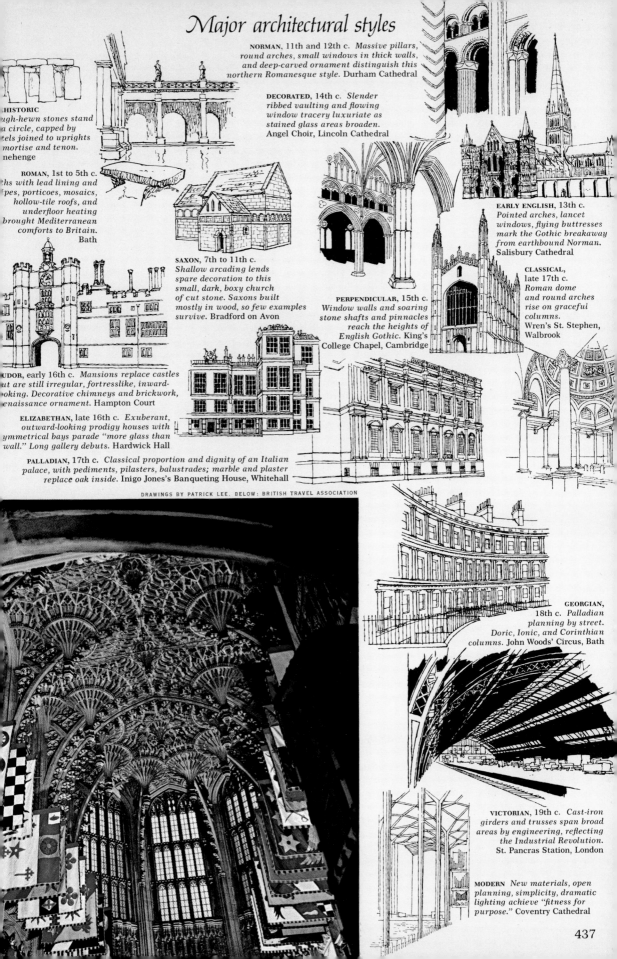

NORMAN, 11th and 12th c. *Massive pillars, round arches, small windows in thick walls, and deep-carved ornament distinguish this northern Romanesque style.* Durham Cathedral

HISTORIC
ugh-hewn stones stand a circle, capped by tels joined to uprights mortise and tenon. nehenge

DECORATED, 14th c. *Slender ribbed vaulting and flowing window tracery luxuriate as stained glass areas broaden.* Angel Choir, Lincoln Cathedral

ROMAN, 1st to 5th c. *hs with lead lining and pes, porticoes, mosaics, hollow-tile roofs, and underfloor heating brought Mediterranean comforts to Britain.* Bath

SAXON, 7th to 11th c. *Shallow arcading lends spare decoration to this small, dark, boxy church of cut stone. Saxons built mostly in wood, so few examples survive.* Bradford on Avon

EARLY ENGLISH, 13th c. *Pointed arches, lancet windows, flying buttresses mark the Gothic breakaway from earthbound Norman.* Salisbury Cathedral

CLASSICAL, late 17th c. *Roman dome and round arches rise on graceful columns.* Wren's St. Stephen, Walbrook

PERPENDICULAR, 15th c. *Window walls and soaring stone shafts and pinnacles reach the heights of English Gothic.* King's College Chapel, Cambridge

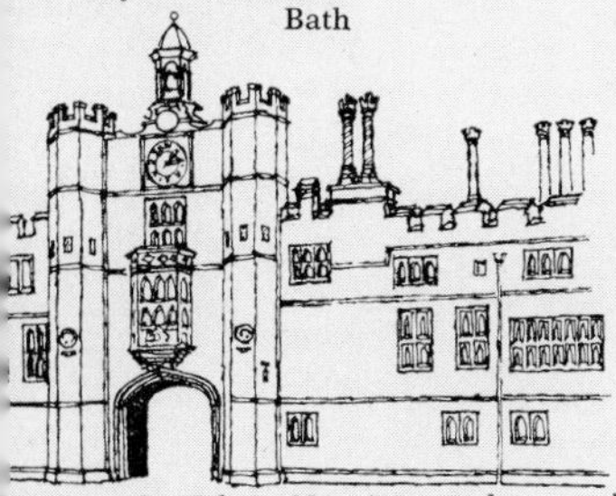

UDOR, early 16th c. *Mansions replace castles ut are still irregular, fortresslike, inward- oking. Decorative chimneys and brickwork, enaissance ornament.* Hampton Court

ELIZABETHAN, late 16th c. *Exuberant, outward-looking prodigy houses with ymmetrical bays parade "more glass than wall." Long gallery debuts.* Hardwick Hall

PALLADIAN, 17th c. *Classical proportion and dignity of an Italian palace, with pediments, pilasters, balustrades; marble and plaster replace oak inside.* Inigo Jones's Banqueting House, Whitehall

DRAWINGS BY PATRICK LEE. BELOW: BRITISH TRAVEL ASSOCIATION

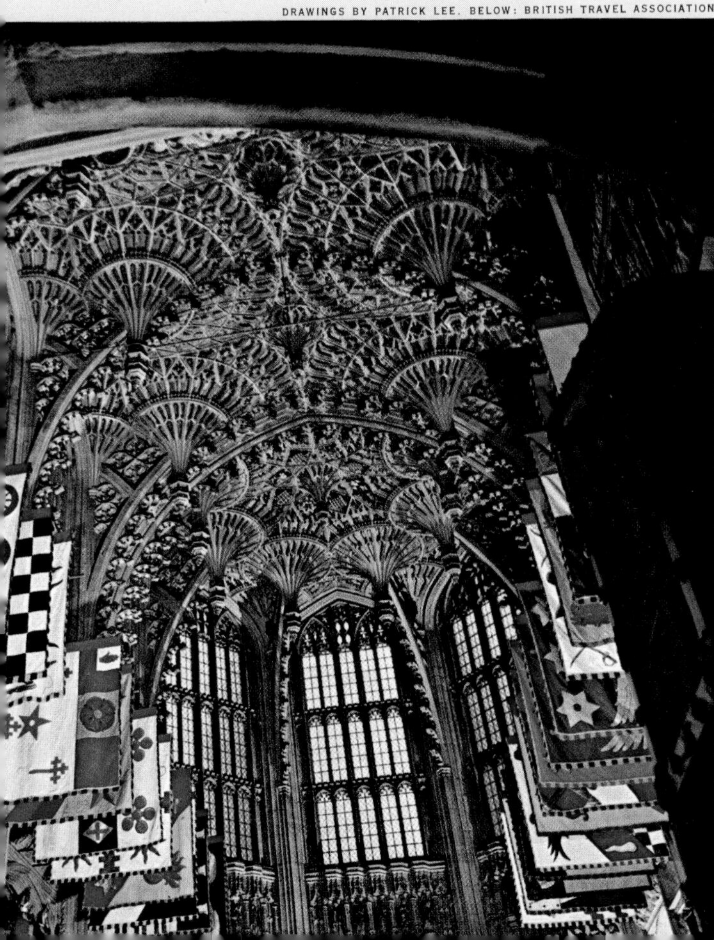

GEORGIAN, 18th c. *Palladian planning by street. Doric, Ionic, and Corinthian columns.* John Woods' Circus, Bath

VICTORIAN, 19th c. *Cast-iron girders and trusses span broad areas by engineering, reflecting the Industrial Revolution.* St. Pancras Station, London

MODERN *New materials, open planning, simplicity, dramatic lighting achieve "fitness for purpose."* Coventry Cathedral

Styles in Dress and Furniture

IN HOSE AND DOUBLET, *the Elizabethan enjoyed his oak armchair. It lost its arms so milady's farthingale would fit it. Stuarts brought coat and vest from France. Elegant Georgians lived amid Chippendale and Sheraton. Regency ladies, classically draped, sat on scrolled sofas, sober-clad Victorians on chairs that grew progressively overstuffed.*

COURTESY GREATER LONDON COUNCIL

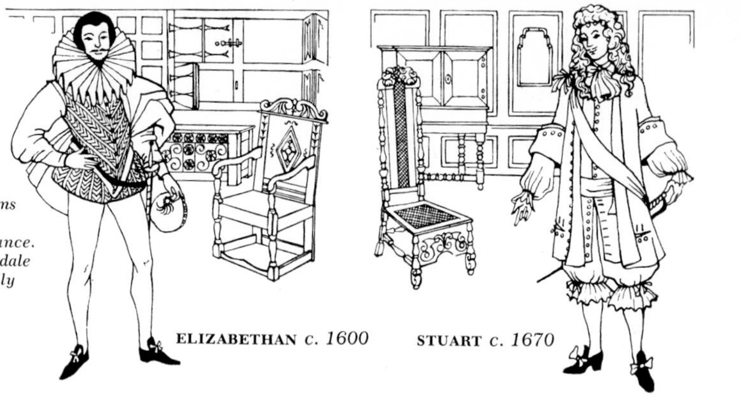

ELIZABETHAN *c. 1600* STUART *c. 1670*

GEORGIAN *c. 1760*

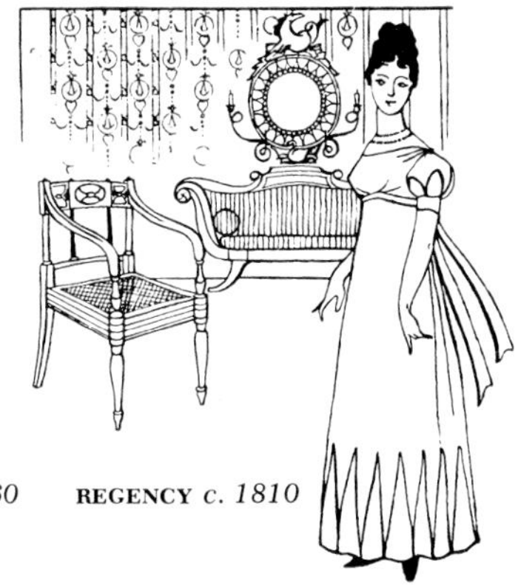

REGENCY *c. 1810*

VICTORIAN *c. 1860*

Acknowledgments and Reference Guide

THE EDITORS are grateful to many individuals and organizations for the wealth of information they provided. Town officials, from Scrooby in Nottinghamshire to St. Mary's in the Isles of Scilly, helped check local details. Specialists in heraldry, Anglo-Saxon linguistics, Roman archeology shared their knowledge – as did clergymen, curators, owners of historic houses. In London, the British Museum, the Bank of England, the College of Arms gave help. In Washington, the Folger Shakespeare Library, the Smithsonian Institution, the British Embassy, and in New York the British Travel Association verified facts. The Library of Congress opened its rich collections.

Books of general scope frequently consulted included: *Anatomy of Britain Today* by Anthony Sampson; *The Character of England* edited by Ernest Barker; *Britain, An Official Handbook; Illustrated English Social History* and *History of England* by G. M. Trevelyan; *The Oxford History of England* (14 vols.); *The Pelican History of England* (9 vols.); *English Life Series* (8 vols.) edited by Peter Quennell; *A History of the English-Speaking Peoples* by Winston S. Churchill; *Historic Britain* edited by Graham Fisher; *England Before Elizabeth* by Helen Cam; and *A New Dictionary of British History* by S. H. Steinberg.

Informative historical companions were: *Stonehenge Decoded* by Gerald S. Hawkins and John B. White; *Seeing Roman Britain* by Leonard Cottrell; *Anglo-Saxon England* by Peter Hunter Blair; *Alfred the Great* by Eleanor S. Duckett; *The Normans in European History* by Charles H. Haskins; *William the Conqueror* by David Charles Douglas; *The Reign of King John* by Sidney Painter; *The Medieval Scene* by G. G. Coulton; *Six Medieval Men and Women* by H. S. Bennett; *Chaucer's World* compiled by Edith Rickert; *The Hundred Years' War* by Edouard Perroy; *The Yorkist Age* by Paul Murray Kendall; *How They Lived 55 B.C.-1485* by W. O. Hassall and *How They Lived 1485-1700* by Molly Harrison and O. M. Royston; *The England of Elizabeth* by A. L. Rowse; *Middle-Class Culture in Elizabethan England* by Louis B. Wright; *The Elizabethans* by Allardyce Nicoll; *The Elizabethan Journals* by G. B. Harrison; *Queen Elizabeth I* by J. E. Neale; *Elizabeth the Great* by Elizabeth Jenkins; *The King's Peace 1637-1641* and *The King's War 1641-1647* by C. V. Wedgwood; *Johnson's England* edited by A. S. Turberville, and his *English Men and Manners in the 18th Century; The Augustan World* by A. R. Humphreys; *Kings and Desperate Men* by Louis Kronenberger; *England in Transition* by Dorothy George; *Queen Victoria* by Elizabeth Longford; and as antidote to too much serious history, *1066 and All That* by W. C. Sellar and R. J. Yeatman!

A Land by Jacquetta Hawkes heads a geographical list: *The British Isles* by L. Dudley Stamp and Stanley H. Beaver; the *Cambridge Air Surveys; An Historical Geography of England Before A.D. 1800* edited by H. C. Darby; *English Villages* by F. R. Banks; *The English Village* by Victor Bonham-Carter; *The Concise Oxford Dictionary of English Place-Names* by Eilert Ekwall. Among regional works used: *York* by John Rodgers; *Lancashire Ways* by J. Cuming Walters; *The English Lake District* by Molly Lefebure; *A History of Cornwall* by F. E. Halliday; *Portrait of Devon* by D. St. Leger-Gordon; *The Mendips* by A. W. Coysh, E. J. Mason, and V. Waite; *Sussex* by Barbara Willard; *Cambridge* by F. A. Reeve; *Oxford* by James Morris; *A History of London Life* by R. J. Mitchell and M. D. R. Leys; *London's Riverside* by Eric de Maré; *The Companion Guide to London* by David Piper.

Literature and Locality by John Freeman; *Hardy of Wessex* by Carl J. Weber; and the *Oxford Companion to English Literature* make good literary friends, as do *The Diary of Samuel Pepys; A Tour Through the Whole Island of Great Britain* by Daniel Defoe; *Our Old Home* by Nathaniel Hawthorne; *English Hours* by Henry James; and the Shakespeare biographies by A. L. Rowse, Marchette Chute, and Peter Quennell.

On special subjects we turned to *The Cathedrals of England* by H. Batsford and C. Fry; *The English Cathedral Through the Centuries* by G. H. Cook; *Stained Glass of the Middle Ages in England and France* by Hugh Arnold and Lawrence B. Saint; *The English Abbey* by F. H. Crossley; *Castles* by Charles Oman; *English Castles* by R. Allen Brown; *Great Palaces of Europe* by Sacheverell Sitwell and others; *Great Houses of Britain* by Nigel Nicholson; *The English Garden* by Edward Hyams; *The English Inn* by Denzil Batchelor; *The Architecture of England* by Doreen Yarwood; *A History of Architecture on the Comparative Method* by Banister Fletcher; *The Buildings of England* series and *The Englishness of English Art* by Nikolaus Pevsner; *Theatre* by Harold Hobson; *English Spas* and *English Fairs and Markets* by William Addison; *The Canals of England* by Eric de Maré; *The English Parliament* by Kenneth Mackenzie; *The English Constitution* by Walter Bagehot; *Our Language* by Simeon Potter; *Boutell's Manual of Heraldry* revised by V. Wheeler-Holohan; *Historic Heraldry of Britain* and *English Ancestry* by Anthony R. Wagner.

The visitor to England will find ready reference aids in the Blue Guides to *England* and to *London; The Shell and BP Guide to Britain;* the Ward Lock regional *Red Guides;* the Pitkin pictorial guides; and British Travel's monthly *Coming Events in Britain.*

National Geographic Society staff members in many departments contributed significantly to this book. See listing on following page. The more than 880 issues of NATIONAL GEOGRAPHIC contain a store of information on England. Consult the National Geographic Index.

NATIONAL GEOGRAPHIC SOCIETY

WASHINGTON, D. C.

Organized "for the increase and diffusion of geographic knowledge"

GILBERT HOVEY GROSVENOR
President, 1920-1954; Editor, 1899-1954
Chairman of the Board, 1954-1966

The National Geographic Society is chartered in Washington, D. C., in accordance with the laws of the United States, as a nonprofit scientific and educational organization for increasing and diffusing geographic knowledge and promoting research and exploration.

Since 1890 the Society has supported more than 350 explorations and research projects, adding immeasurably to man's knowledge of earth, sea, and sky. It diffuses this knowledge through its monthly journal, NATIONAL GEOGRAPHIC; more than 26 million maps distributed each year; its books, globes, and atlases; 30 School Bulletins a year in color; information services to press, radio, and television; technical monographs; timely exhibits from around the world in Explorers Hall; and now a nationwide series of programs on television.

NATIONAL GEOGRAPHIC MAGAZINE

MELVILLE BELL GROSVENOR, *Editor*
MELVIN M. PAYNE, *Executive Vice President*
FREDERICK G. VOSBURGH, *Associate Editor*
FRANC SHOR, *Associate Editor*
JAMES M. DARLEY, *Cartographer Emeritus*